Russian Political Thought

An Introduction

RUSSIAN POLITICAL THOUGHT

An Introduction

THORNTON ANDERSON

University of Maryland

Cornell University Press

ITHACA, NEW YORK

CORNELL UNIVERSITY PRESS

First published 1967

Library of Congress Catalog Card Number: 67–12902

PRINTED IN THE UNITED STATES OF AMERICA
BY KINGSPORT PRESS, INC.

Preface

THE Greek, Roman, western European tradition continues to domi-
nate our study of the history of political thought. The brilliance of that
tradition has blinded us to other independent starts in political thinking
made in China, India, and elsewhere, and even to the other streams of
thought to which the Greeks contributed, those of the Moslems and
the Slavs. In consequence, there has been a general neglect in the West
of the history of Russian political ideas. The opinion, justified or not,
that Russian thought in this field has lagged behind that of western
Europe has been accompanied by the dubious assumption that the main
lines of development are the same, and that current differences are the
work of a few perverse individuals (such as Pobedonostsev and Lenin)
who have prevented their compatriots from accepting the norms of
Western politics. From this assumption it is deduced that a knowledge
of the streams of thought which have entered Russia from Scandinavia,
from Byzantium, and from Mongolia is unnecessary to an understanding of modern Soviet policies, and that the perspective of the nineteenth century, or at most that of the two centuries since Peter the
Great, is sufficient. Opposing that conclusion, the present work seeks to
delineate the Greek-Mongol-Russian tradition of political thought, as
distinct from, and only in part related to, the Western tradition.

The genius of the ancient Greeks lies at the root of both Russian and
Western thought. For the West, the Greek element of its tradition
might be said largely to have ended its creative contribution with the
migration of the Stoics Polybius and Panaetius to Rome in the second
century B.C. From that point onward Greek philosophy was gradually
integrated into Roman law, and Greek politics into the Roman administrative system. These two enduring influences, coupled with those of

v

Christianity and of the Germanic invasions, gave definite direction to Western thought. During these centuries, to be sure, the reverse migration under Constantine made Greece the center of empire and added Roman elements to the Eastern tradition; but the Romans were gradually submerged as Constantinople became more and more Asiatic. Even the common religion became differentiated as Rome itself slipped gradually toward the final schism of 1054, and Western political thought steadily diverged from the pattern developing at Byzantium and in eastern Europe.

For the Russians, on the other hand, the Greek element did not begin its influence until the tenth century, when this divergence was already well advanced. The secular and speculative thought of the classical age had been diluted and transformed by Asiatic immigration and by an intellectual preoccupation with religious subjects. Byzantium, by that time, saw itself as an isolated citadel of religion and culture beleaguered by surrounding infidels; the ideal of a Roman and Christian ecumene remained, but in practice something akin to the old Greek concepts of civic membership and of distinction from the barbarians had returned. It was this psychology and the attendant almost inflexible ideas which were passed on to Russia, largely through the church. Furthermore, this Byzantine influence in Russia came to a virtual end with the Florentine Union of 1439, just when the Renaissance was reinforcing the connection of the West with the heritage of the pagan Greeks and Romans. The Greek contribution to Russia, therefore, was markedly different from the Western heritage. Instead of the stimulating and controversial writings of long-dead philosophers, it came in the form of living priests and monks bearing a dogmatic and eternal truth.

Russian and Western lines of development are also related through a common experience of Norse invasions, yet here again the effects upon political thought were different. In western Europe, although Charlemagne's empire had already been divided, a degree of organization remained capable of keeping the vikings on the periphery of the continent, where, as in Normandy, they rapidly absorbed the feudal institutions of their neighbors. Even in England, which they subdued as they did Russia, they were soon assimilated, the Anglo-Saxons being, like themselves, an agrarian people who had long since destroyed the Roman cities and cleared the ground for feudalism. In Russia, by contrast, neither the history of Roman unity nor the actuality of feudal subordination existed to give the Slavs military cohesion. They had, however, cities of considerable individual strength, although these were linked mostly by commercial, rather than political, ties. The efforts of the invaders to subjugate and control these cities produced an enduring caste system differing fundamentally from the feudal order. Not based on landholding, this system discouraged the growth of an independent nobility and led to a centralization and autocracy unknown in the West.

This development was accentuated and complicated by another influence which set Russia apart—her subjection to the Mongols. Cleverly utilized by her princes in their struggles with the cities, the Mongol, or Tatar, domination deurbanized Russia and sentenced her to the intellectual stagnation of both rural and international isolation, just at a time when the cities of the West were emerging to aid the kings in the destruction of feudalism and the building of modern Europe.

These well-known facts of history might seem remote from the Soviet Union and from its political thought. Yet this study suggests that numerous analogies and perhaps even continuities link modern Russia with her distant past.

For one thing, there has been a continuous tradition of separation of the government from the governed. Beginning with the successful effort of the Norse princes to set themselves above the Slavic towns, this separation was aggravated by the equally successful effort of the tsars to exalt themselves above the nobility. Noble rank was, from 1722, open to foreigners and to commoners; but this innovation, instead of forming a link with the people, actually increased the separation through an influx of Germans and the drawing off from the people of the more capable commoners. Molded with time into a subservient bureaucracy under an unlimited autocrat, the old ruling class yielded its power in 1917. The gulf that stood between it and the people, however, apparently still stands between Communist Party members and nonmembers, and the drawing-off process continues.

A corollary of this separation has been centralization and the discouragement of local initiative. Phrased another way, decision and administration from above, and not competition of opinions and variety of experimentation from below, have characterized Russian history even from the first Vladimir in the tenth century. Thus, the Kievan provinces were administered by the brothers of the grand prince, and Muscovy, and later the whole empire, by military governors, always appointed from the center; the bureaucracy of the capital remained almost undiluted even by advisory bodies representing the provinces. In modern times this centralization has also impressed itself upon the revolutionary movement, the more tightly knit Marxists prevailing over the *narodniki* or populists, the Bolsheviks over the Mensheviks, and the Communist Party apparatus over the decentralized "workers' opposition" of 1921.

A third continuing tradition is that of the ruling class as the guardian of a true faith in an exposed and threatened outpost of civilization. In the beginning this trusteeship was a matter of guarding Christianity against paganism and, almost from the beginning, of protecting Greek Orthodoxy against Roman Catholicism. The coming of the Mongols deepened this defensive sense of righteousness and mission. With the Florentine Union, Russian Orthodoxy closed ranks against both Greeks and Romans. Whenever the leadership on occasion made efforts to break out of this psychology of isolation, as with Nikon or with Peter I, the tradition always reasserted itself strongly, in the *Raskol* or schism under Nikon and in the Slavophils after Peter. At present, of course, as the ground for suspicion and dislike of the West, Russian leaders have replaced the Latin heresy with the capitalist heresy.

Additional illustrations of such recurring or continuing themes could be sketched, but it should be clear that many of the features of current Soviet thought and practice which the West finds so repellent—the unrepresentative bureaucracy, the suppression of unofficial opinion, the unyielding self-righteousness, the messianism—are not the effects of Marxism. It may well be, on the contrary, that Marxism gained control in Russia, in spite of the impossibility of fitting its economic theory to the facts, because some aspects of its political theory fitted the Russian heritage so well. If the result has been a distortion of Marx, this may simply mean that that heritage has a stronger grip on Russian thought than has the imported system.

A study of the Greek-Mongol-Russian tradition, as a distinct body of political thought, may therefore provide an advantageous perspective from which to examine Soviet developments. Russian studies in the West, developing since 1917 under the influence of antagonistic émigrés and in an atmosphere of fear and hatred of Communism, have rarely equaled either the objectivity or the understanding exhibited by Professor Masaryk in *The Spirit of Russia*, a work completed in 1913 and still the best analysis of Russian political thought. Western policy, as a result, suffers from wishful thinking and other irrationalities.

PREFACE

Since these and related matters are subject to controversial interpretation, however, I have not thought it wise to present only one more point of view. My aim, instead, has been to supplement the exposition with the words of the Russian thinkers themselves in some of their most representative passages. Unfortunately this method has not always been feasible for the earlier centuries, political thought then being more implicit than explicit. Attention is therefore given in the early chapters to institutions as expressions of political ideas, but such efforts at the derivation of theory from practice are not so necessary after the Russians begin to express their ideas in theoretical writings.

Implicit in an undertaking such as this is the belief that knowledge of the traditions of others is more promising, as a first step toward mutual understanding, than a demand that others accept our traditions. Western thinkers have suffered from the hypnosis of national sovereignty and have failed to give adequate answers to the problems of the economically underdeveloped, as individuals or as peoples. These and other shortcomings make our political thought unacceptable in large areas of the world, and Western complacency in the face of these deficiencies has induced in non-Western peoples an increasingly critical attitude. In these circumstances we need to explore other traditions of political thought, not in search of new solutions, but to improve our perspective and our awareness of the basic opinions of others. When problems are world-wide rather than specifically Western, a cross-fertilization of ideas may lead to more readily acceptable policies, while exclusive absorption in any one body of thought may be tantamount to an abdication of world leadership.

I wish to express my appreciation to my friends in the field of Russian studies and to the many librarians who have helped me. I want especially to thank Elizabeth Anderson for her help with early drafts of this manuscript and Erwina Godfrey for her comments on later ones.

THORNTON ANDERSON

College Park, Maryland
August 1966

Contents

CONTENTS

Part Five
THE ROADS TO 1917

Part Six
THE SOVIETS

A Note on Procedure

A FEW procedural matters should be clarified. This book uses the Library of Congress system of transliteration (without its diacritical marks); however, the final 'i' of the 'ii' ending and the final soft sign (except in Rus') are omitted. A few well-known nouns like soviet and Trotsky appear in their usual forms. Russian words adopted by Webster are printed without italics; others are explained in the text. The numbered notes, printed at the back, are always citations; substantive notes appear as footnotes.

PART ONE

Kievan Rus'
(ninth to thirteenth centuries)

CHAPTER I

The City-States: The Slavs

FROM the ninth through the twelfth centuries three very different sources fed political conceptions into the area between the Baltic Sea and the Black. In this region, and to the west and south, the Slavs had resided since prehistoric times, with ancient and highly developed indigenous customs, many of them similar to those of the Teutonic peoples of western Europe. Into this Slavic sea was poured a stream of Scandinavians called Varangians, contemporary with the viking invaders farther west, and a slightly later stream of Greek Christians from Byzantium, the seat of the highest culture then existent in the Western world.

Little is known of political arrangements in the early centuries although four separate sources from the sixth century touch on this subject. The historian of the Goths, Jordanes, mentions a prince and seventy elders among the Antes, a Slavic people, and the Byzantine Menander Protector makes a similar statement. Procopius of Caesarea says, "For these nations, the Sclaveni and the Antae, are not ruled by one man, but they have lived from of old under a democracy, and consequently everything which involves their welfare, whether for good or for ill, is referred to the people." [1] Another Greek author, Mauricius, agrees: "Both the Sclaveni and the Antes live in freedom and do not let anybody subjugate them. . . . They have no supreme power but always quarrel one with another." [2] From these sources it appears likely that, like other barbarian tribes described by Tacitus, the Slavs chose leaders for times of war but not for permanent authority. Stressing their libertarian attitude, Mauricius goes on to attribute to them an unusual antipathy to the institution of slavery: "They do not enslave their captives for an unlimited period, as other tribes are wont

3

to do." [3] The slave might ransom himself by a payment or might work off an equivalent sum, as is further described in the tenth-century *Court Law for the People*, a Bulgarian legal manual widely used in Rus'.

The Russian chronicler also, although writing later when princely rule was well established, recalled a period when the Slavic peoples lived without rulers. Needing to justify the princes, he wrote of the Slavs that "there was no law among them" and wars arose among the tribes. Yet he saw nothing improbable in his report that the tribes agreed to end these wars by inviting a foreign prince to rule over them collectively "and judge us according to the Law." They then, he recounted, went overseas to the Varangian Russes and said, "Our land is great and rich, but there is no order in it. Come to rule and reign over us." * In the pattern of such chronicles, it is stated that they selected three brothers, with their kinsfolk, who came in 862 and located in three different towns. The eldest was Riurik, from whom, his brothers having shortly died, was descended the Riurikides, the single family that continued in power for over seven hundred years.†[4]

As the Slavs grew in numbers, their position astride the upper Dnieper River and other waterways between the north of Europe and the trading centers of Asia provided commercial opportunities which, when added to the need for fortifications against the nomads of the steppes, drew them together into urban communities. In contrast to the subsistence economy of agricultural feudalism in most of western Europe, their economy included substantial production for the market and they had numerous towns as centers of commercial capitalism. Kievan Rus' was known to the Scandinavians as *Gardariki*, the "realm of cities." Some three hundred towns are named in the chronicles, among them Novgorod, which became the easternmost member of the Hanseatic League.‡ A recent estimate sets the urban population in the

* From this it appears that the name of Russia is derived from that of the Scandinavian tribe from which the ruling family came, but there are several other explanations of its origin (see, for example, George Vernadsky, *Ancient Russia* [New Haven, 1943], especially pp. 275–286, 333–339, and Henryk Paszkiewicz, *The Origin of Russia* [London, 1954], pp. 3–25, 331–335).

† Riurik is frequently identified with Rorik of Jutland, whose life is sketched in Vernadsky, *Ancient Russia*, pp. 337–339.

‡ Even in the second century A.D. the geographer Ptolemy named and located more than a dozen towns in the region of the Dnieper and Dniester Rivers (*Geography of Claudius Ptolemy*, trans. E. L. Stevenson [New York, 1932], pp. 79–80).

twelfth century at 13 per cent, a figure not reached again until near the end of the nineteenth century.* Each of these early towns was a city-state, ruling the surrounding rural areas and smaller towns. The territory of Novgorod, the largest, stretched north and east over an area the size of modern France.

Nine of these towns are mentioned by the chronicles before the tenth century, but it is not until the eleventh that any data are available relating to their systems of government. Historians disagree as to the continuity of these urban arrangements with the old tribal democracy, but it seems likely that a connecting link may be found in the basic political unit of the countryside—the *verv*—a peasant commune, based on blood relationships, that was evolving into a territorial unit later known as the *obshchina* or *mir*. The *verv* was a voluntary combination of families with such collective law-enforcing responsibilities as searching for thieves and paying the wergild for murders committed in the neighborhood when the murderer could not be determined. Decisions of the *verv* were made by the heads of families, each head speaking for those under his roof—sons and younger brothers, wives and children.

The larger the town, the more complex became its political organization, although the old rural unit, the *verv*, influenced the whole. In Novgorod, where the pattern was most highly developed, the city was divided into five sections, each subdivided into streets and these again into rows; and each of these units, at each level, had its own assembly of heads of families presided over by an elected elder. The hierarchy culminated in the city assembly, the *veche* (plural, *vecha*), a highly interesting institution. The Laurentian chronicle remarks that "the men of Novgorod, and of Smolensk, and of Kiev, and of Polotsk, and of all the districts [*vlasti*], from the beginning came together for deliberation into *vecha*." [5]

Similar assemblies had appeared in many places. They had been common among the ancient Greeks, and Greek cities, trading with the hinterland, had dotted the shores of the Black Sea for a thousand years.† There is no evidence of any connection between the Greek and Slavic city-states, however, and there are sharp elements of contrast as well as of analogy between the *veche* and the *Ekklesia* of Athens, the best known of the Greek assemblies. Both were regarded as sovereign

* See George Vernadsky, *Kievan Russia* (New Haven, 1948), p. 105.
† On these cities see Mikhail I. Rostovtsev, *Iranians and Greeks in Southern Russia* (Oxford, 1922).

meetings of the whole citizenry, without distinctions of class or of wealth, but the *Ekklesia* was open to any Athenian over eighteen whereas the *veche* was restricted to heads of families. Debate in both was free, and votes were cast by individuals (not by sections or tribes as at Rome), but decisions were taken at Athens by a majority whereas the *veche* required unanimous agreement.* Under the constitution of Cleisthenes (from 507 B.C.) the powers and procedures of the *Ekklesia* were much more regular than those of the *veche* ever became. Ordinary sessions were regularly scheduled; the order of business was established; and a procedure was provided, the *graphe paranomon*, by which an act of the assembly might be challenged before the people's court, the *Heliaea*. The *veche*, on the contrary, met irregularly, summoned to the public square by the ringing of a bell—usually in emergencies, and not infrequently in the absence of the prince. It was much more active in some towns than in others, and its functions were outgrowths of the basic judicial and defensive requirements of the various communities. Prior to the coming of the Varangians it held all political power, operating somewhat like a constituent assembly; thereafter it shared power with them, remaining as a native, somewhat democratic element in the government. It had, to continue with modern terminology, executive, legislative, electoral, and judicial powers.

Since the routine of government was entrusted to officials, the executive role of the *veche* mostly concerned relations with marauding nomads and neighboring cities: matters of war and peace, use of the militia, and payment of tribute. With the establishment of the Norse princes, the maintenance of defense became more dependent upon the employment of mercenaries. The prince and his retainers, who may originally have been engaged as supplementary troops, gradually assumed a greater share in the defensive duties, and in the process increased their strength relative to that of the militia. Deliberately designed by the princes to improve their position against the *veche*, their policy of increasing participation in defense was generally successful in the long run, although neither the *veche* nor its militia was eliminated during the Kievan period. If sufficiently aroused, the citizenry might assert themselves, and in an emergency, even in a town like

---

* To secure unanimity three main methods were employed: discussion, which sometimes seemed interminable, a direct appeal to God by the use of lots, and physical "persuasion" in a free-for-all that might end with the dissenters thrown into the river.

Moscow, where it was never strong, the *veche* might suddenly don its armor and fight against hopeless odds. In 1382, when the Mongols approached and the ruling prince fled to the north, the *veche* reorganized the defenses of Moscow and almost succeeded in saving the city.

Medieval legislation was characterized by its emphasis on the clarification rather than the creation of law. This characteristic prevailed in Rus' as in the West, although a definite power to legislate was recognized in the *veche*. At Novgorod in 1136, for example, the *veche* resolved that only its own citizens could acquire land in Novgorod, an enactment aimed at preserving the power to get rid of unwanted princes. Thus a new law was designed to protect an old situation against a new threat, just as the "ancient rights of Englishmen" were protected by the Magna Carta. A charter granted to the city of Pskov in the early fifteenth century reviewed the customs and then added, "And if any provision of the customary law is missing in this charter, the mayor may refer the matter to Lord Pskov at the *veche*, advising the insertion of a new clause accordingly. And if any clause in this charter is not satisfactory to Lord Pskov, that clause is to be deleted." [6]

On rare occasions the *veche* might act as a court of final judgment, like the popular juries of ancient Athens, a power normally exercised only in trials of princes or other high officials. Such trials had the nature of impeachments or recall elections. Usually, however, judicial matters, other than those belonging to church or manorial courts (discussed below), were entrusted to elected officers or to the princes and their appointees.

Elective functions were, therefore, among the *veche*'s most important duties. It elected for indefinite terms, subject to recall, a mayor, who also had jurisdiction in cases concerning land, and a commander of militia, who also judged commercial disputes. These two offices were frequently conferred upon members of influential families: five generations of one family were mayors of Novgorod for a total of fifty-odd years during the twelfth and thirteenth centuries. The institutions of democracy thus might have aided the consolidation of an aristocracy, but these offices did not become hereditary. The commander, like the Roman tribune, was the regular spokesman for the people of the city in their dealings with the prince. Military necessity, however, required that he cooperate with the prince in wartime, and for this reason the prince brought influence to bear upon his election and eventually was able to fill the office by appointment. Yet even after it became appointive, this office continued to be regarded as peculiarly representative of the people, and as such it was a special target of ambitious princes; in Moscow, for example, it was abolished in 1375. There seems to be no record that the office was ever held by a member of the princely family.

In Novgorod (in 1193, for example) and at times elsewhere the *veche* might even select the bishop:

The people of Novgorod, with Prince Iaroslav and the hegumens and the people of St. Sophia and the priests, deliberated together . . . and there being a disagreement they placed on the holy altar three lots and sent from the *veche* a blind man . . . and he chose Marturi by God's will; and they at once sent for him and brought him from Rus' and seated him in the court of Holy Sophia, and sent [word] about him to the metropolitan, saying, "Appoint this bishop to us. . . ." [7]

Yet here, too, other influences were apt to intrude. Choices by the local prince, by the metropolitan at Kiev, or even by the patriarch of Constantinople might confront the city with the dilemma of acquiescence or rebellion.

The *veche* could also, and in Novgorod frequently did, in effect, elect the prince. Hearing, in 1102, that the grand prince proposed to appoint his son as prince in the northern city without having obtained the approval of the *veche*, the Novgorodians sent him this message: "We were sent to you, oh Prince, with positive instructions that our city does not want either you or your son. If your son has two heads, you might send him." [8] This privilege of Novgorod was confirmed by a council of princes in 1196:

And Vsevolod [III, of Suzdal,] having gone into their land, God did not allow more bloodshed between them, and they took peace between each other, and all the princes set Novgorod at liberty: where it pleased them, there they might take to themselves a prince. . . . And having taken counsel, the men of Novgorod showed Iaroslav [son of Vsevolod] the road out of Novgorod, and drove him out on St. George's Day, in the Autumn. [9]

The *veche* of Novgorod, moreover, was able to impose rather stringent restrictions upon the princes it chose. Each of them had to kiss the cross, taking an oath to abide by the formal limitations set forth in a treaty, such as this of 1270:

You are to rule Novgorod as formerly, according to custom. You, prince, are not to rule the Novgorod districts with your own men but with men of Novgorod; but you will receive a revenue from the districts. And without the mayor you, prince, are not to judge cases, nor to give away territories, nor to grant charters. . . . And in Bezhiche, and in all the [other] districts of Novgorod, neither you, prince, nor your princess, nor your boyars, nor your servitors are to own villages or to buy them or to take them as gifts. . . . And, prince, neither you, nor your princess, nor your boyars, nor your servitors are to deport people from Bezhiche or from any [other] Novgorod district into your own territory, or to give charters, or to accept indentured debtors, either peasants or merchants.[10]

Other towns were less successful in defending their elective powers. The idea refused to die, however, and on several occasions the *veche* of Kiev was able to influence the succession or to impose treaty limitations on the prince. In 1146, speaking through the commander of militia, the Kievans rejected the ruler chosen for them by their dying prince, Vsevolod Olgovich, and invited instead Prince Iziaslav II from another branch of the Riurikides: "Thou art our prince; we do not want any princes of the Olgovichi branch. . . . We do not like to be disposed of as if we were part of the deceased prince's estate."[11]

These great popular gatherings were at times stormy and in the heat of emotion might erupt in riot, sacking and burning the houses of officials and others who had aroused their wrath. On such occasions monasteries were usually plundered, a practice that indicates not only monastic wealth but also the identification of monasteries in the popular mind with the ruling group against whom the people were asserting themselves.

On normal occasions, however, the *veche* was reasonable and orderly. This harmony was accomplished in part by previous preparation and the presentation of issues and proposals by what might be called natural leaders and by officials, including the prince and the bishop. Former mayors and commanders might remain as city elders or, as at Novgorod, members of "the lords" (*Gospoda*), a body similar in function to the Council of Five Hundred (*Boule*) at Athens. The *Gospoda* was never so formalized as the *Boule*, and it was not based on the five sections of the city as the *Boule* was based on tribes. Nor was it in any sense a second chamber; it was rather of the nature of a steering committee within the *veche*. It carried great weight, however, because of its large size (three hundred or more), which permitted it to include most of those who had leadership abilities.

What conscious or unconscious political ideas or attitudes underlay these institutions? Seven political assumptions are apparent: (1) Community solidarity. Individualism and initiative were acceptable only when they had general support; the common welfare was expected to take precedence over personal desires and ambitions, no matter how highly placed. (2) Collective wisdom. The decisions of greatest importance were not entrusted to individuals, but individuals contributed to the decision-making process in proportion to the confidence of the public in their wisdom. (3) Voluntary participation. Both attendance and activity were voluntary, no quorum was required, and residents of the hinterland belonging to the city could speak if they happened to be present, although no provision was made for their attendance. (4) Absence of representation. Except in so far as a family could be said to be represented by its head, no one could speak, any more than he could think, for another. Since wise decision was the objective, machinery which would exclude anyone considered able to contribute wisdom was undesirable. (5) Unanimity. Acquiescence or constructive agreement, rather than the expressed assent of every individual was required, just as in medieval Europe. Yet there was no belief that any group, even a majority, had a right to take action over the head of an unconvinced minority (although the methods of "convincing" might be physical as well as mental). (6) Delegation of executive and judicial functions. In contrast to the use of committees at Athens, the Slavs had confidence in the modern method of single administrators. (7) Responsibility of officials. The indefinite term of office, coupled with the recall, could be applied effectively even to the prince when the *veche* felt sufficiently strong and aroused.

To these can be added, at least from the late tenth century, the acceptance of the exclusive claim of the house of Riurik to the office of prince. Thenceforward there is no evidence of attempts by the *veche* to elect princes from other families or by powerful aristocrats to assume the office. The result, no doubt, of Riurikide strength rather than of Slavic political wisdom, this practice did, nevertheless, unite the cities of Rus' with a family bond that minimized interurban warfare such as that which had exhausted the cities of Greece. Only as that bond became remote and uncertain did such strife appear and open the gates to the Mongols.

CHAPTER II

Fraternity: The Varangians

WHEN the Scandinavians first came to the "realm of cities" they came as raiders, as merchants, and as mercenary soldiers; and they appear to have been employed in the latter capacity by the Rus' cities against wandering nomads and jealous neighbors for a considerable period before any of them were, as the chronicles put it, "invited" to become their princes. The name, Varangian, is derived from an old Norse term meaning "confederate," and these bands of confederates, fully armed, were highly mobile, turning up in Bagdad in the ninth century, and attempting to raid Constantinople in 860.* Even after three generations of their rule in Kiev, the Prince Sviatoslav who rowed across the Danube in 971 to meet a Byzantine emperor in golden armor was still a viking with a huge gold ring in one ear. The parallel with the conquests of Normandy and England is tempting, therefore, and the chronicle account reads like a construction put on the affair by the appeasement party.

Yet the subsequent relations of the princes to their cities do not follow closely the viking parallel. The strength of the indigenous political institutions enabled the Slavs to develop, and to some extent to maintain, a concept of the office of prince resembling in some respects the attitude of a modern community toward its city manager. The Slavs believed that the *veche* engaged the prince, with his retinue, not to rule as a sovereign but to perform very limited functions, frequently stipulated by treaty, chiefly aimed at protecting the city and its subsidiary territory from foreign marauders and domestic criminals. For these

---

* Although belonging specifically to mercenaries in the tenth and eleventh centuries, this name is now generally applied to Scandinavian residents in Rus' throughout the Kievan period.

purposes he was permitted to collect taxes and fines. Thus the administrative duties of the prince and those of the other officials were, and in theory remained, separate; but the sources of revenue and the nature of the functions of the princes were such that the princes were able gradually to absorb additional duties and influence.

To the princes, on the other hand, the office had a different meaning. The chronicles themselves, while stating in general terms the thesis of invitation to the Varangians, recount in particular the conquests by them of many of the cities. As military men the princes based their positions in the beginning upon the power of their retinues, and later also upon grounds of inheritance. In Scandinavia they had been familiar with elective kingship and with popular assemblies called *thing*'s; but they knew too that the candidates in such elections were usually limited to the family of the deceased king, which in practice tended toward hereditary monarchy. Moreover, the *thing*'s of Scandinavia—unlike the *vecha*—had broad bases in the rural freeholders, and the absence in Rus' of a national *veche* or *thing* encouraged the grand princes of Kiev, who claimed all Rus', to consider the *veche* of the capital city as a source of cooperating man power (or, at worst, a source of trouble), but not as the source of their authority. Yet its cooperation was needed and as politicians the princes generally avoided offending the *veche* too seriously. Their rule was, therefore, neither that of responsible employees nor that of occupying conquerors, but something of both, in different proportions at various times and places.

In Kievan Rus', as among the Germanic peoples of the West, two conflicting principles of princely power existed: family inheritance and popular choice. Whenever the system of inheritance (if as yet it could be called a system) worked without internal quarrels and provided the sort of administrative and military efficiency the *veche* wanted, the people were willing to acclaim, or at least acquiesce to, new reigns. On the other hand, whenever the incumbent led the city to defeat or the succession provided a highly undesirable candidate, the *veche* felt itself justified in ejecting or rejecting him, as the case might be, provided, of course, it felt itself strong enough to do so. If it did not acquiesce, the prince it chose instead was certain to be opposed by a hereditary claimant and the result might be almost continuous war, which, of course, the *veche* did not want either. In the course of time, therefore, the principle of election tended to be subordinated to family inheritance.

There was no accepted formula, however, for deciding the inheritance. Among the Germanic peoples, in so far as the elective principle did not interfere, the sons of a king usually inherited his kingdom equally, either dividing it or ruling it jointly. The Merovingians and the Carolingians, as well as the Scandinavian dynasties, provide examples of both division and joint rule. The exact nature of a division, which might be made by the old king or by treaty among his heirs, was not always understood or agreed upon although it was of great importance. If the kingdom was permanently divided, each part would pass by inheritance to the sons of its ruler; but if the division was only one of administrative convenience, or if they ruled jointly, the brothers would inherit from each other, to the exclusion of such sons, until the last survivor again ruled the whole.

Conflict was inevitable with such uncertain patterns of succession. On the death of Grand Prince Vladimir, his son Sviatopolk embarked upon a contest of methodical elimination with his half brothers, disposing of three before being himself eliminated by a fourth, Iaroslav. Wishing to avoid a repetition of this, Iaroslav attempted to establish, by testament, joint rule and seniority among his heirs. Having ruled for thirty-five years he felt himself strong enough to assign the cities of Rus' to his sons without consulting the *vecha* (1054):

My sons, I am about to quit this world. Love one another, since ye are brothers by one father and mother. If ye abide in amity with one another, God will dwell among you, and will subject your enemies to you, and ye will live at peace. But if ye dwell in envy and dissension, quarreling with one another, then ye will perish yourselves and bring to ruin the land of your ancestors, which they won at the price of great effort. Wherefore remain rather at peace, brother heeding brother. The throne of Kiev I bequeath to my eldest son, your brother Izyaslav. Heed him as ye have heeded me, that he may take my place among you. To Svyatoslav I give Chernigov, to Vsevolod Pereyaslavl, to Igor the city of Vladimir [-Volynsk], and to Vyacheslav Smolensk.[1]

Rus' was thus not divided but remained a political unit with seniority at Kiev, and Iaroslav hoped that fraternal cooperation in its government would replace the pagan practice of fratricide which had destroyed his own generation. This system of inheritance, derived from the old Germanic joint kingship, meant that the succession to Kiev should pass to the eldest surviving brother and after the last brother to the eldest son or nephew. Awaiting their turns the brothers were distributed to the other cities, both for their own support and for the coordination of the administration, but their tenures were expected to be temporary, for each was expected to move to the next more important throne as vacancies arose. Historians have seen in Iaroslav's testament an attempt to establish a permanent hierarchy of cities, but this is a doubtful reading. Society was too fluid and the importance of cities too fluctuating for any one pattern to become stabilized.*

Iaroslav's solution to the problem of fratricide was accepted by his sons, but not by the *veche* of Kiev. The city accepted his eldest son as prince, but in 1068, after a military failure by Iziaslav and his brothers, the *veche* revolted, expelled its prince, and established his cousin Vseslav. Iziaslav returned a year later, but he so mismanaged relations with the citizenry that his brothers themselves expelled him again. In these struggles it became apparent that relations within the princely family were strongly influenced by the attitudes of the *veche*.

Although the rotation of thrones was never successful, the more basic concept of family seniority had great strength among the Rus' princes. A hundred years later a great-great-grandson of Iaroslav, firmly in control of Kiev, said to his uncle, offering him the throne, "Thou art my father; here is Kiev; take whatever pleases thee and give me the rest." [2]

Inheritance through brothers and nephews is subject to insuperable complications within a few generations, and in Rus' from the middle of the twelfth century the princes could not agree upon seniority. Moreover, it is doubtful that the concept of national or dynastic unity of "all Rus' " was as firmly fixed in the minds of the princes as in those of the churchmen who wrote the chronicles under the influence of Byzantine ideas of unity. Iaroslav himself, in drawing up his testament, left out of his system the descendants of his brother and of his own eldest son, who had died before him. His sons, therefore, inherited discord with their thrones.

Moreover, as the difficulties of the rotation system became greater, the princes thought more and more in patrimonial terms. The chronicle reports that Iaroslav's grandson, Oleg of Chernigov, demanded that his nephew depart from Murom with this message (1096):

* Some have doubted the theory of "rotation of thrones" since in practice there were so many deviations from it (see Alexander E. Presniakov, *Kniazhoe pravo v drevnei Rusi* [St. Petersburg, 1909]). Description of the system as a federation, however, seems to be anachronistic.

Return to your own father's district in Rostov, for this is my father's territory [*volost*] here. I intend to abide here and settle my account with your father, for he expelled me from my father's city. Are you unwilling to let me eat my daily bread here? [3]

The nephew, opposing the demand, was killed in the ensuing battle, and "Oleg entered the town and was well received by the citizens" for, in the chronicler's opinion, "he was justified in his contention." Thus rotation never really became standardized before it was supplemented, and challenged, by the patrimonial principle.

The conflicts in interpreting these principles led repeatedly to open fighting among the grandsons of Iaroslav until, in 1097, they held a council and made an important agreement:

Why do we ruin the land of Rus' by our continued strife against one another? The Polovcians harass our country in divers fashions, and rejoice that war is waged among us. Let us rather hereafter be united in spirit and watch over the land of Rus', and let each of us guard his own domain [*otchina*]; with Svyatopolk retaining Kiev, the heritage of [his father] Izyaslav, . . .[4]

and so on through the list of princes, assigning to each (and to brothers jointly) the domains which their fathers had received from Iaroslav. Still Rus' was not formally divided, since the ideal of cooperation remained; but the attractive principle of patrimony in the assignment of territory was established. The concept of seniority continued to apply within particular branches of the family, but the hierarchy of cities and the rotation of princes gave way to the simpler attachment of each branch to one geographical area. Kiev, now regarded by the princes as a patrimony, continued to enjoy the prestige of the senior city.

The concept of patrimony had long been applied to landed estates. Iaroslav's code of laws recognized equal inheritances by male heirs and the right of their father to make their shares unequal by will. But were the Russian provinces landed estates? The old Norse sagas and early laws indicate that, at times at least, the kings did own the land. Harald the Fairhaired, for example, after conquering Norway in 872, expelled the former owners and held the whole country as an *odal*, an alodium. With this background it is not surprising that the thinking of the princes gives evidence of a tendency to equate ownership with political authority. Just as in the early middle ages the Latin word *dominium* meant both "ownership of" and "authority over," so in Russian there were several words—*gospodar, gospodin, obladati* and *obladatel, volodeti* and *volodetel*—all carrying the connotations of both ownership and rule.* In the West the two meanings of *dominium* were combined in the institutions of feudalism and were not effectively distinguished until late in the twelfth century, when the revived study of the Roman law clarified some of the ambiguities of Germanic tenures; and even then some civil lawyers continued to believe that the Holy Roman Emperor held *dominium* in both senses. In medieval Rus' on the other hand, the relations were not feudal.† So long as all the affairs of government had remained in the hands of the *veche*, owners and rulers may have been practically synonymous, and in these conditions the vocabulary had developed. But with the coming of the Varangian princes this identity, for the native peoples, began to break down. In the minds of the *veche* the princes were outsiders, hired employees, neither owners nor rulers; yet as their power grew, as their position became customary, even the *veche* had to concede that they were rulers. In the minds of the princes, at least from the time that Oleg established the dynasty in Kiev around 880, they were definitely rulers, and the existent language encouraged them to think of their domains also as property. In relation to the private landed estates that they acquired this was certainly legitimate; the *veche*, however, as has been seen, sharply distinguished such patrimonial estates from the prince's political domain. Nevertheless the fact that Iaroslav wrote a will assigning the parts of his domain to his sons is an indication that this sharp distinction was not accepted by the princes, and that patrimonial thinking in political matters had already begun.

The council of princes in 1097, therefore, in formalizing the patrimonial relationship of princes to provinces, gave expression to a very deep-seated princely attitude which had been previously restrained by the idea of rotation and by the powers of the *veche*. With this new arrangement the princes were encouraged to build up the strength of their own provinces, and to indulge less their roving eyes for their cousins' weak spots. Thus the foundation for separatist thinking was laid.

Like Iaroslav's testament, however, the agreement of 1097 was made

---

* With slight changes in spelling and value these are all found in modern Russian, still largely retaining their double meanings.

† For an analysis of this widely disputed subject see Rushton Coulborn, *Feudalism in History* (Princeton, 1956), pp. 167–182, 344–363.

without the *veche*. On occasion, therefore, the *veche* felt itself as free to violate the patrimonial principle as that of seniority, and this it did in 1113 when Vladimir Monomach was invited to the throne of Kiev. By such an election, coupled with sufficient strength in the elected prince, the *veche* could upset the arrangements made by the princely family.

The princes, moreover, were not reluctant to use a tenure gained through election as the basis for later patrimonial claims. Thus the descendants of Vladimir Monomach continued to claim Kiev against the senior branch of the Riurikides descended from Sviatopolk II. If, on the contrary, an election went against a prince who had patrimonial or seniority claims, he might refuse to recognize it. When the Kiev *veche* asserted itself in 1146 and called Iziaslav II to the throne in defiance of both patrimonial and seniority principles, one of his disappointed uncles was Iuri of Suzdal, who continued to claim, on both grounds, authority over Kiev and all of Rus'. From him the later claims of Muscovy were derived.

The trend of patrimonial thinking toward the partition of Rus' progressed most markedly in Suzdalia, Iuri's province far to the northeast, along the upper Volga. On rare occasions he and his descendants were able to enforce their claim to Kiev, but their hold upon Suzdalia was so much more secure that even when they were in control of Kiev they refused to accord it its former prestige, asserting that the capital must follow the prince, and they governed Kiev through appointed junior princes. They preferred the realistic policy of consolidating the strength of their province, knowing that their influence in the brotherhood of princes had become as precarious as the family relationships had become complicated. An indication of their attitude toward the brotherhood is found in their heraldic device: all branches of the family had used a common emblem, the trident; they replaced it with the lion. Further, Iuri's son, Vsevolod III, assumed the Kievan title of grand prince although he did not rule that city, and permitted the princes of Galicia and Riazan to address him as lord (*gospodin*), a form never before used among members of the princely family.

Since Suzdalia was a frontier area, largely settled after its princes were firmly entrenched, it provided this branch of Iaroslav's descendants with opportunities to assert almost feudal claims over later arrivals. Vsevolod's older brother, Andrei, had assumed an attitude of suzerainty toward the weaker princes. He also obtained control of Kiev but refused to go there, installing instead some of his cousins. It is recorded that, becoming displeased with their activities, he told them bluntly, "If thou [Roman], with thy brothers, do not obey my will, then get out of Kiev and David, out of Vyshegorod, and Mstislav, out of Belogorod; and then go to Smolensk and divide it among you." [5] The princes protested that they were not his vassals and should not be treated as such, but they obeyed. Vassalage was precisely the status to which Andrei and Vsevolod reduced the lesser princes within Suzdalia: protection was offered in exchange for obedience. Still, however, there is no evidence that reciprocal rights and duties attained the settled status which they reached in feudal Europe.

The Suzdal princes were careful also to reduce the power of the *veche*. The old towns like Rostov and Suzdal where the *veche* had gathered strength and become troublesome were rejected as capitals in favor of the newer places Vladimir and Moscow, where the princely power had preceded that of the *veche*.

This universal subjection did not exempt even the sons of the grand prince. Angered by his eldest son in 1211, Vsevolod determined to pass the scepter to his second, Iuri. Displaying some political imagination, he is said to have gathered "all of his boyars, from the cities and from the countryside, Bishop Ioan and the hegumens, and the priests, and the merchants, and the courtiers, and all the people." [6] Then, utilizing the religious sanction to forestall future conflicts, he led them to kiss the cross, thus swearing allegiance to Iuri. Referred to as the prototype of the Muscovite consultative assemblies, the zemski sobors, this gathering combined the earlier councils of princes, the advisory council of boyars, and the *veche;* the combination itself indicates the common element of subjection to the grand prince which Andrei and Vsevolod had imposed. It has been suggested that not all the people of Suzdalia could have attended and that therefore some kind of representation was implied. Such an unusual phenomenon would hardly have been passed over in silence by the chronicle, however, and it is easier to imagine that the meeting was announced ahead of time (which was not done for ordinary *veche* meetings) and that those from other cities who wished to made the journey to Vladimir. It is not recorded, and it is highly unlikely, that Vsevolod consulted all these social levels on any additional matters.

Not much has so far been said about the aristocratic element of Kievan Rus'. When the Varangians arrived there were already persons, and perhaps families, distinguished by the accumulation of commercial wealth, by descent from former chieftains, or by election to public office. To these aristocrats the princes added not only the royal family, but also another élite in the form of their retinues (*druzhina*), those who served them effectively in war or in the management of landed estates and commercial affairs. The *druzhina* early became differentiated, its stronger members acquiring retinues of their own, as did some of the local aristocrats. The name *boiar* or boyar was applied to a member of this upper stratum, whether local or a retainer in origin, to distinguish him from a member of the ruling Riurikide family, called a *kniaz*—a word widely translated "duke" although related to the German *könig* and the English "king" and best rendered "prince." * Boyars were also distinguished from the other members of the retinue known as the *grid*. The entire retinue, whatever their individual origin, were free men and served their prince voluntarily, the word *druzhina* meaning "friends"; but in Suzdalia in the twelfth century the *grid* began to lose their liberty and a new name was applied to them: *dvoriane*, "courtiers." Unlike the princely family these élite groups did not soon become exclusive, but remained open to ability through princely service (the broadest gateway), through the *veche*, and through private wealth.

As the exploring, plundering phase of the Scandinavian occupation gave way to local residence, good service to the prince came to be rewarded by a grant of land in patrimonial tenure, an *otchina* (or *votchina*). While frequently resulting from service, these estates were not held, as were fiefs in western Europe, on any condition of further service. The local, nonservice boyars also acquired land, as did even the peasants, since land was plentiful and there were no legal restrictions on its acquisition by any social class. It is important for later developments, however, to remember that the prestige and powers of the nobility, and frequently their lands, were derived from service to the *veche* or to the prince; nobility and service were not derived from landownership.

The local boyars participated in the *veche* and some of them, for example, the former mayors and commanders at Novgorod, acted as a formal or informal steering committee for the *veche*. The most influential of them, including the commander of militia, continuously partici-

---

* Although meaning, in recent times, a male monarch, the word "king" is closely related to the word "kin," and it originally signified simply "a member of the (royal) family." This meaning the cognates long retained in Scandinavia and in Rus'.

pated in the administration and gave counsel to the prince. They are mentioned separately as having agreed to the elections of princes, to treaties with Byzantium, to city charters, and to codes of laws. Five of them are referred to by name as having helped Iaroslav's three sons revise his code. One of them was the head of the guild of builders.

The practice of the princes in consulting the boyars on major matters rested upon expediency and necessity rather than upon any legal right of the boyars to be consulted. Without his retinue the prince was almost helpless, and unless they were satisfied with their treatment they might desert him. It is recorded that Prince Vladimir of Dorogobuzh arranged with certain allies to attack Kiev in 1169, and then approached his boyars with the completed plan. They flatly refused to help: "You have conceived this plan for yourself, Prince. We will not follow you, for we knew nothing about it." [7] His allies, seeing him come without the boyars, chased him away with arrows.

Dissatisfied boyars, individually or in groups, could take service elsewhere. This freedom of departure, based on the old Scandinavin comradeship in arms, was so firmly established as to be one of the chief forces preventing the development of feudal relations in Kievan Rus'. A boyar who was rewarded with a grant of land often sank local roots and might not wish to accompany the prince when he moved to another city. Thus became established the freedom of boyars to leave the service of their princes without losing their lands, a practice sharply differing from the feudal customs of western Europe, where tenure was conditional upon service. This freedom rested not only on the alodial character of *otchina* tenure, but also on the concept of brotherly cooperation within the princely family: departure to serve a nephew or a cousin was not desertion to an enemy.

Yet this one freedom was instrumental in the failure of the aristocracy to secure others. The ease with which conflicts between boyar and prince could be resolved by departure hindered the search for other solutions. Furthermore, the ease of entry into the aristocracy reduced its solidarity, as did the diversity of the paths by which that entry could be achieved. The fluidity of the group prevented the consolidation of any general structure of privileges as against the princes: it had no Magna Carta and lacked the cohesion to secure one.

On the other hand, the power of the princes, even of the grand princes, in sharp contrast with later developments around Moscow, never became absolute in Kievan Rus'. At least seven practical limitations restrained the princes. (1) They were dependent for active support upon their retinue as a group, although not as a separate, corporate organ of government, and not upon individual members of it. (2) The boyar freedom of departure restricted invidious attitudes and actions of princes toward the aristocracy. (3) The alodial tenure enjoyed by the holders of *votchiny* effectively removed such lands from the princely administration. (4) The princes were dependent upon the *veche*, at times for active support, but always for at least passive acquiescence, a dependence frequently defined closely be treaty. (5) The princes were restricted by the testaments of their fathers, which divided the land into shares, *udely*, among them, and exhorted mutual cooperation and respect. These wills were enforced both by religious considerations and by the arms of the other heirs. (6) Similar restraints were contained in the treaties between princes, and the same sanctions were applicable against violators. (7) The church, in its formal jurisdiction and in its general influence, was partly independent of the princes by virtue of its connection with Byzantium and its possession of a higher culture—an independence it had not enjoyed in Byzantium itself.

The practical nature of these limitations is apparent; there was no corresponding body of theoretical limitations which the princes recognized. As contributors of political ideas the Varangians stressed the elements of power, not the restrictions upon it. Against the earlier community solidarity of separate cities they asserted the solidarity of a ruling family, with a number of corollaries. For one, the unity of Rus': to the old linguistic ties they added, in spite of their internal differences, an idea of political cohesion which helped to prevent the fragmentation that overtook western Europe. For another, the chief political office, that of the grand prince, was considered a monopoly of the Riurikides, to be assigned by family rules, not by election of the *veche*. And for a third, all members of the family considered themselves entitled to a share in the cooperative ruling of Rus'. Against the democratic methods of the Slavs the Varangians set their own comradeship in arms. Although itself somewhat democratic when restrained by the independent farmers and folk *thing* of Scandinavia, this comradeship led in Rus' to the gradual replacement of the militia by the military profession (with its concomitant discrimination against nonfighting men and its distortion of public administration in favor of military considerations); more important, it led to the gradual proliferation of aristocracy (with its class and rank consciousness and its individual tenures of land). And finally, against the responsibility of public officials the princes asserted irresponsible government or, euphemistically, with the help of the church, government responsible to God, not to men. For authority emanating from the people they substituted hereditary authority with its subsidiary features: family seniority, patrimonial territorial claims, and a power of political testament.

CHAPTER III

Symphonia: The Byzantines

A THIRD body of political concepts was brought into Rus' from Byzantium, largely by monks and priests. They gave the pagan Russes not only Christianity but also a connection with a very old and highly developed culture. Byzantium, the second Rome, was then the center of the Christian world, the western parts of the Roman empire having fallen to the barbarians and the Mohammedans. It was proud of its inheritance of ideas and institutions both from the first Rome and from the ancient Greeks.

Of the many elements of this intricate civilization that were influential among the Russes, perhaps the most important for politics were their ideas of harmony and of kingship, which include the relations between church and state.

The first of these goes back to the shadowy figure of Pythagoras in the sixth century B.C., who expressed a conception of the universe of which the essence was the order of number and proportion. All things in heaven and earth were made to fit together, to work in harmony, each in its proper sphere. First worked out in the mathematics of musical sounds, such relationships were believed to obtain quite generally—in cosmology, in religion, and in politics.* So appealing were the ideas of proportion and harmony that they pervaded Greek society, as is clear from their achievements in architecture and sculpture. Many of the disciples of Pythagoras went astray in the mystical pursuit of symbolic numbers, but his main concept was seized by Plato and carried to great heights in the *Republic*. In Plato's theory of forms, and even more explicitly in the later Stoic ideas of natural law, the concep-

* His famous theorum about the right triangle Pythagoras regarded as another illustration of the harmony of nature.

23

tion gradually matured of an ordered, harmonious universe, rational and unchanging, in which the best man, the philosopher king, should rule as a servant of the universal community. In politics it was a hierarchic, not a democratic, conception; men were in a sense equal, but equality must be proportional, rewards must be in harmony with merits. Each class or rank had its place in society, and justice required that each remain in its place. Moreover, when connected with the concept of a divine plan of the universe, such ideas provided a firm basis for conservatism: any change would destroy the harmony, and might also offend the gods.

The practical application of this thinking came with the empire of Alexander, wherein even the old conflict between Greek and barbarian was integrated into a harmonious whole. The influence of Pythagorean ideas on the development of the Hellenistic kingship, and the continuity of these ideas in the Roman and Byzantine periods, have been stressed by competent scholars.* Diotogenes, a neo-Pythagorean of uncertain date, clearly expressed the prevailing theory: "The State, which is a body joined together in harmony from many different parts, imitates the system and harmony of the universe; and the emperor (*basileus*), who exercises an authority which is not responsible [to any earthly superior], and who is in himself Animate Law, thus becomes the figure of a God among men." † When Eusebius, in the fourth century, undertook to explain the position of the Christian emperor, Constantine, he found the well-established pagan theory to be quite acceptable. It was necessary only to regard the emperor, not as a god, but as the vicegerent of God; all the rest of the old explanation remained intact. The earthly empire was a copy of the heavenly, just as the pagans had said. As in heaven there was one God and one divine law, so on earth there could be only one emperor in a universal empire, centralized and autocratic, yet ruling by one law. It was the duty of all men to cooperate in the reproduction, so far as was possible, of

---

* See, for example, Erwin R. Goodenough, "The Political Philosophy of Hellenistic Kingship," *Yale Classical Studies,* I (1928), 55–102, and Norman H. Baynes, "The Byzantine State," in his *Byzantine Studies and Other Essays* (London, 1955), pp. 47–66.

† As preserved in Stobaeus, *Florilegium;* translated in Ernest Barker, ed., *From Alexander to Constantine* (Oxford, 1956), pp. 364–365. Diotogenes is dated variously from the fourth century B.C. to the third A.D. This in itself, since his fragments are fairly comprehensive, indicates the similarity of thought during this long period.

the harmony of the heavenly government. Moreover, the celestial arche-
type could not change; therefore, the earthly copy should not. Thence
came the intense conservatism of the Byzantines, whose thousand years
of empire were characterized by an almost complete absence of original
political thought.

The imperial power, held as a trust from God, carried with it a duty
to imitate God. God was conceived as the prime mover, the original
energy, and also to be benevolent; therefore it was the emperor's duty
to accomplish things and to be beneficent, to take on himself the
burden of empire and to be a public-spirited servant of his people. He
was expected to take the initiative in providing for the public needs,
and personally to lead the armies, to administer justice, and to relieve
the distressed.* "It is our care," said Emperor Marcian (d. 457) in his
Second Novel, "to provide for the welfare of the human race." The
doles of bread and circuses were later discontinued in Byzantium, but
the psychology of dependence upon the emperor was never lost.

With the world conceived as partaking in the celestial harmony, and
the emperor in the role of the good shepherd, the relations of church
and state were also conceived to be harmonious. Further, the purposes
of the two were not viewed as being distinct or separate but rather
mutual and united. The doctrine of the separation of church and state,
developed in the West by Ambrose and Gelasius, had few adherents in
the East. In Constantinople the church had never exercised authority
over secular affairs as it had in Italy when the temporal power collapsed
during the barbarian invasions. Struggles between sacred and secular
rulers, such as those that agonized Europe for centuries, had not
occurred in Byzantium. To be sure, the East also had had its theorists
who exalted the spiritual power above the temporal. Patriarch John
Chrysostom (d. 407), later very popular in Rus', had spoken of "the
priesthood, which is as much more sublime than a royal dignity as the
soul is more sublime than the body." He continued, "Hence, we should,
by rights, regard them [priests] as more august than kings and
princes." [1] But as a practical matter Chrysostom, when he set his will
against that of a reigning emperor, found that a patriarch could be
removed from office; and similar discoveries were made by others.
Perhaps the priesthood was "more sublime," but in conflicts the emperor might prove to be a higher priest than the patriarch.

* In the days of Augustus the inclination of the Romans to depend upon him
had played a large part in the transition from the republic to the principate.

The early church had helped the emperors to a kind of sacerdotal position. Constantine, baptized only on his deathbed, had retained his pagan title of *pontifex maximus,* the highest priest, and was regarded as the bishop of those outside the church, the pagans and heretics. The church, grateful for its legal status after so many persecutions, accepted this anomaly and helped him determine the orthodox doctrines through the great councils. The Eastern emperors later abandoned the pagan title, but they never forgot their special position within the church. The iconoclast Emperor Leo III (d. 741), who had written to Rome, "Understand, O Pope, that I am both emperor and priest," summarized in the preamble to his digest of Roman law, the *Ecloga,* his conception of the imperium:

Since, then, having placed the power of imperial rule in our hands as was His pleasure, He has made this sign of recognition of our love in fear for Him, ordering us, after the manner of Peter, the most exalted acme of the apostles, to shepherd the most faithful flock, we trust that in His eyes there is nothing before or greater than the governing, in legality and justice, of those who, for redress [of grievances], have been entrusted to us by Him. . . .

Wherefore, busied with concerns such as these and tirelessly directing our thoughts toward the discovery of those things that are pleasing to God and beneficial to the common weal, and respecting, before all things on earth, justice, as the ambassador of Those on high and as being sharper than any sword against the enemy for his strength who avails himself of it, . . . we have decided to gather together in orderly fashion, both more clearly and more precisely, in this book the decisions on frequently arising affairs and contracts and the penalties corresponding to the complaints.[2]

Leo represented an extreme, leaning further than other emperors in the direction of the doctrine of caesaropapism. The usually prevailing doctrine was better balanced and was clearly expressed in the preamble to Justinian's Sixth Novel, a high authority frequently quoted in Russian sources:

The priesthood and the Empire are the two greatest gifts which God, in His infinite clemency, has bestowed upon mortals; the former has reference to Divine matters, the latter presides over and directs human affairs, and both, proceeding from the same principle, adorn the life of mankind; hence nothing should be such a source of care to the emperors as the honor of the priests who constantly pray to God for their salvation. For if the priesthood is everywhere free from blame, and the Empire full of confidence in God is administered equitably and judiciously, general good will result, and whatever is beneficial will be bestowed upon the human race. . . . We think that this will take place if the sacred rules of the Church which the just, praiseworthy, and adorable Apostles, the inspectors and ministers of the Word of God, and the Holy Fathers have explained and preserved for us are obeyed." [3]

Along these lines the Eastern Church developed the theory of *symphonia*, a theory of judicious consultation and mutual respect that did not separate but rather combined the two powers in the apostolic task of conducting the people to salvation, on earth and in heaven.

This old and well-tried theory the bishops brought and applied to Rus', even though conditions there required that it rest upon somewhat modified bases. For one thing, the church in Rus' was not autocephalous, since the metropolitan was responsible to the patriarch at Constantinople. This might, on occasion, hamper the flexibility of church policy; but it also provided outside support for the metropolitan. He and his bishops, and of course the patriarch, tended to view the church in Rus' as a Byzantine civilizing mission to a benighted, almost barbaric, land. Moreover, the princes were not well versed in theology, as some of the emperors had been, and this tended to give the bishops further advantage. The princes, however, had two great assets. The first was their independence of the Byzantine emperor, an anomalous fact never quite digested by the bishops, who regarded both the church and the empire as universal. Their second lay within the church itself—the Pauline doctrine of subjection to secular powers. The result avoided both extremes: it was never so near caesaropapism as Leo III had been, nor was it the theocracy of an Innocent III, since the secular power really ruled. The scales in Rus' may have tipped a bit in favor of the princes, as compared with Byzantium, but the balance of forces, while differing in detail, did not differ in essence, and the *symphonia* in Rus' retained its primary quality of cooperation between prelates and princes. Religious affairs were a legitimate concern of the princes, and the bishops were expected to serve as advisers to the princes even in regard to secular problems.

Much ambiguity clouds the historical record of the earlier conversion of Rus' to Christianity.* The seeds seem to have been planted three times before they finally took root under Vladimir about 988.

* The literature is vast (see Evgeni E. Golubinski, *Istoriia Russkoi tserkvi*, I, part 1 [2d ed.; Moscow, 1901], 105–187).

Vladimir, seeing in religion a means toward national unity, first tried to establish a pagan pantheon. He then turned to Christianity. The Byzantine empire was shaken by internal and external conflicts, and Vladimir secured with his new faith a new wife, Anna, a sister of the emperor, whose hand had already been haughtily refused to the German emperor. One of the problems of the new religious policy was to avoid dependence upon Byzantium: the unity of church and state must not mean political submission to the emperor. The creation of a trained native clergy was therefore essential. For this reason, the energetic Vladimir, a worthy precursor of Peter the Great, not only ordered his people in masses into the rivers, where they were baptized. He also "took the children of the best families, and sent them [to Constantinople?] for instruction in book learning. The mothers of these children wept bitterly over them for they were not yet strong in faith, but mourned as for the dead." [4] Only after his time was the regular hierarchical relationship to Constantinople established. The problem of independence remained, as will be seen.

Vladimir is also credited with the establishment of the basic immunities and privileges of the church in Rus'. His church statute, supposedly issued in 996 and revised a few years later, although actually of uncertain age, was none the less of prime importance in regulating the relations of church and state. It said, in part,

And then, having opened the Greek *Nomocanon*, we found in it that it is not proper for the prince to judge these [church] trials and suits, nor for his boyars nor for [his] judges. And I, having consulted with my princess Anna and with my children, granted this jurisdiction to the churches, to the metropolitan and to all the bishoprics in the land of Rus'.

And accordingly neither my children, nor my grandchildren, nor any of my descendants need interfere with either the church people or any of their courts; that is all given for all towns and for districts and villages, wherever Christians may be. . . .

And these are the church cases: divorce, marriage agreements and dowries, adultery, rape, abduction, [those] between husband and wife about property, marriage of consanguines or affines, witchcraft, enchantment with herbs, divination, incantation, magic, three insults: whore [and fool(?)] and poisoner, heresy, biting, a son beating his father or a daughter her mother or a daughter-in-law her mother-in-law, brothers or children contending about an inheritance, theft of church property, grave robbing, . . . sodomy, praying [as pagans] in a barn or in a grove or by waters, or a girl abandoning her child. . . .

And my judicial officials I command not to offend the church courts, and from the [civil] courts to give nine parts [of the fines] to the prince and the tenth to the holy church. . . .

And from ancient times are established and entrusted to the holy bishops all public and commercial standards and measures, scales [and] weights; from God thus anciently established, the bishop must guard [them] without dishonesty, neither diminishing nor increasing, [and] for all that he will give [account] to Him, word for word, on the great judgment day, just as for men's souls.

These are the church people: hegumen, priest, deacon, their children, priest's wife, those who belong to the choir, hegumene, monk, nun, woman who bakes sacramental bread, pilgrim, physician, person healed by a holy miracle,* [widow], person bequeathed to the church, stranger, blind person, cripple, (people of) monastery, hospital, inn, hospice.

Between the people of the church of God the metropolitan or the bishop judges the offenses or differences or quarrels or inheritances. But if there is a suit between other people and these people, then a mixed court. . . .[5]

Parts of this text may have been inserted after the time of Vladimir, but the document established an extensive precedent for the acceptance of Greek canon law, a very elaborate and intricate body of rules upon which the church later drew on numerous occasions for additional support of its privileges. It should be noted that church jurisdiction fell into two general categories, one covering certain kinds of crimes and disputes (including the important one of succession to property by will †) regardless of the status of the parties, and the other covering certain kinds of persons (including all peasants tilling monastery lands) regardless of the nature of their disputes or crimes—except when laymen were involved. This statute became a model for many others issued by the princes throughout Rus', cementing the interdependence of church and state. Very similar wording appears, for example, in the fifteenth-century charter of Pskov, with this telling addition (Article 2): "And the [archbishop's] lieutenants shall not interfere with the princely court."[6]

If Vladimir opened the Greek *Nomocanon* he found in it not only

---

* Or, more probably, "freedman," reading instead of *proshchenik, pushchenik,* as found in some other lists of church people.

† Scholars differ on this point, since the approximately contemporary *Russkaia Pravda*, Art. 92, appears to place successions under secular jurisdiction (*Medieval Russian Laws*, ed. and trans. George Vernadsky [New York, 1947], p. 51). Some resolve the dilemma by restricting church jurisdiction to the property of church people, others by restricting the secular law to succession in the absence of a will.

canons of the church but also substantial portions of the Byzantine secular law, for the *symphonia,* far from requiring a separation of the two, caused church rules to be enforced by civil sanctions, and civil law to reflect religious prejudices. These interrelations were apparent in the sixth century in the great code of Justinian, although in it the pagan Roman element was still dominant, and by the eighth century, in the *Ecloga* of Leo III, the Christian influences were especially marked. The emperor Basil I turned back from some of the more caesaropapal positions of Leo, but the digests prepared in his reign, the *Procheiron* and the *Epanagoge,* still reflected strong religious influences, the latter containing a singularly clear description of the parallel positions of patriarch and emperor.* All these legal manuals, however, were essentially simplifications of the code of Justinian, and separately and through the *Nomocanon* thus served to transmit to Rus', which had never been ruled by the Romans, some elements of the Roman law. Therefore, in the centuries when the school of Bologna was reviving the study of Roman jurisprudence with such vigor that all of western Europe (except Britain) eventually adopted it, it is not surprising that some parallel modifications were to be found in the legal enactments of the Russes; yet in the whole body of their civil law these modifications remained relatively minor—which indicates the independence of Rus' legal thought.†

In religious law, on the other hand, Byzantine influence was dominant from the beginning. The Eastern Church, unlike the Roman, encouraged the use of vernacular languages in religious services, and in translation as the *Kormchaia kniga,* or "Steering book," the *Nomocanon* was known, by the thirteenth century, to many who could not read Greek.‡ The great commentators upon the canons, Aristinos, Balsa-

---

* Translated in part in William K. Medlin, *Moscow and East Rome* (Geneva, 1952), pp. 232–233.

† In view of the reputation for brutality that Russia later earned by the extensive use of flogging and similar punishments it is striking to note, as an illustration of this independence, that the codes of Kievan Rus' prescribed money fines wherever the Byzantine law called for corporal punishment, mutilation, or execution. Not until the fourteenth century was capital punishment exacted by any Russian law, and then on a very restricted scale, and only in the western provinces, to which it probably penetrated from Europe. By 1649 over fifty offenses were so punished—in this regard Russia had become quite Western. The Tatars, too, used capital punishment, and may have influenced the Muscovites.

‡ It included, in Chap. 42, the quotation from Justinian's Sixth Novel given above.

mon, and Blastares, were also translated. And, aside from such books, the Greek bishops themselves, accustomed to think in terms of a Byzantine background, applied the rules they had learned to the training of native clerics and to the advising of princes and thus spread the attitudes and values of Byzantium. In this process many secular matters also were involved, either through their implications for religion or through the implications of religion for them.

Through these channels the mature political concepts of Roman and Greek civilization, always in their Christian coloring, were introduced. Moreover, the long experience of that civilization had provided solutions to many problems, and as similar situations appeared in the development of Rus', the bishops were ready with these solutions, ready to direct the thinking of princes and people along the well-tried pathways.

The ambiguous position of the princes as hereditary rulers and as employees of the *veche* obviously presented a problem which Byzantine experience had long since settled. The pagan Romans had created a prince, the emperor, and according to their theory he was elected by the Senate, the army, and the people of Rome, although heredity and the will of the reigning emperor were also influential. After the coming of Christianity the clerics stressed the pervasive influence of God over all elements of this selective process, bringing them into harmony, and indicated that any conflicts among them were probably the work of the devil. The Roman Senate, army, and people were all included, *mutatis mutandis*, in the *veche* of Kiev, and, as at Byzantium, God spoke through it. But with much less ambiguity, and therefore much more reliably, he spoke through heredity and the sworn testament of a departed prince.* Thus the bishops recognized the voice of the people in the choice of princes, but to them, as at Byzantium, it was usually a voice of acquiescence, not of deliberation, since God did not need to deliberate. On the whole then, by emphasizing the divine selection of rulers, the clerics threw the prestige of their religion behind the hereditary claims of the princes and against the freedom of choice of the *veche*.

In other ways as well, drawing on the Bible and on established Byzantine traditions, the bishops reinforced the growth of princely

---

* These same four claims to kingly power—selection by the reigning king, by inheritance, by the people, and by God—had also been combined in Western thought and practice, for example, in Charlemagne's empire.

power and of cohesion in the realm. As in western Europe, full use was made of Paul's "Be subject unto the higher powers. For there is no power but of God: the powers that be are ordained of God" (Romans, 13:1). An aphorism of Deacon Agapetus of Constantinople (ca. 527) was widely repeated: "By the nature of his body an emperor is like any man, but by the power of office he is like God." [7] The patriarch Gennadius (d. 471), some of whose writings were also translated, advised the people, "Fear the prince with all thy strength. . . . The pupil fears the master's staff, and all the more so the master himself; so fear God and the ruler by whom the sinful are punished. For the prince is the servant of God for human mercy and punishment." [8] By such expressions the bearers of the divine word gave to the people of Rus' a picture of their place in the cosmic order very different from that of the pagan days when the *veche* had been supreme. Moreover, the bishops had other expressions which could be used to clarify that picture, if necessary. In 1135, for example, Metropolitan Michael threatened the city of Novgorod with an interdict if the *veche* did not restore order.

Quite apart from such sentiments and activities, the unified organization of the church itself strengthened the dynastic unity of Rus'. All the bishops were under the single metropolitan at Kiev, and although the branches of the princely family drew apart, the ecclesiastical unity remained. In addition, the church constantly presented, before the eyes of both princes and people, a definite pattern of centralization and subordination that eventually, in Muscovy, became also the pattern of the state.

From this symbiotic relationship, however, one should not deduce that harmony always obtained between the bishops and the princes. The institution of princely rule the bishops approved, but not always did they approve the actions of individual princes. Chrysostom himself had distinguished the power of ruling from the person of the ruler, as had Ambrose in the West, and thus had provided a basis for a modification of the accepted interpretation of Paul's "The powers that be are of God" to a more active, responsible one, namely, that an unjust ruler, God's punishment for the sins of the people, was himself liable as a sinner to correction by the bishop. This was still a doctrine of submission, but the spiritual shepherd might rebuke his princely sheep and, praying God to withdraw his wrath from the rest of the flock, might see an answer to that prayer in a rebellious *veche* that turned out its prince on less sophisticated grounds.

A more general source of friction between bishops and princes, however, lay in the fact that most of the metropolitans and many of the bishops were Greeks. Imbued with the Byzantine idea that the emperor was the ultimate head of both church and state, they were not always inclined to view the princes of Rus' with due respect. At the same time, the influence enjoyed by the high clergy over the people, coupled with their intimate relationship as advisers to the princes, made their selection a matter of both personal and political importance to the princes.

In the beginning Vladimir may have maintained a degree of independence for the church at Kiev by selecting a bishop not derived from Constantinople, but under Iaroslav the acceptance of metropolitans designated by the patriarch at Constantinople became the normal pattern. There was, however, one noteworthy exception. In the year 1051,

there was conflict and lack of harmony between Iaroslav . . . and the Greeks, and so Iaroslav met with his Rus' bishops and they decided thus, according to the sacred, apostolic laws and regulations . . . : two or three bishops may appoint a bishop; and according to this sacred law of the divine apostles the Rus' bishops convening together appointed Hilarion,* a Rus', as metropolitan of Kiev and all Rus'—not separating from the orthodox patriarchs and the piety of the Greek law [and] not being proud in appointing from them [the Russes], but avoiding enmity and malice as it was then.[9]

Hilarion was later expelled, and thereafter, under Iaroslav's successors, Greek influence increased until his great-grandson, Vsevolod II, undertook to reverse this trend and to persuade the metropolitan to appoint Russes as bishops. The metropolitan, the Greek Michael, departed for home instead, laying all Rus' under a ban (1145). Iziaslav, who followed Vsevolod and continued his church policy, convened the bishops and thus elected a Rus', the well-educated Clement of Smolensk, to succeed Michael. By that time, however, Greek control of the office had

---

* His sermon "On Law and Grace" is a monument of early Russian literature and religious thought. For a translation see Karl Rose, *Grund und Quellort des russischen Geisteslebens* (Berlin, 1956).

become so customary that the bishop of Novgorod, the fiery Niphont, refused to recognize a metropolitan so chosen. Instead he wrote to him:

There is nothing in the law, that the bishops may appoint a metropolitan without the patriarch; but the patriarch appoints the metropolitan. We will not honor thee here, nor worship with thee, if thou hast not received benediction at holy Sophia nor from the patriarch. If thou correct this, receive benediction from the patriarch, then will we honor thee.[10]

The controversy continued and reached a climax under Grand Prince Rostislav, who sent back to Byzantium a metropolitan named by the patriarch without Rostislav's approval. On that occasion he wrote to the emperor, "If the patriarch henceforth without our knowledge appoints a metropolitan to Rus', then not only will I not accept him but we will also resolve once and for all that the metropolitans be selected and appointed by the Rus' bishops by order of the grand prince." [11] This strong statement he followed in 1166 with a call for another synod of Russian bishops, which elected a third Rus' metropolitan, Constantine II.

Similar difficulties appeared also on the local level in the selection of bishops. The Suzdal princes, strong personalities, were especially prone to these altercations. Vsevolod III, objecting to the designation of one Nicholas to be bishop of Rostov, wrote to the metropolitan in 1183: "The people of our land have not chosen him; but if thou hast appointed him, then keep him where thou wilt; but to me appoint Luke." [12] It was typical of Vsevolod that he did not write, "to Rostov appoint . . ."; his reference to the people should not be taken as support for democracy. His older brother Andrei had gone a step further: he had actually removed his bishop from office, after several disagreements, and thereby brought down upon himself a sharp reprimand from the patriarch:

If you will not submit to his teaching and instruction, but still will persecute him, the savior given to you by Christ, . . . even if you fill the whole world with holy churches and monasteries,* and if you build innumerable cities, you are persecuting a bishop, head of the church and of the people, and therefore they are not churches but cattle stalls, and not one of them will be your reward and salvation. . . . Ask your head, who is your bishop, and whatever he says, do it, believing, as the Lord says, in your bishop's

---

* These were cutting words, for Andrei was widely known as a builder of churches.

lips. . . . If you honor the bishop, you honor Christ, for he bears the image of Christ and sits in the seat of Christ.[13]

This letter of Patriarch Luke Chrysobergos represents an extreme both in its acrimony and in its ecclesiastical claims. He was asserting for the bishops of Rus' a superiority over temporal rulers greater than any that he could make good for himself against the emperor.

With these and similar altercations between princes and prelates, and with both the metropolitan and the local bishops drawing support from the patriarch (who might, to the princes' way of thinking, have very exaggerated conceptions of the bishops' powers), it is not surprising that the princes desired to break the link with Constantinople. It would appear that in the mid-twelfth century the princes were about to prevail in the contest, as two metropolitans were elected in Kiev within twenty years. At the death of Rostislav, however, conflicts among the princes reduced the importance of Kiev, which was sacked and burned by Andrei, and the center of power shifted toward Suzdalia. While these conflicts were still in progress, and before the trend toward the election of metropolitans and their subsequent confirmation in Byzantium could be resumed, a new force supervened—the Mongols. As a result of these distractions the church "of Kiev and all Rus' " continued under the control of Byzantium until the fifteenth century.

Another aspect of the connection with Constantinople had an even more enduring effect upon the political thinking of Rus'. When the Roman pope placed an imperial crown on the head of Charlemagne in 800 without the consent of the reigning Byzantine empress, Irene, he drove a wedge between Rome and Constantinople, widening the gap that mutual jealousies had created over the centuries. The Byzantines regarded this as pure usurpation, another perfidious act of Rome; it was followed by the Photian Schism later in the century and by mutual recriminations leading to the formal separation into two churches in 1054.* Thus, when Vladimir accepted Christianity for Rus' around 988 the schism was not complete, but the Eastern clergy had had ample time to formulate their conception of the errors of the West. The "Latin heresy" may never have been expounded, as the chronicles relate, to Vladimir himself, and the Russes certainly did not

---

* An important theological issue in the conflict was the unilateral insertion into the Latin creed of the word *filioque*, so that the Holy Ghost is said to proceed "from the Father and the Son," whereas the Nicene creed, retained by the Greeks, said "from the Father" alone.

shun the West like a blighted area; yet knowledge of Rome and of the Roman Catholic countries entered Rus' under a cloud which produced there a feeling of antagonism more pronounced even than that at Byzantium. From the time of the coming of Constantine to the Bosporus, Greece and Constantinople had been proud of their prominent role in the Roman Empire, which continued to be a unity even when ruled by separate Eastern and Western emperors. After the cultural decay of the Western areas, the great heritage was zealously guarded by the East, and in spite of all admixtures of Asiatic peoples the Byzantines to the end called themselves Romans. None of these historical ties drew the Russes to the West. When they appeared on the historical stage the great days of Rome were over and Byzantium was the fountainhead of culture and truth, while Rome, their priests told them, was far away in the land of error. Therefore, to geographic and linguistic isolation was added a religious antagonism unmitigated by the memories of cooperation and the continuing intellectual exchanges which softened the effects of the schism in Byzantium itself. By the time of the Florentine Union (1439) this feeling was strong enough to be turned even against Byzantium. When the Hanseatic League and the Byzantine Empire collapsed, cutting her firmest links with the outside world, Rus' began a separate existence that has never been entirely abandoned. The psychological effects of this defensive isolation are still strongly felt.

The Byzantine contributions to the political thought of the Russes may now be summed up as five major attitudes. (1) A tendency prevailed, like that within the empire, toward centralization and against feudalism and local autonomy. Temporarily successful at Kiev, and permanently so at Moscow, this tendency has not yet been reversed. (2) The Byzantines brought an emphasis upon the value of monarchy and hierarchy, of the harmony of different orders of men, and a complementary discouragement of democracy and equality as embodied in the *veche*. The bishops and monks continually encouraged both the princes and the people to think that authority and submission were prescribed by God's plan. (3) The Hellenistic and Roman attitude of dependence upon the prince, already present, was reinforced. Local or popular initiative was regarded as an anarchistic violation of the centralization and monarchy of the divine plan. (4) The Byzantine pattern of *symphonia*, of cooperation between church and state, rather than their separation, became the Russian pattern. Mutual aid linked the two together irrevocably, both in institutions and in the minds of the people, while the princes' problem of maintaining political independence from emperor and patriarch left the church perhaps less independent of the state than at Byzantium. (5) The attitude of trusteeship toward truth, which stifled originality among the Byzantines, similarly discouraged among the Russes any tendency toward free speculation or exploration. The Byzantine "civilizing mission" was a transmission of knowledge already acquired, not of the techniques of thought by which it might be increased. Christianity and civilization were treasures to be preserved; orthodoxy and conservatism, the essential means.

PART TWO

Mongolian Rus'

(ca. 1240 to 1480)

CHAPTER IV

World Empire: The Mongols

THE great horde of bowmen on horseback that poured over Asia in the thirteenth century conquered, in the name of Chingis Khan (1167–1227), and with devastation only recently equaled, the largest empire the world had ever seen. For administrative purposes it was early divided into regions called *ulus*'s, assigned to Chingis Khan's sons. The eldest son, Juchi, was assigned the western portion with its largely Turkish population. Juchi died before his father, and the family elected Chingis' third son, Ugedey, to succeed as great khan. Juchi's *ulus*, similarly divided among his sons, was legally subject to Ugedey, at Karakorum, and Juchi's second son, Batu, was commissioned to continue the Mongol drive to the west. Using supplementary Turkish troops he overran almost all of Rus' and, at the death of Ugedey, became virtually independent, with headquarters at Sarai on the lower Volga. Due to the Turkish element these conquerors were known as Tatars, but the leadership continued to be Mongolian.

The subjection of Kievan Rus' to the Golden Horde * was not the political eclipse that it might have been. For one thing subjection meant quite different things in different places and at different times; for another, its effect on different parts of the country lasted for varying periods of time. During the period of the conquest, it frequently meant much slaughter, and many cities were razed; later it meant Mongol and Tatar tax and conscript gatherers; finally it meant tributes of men and money collected for the Mongols by the Russes themselves. The cities

* This term, in use only since the sixteenth century, customarily designates not the Mongols and Turks of the whole empire but only those of Batu's khanate. As a geographical term, it applies to the large area west of the Urals, also called the khanate of Kypchak from the Tatar inhabitants.

of Polotsk and Pskov escaped subjection; Novgorod paid tribute but retained its own administration; most of the cities of the southwest and far north had partly Mongol and partly Rus' government, becoming entirely Rus' early in the fourteenth century; Kiev and the surrounding towns not only were destroyed but were administered directly by the Mongols until 1363. In the southwest subjection lasted about 100 years; in the central Kievan area, some 160; in the northeast, well over 200.

Nor were the Mongols themselves quite the soulless barbarians they are sometimes pictured. They commanded not only rugged horses and accurate bows but also a highly organized system of public administration and a respectable body of political philosophy. They were both raiders and rulers, conquering most of the land mass of Europe and Asia, and holding it for varying periods down to the present time. The extent and quality of their influence upon Russia are still subjects for debate among the historians, and the presentation here of Mongol ideas available for absorption by the Russes does not necessarily imply that the reappearance of some of these ideas in Muscovy was due to such absorption.

Since the beginning of history the great plains of central Asia had been the home of nomadic herdsmen who roamed over vast areas, coming into contact, through trade and war, with the centers of high culture to the east, west, and south. To the southeast lay China, conceiving herself the center of a world empire with a divinely appointed ruler. In the southwest lay Iran, ancient center of empire and of the idea of divine kingship, which more recently had been the transmitter of two universal religions, Nestorian Christianity and Islam. Periodically the nomads irrupted into these settled areas with great military force. They already had generated one great empire, that of the Huns, whose conquests, reaching from China to Roman Gaul, may have left a legend of universal empire among the steppe peoples even before the Mongols themselves came into contact with either China or Iran. The Hun chieftain, Attila, according to the historian Priscus who visited him, held an important idea that was later to reappear in Chingis Khan's beliefs. He believed himself, after his legendary finding of the sword of Mars, to be called by God to be ruler of the whole world. He also felt himself to be irresistible in war—a notion that the Mongol was careful to disclaim. In any case, this central Asian milieu synthesized toward the end of the twelfth century a messianic Mongol vision that became focused with religious fervor in the person of Chingis Khan.

The meaning of the name "Chingis," applied to Temujin as emperor of the Mongols, still eludes scholars, but he was also called T'ien-tze, "Son of Heaven," in Chinese, a name given to their emperor. The medieval Latin translators rendered this as "Son of God," a personalization that did violence to the level of abstraction that had been attained in central Asia, probably under the influence of China. The unbroken sky above the steppes was itself abstract, and although a primitive shamanism prevailed among the Mongols, Chingis Khan conceived the Eternal Blue Sky as the supreme deity, a deity as impersonal and abstract as the Chinese heaven.

The religious elements of the Mongol ideology were deeply rooted and very important. According to the *Secret History of the Mongols*, written by 1240, there were certain supernatural features in the immediate ancestry of Chingis Khan, and he early became convinced that he was personally under the protection of the Eternal Blue Sky.[1] On occasions of great moment he would withdraw alone to seek guidance from this highest deity. He made use of shamans, but he also felt himself to be in direct communication with the heavenly power. For his followers, too, his military successes were convincing evidence of the validity of this belief.*

Another religious element of a more sophisticated kind was the concept of direct divine appointment, bringing with it not privilege but inescapable duty. This idea was quite different from the Western divine right theory of kingship, which stressed the freedom of the king from earthly control. It was closer to the Chinese theory of the "mandate of heaven" or to the old Babylonian concept of the king as the servant of God, concepts which limited the ruler by instructions from on high. Its effect was to give the campaigns of the Mongols the quality and fanaticism of religious crusades. Their military opponents were not simply enemies; they were sinners, enemies of God. The

---

* The popular appeal of Chingis Khan was based on supernatural notions as well as on lust for booty. One of these made him a smith, "the great smith of the universe." In more primitive times the almost miraculous achievements of metallurgy established among the peoples of central Asia, as elsewhere, a belief in the great natural and supernatural powers of smiths. The cult of the ancient Greek smith-god, Hephaestus, or his equivalent, was widespread, and hammers, anvils, and forges were used in devout observances. The name "Temujin" derived from *temur*, "iron," and meant "blacksmith." According to William of Rubruck, who visited the Mongol court in 1254, Temujin was, in his youth, a smith. Whether a smith or not, he was thus connected with the supernatural in the minds of his more primitive followers.

almost contemporary Moslem historian Juvaini records that Chingis Khan explained this to the conquered citizens of Bukhara: "O people, know that you have committed great sins, and that the great ones among you have committed these sins. If you ask me what proof I have for these words, I say it is because I am the punishment of God. If you had not committed great sins, God would not have sent a punishment like me upon you." [2]

Chingis Khan thus believed himself, and was believed by his followers, to be sent from heaven, charged with the great mission of bringing peace and unity to mankind. This belief carried all before it, not only in terms of the march of the Mongol armies but also in terms of the philosophy those armies supported. As Eric Voegelin's studies indicate, "The Mongol Empire is, according to its self-interpretation, not a state among states in this world, but . . . a World-Empire-in-the-Making." [3]

God having declared his will, there was no longer room on earth for independent nations. Only three relationships to this universal empire were possible: a nation could make its submission to the great khan; it could possibly be so far away as not yet to know about the decision of God; or, knowing but not submitting, it could be in rebellion. An equality of nations was inconceivable, since there was only one God. Yet it is important to note that no tribal God of the Mongols was implied; many nations might have many names for him, but as there was one blue sky above, one heaven, so there was one God. There was no need, therefore, that any particular body of religious beliefs either be accepted by those who submitted to the Mongols or be eradicated by the Mongols from the nations they conquered. The purpose of their armed evangel was to bring peace, so they must always offer peace; if the offer was rejected, if a contumacious prince was unwilling to play his role of subjection in God's great plan, then the issue was up to God. As faithful and self-sacrificing servants the Mongols would do their part.

These well-integrated ideas, reduced to almost invariable formulas, were expressed in the messages which the Mongols apparently felt obliged to send to prospective candidates for inclusion in the khan's empire, informing them of God's will. One of these was sent in 1246 to Pope Innocent IV, another bearer of God's will, who had taken the trouble to send envoys to the khan's court exhorting him to embrace Christianity and threatening him with the divine wrath.

In the power of the eternal sky, the universal [*dalai*] khan of the whole great people: our order. This is an order sent to the great pope that he may know it and understand it. . . .

Another point: you have sent me these words, "You have taken all the realms of the Magyars and the Christians. . . . Tell us what has been the fault of these?" These your words, we do not understand them. . . .

The Order of God, both Genghis Khan and the Kha Khan have sent it to make it known, but the Order of God they did not believe. Those of whom you speak did even meet in a great council; they showed themselves arrogant and have killed our envoy-ambassadors.

The eternal God has killed and destroyed the men of those realms. Save by order of God, anybody by his own force, how could he kill, how could he take? . . .

By the virtue of God, from the rising of the sun to its setting, all realms have been granted to us. Without the Order of God how could anyone do anything? . . .

Now, you ought to say from a sincere heart: "We shall be your subjects; we shall give unto you our strength." You in person, at the head of the kings, all together, without exception, come and offer us service and homage; then shall we recognize your submission.

And if you do not observe the Order of God, and disobey our orders, we shall know you to be our enemies. That is what we make known to you.

If you disobey, what shall we know then? God will know it.[4]

Such letters were based on formulas and instructions which had been laid down in a code of statutory law, known as the Great Iasa, in which Chingis Khan had attempted to improve the customary law of his peoples by some additions. How much of this legislation was his own invention cannot be determined, but it attained the sanctity among his followers which the words of Jesus and Mohammed have among theirs. No full text of the Iasa has been found, but fragments preserved by various historians include the following.

1. When [the Mongols] have need to write any letter to rebels, and they must send an envoy, let them not threaten them with the great size of their army and their numbers, but let them say only, "If ye will submit yourselves obediently ye shall find good treatment and rest, but if ye resist—as for us what do we know? The everlasting God knoweth what will happen to you."

5. There is no other army in the world like that of the Tatars; in war time it hunts as it were for victory over the wild beasts of prey; in peace time it

is like a flock of sheep contributing milk and wool . . . ; among labors and calamities it is free from any division or opposition. It is an army of serfs who are liable to diverse contributions and show no annoyance with what has been ordered. . . . And even during a campaign . . . if some personal labor service was required from the man and he is not there, his wife is liable to appear and to do his work. . . . All of the men are divided into units of ten, and among each ten one man is appointed chief of the other nine; and among ten chiefs of the ten units one is called centurion and the whole century is under his command. And so it goes through the unit of one thousand up to the unit of *tuman* [10,000], and the chiefs are called chiliarch [and myriarch, respectively]. . . . There is equality. Each man works as much as the other; there is no difference. They do not pay attention to wealth or importance of a man. . . .

7. No man of any thousand, or hundred, or ten in which he hath been counted shall depart to another place; if he doth he shall be killed and also the head who received him.

10. He [Chingis Khan] decided that no taxes or duties should be imposed upon . . . fakirs, readers of the Al-Koran, lawyers, physicians, scholars, people who devote themselves to prayer and asceticism. . . .

11. He ordered that all religions were to be respected and that no preference was to be shown to any of them. All this he commanded in order that it might be agreeable to God.

13. When a wayfarer passes by people eating, he must alight and eat with them without asking for permission, and they must not forbid him this.

24. He forbade emirs to address themselves to anyone except the sovereign. Whoever . . . [did] was to be put to death, and anyone changing his post without permission was also to be put to death.

34. Children . . . receive their share of the heritage according to the disposition of it made by the father. The distribution of property is to be carried out on the basis of the senior son receiving more than the junior, the younger son inheriting the household of the father. . . .[5]

In these laws the features of messianism, bound service, religious immunity, decimal administrative subdivision, unequal inheritance, and capital punishment are noteworthy. All of these were found in post-Mongol Muscovy. This does not prove conclusively that the Mongols were responsible for the advent of these features. The Mongols were certainly not the only source from which they may have been derived. Serfdom, unequal legacies, and severe punishments were settled usages in parts of western Europe at the time, and may well have spread from there into Rus', particularly into the southern and western parts during the period of Lithuanian rule. Yet supporting the thesis that there was some borrowing from the Mongols is the fact that contact with the West had been extensive in the Kievan period without producing such practices.*

* For a review of the opinions of leading historians on this complex subject, see B. D. Grekov and A. Iakubovski, *La Horde d'Or*, trans. François Thuret (Paris, 1939), pp. 240–251.

CHAPTER V

The Church: Autonomy

HOW did the conquered fare under a regime so alien? Especially after the Mongols became Mohammedan (ca. 1255), the church in Rus', not yet firmly established among the lower classes or outside the cities, might have been expected to fall victim to a holy war, or at least to suffer a pervasive deterioration. If it failed to hold its own, and much more to parallel the flowering of religious thought and writing in the West during this period—a period that produced Aquinas, Duns Scotus, Dante, and Occam—it might be excused in its circumstances. In fact, its subsequent deficiencies, which led to the internal disputes of the sixteenth and seventeenth centuries and eventually to the complete subjection of the church to the state, might all be blamed upon the demoralization of Mongol domination.

It appears, however, that on the contrary the Mongol period experienced an unprecedented growth of the church, an extension of its influence among the ordinary people, and a great expansion of its wealth and prestige.

While Rus' was in "rebellion" the churches and clergy suffered with the rest of the population. After the conquest, however, they had the advantage of the Great Iasa's requirement of tolerance toward local religions. Although based on principles very different from those of the canon law, it provided the church with immunities similar to those normally enjoyed on the basis of Vladimir's church statute. At a time when such immunities were breaking down in western Europe, as in the conflict between King Philip of France and Pope Boniface VIII over church lands, in Rus' they were even more firmly secured by a charter (*iarlyk*) granted in 1267 by the khan Mangu-Temir:

By the power of the supreme God and by the will of the supreme Trinity,* the word of Mangu Temir to the people's tax inspectors and [to] princes and commanders and to collectors of the tribute and to census takers and to passing emissaries and to falconers and to huntsmen.

Chingis Khan [*tsar*] then [decreed] that tribute or food not be taken from those who, with upright heart, pray to God for us and our family and bless us. So also spoke later tsars, in the same manner favoring priests and monks. Tribute or any other levy, customs, taxes on tilled land, post-station supplies, conscripts, whoever demands anything and should say to give—who among us does not know this?—we all know [it]. And we, praying to God, did not change their charters. So we speak in the original manner, that tribute or taxes on tilled land or cartage or maintenance of any kind, let no one demand [of them]; post-station supplies, conscripts [or] customs let them not give. Or church lands, waters, gardens, vineyards, mills, winter or summer pastures, let them not be touched. And whatever may have been taken, let it be returned. And church craftsmen, falconers, huntsmen of any kind, let them not be touched, nor restrained. Or things that concern their law, their books or other things, let them not be touched, nor taken, nor torn, nor destroyed. And whoever blasphemes their faith,—that person will confess and will die. If priests have a brother or a son eating the same bread and living in the same house, to him the same favor is granted as long as he does not depart. But if he depart, tribute or any other [taxes] he will pay. And the priests are favored by us according to the first charter, properly praying to God and blessing us. But if you have not an upright heart and pray concerning us—to God that sin will be on you. Thus we speak. And if other people, who are not priest[s], although praying to God, take on themselves to have [these immunities], that [same sin] will be in that.†

Thus speaking, we have given this charter to the metropolitan. Tax inspectors, princes, census takers, collectors of the tilled land tax [and] customs collectors seeing and hearing this charter shall desire neither tribute nor anything else from the priests [or] from the monks, nor disturb [them] —if any disturb [them], according to the Great Iasa he will confess and will die.

Thus we speak in the year of the hare, the first month of autumn, the fourth [day], at Taly. Written.[1]

---

* The Mongols not being Christian, these words are suspect. The original *may* have been, "In the might of everlasting Heaven, in the protection of the great fortune flame. . . ." Cf. F. W. Cleaves, "The Mongol Documents in the Musée de Teheran," *Harvard Journal of Asiatic Studies*, XVI (June 1953), 26.

† An alternative, less probable, reading is, "And if one who is not a priest take unto himself other people desiring to pray to God, that [sin] will be on him."

This charter was binding upon Rus' and Mongol alike, although relationships within Rus' were more closely regulated by immunity charters granted by the princes to monasteries and churches. It appears from such grants that the clergy were not always exempt from exactions by the princes, yet they refrained from invoking the khan's charter against their fellow Christians.

The khans renewed the metropolitan's charter in successive reigns. It is recorded that, six reigns later, Janibeg Khan asked the metropolitan to release him from the obligation of these decrees so that he could tax the clergy, but was dissuaded from that enterprise.[2] The story is doubtful, since the immunity rested ultimately upon the Great Iasa rather than upon the khan's charter; yet its preservation serves to illustrate how strictly the Mongols adhered to the immunity charters. They had, of course, political as well as ideological reasons: mention of the khan in prayer meant valuable church sanction for their administration.

The contents of the Mongol franchise were not quite the same as those of Vladimir's statute. The prime provision of the former was the protection of those especially connected with God against taxation and conscription, while Vladimir stated primarily the exemption of these same people from the civil courts; yet in both motives and general effects the differences were not important. Each ruler hoped by his grant to please the heavenly powers, and Mangu-Temir perhaps felt himself under the same compulsion from the Iasa that Vladimir felt from the canon law, although evidence of this feeling is absent from the two charters. Vladimir did not mention exemption from taxation, but, with the help of the canon law, the judicial exemption could be read to include it; and Mangu-Temir mentioned neither secular nor sacred courts, yet the injunction against disturbing the church people applied, of course, to their courts.

In their particular effects on the non-Orthodox, however, the two charters differed markedly. Vladimir, guided by his new religion, proceeded positively to confer upon the bishops jurisdiction over charges of heresy and pagan practices, effectively placing all dissenters and adherents of other religions in the hands of their enemies. Mangu-Temir, on the contrary, proceeded negatively and thereby exempted from molestation, if not all practitioners, at least the rabbis, fakirs, and priests of non-Orthodox religions. Moreover, he modestly left to God the judgment of any who might lay unfounded claims to the immunities. Invocations by the non-Orthodox of such immunities against the bishops have not been recorded for us, for understandable reasons; yet the idea of religious toleration took root in Rus' long before it reached the West and, as will be seen, played a conspicuous part in the great religious controversy which emerged when the Mongol yoke was broken.

In the long run, the Orthodox church profited both spiritually and materially from the Mongol period. Taking the general position that the calamities and oppressions attendant to the subjection were God's punishment for the sins of the people, a position for which a foundation had long been prepared in church doctrine, the clergy was provided with a sharp weapon against those who professed, but did not practice, Christianity. Remorseful consciences smitten by this weapon were responsible for many of the donations of land that built the wealth of churches and monasteries during this period. Others, in no position to give land, could give themselves, by becoming monks or peasants on the monastery lands; still others, unmotivated by twinges of conscience, might take this road since it led to exemption from conscription by the Mongols. Tax exemption, added to the foregoing, enabled the church to build an economic position that would, in time, excite the jealousy of both the aristocracy and the state.

The political position of the church, vis-à-vis the princes, was also strengthened. The church now had a charter of its own which was in no way dependent upon the princes. While the metropolitan still had to be confirmed at Constantinople, the princes now also had to obtain patents for their offices from the khan. Clinging precariously to these patents, which had to be renewed at each Rus' or Mongol succession, the princes made frequent trips to the capital at Sarai in order to prevent rival claimants from gaining the favor of the khan. Moreover, acting as agents of the Mongols, they earned the enmity of the lower classes not only by collecting tribute and conscripts but also by restraining the urge toward rebellion frequently expressed by the townsmen. During this time the bishops, supported by the prestige of their religion, the unity of their hierarchy, and the intricacies of the canon law, had an advantage which the pope never enjoyed over the kings of Europe.

The question may be asked, therefore, why the church in Rus' did not attain a position of dominance over the secular power comparable to that of Innocent III, who had shown the way by reducing King

John of England to vassalage in 1213. The doctrines of Chrysostom on spiritual superiority were ready at hand, and there were some who were pleased to employ them. The metropolitan Alexis (r. 1354–1378), for example, who served during the weak reign of one prince and the minority of another, exercised extensive secular power and influence. Although a godson of Ivan I and well groomed for his office, he was far from subservient and in both word and action asserted the independence of his pastorate. By and large, however, the powers and opportunities of the clergy, subordinate as they were to a foreign patriarch, were not such as to attract persons of inordinate ambition. Perhaps, too, there was a feeling that a time when the country was overrun with the pagan and then Moslem Mongols was no time for a trial of strength between God's spiritual and secular stewards. Alexis had been well trained by his Greek predecessor in the thousand-year-old Eastern tradition concerning the relationship between them. The concept of *symphonia* was much stronger than the example of Innocent, who after all was regarded as a heretic, and long usage had so sanctified this concept that even most favorable opportunities did not change it. Byzantium itself had not been noted for radicalism of thought; it should not be surprising if it failed to teach the Rus' clergy to deal independently with its own religious traditions.

The temporal powers were less completely satisfied with the existing *symphonia*. The tie with Byzantium had a secular as well as a spiritual side in that the empire still claimed to be universal, and this "subjection," although only symbolic, grew less acceptable to the princes as the prestige of the empire declined. Moreover, the metropolitan, in his occasional differences with the grand prince, sometimes drew support from the old idea of universal empire. This was illustrated in 1393 when Metropolitan Cyprian, a Greek, wrote to Constantinople accusing young Prince Vasili I of Moscow (r. 1389–1425) of preventing the mention of the emperor's name in divine services. The patriarch, Antonius IV, himself rose to the defense of the emperor. The prince, apparently needing instruction, was sent a very enlightening letter (1393) setting forth once more the old Byzantine conception of church-state relationships:

It is with sorrow that I hear of some words spoken by thy highness about the most high and holy autocrat and emperor. It is said that thou dost not allow the metropolitan to mention in the diptychs the holy name of the emperor (a thing that has never before been possible) and that thou sayest,

"We have the church but we do not have the emperor, and we do not wish to know him." This is not good. The holy emperor occupies a high place in the church; he is not like the others, the local princes and authorities. The emperors in the very beginning strengthened and established piety in the whole world; the emperors convoked the ecumenical councils; they also sanctioned, by their own laws, obedience to the divine and holy canons. . . . Finally, the emperors, together with the councils, decreed the rank of the episcopal sees and set the boundaries of the metropolises and of the dioceses. For all this they have great honor and occupy a high place in the church. If, by the will of God, the pagans have surrounded the domains and lands of the emperor, still to this day the emperor receives the same consecration from the church; with the same ceremony and the same prayers he is anointed with holy oil and established emperor and autocrat of the Romans, that is, of all Christians. In every place where people call themselves Christians the name of the emperor is mentioned by all patriarchs, metropolitans, and bishops. . . . It is impossible for Christians to have the church and not to have the emperor. For the empire and the church are in a close union and relationship, and it is impossible to separate one from the other.[3]

This forceful restatement of the role of the emperor, stressing the unity of the Orthodox patriarchates and the uniqueness of the emperor's position, also pointed up the quandary in which the Muscovites found themselves. Vasili had no desire to overturn the hallowed spiritual-temporal cooperation, or to separate from the brotherhood of the Orthodox patriarchs, as Rome had done. His wish was to transfer to Moscow the relationships that had been long established at Constantinople, so that the head of the church "of Kiev and all Rus' " would look to the grand prince, as the patriarch had long since learned to look to the emperor, as the ultimate authority and final repository of earthly power in things both temporal and spiritual. But unless Moscow became the seat of a patriarch recognized by the other patriarchs, and unless the grand prince could, in some way, claim succession to the Byzantine empire, these exact relationships could not be transferred. And such aspirations were in the realm of dreams. The anomaly of a metropolitan leaning on Byzantium and a prince aspiring to sovereignty seemed destined to continue.

Within fifty years, however, events rather than thought had drastically altered the situation. Without deliberate intent, it would seem, the Muscovite church became autocephalous.

When the pressure of the Ottoman Turks became unbearable, and the fall of the empire perhaps already unavoidable, the emperor and the patriarch, in 1439, finally agreed to the only terms under which they could hope for help from western Europe: a union of the Eastern and Western churches, with recognition of the supremacy of the pope, the Latin creed, and other almost equally hated concessions. In these negotiations at the Council of Florence, the Greek Isidor, recently appointed as metropolitan of Rus', participated and advocated the concessions, emerging from the agreement as a cardinal of the united church. When he returned to Moscow, however, the Muscovites, who had been reluctant to see him go to negotiate with the heretical Latins, immediately turned him out of the Uspenski Cathedral. Convinced of their own orthodoxy, they were thus cut off from a heretical world, in the wilderness without a shepherd, and they could not appeal to Constantinople for a new appointee for he would be similarly contaminated.

Yet the bishops and the prince could not seize this apparent opportunity to make their church independent of foreign entanglements without danger of going the way of the Latins into heresy. It was with much hesitation and trepidation that the decisive steps were taken. Did the bishops realize how dependent upon the grand prince a national church would be? Our sources do not say. But would not the prince then have been correspondingly eager? More likely the ecumenical concept was simply so deeply instilled that the idea of an isolated national church seemed actually repugnant. The grand prince, Vasili II, wrote a letter to both emperor and patriarch asking permission for the election of a metropolitan by a council of Rus' bishops; but this letter, like a similar letter two years later, was not sent. Neither an affirmative nor a negative reply from the Greek heretics could be expected to bring with it God's blessing. Only in 1448, after a delay of seven years and assurances from his coreligionists in Lithuania, did Vasili call the bishops for an election.* Still seeking to avoid religious isolation, he announced the result to Constantinople as motivated not by "pride or insolence" but by "great necessity"—i.e., the dire straits of Moscow in the civil war (below, pages 61 ff.); and the new metropolitan, Iona, was careful to insist that he wanted the blessing of the patriarch, as soon as the patriarch should return to the faith. Toward the end of his

* Grand Prince Vitovt of Lithuania had already held a local election in 1415 (see Gustave Alef, "Muscovy and the Council of Florence," *Slavic Review*, XX [Oct. 1961], 384–401).

life Vasili still felt the need for the universal church: he asked absolution of the patriarch of Jerusalem.

From that time dependence upon the patriarch of Constantinople was nominal rather than real, even after his union with Rome was abrogated. Yet the Muscovites, satisfied as they were of their own doctrinal purity, still hoped for a firmer link with the ecumene in recognition of their great steadfastness in the faith. An adequate conception of their new position was to come only in the following century. Then arose the doctrine of the Third Rome, making Moscow the capital of Orthodoxy. Then came also ecumenical approval for the establishment of a patriarchate at Moscow.

CHAPTER VI

The Rise of Moscow

WHILE the church continued thus to grow in wealth and independence, and at the same time to adhere firmly to its traditional political doctrines, the strength of the princes, although more hampered by the hegemony of the conquerors, also improved. Indeed, it can be argued that the most influential development of the Mongol period was the growth of the power of the prince of Moscow. Many influences contributed to this, only a few of which have importance for political theory.

The policy of cooperation with the Mongols, initiated by Alexander Nevski, gave the Suzdalian princes (located at Vladimir and later at Moscow) a degree of independence not enjoyed by those in the south, and this provided them an opportunity to continue the local consolidation begun during the previous century. This northern branch of the Riurikides, however, was itself soon divided into several important branches. Among them struggles for the grand-princely patent to Vladimir began in 1280 and lasted throughout the period of Mongol rule. The Mongols tried to pursue something of a balance-of-power policy among them, but tended to support those who were most pliable or cooperative.

An important advantage gained by the diplomatic skill of the Moscow branch of the family was the presence of the metropolitan. The devastation of Kiev and the absence of a resident prince after 1240 had rendered that city undesirable as an ecclesiastical center, so in 1299 the metropolitan had moved to Vladimir. The next metropolitan, Peter (r. 1308–1326), strongly incensed against the grand prince, Mikhail of Tver, who had opposed his nomination at Constantinople, spent much time, instead, in Moscow and was friendly with its prince, who supported him against the accusations of Mikhail. Solov'ev has called this move "more important than all the *iarlyki* of the Khans" for the strength of Moscow.[1] According to the biography of Peter by his fifteenth century successor, Cyprian, Peter had made an agreement with his friend, Ivan I of Moscow, later grand prince:

> My son, if thou shouldst hearken unto me, and shouldst build the Church of the Holy Mother, and shouldst lay me to rest in thy city, then of a surety wilt thou be glorified above all other princes in the land, and thy sons and thy grandsons also, and this city will itself be glorified above all other Russian towns, and the Saints will come and dwell in it, and its hands will prevail against the breasts of its enemies. Thus will it ever be so long as my bones shall lie therein.[2]

The earlier life of Peter, compiled by his friend Bishop Prokhor of Rostov, does not mention this "agreement" and it is probably an *ex post facto* explanation of the success of Moscow. When Peter's immediate successor did move his seat permanently to Moscow, he brought the city some important advantages. The policies of the Moscow princes gained prestige, since it was presumed (usually rightly) that the metropolitans had participated in their formulation. The great weapon of excommunication was available, and used, against Moscow's enemies. The bishop of Sarai, serving under the metropolitan, became a permanent representative of Moscow in the Mongol capital, the only one with this rank. And, of course, the religious establishments of all the other cities were subordinate and not free to deal independently with either Sarai or Byzantium.

Although the Mongols' respect for priests was genuine, it is not known to what extent, if any, their support of Moscow was induced by either the Sarai bishop or the prestige of the metropolitan. In their dispensation of the princely patent to Vladimir they had reasons other than the prayers of Peter for preferring Moscow to Tver, a town more favorably located for commerce * and Moscow's principal rival. They had had unhappy experiences with three successive Tver princes, and Moscow seemed more dependable.

The devastation of Kiev and the regime of direct Mongol rule

---

* V. O. Kliuchevski and others, on the contrary, have considered Moscow to be more favorably located; see his *History of Russia*, trans. C. J. Hogarth, I (London, 1911), chap. 17.

there * expelled also many of the princes and boyars from southern Rus', and a number of them entered the service of Moscow. The policy of Andrei and Vsevolod in reducing the weaker princes of their own family to vassalage could, therefore, be continued with ease by the Moscow princes. The newcomers had no claims in the north and were given lands or positions at court only after taking oaths that they and their descendants would serve permanently the Moscow house. The princes among them became known as "servitor princes" and did not have the old boyar freedom of departure. Below the level of the boyars the princes of Moscow were also able to develop a class of servitors, known as the *dvoriane*, bound for definite periods or for life, some of them holding land on condition of service. Although the nobility in general was increasing in wealth and was important in the princely administration, the pressure of the Mongols thus created the conditions in which its independence could be curtailed. In the treaties of the fourteenth and early fifteenth centuries the princes continued to agree that "free servants ought to enjoy the liberty to go or stay with us as they like," but in practice this liberty began to be conditional. The political position of the servitor princes, who were socially above the boyars, became a precedent for restricting also the rights of the boyars. Two boyars who left Moscow in 1374 and 1433 had their estates confiscated on grounds of treason, and one of them was later executed when caught. Moscow was in grave trouble at both of these periods but she was not at war, and the confiscations violated the ancient right of departure. The old theory of boyar freedom was giving place to a new theory of duty to the prince.†

Closely related to the restriction of the right of departure was the grand-princely desire to make service a positive requirement. Perhaps inspired by Mongol ideas of universal service to the khans, the Moscow princes, in their construction of autocracy, moved gradually toward a similarly universal service. At least from the reign of Ivan I some

* Thus M. S. Grushevski [Hurshevsky], *A History of Ukraine*, ed. O. J. Frederiksen (New Haven, 1941), pp. 106–111; but cf. B. D. Grekov and A. Iakubovski, *La Horde d'Or*, trans. François Thuret (Paris, 1939), pp. 221–224. Grekov doubts that Mongol methods around Kiev differed greatly from those used elsewhere.

† The term "boyar" underwent a contemporary change. It had previously carried largely a social significance, meaning a high aristocrat who was not a prince. It now came to have a more official meaning, namely, a member of the Boyar Duma (the grand prince's council) of the highest rank. It was applied to both boyars and princes who attained that rank in the Duma.

tenures of land had been conditional upon continuing service. Holders of *udely* and *votchiny*, however, unlike the holders of fiefs in western Europe, had owed no service to any lord for them. Yet so effectively did the grand princes restrict such holders in the last half of the fifteenth century that in his will (1504) Ivan III could say:

And the boyars and boyars' sons of Iaroslavl, along with their *votchinas* and goods, are never to leave my son Vasili to go to anybody. If any leave, their lands go to my son; but if they serve him he will not transgress their lands nor those of their wives or children. . . . And the servitor princes in the Moscow and Tver territories who serve my son Vasili will retain their *votchinas* as they did under me. But if any of those servitor princes leave my son Vasili for my younger children or anyone else, the *votchinas* of those princes go to my son Vasili.[3]

Service was not yet universally required, but the old rights and immunities of *udel* and *votchina* holders were now privileges, conditional on the will of the grand prince. A boyar could lose his estates not only by departure to serve another prince, but also by simply ceasing to serve Vasili. As these new concepts gradually were enforced, through the reigns of Vasili III and Ivan IV, the distinction between free service and bound service disappeared. As will be seen, Ivan used the word *rab*, slave or unfree servant, indiscriminately for both. Service to the prince was no longer simply the traditional and broadest pathway to individual advancement; it was now becoming obligatory for all the higher ranks of society.

The contemporary result of the astute manipulation by the Moscow princes of the conditions of Mongol suzerainty was a dominance within their principality even more complete than that which the kings of France and England had achieved with the aid of the burghers. This consolidation of power required the suppression of two old institutions: the *veche*, an expression of popular sovereignty and potential rebellion, and the seniority (collateral) system of succession, with its tendency toward fragmentation and dissension.

The townsmen of Muscovy, like those of the West, displayed a dislike for the aristocrats, and the grand princes used this friction for their own advancement; but the princes did not need the help of the lower classes, armed as they were with the patents of the khans and with lands to distribute. Thus, while the towns of western Europe were growing in importance, building its commercial and industrial future, the towns of Rus' were receiving a series of blows that removed them from the list of important political forces. Aside from the devastations of conquest and of punitive expeditions, the Mongols conscripted builders and other artisans for the purposes of their empire, conscription that not only fell most heavily upon the towns but even discouraged the acquisition of skills.

Mongol theories of government could accommodate subservient princes—even the single dynastic family was paralleled in their own ruling family—but not the unruly *veche*, so under the Mongols it had no status and no rights. When, for example, the Novgorodians chose as their prince in 1272 Dmitri of Pereiaslavl, the Mongols sent an army to compel them to recognize the grand prince of Vladimir instead. The princes, in their turn, instead of attempting to harness the indignation of the cities in a concerted movement of resistance to the Mongols, saw in the new situation an opportunity to relieve themselves of their former partial dependence upon the *veche*. Their policy of cooperation with the conquerors, expedient though it was, was also a policy of keeping the impatient townsmen under control. Sometimes the princes even devastated the cities that rose against the Mongols. The boyars also, who had more to lose in unsuccessful revolts than their fellow-townsmen, tended to dissociate themselves from the *veche*, to support the princes' policy, and to give their attention to their manorial estates. Deserted thus by their former leaders the *vecha* rose, at times, in isolated revolts, usually with disastrous results, but they did not achieve any coordinated uprising, and so they emerged from the Mongol period unable to resist the consolidated power of the Moscow princes.

The suppression of the collateral seniority system of succession was a second step in the consolidation of the power of the princes. It will be recalled that the Suzdal princes had thought in patrimonial terms, had built up their *udel*, and had effectively separated it from the remainder of Kievan Rus' (page 17). They claimed Kiev, however, on the basis of collateral seniority, and they did not attempt to abolish seniority as the pattern of succession within their branch of the Riurikides until the fifteenth century. For four generations, from two to five brothers in each generation held the throne of Vladimir, no brothers being passed over in favor of sons, in spite of almost continuous family strife.* The

---

* It might be said that the prevalence in the treaties among the princes of "elder brother," "brother," and "younger brother," meaning superior, equal, and inferior, was a reflection of thinking in collateral rather than in lineal terms. "Father" and "son" were also used, however.

same pattern was continued for two more generations under the Moscow house of the family, but without the strife. In these two centuries the seniority principle would seem to have been established, in part on Kievan precedents such as the will of Iaroslav and in part on Mongol favor since, like their own method, it produced mature rulers.

Collateral seniority became clouded at Moscow, however, by a frequent absence of nephews.* Dmitri Donskoi (d. 1389), therefore, having numerous sons, made an important will, attempting to fix the succession by seniority for at least two steps: "And if, for his sins, God takes away my [eldest] son, Prince Vasili, then whoever of my sons will be next [eldest] under him, to that son belongs the *udel* of Prince Vasili." [4] At that time Vasili was unmarried. Later, as his children approached maturity, he took a decision of great significance for the development of autocracy at Moscow. He resolved to supersede Donskoi's intent and, with the support of the metropolitan and the Moscow boyars, to bequeath the throne of Vladimir to his own eldest son, possibly with the prior approval of the Mongols. It was argued that Donskoi had not meant to disinherit any sons Vasili might have, but only to provide a successor if Vasili should die childless. This, however, is a later interpretation, read into Donskoi's will after Vasili determined to follow the lineal system; in 1389 there were clearly many more precedents for succession by brothers in the presence of sons than for the succession of sons in the presence of brothers of the reigning prince.

In the civil war that resulted seniority was defeated. If any principle of succession emerged victorious, it was not a stable primogeniture but an unstable patrimony dependent upon the will of the reigning prince, and this important matter was thus left to be determined not by law but by personal decision. Moreover, collateral seniority was not completely extinguished as a claim to the throne. Repeatedly it had to be suppressed by the exercise of the grand princely will, a practice that significantly contributed to the development of the habit of arbitrary decision. The resulting psychology was well expressed by Ivan III, who personally "favored and blessed" his grandson Dmitri with the grand principality. He later removed Dmitri in favor of his second son, Vasili, and said, "Do not I, the grand prince, have authority over my own

---

* The small number of surviving sons has been noticed by historians as an explanation for the rise of Moscow. The patrimony was less fragmented among heirs than elsewhere.

children and my own principality? To whom I will I shall give the principality." *5 His two surviving sons made a treaty recognizing the succession of Vasili III not by his own seniority but by virtue of his father's will.

To reinforce the position of the son chosen by such personal decision the grand princes introduced two foreign practices: unequal patrimony and co-optation. The former was in use among the Mongols and in western Europe, and the old Rus' private law had permitted unequal legacies, but in practice both nobles and princes had usually made them equal. Dmitri Donskoi began the change; later his grandson Vasili II granted fourteen towns to Ivan III, as against twelve distributed among his other four sons; and Ivan in his will increased the inequality to sixty-six as against thirty. The resources for resistance to the favored son, normally the eldest, were thus denied to the younger ones. Co-optation, an old Byzantine maneuver, used too by the Mongols, was also adopted: Vasili II proclaimed Ivan grand prince and coruler, in order to assure his succession.† Later Ivan co-opted in turn his son, his grandson, and his second son, aiming to safeguard the throne against his brothers. Both of these practices served to reinforce the element of personal power in the Muscovite government, which in this period was building up to a climax in the autocracy of Ivan IV, known as *Grozny*, the Terrible.

One of Vasili's motives in superseding his father's will may have been the clear assertion of the rights of ownership as well as of rulership over his realm. The private law had, from early times, provided for lineal successions to land, and thus the custom of collateral succession to the grand princely throne had effectively set this apart as a political position, not a private tenure. The elimination of this special characteristic, succession by brothers, meant the application to the grand principality itself of the ideas of the private law. Vasili's wills, therefore, were not simply expressions of exceptional paternal solicitude. The exclusion of his brother Iuri was a necessary step in the process of approximating Muscovy to a private alodium.

The respected historian Gradovski believed that this conception of

---

* The chronicler quotes this in relation to Pskov, but Ivan's reasoning was general.

† This co-optation followed closely upon the blinding of Vasili in the civil war and may have reflected in part another Byzantine idea, that a blind man was ineligible to rule.

ownership of the land was derived primarily from the Mongols.[6] Among these nomads little distinction was needed between authority and ownership, power over both land and people being assigned from the khan down through his hierarchy of officials. By Gradovski's analysis the Rus' princes were rulers but not owners of the land before the coming of the conquerors, but as lieutenants of the khans, they were placed by their patents in positions of control over their lands quite apart from any claims by other previously recognized owners. As heirs of the khans, they remained after the liberation both rulers and owners of the land. He might have added that by the same logic they became owners of all the people.

Certainly the princes, in their frequent visits to the capital of the Golden Horde, may have absorbed or become aware of these Mongol concepts. While still administrators in the Mongol hierarchy, however, they could not use their patents as bases for claims to ownership of either land or people, since this was vested ultimately in the family of Chingis.* Moreover, these claims would conflict with ancient Rus' customs, such as the right of departure, that could be infringed only gradually as the grand princes grew in strength. Only when the Mongols were defeated could these concepts be implemented. When that defeat came, the positive powers they had enjoyed over land and people, and not simply their high title of "tsar," may well have stimulated the grand princes to claim the succession to the khans, and with it equally complete ownership.

It may be concluded, then, that the Mongol example was influential in the Moscow princes' embarkation upon the long, gradual, yet very bitter process of appropriating, in addition to their political authority, the authority of the land owner. In this process the Mongol patents themselves were also indirectly useful. In them, including that of the grand prince of Vladimir, the Mongol terms for the territory were, from the fourteenth century, translated as *"otchina"* or *"votchina,"* words that, unlike *"udel,"* stressed independent, alodial ownership and lineal inheritance.† These patents thus provided a basis for the assertion, when the grand princes came to feel strong enough, of hereditary

---

* On Mongol tenures see B. Vladimirtsov, *Le régime social des Mongols,* trans. Michel Carsow (Paris, 1948), esp. pp. 144 ff.

† Concurrently, the granting of *otchiny* to boyars and servitor princes became rare, *kormleniia,* "feedings," being assigned instead on an annual basis; and alodial tenure was confined more and more to the holdings of the grand prince.

ownership of Vladimir itself. As has been pointed out, Donskoi used *"udel"* in his will, but his son, Vasili I, said in 1417: "And to my son, Prince Vasili, I bequeath my *votchina*, the grand principality, which my father bequeathed to me." [7] Vasili II followed the precedent thus established, and thereafter the grand principality continued to be treated as a possession and bequeathed in proprietary rather than in political or administrative terms.*

"Votchina" was derived from *otets*, "father," and thus stressed not simply alodial tenure but specifically patrimony. When, therefore, due to an absence of surviving brothers, the Moscow throne passed from father to son through three generations, each also receiving the patent as grand prince of Vladimir, it is not surprising that the whole grand principality became in their minds a *votchina*. They chose to believe that the method of succession brought with it the rights of the *votchinnik*, and consequently that any land that had been owned or ruled by a direct ancestor could be claimed as patrimony. Ivan III, seizing Novgorod in 1478, explained, "We grand princes want our realm; as we are in Moscow so we want to be also in our *otchina*, Great Novgorod." †[8]

This collapse of Novgorod, the strongest of the city states, marked a milestone in the development of Russian governmental institutions. A gradual process, it was the result of internal dissension and military weakness. The retreat of the Mongols and the emergence of Muscovy and Lithuania as the two major powers in the territory of the old Kievan state fundamentally changed the position of Novgorod. As in classical times, the republican government of the city state, in spite of its vast territories, failed to compete with the monarchial systems of its neighbors. The government of Lithuania was largely controlled by its aristocracy while that of Moscow tended toward autocracy. This difference aggravated a conflict that was then developing within

---

* The identification of an *udel* with a *votchina* was made easier by the fact that the rights of the landlord, the *votchinnik*, ordinarily included matters that to the modern point of view are definitely political. He took not only rent or services from those who used his land but also taxes to be paid over to the grand prince (in theory, anyhow, for the Mongols) and judicial fees and fines collected through his administration of justice.

† With fine irony, reflecting their contempt for autocracy, the ambassadors of the proud republic told Ivan, "You order us to conform to the laws of Moscow, but we *are not acquainted with the laws* of Moscow; teach us to know them" (quoted in A. I. Herzen, *Les idées révolutionnaires en Russie* [2d ed.; London, 1853], p. 21).

Novgorod as the growing wealth and power of the boyar class separated it further and further from the other citizens. The boyars saw an alliance with Lithuania as the best means to preserve their own and the city's freedom against an expanding Muscovy. The lower classes, on the contrary, saw this policy as a boyar plot. Since the time of Ivan I the city had normally chosen the grand prince of Moscow as its prince—an arrangement that had worked fairly well. His powers, subject to treaty limitations (above, page 8), could be exercised only when he was present in the city, but the lower classes now turned to him for protection, inviting him to intervene in the city's affairs even when absent. Given such opportunities the Moscow princes moved steadily toward the elimination of Novgorod's independence. After a military defeat in 1456 the *veche* was deprived of control over the city's foreign policy: all treaties had to be signed by the Moscow prince. In 1471 the Novgorodians had to agree never to engage service princes from Lithuania. Then, seven years later, Ivan III demanded that Novgorod recognize him as its sovereign (*gospodar*), that is, without any treaty limitations on his power. The *veche* was abolished and Ivan ordered the removal of its bell to Moscow. In 1510, after similar internal disputes, Pskov was also annexed and its bell removed.

In the reduction of these free cities to submissive obedience Ivan and his son Vasili III employed a most effective technique: mass deportations. After 1478 the upper classes of Novgorod continued to seethe in spite of executions of ringleaders, so Ivan scattered over 7,000 of them throughout Muscovy, granting their houses and lands to Muscovites. In 1489, after a revolt, the whole population of the free city of Viatka was deported. Vasili removed 6,800 from Pskov and thousands more from Riazan and replaced them with Muscovites.[9] The cities were thus deprived of leaders rooted in local traditions, and the gentry, resettled in new surroundings, their groups broken up, their independence shattered, were unable to unite in resistance. Local particularism was repressed in favor of imperial unity, and the roots of the later exile system were firmly planted.

Ivan III took another important step toward the unification of his realm in the compilation of a standardized code of judicial procedure, the *Sudebnik* of 1497. This code contained little substantive law; the existing customs and charters were largely left intact. Local peculiarities were even reinforced by the requirement of participation by local people in trials in the provinces. Yet the code reflected and exerted a

strong centralizing influence. The independence of the boyars and other aristocrats as judges was restricted by the prescription of exact judicial fees and by the requirement of a second judge, a *d'iak* (clerk).*
These clerks, elevated from the lower classes for their literacy and their administrative abilities, were dependable servants of the grand prince, restraining the impulses and the avarice of the aristocrats and promoting a uniform administration of justice.

By the end of Ivan's reign (1505) the process of centralization was still incomplete. *Udely* and *votchiny* retained some independence; the *Sudebnik*, for example, did not apply within them. Yet the pursuit of power had carried the grand princes, through dynastic cooperation in the Kievan period and shrewd manipulation of the Mongol relationship, to centralized personal authority that combined the powers of both proprietor and sovereign. The foundation was laid for an autocracy beyond any then known in the West.

* This is the interpretation of Sergeevich. The *Sudebnik* of 1550 states clearly that the *d'iak* is to judge, although that of 1497 says only that he will be present (V. I. Sergeevich, *Russkiia iuridicheskiia drevnosti*, I [St. Petersburg, 1902], 408–414, 524–526).

PART THREE

Muscovy: Autocracy
(1480–1682)

CHAPTER VII

The Third Rome

RELAXATION of the Mongol grip permitted Ivan III to succeed to his father's throne without a patent, and to assert his complete independence in 1480. He was also the first prince to claim the whole of Rus' as his patrimony "from father and grandfather [*votchina i dedina*]." The division and decline of the Golden Horde brought independence for northeast Rus', but not before the growing power of Moscow was capable of reducing and absorbing the remaining principalities, as well as the free cities. In the previous century the khan had granted the title of "grand prince" to several princes in the cities around Moscow. Ivan I had then added the words "and all Rus'" to his own title to Vladimir, imitating in this the title of his friend, the metropolitan "of Kiev and all Rus'," and significantly expressing the ambition of his house. But Ivan I did not intend to claim sovereignty over the other principalities. It was a hundred years before the term *gospodin*, "lord," appeared in the interprincely treaties, and even longer before *gospodar*, "sovereign," was used. Ivan III, however, used both freely, requiring in 1478 that Novgorod recognize him as its sovereign. The Mongols had declined in power, and Ivan planned to step into their place.

The title "tsar" was also occasionally used by Ivan III. It had previously been reserved for the Byzantine emperor, whose capital was called Tsargrad, and for the Tatar rulers who were descendants of Chingis Khan. There were thus two sources, two patterns, from which the Muscovites could copy this office, one Christian and the other pagan and infidel.* Partly for this reason, perhaps, their adoption of it

* For a perceptive analysis of the two influences see Michael Cherniavsky, "*Khan* or *Basileus*: An Aspect of Russian Mediaeval Political Theory," *Journal of the History of Ideas*, XX (Oct.–Dec. 1959), 459–476.

was slow and hesitant. In 1498, the ceremony installing Ivan's grandson Dmitri as coruler was patterned after the Byzantine ceremony for the installation of a junior coruler, a *caesar*, which implied that Ivan himself was emperor, the *basileus*. He was called by the metropolitan "Tsar Ivan, Grand Prince, Autocrat of all Rus'," and Dmitri was admonished to "care with all thy heart for all Orthodox Christendom." [1] In 1505, however, Vasili III (Ivan having ousted Dmitri) was crowned as "grand prince," so Ivan IV in 1547 became the first actually crowned as "tsar."

The Muscovites had several theories by which they justified the new title. The most obvious might seem to be the fact that Ivan III had married Sophia Paleologa, a niece of the last Byzantine emperor, who had lost his throne and his life to the Turks in 1453. By this marriage Ivan and his descendants could and did claim to be heirs of Rome. Little weight, however, seems to have been placed upon this circumstance at the time. Apparently more substantial to Muscovy were two further justifications, now regarded as legendary. It was claimed that the Byzantine emperor had given an imperial crown (along with his sister Anna) to the first Vladimir at the time of his conversion. And it was said that the second Vladimir (Monomach), son of a Byzantine princess, had similarly been given certain insignia of empire. As court etiquette became more Byzantine, these legends became part of the coronation ceremony. Still more substantial was the justification based on the decline of the Tatar power. After preaching submission to the khans for 250 years, the church needed to abandon that part of its ritual and apparently thought it necessary, or at least desirable, to replace the Tatar tsar with another. In the absence of a tsar at Byzantium, the grand prince was the obvious candidate. This reasoning lay behind the argument attributed to Archbishop Vassian of Rostov in 1480 in persuading Ivan III to resist the khan:

And if some will argue that you are under the oath of your ancestors not to raise your hand against the tsar, listen God-loving tsar! If an oath is made because of necessity, we are allowed to forgive the breaking of it. . . . And who of the prophets of the prophecies or who of the apostles or saints have taught you to obey this God-shamed and most evil so-called tsar, you, the great Christian tsar of the Russian lands? [2]

Such denigrating of the khans and elevating of the grand princes was paralleled by military victories of Ivan III and Vasili III over the khans of Kazan, so that, in anticipation of the final subjugation of Kazan and

Astrakhan, Ivan IV was crowned as tsar before setting off on that campaign. The absorption of these two Mongol succession states into Muscovy made Ivan the successor to these two khans. The wide dissemination of this argument indicates that the princes of Moscow felt little distaste in deriving their claim to power from the devastators of Rus'.*

The title "tsar" itself was of less significance than the implications, both Byzantine and Mongol, that came with it. As a successor to the khans, the tsar could with some justification later claim authority over additional parts of the Mongol empire. The basis for Russian imperialism toward the east was laid, and in fact the tsar did later acquire the largest segment of the heritage of Chingis Khan. Moreover, Mongol concepts of the khan's ownership of all the land and the people, universal slavery, and other aspects of oriental political thought were involved.† Yet the church was alive to the problem of power claimed from a non-Christian source. The crowning of Ivan before the conquest of Kazan is one indication of this. Another is found in the effort to connect the Moscow throne more closely with that of Byzantium. For this purpose the legend of Monomach's "crown" or cap was created early in the sixteenth century.‡ And for the same purpose the more general doctrine of Moscow as the Third Rome was advanced.§

As we have seen, when the Emperor Constantine deserted the Tiber for the Bosphorus about 330 he built there a "New Rome" which became the cradle of official Christianity, the center of the seven ecumenical councils, and the home of the Orthodox emperors and patriarchs. For over a thousand years it dedicated itself to a great duty, the preservation of three great heritages, that of the classical Greeks, that of imperial Rome, and that of the church fathers—together encompassing all that God had given man to know in this world. During that time the empire and the church became so inextricably interrelated that

* Among the princes serving the Moscow rulers in the sixteenth century, those who had come over from the Mongols were given the highest rank, a practice still prevailing in the nineteenth century.

† On Russia as an oriental despotism see Karl A. Wittvogel, *Oriental Despotism: A Comparative Study of Total Power* (New Haven, 1957), pp. 219–225 and *passim*.

‡ This cap, first mentioned in the will of Ivan I (1339), is now regarded by scholars as of central Asian origin, possibly given to Ivan by Khan Uzbek, and clearly unlike any Byzantine conception of a crown.

§ On the political thought of the church in this period see Igor Smolitsch, *Russisches Mönchtum* (Würzburg, 1953), esp. pp. 119–144.

the clergy could not imagine Christianity without the emperor. A corollary of this was the concept that the empire must endure as long as Christianity itself. But Constantinople had fallen to the infidels; the empire was no more. Bulgaria too, which had claimed a tsar of its own, was subjugated.

Of course, there was an emperor in the West, but the West had become heretical. The tsar of Moscow was the only reigning Orthodox emperor, and there were enough historical connections to give color to his claim of being the legitimate heir of Byzantium. During the previous centuries, as already pointed out, the Rus' clergy had aided greatly the strengthening of the princes, and they had assumed a leading role in bestowing high-sounding titles upon the Moscow princes long before the princes themselves, as dutiful sons of the church, began to use them. Similarly, in the new post-Mongol situation, they were most eager to grasp for Moscow the Byzantine heritage. They may have been assisted to their new doctrine by the influx of south Slavic clergy who had moved northward as the Turks overran the Balkan area, for as early as the fourteenth century the Bulgarians had thought of their capital, Turnovo, as a successor to Constantinople. In any event it was a monk of Pskov who presented the new vision, full blown, in a letter to the grand prince toward the end of the fifteenth century.* Said Monk Philotheus:

As it is from the supreme and the all-powerful, the all-supporting right hand of God, that tsars reign, and that the great are glorified and the mighty administer justice,—[so] to thee, most serene and supreme sovereign and grand prince, Orthodox Christian tsar and lord of all, ruler [lit., rein-holder] of God's holy thrones, [is] the holy, ecumenical and apostolic church . . . , which has shone through in the place of those of Rome and Constantinople. For the church of ancient Rome was destroyed through the apostasy of the Apollinarian heresy; and the doors of the church of the second Rome, the city of Constantine, were cut asunder by the battle axes of Hagar's posterity. But the holy, apostolic church of the [ecumenical] councils, of this third new Rome of thy sovereign power, which [extends] to the ends of the earth in the Orthodox Christian faith, shines everywhere under the heavens more brightly than the sun. And may thy dominion realize, O pious tsar, that all the empires of the Orthodox Christian faith have come together into thy sole empire: thou alone in all the earth art tsar

* On the dating of his letters see Nikolay Andreyev, "Filofey and his Epistle to Ivan Vasil'yevich," *Slavonic and East European Review*, XXXVIII (Dec. 1959), 1–31.

to the Christians. . . . Observe and take heed, O pious tsar, that all Christian empires came together into thine alone, that two Romes fell, but the third stands, and there will be no fourth: for thy Christian empire "shall not be left to other people" [quoting Daniel, 2:44].[3]

The great duty, then, had come to the Moskva, the duty of preserving the world's cultural heritage. The Muscovites knew little of the glory of Rome and perhaps less of the wisdom of ancient Greece, but that had all been overshadowed by the wisdom and glory of the great religion which they had made their own. It was the Christian tradition, fundamentally, which they must preserve. The duty was both universal and exclusive. It was universal because God had established only one church, and that in a universal empire. In the time of Byzantium many forms of heresy and a new religion had lured people away; the church had become almost a national church, and many barbarians and infidels had detached segments from the empire; yet the idea of universal church and empire remained. Perhaps as a reward for greater piety God's grace might restore what had been lost. There could be only one universal empire, hence the duty must belong exclusively to Muscovy since she alone had preserved the true faith. Thus the feeling of isolation that descended upon the Muscovites after the Council of Florence was submerged in a new enthusiasm for the religious mission of Moscow. With the Mongols in retreat a beginning could be made by "gathering" unto Muscovy all the lands that had once been parts of Kievan Rus'. In the coregency ceremony of 1498, mentioned above, the willingness of the church to see the tsar take jurisdiction over all Orthodox Christians is evident. Even into the nineteenth century this religious mission remained one of the main springs of Pan-Slavist thinking; it was not naval strategy alone that sparked Russia's urge toward Constantinople and the Dardanelles.

In Byzantium, however, the emphasis had not been upon expansion. The Byzantines had emphasized conservation: fascinated by the perfection and stability of the theoretical and institutional structures they had inherited, the strength of the most capable minds was devoted to their preservation. A similar conservative attitude was another of the effects of the Third Rome concept in Moscow. Even the circumstances of the fall of Constantinople aggravated this tendency. The defeat had occurred only fourteen years after the Greek church had submitted to Rome, deserting its duty, from the Rus' point of view, and going into heresy. The lesson was driven deeply—the lesson of the double danger of deviation from the true faith and of contact with the "Roman heresy." Thus, at the beginning of her new autonomous existence, Muscovy was given a sharp thrust toward conservatism and an admonition to watch warily against perverting influences from outside, especially from western Europe. It is well to remember, in interpreting subsequent ideas and events in Russia, that for nearly a thousand years she has considered herself the possessor of absolute truth, and for half that long its exclusive custodian.

At the same time the West itself was becoming both more intrusive and more attractive. The advance of the Ottoman Turks into the Balkans sent many somewhat westernized Slavs northward to Kiev, to Pskov, and to Novgorod, and also helped to stimulate the Renaissance in Europe. Moreover, the dangers of the Roman heresy themselves were lessened as northern Europe accepted the Reformation. The growing independence of the Muscovites thus coincided with a time of great cultural and commercial activity in the West. Habits of isolation, reinforced by the Third Rome doctrine, could not be suddenly discarded, but gradually and irrepressibly contacts with the West multiplied.

In this context, and partly as a response to ideas brought from the Balkans, the Muscovite church experienced its first indigenous intellectual ferment, foreshadowing the great schism under Patriarch Nikon over 150 years later. Two strains of Christianity appeared, one spiritual and ascetic, the other administrative and dogmatic. These had always been present but were now aroused to differentiate themselves more strongly by two new circumstances: the spread of heresy in Novgorod and Pskov, and the increasing interest of the grand prince and the boyars in church land.

The new power and freedom of action of the Moscow prince led him to need and to covet, like the contemporary rulers in western Europe, the land which had accumulated in the hands of the church as a result of the immunity it enjoyed in the Mongol and earlier periods. After the conquest of Novgorod, Ivan III secured the approval of the metropolitan for the seizure of much monastery land there and its distribution among his supporters. Strangely enough, a group of the clergy urged the general secularization of church property about the same time, and thus earned the appellation of "noncovetous." This was the ascetic group, known as the Trans-Volga Elders from their residence in hermitages and small monasteries in the northeastern wilderness. Their strongest spokesman was Nil Sorski (Nilus of Sorsk) who insisted:

We have been instructed by the holy fathers to gain our daily bread and other necessities by manual labour, as Our Lord and His Immaculate Mother have commanded. "If any man will not work, neither shall he eat," says the Apostle. . . . It is not to be thought of that we should take the fruit of other men's labour by force. . . . We must resist and avoid like deadly poison the desire to possess earthly goods.[4]

The church must avoid temptation, must surrender its lands—not because Ivan wanted them, but because piety demanded poverty.

Such doctrine would seem ready made for Ivan's purpose, and the grand prince leaned toward it; but with this rose there were thorns. What Sorski wanted was to withdraw the church from worldly affairs, to emphasize its spiritual mission, and consequently to reduce all secular influence over it. Moreover, he advocated reducing the influence of the hierarchy within the church in the interest of individual prayer and study, which he stressed. This was new and untried doctrine, leading no man knew where. Far from being the pure reactionary he is sometimes pictured, Sorski was a reformer with high standards of scholarship and of morality. He was strongly influenced by the Hesychasts of the Mt. Athos monasteries in Greece and was intent upon the search for salvation through an understanding of the scriptures, to which, he believed, worldly interests barred the way. The church under his influence would not easily bend to the princely will.

These opinions seem like a delayed echo of the fourteenth-century controversy over evangelical poverty between Pope John XXII and the Franciscan Order. Indeed, there was much similarity of attitude in Sorski and the great Franciscan, William of Occam, and to a lesser extent Marsilio of Padua. William had defended poverty, had stressed the need for study and research into religious truth, and had attacked the synthesis of faith and reason with which Thomas Aquinas had, in the opinion of the hierarchy, crowned the intellectual achievements of the Middle Ages—and William had done this with the prime motive of setting faith rather than reason free from papal domination. Both property and reason involved the church too much in things of this world, obstructed its spiritual mission, and invited—even compelled— secular interference.

There is no direct evidence that Sorski was familiar with the work of the scholastic philosophers although he was well educated in Greek monastic schools and a few Western scholars were present in Muscovy in those days. Nor did Sorski, by any means, have Occam's power of theoretical construction, but on one point he was in advance of the West. Even Marsilio, who denied the right of the church to punish heresy, had not wished to exempt it from punishment; he held it instead to be a secular offense. Sorski went further; he denied the validity of corporal punishment, secular or spiritual, for heresy. Only spiritual methods of persuasion should be used to recover deviating souls, since the realm of the church is spiritual.

The question arises as to whether this doctrine of toleration owed its origin to the tolerant attitude of the Mongols. While their example may have been appreciated in the Muscovite church, they were, none the less, infidels; it is more probable that Sorski derived his position from Chrysostom, who had denied the use of force before Augustine, in the West, had found a justification for it.*

Although the thought pattern of the Trans-Volga Elders included some Western elements, these elements were not, by and large, the dominant opinions either in the West or among the Elders. As a whole Sorski's followers stood for the Greek monastic tradition with its mysticism, morality, and decentralization. It was in Sorski's chief opponent, Joseph Sanin, or Volotski, hegumen of the Volokolamsk Monastery near Moscow, that prevailing attitudes of European Christianity were most nearly paralleled. Joseph's opinions, the administrative and dogmatic strain of Muscovite Christianity, became the official opinions of the church.

Variously interpreted as the earliest Russian advocate of revolution and as an exponent of tsarist absolutism, Joseph faced a difficult situation and found for it a very successful solution. On the one hand he wanted to protect the landed interests of the church against secularization; on the other, he wished to protect both the hierarchy and its flock against the heresy and dissension that had gained a foothold even in the royal family. For this he needed the help of the grand prince.

* Chrysostom had said, "The laws confer upon us no such power of coercing the wayward: nor could we use it even if they did. . . . If a man, however, stray from the true faith, a work of great diligence, patience and perseverance is required of the spiritual shepherd. Such a one can neither be brought back by force nor can he be constrained by fear. He must be led back by argumentation to the truth from which he originally swerved" (*The Priesthood*, trans. W. A. Jorgens [New York, 1955], verses 105, 118; cf. also verse 104).

When Ivan III raised the issue of the lands at the church council of 1503, knowing that he could count upon the support of Sorski and his followers, Joseph scored a lasting victory. Judging shrewdly that the aging prince was really more interested in his own salvation than in the church lands, Volotski persuaded the council to oppose Ivan on this issue, but in so doing he managed to appear to be a model of obedience. He made his requests for immunity from secularization and for civil prosecution of the heretics to hinge upon the canon law and Ivan's desire to remain orthodox. His attitude in the council he described clearly:

The divine rules command you to revere the tsar and not to quarrel with him. At the ecumenical and local councils the ancient bishops did not dare to do this; neither did the four patriarchs, nor the Roman pope. . . . And if on occasion they happened to want to converse with the emperor or prince at the council, they would first beg the emperor to be permitted to speak; and when the emperor ordered, they would speak humbly and in all humility from the holy scriptures.[5]

As the Byzantines had known, the prince is the chosen of God and is to be obeyed and cooperated with in *symphonia*. This close relationship allowed the church to give spiritual guidance to the prince, and through the council Joseph guided Ivan to a better understanding of Vladimir's church statute and the Donation of Constantine, both considered canon law, as sacred barriers against the secularization of church land. Since Ivan badly needed clerical support for the consolidation and expansion of his realm, he felt obliged to yield.

But still the guidance was not finished:

Harken then, and understand that it is from God that power is given you; you are the servants of God. He placed you here as the shepherds and guardians of his people to keep the flock intact from the wolves. God chose you in His own stead and put you on His throne and gave life and mercy into your hands, and it was God's hand that gave you your sword; for your part, do not prefer lies to the truth, fear the heavenly scythe, and do not give free rein to the will of the evil doers. . . . And if they commit evil, sin comes upon the soul of those who permitted it, that is, the king, the princes and the worldly judges, and if these rulers give power to an impious man, they will suffer torment from God on the dreadful day of the second Advent.[6]

The prince, in other words, should use his sword for the correction of the heretics. "The king is the servant of God to punish and to pardon men. But if the king who rules men is himself ruled by evil passions and sins, such as rapacity and violence . . . such a king is not a servant of God but of Satan, not a king but an oppressor." And he admonished the subjects, "And you too, do not obey such a king or prince who leads you to dishonorable and deceitful acts, even though he torture you or threaten you with death. . . . It is in this way that you should serve kings and princes." [7]

Yet this was no new doctrine of revolution; many parallel statements are found in the early fathers, based on Peter's "We ought to obey God rather than men." Nor was it a new submissiveness, although it served to impress once more upon the rulers of Moscow the idea that their powers were of God. Rather was it an effective reaffirmation of the Byzantine doctrines of church and state, necessary after the long period under the shadow of Mongol domination. In his revisions of monastic rules, in his preservation of the worldly interests of the church, and in his justification of civil punishment of heresy, Joseph brought Muscovite practices closer to those of Europe; yet he distinctly avoided any unnecessary assertion of the superiority of spiritual authority over temporal, such as lay inherent in the attitude of Sorski and would culminate one day in the anarchism of Leo Tolstoi.

Between these two schools of thought the struggle continued, with the church hierarchy, in protection of its wealth, largely supporting Joseph, and the boyars seeing much merit in clerical poverty. A decisive turn came, however, when Ivan's son, Vasili III, needed a divorce which the "noncovetous" Metropolitan Vaarlam refused to sanction. Vaarlam was removed and (without the usual formalities of election) the Josephite, Daniel, was appointed by Vasili.

Daniel was an effective expounder of his master's political doctrines and even more subservient to the prince than Joseph had been. He argued, from the scriptures and the fathers, that God acted through the secular power as well as through the church, and that obedience to both was obligatory. Those who deserted the faith, therefore, were enemies not only of the church but also of the state: heresy was treason.

One of the victims of Daniel's campaign against dissenting thought was Maxim the Greek, a tragic figure who came to Moscow from Mt. Athos as a translator at the request of the grand prince, bringing a breath of the western Renaissance to a land so long isolated.* He had

* See Elie Denissoff, *Maxime le Grec et l'Occident* (Louvain, 1943).

studied for some ten years in Italy, had heard Savonarola, and had absorbed some of the ideas of Marsilio, of William, and of the theorists of the church councils, by then imbedded in the Western theological heritage. The need for correction of Muscovy's religious books had frequently been noticed, and Maxim went industriously to work. But such enterprise is fraught with danger, and unfortunately Maxim had identified himself with the followers of Sorski; so when Sorski's enemies gained control of the metropolitanate, Maxim was imprisoned.

At his trial Maxim was accused, among other charges, of calling Vasili III a "persecutor and Godless oppressor," and he appears to have brought with him the Roman doctrine that "the clergy anoints and crowns and confirms the tsar, but not the tsars the prelates. . . . For the priesthood is greater than the temporal tsardom [and] the lesser is blessed by the greater without contradiction." [8] He was, therefore, an opponent of the current exaltation of the throne that had begun under Ivan III and Sophia, and both before and after his imprisonment he was a focus for dissident thought, political as well as religious.

The growing dissatisfaction of the service princes with their diminishing influence in the government, aggravated by the arbitrary quality of Vasili's temperament, was gradually dividing the ruling class of Muscovy into two covertly hostile camps—the grand prince and the Josephite clergy in one and the boyars and Trans-Volga Elders in the other. As yet the contradiction between autocracy and aristocracy was not clearly drawn, and Maxim's friends united several shades of opinion in their shared antagonism to Vasili and the Josephites. They sensed vaguely that the political situation was deteriorating, but none of them seems to have understood the significance of the trends.

The most outspoken of the disaffected boyars, as well as one of the most conservative, was Ivan Bersen-Beklemishev. He is said to have told Maxim,

Thou thyself knowest (even as we also have heard it from prudent men) that the land which doth forsake its ancient customs standeth not for long. Behold, here is our Suzerain Prince beginning to change our ancient usage! What honor, therefore, should he look for from us?

His explanation of these developments was this:

Since the time that the Greeks came hither our land hath been thrown into confusion, even though it did once live in peace and quietness. Straightway when the Suzerain Princess Sophia did come hither with those Greeks of thine there hath risen among us such a strife as there is in Tsargorod, under your Tsars.[9]

Bersen thus saw the crux of the boyars' discontents in the conversion of the old, cooperatively governed grand principality into a Byzantine autocracy.

CHAPTER VIII

The Reign of Ivan IV

REMOVED by the boyars after Vasili's death, Metropolitan Daniel was followed in 1542 by Macarius, another Josephite, who helped to educate the orphan prince, Ivan IV. Ivan's grim half-century reign (1533–1584), which earned him the epithet *Grozny*, the Dread or Terrible, continued the policy of territorial expansion and brought to a critical point the conflicts between old ideas and habits and the new requirements of stronger central administration.

In his boyhood, while the boyars contended for power, Ivan read. Of the few chronicles and religious books available the Old Testament interested him most, and so thoroughly did he apply himself to this material that he became able to conduct theological controversies in the prevailing style. The Old Testament seems to have attracted him because he saw in the accounts of the Hebrew kings a description of his own office and his own relationship to God, and in their rewards and punishments the evidence for his own personal responsibility. The figure of Moses, in particular, appealed to him as a leader who had successfully unified the priestly and kingly offices, an example of the two forms of God's power cooperating toward his ends.

This study enabled him to formulate more clearly than any of his predecessors Moscow's claim to power, and to understand the Josephite interpretation of *symphonia:* the priests must both instruct and obey the prince, yet he, as prince, having heard their instruction must, logically, be free to reject it since to him alone is the responsibility of government entrusted. God will reward or punish the execution of that responsibility, but no one on earth may judge the prince. Ivan's strange reign is best understood, therefore, as the conscientious work of a man who accepted, more literally and logically than Volotski had intended, the Josephite teaching that he was God's vicar on earth. From this source also came an element of Ivan's political thought that most of his contemporaries, and many later students, failed to understand: as the carrier of God's will he acted with a sense of duty even in the most deliberately bloody of his punishments. It was to this element that Prince Kurbski referred when he accused Ivan of having a "leprous conscience." His sense of objective purpose relieved and satisfied his conscience and enabled him to commit atrocities that to some interpreters required an absence of conscience if not of sanity itself.* There is no evidence that Ivan knew the Mongol theory of the Order of God, but it is instructive to see how closely parallel are the two concepts of divine mission and the consequences of resistance.

Thus, to the other forces enhancing the power of the Moscow prince, Ivan added a conviction of more active and personal responsibility to God. To Ivan's mind this called for a reinterpretation of the prince's new title "autocrator" (*samoderzhets*), borrowed from Byzantium and used along with "tsar" and "grand prince." As employed before it had connoted independence from external or foreign powers. Ivan was more literal; as he used the term it also required independence from internal, domestic restraints, authority unlimited by laws, institutions, or customs.

Ivan also reinterpreted the concepts of Muscovy as a *votchina* and of his powers as *votchinnik*. His ancestors had treated the land of the principality as their private property, but they had respected the liberties of "free servants." † Ivan treated the people also as property—without discrimination or exception all were his "slaves." This went beyond the powers of the ordinary *votchinnik*, from whom free peasants might depart. It resembled instead, and may have been derived from, the tenures of land and people among the Mongols.

These interpretations were parts of Ivan's solution to the inherited frictions between the suzerain prince and the boyars. The title of autocrat and that of tsar, the Third Rome idea, the new coronation ceremony, and the double-headed eagle (also borrowed from Byzan-

---

* Novgorod, for example, which had escaped the Mongol ravages, never recovered from Ivan's pillage of 1570.

† When Bersen-Beklemishev opposed a campaign against Smolensk, Vasili III had lashed out with, "Away from me, peasant! I need you no more." Yet even in anger Vasili did not use the word *rab* (slave), but *smerd*, which, although very derogatory, still connoted a degree of freedom.

tium), all tended to elevate the prince, to meet the difficulties of government in an expanding realm by concentrating power in his hands. There was, at the same time, another approach that called for the participation of increasing numbers of persons in the governing process. The Boyar Duma, now called the *synklete,* the Greek name for the Senate, was expanded; a new code of laws was promulgated; administrative bureaus were established; local government was reorganized; and a new and larger council, the zemski sobor, came into intermittent existence. Ivan supported this second approach, but he was careful to avoid the danger that it might bring about a dilution of his autocratic power in favor of the boyars.

Ivan saw clearly the two alternative systems of government that history had prepared. Would the government of Muscovy, like the contemporary governments of Lithuania, Poland, and Sweden, develop in the direction of aristocracy, with only the strongest of their kings able to overcome the myopic policies of their nobles, or would it develop in the direction of authority and unity, with centralized power able to fix and pursue constructive goals? * For a century power had been concentrating in the hands of the grand prince, and the nobles had been losing strength. Dmitri Donskoi, reflecting the earlier tradition, had instructed his sons in his will (1389), "Love ye your boyars, and grant unto them honor meet unto their services; nor do aught without their will." [1] Four generations later their position had so deteriorated that the boyar, Bersen-Beklemishev, accused Vasili III of locking himself in his bedroom alone and there deciding everything. All through Vasili's reign the conflict of grand prince and boyars had smoldered; on Vasili's death, however, the pendulum had swung to the opposite extreme. From 1533 to 1547, during the childhood of Ivan, the boyars ruled. Only factional struggles among them prevented the consolidation of their position. To bring them under control and to establish the autocracy irrevocably were Ivan's prime objectives.

* Ivan repeatedly contrasted these alternatives in insulting letters to foreign rulers. For example, in 1572 he wrote to King John of Sweden: "If thy kingdom were a complete one, the counsellors and the archbishop and all the land would not have been comrades to thy father, and everybody would not [thus] be enrolled as great sovereigns. . . . And thy father was at their head like an elder in a *volost* . . . and it is therefore impossible for thee to be equal with great sovereigns, [for] in great states those customs are not maintained" (*Sbornik imperatorskogo Russkago istoricheskago obshchestva,* CXXIX [St. Petersburg, 1910], 236–237).

But autocracy, interpreted as an absence of domestic restraints, required that the tsar be free to choose his administrators, to consult or not to consult whom he chose, and to take or leave their advice. On these points he came into conflict with both the boyars and the church.

The "titled" boyars (those who were also princes) believed they had prescriptive rights to the highest administrative positions and to a monopoly of lay advisory functions. These were among the remnants of the old authority of the *udel* princes. They no longer ruled separately parts of Rus', but coming to Moscow as the *udely* were gradually "gathered" by the grand princes, they tried to apply to the cooperative ruling of the whole the same system of seniority that had governed the allotment of *udely*. The result, from the early fifteenth century, was the *mestnichestvo*, the allotment of public offices, including military commands, by right of birth without regard to other qualifications. The system was designed to protect the servitor princes and other boyars against upstarts and against the arbitrary favoritism of the grand prince, but it also protected them against each other and thus stifled ability and enterprise beneath constant petty quarrels over precedence. It dissipated the cohesiveness of the nobles and weakened their resistance to autocracy, while at the same time, by its ingrained inefficiency, it stimulated the autocrat to seek to break the ties of custom.

The distinction between administrative and advisory functions not being drawn with modern clarity, the boyars wished also to apply the *mestnichestvo* to membership in the Boyar Duma, the council of the grand prince. In this institution two separate, and in part conflicting, lines of thought and of historical development were amalgamated.

The older of these lines derived from the relationship of the Varangian retinues to the early Riurikides. These early companions-in-arms were all "free servants" with both the right and the practice of departure at will, and there were no members of the ruling family among them. Entry into the group was at the discretion of the prince. Theoretically, he consulted them at will, but in practice they were consulted on all important decisions—not as a matter of legal obligation but as a matter of practical politics. It has already been noted that they might refuse their cooperation, and if they or their advice was ignored too much they might take service elsewhere. On the other hand the prince might, directly or indirectly, dismiss those whom he disliked. In these circumstances both prince and boyars were partly independent and partly dependent: neither could accomplish much without the other, yet the freedom of departure, matched by freedom of recruitment, gave each an easy path for the resolution of personal differences.

A second line of thought had gradually come to bear upon this *modus operandi* with the coming of the servitor princes. They were Riurikides (although to them were later added Mongolians, Lithuanians, Germans, and others) who leaned heavily upon their family relationship to the grand prince. They believed they were entitled by family custom, going back to Iaroslav's will, to a share in the government of the country. If the grand prince no longer provided them with separate *udely*, he was at least obligated to admit them to his council, to consult them on all important matters, and generally to heed their advice. From their point of view the relations of Duma to grand prince were not so much a matter of separate rights or prerogatives as of the division of labor among cooperators. Yet as they became more numerous they could not all be included in the Duma without radically altering its nature. Gradually they learned that with their independence they had surrendered more than they thought.

By the sixteenth century the position of the grand prince had so improved, and that of the boyars had so deteriorated through the bound service of the princes and the loss of the boyars' old freedom of departure, that the grand princes were inclined toward the earlier interpretation of the Duma, denying any prescriptive rights to the Riurikides. Having no fear that those excluded would take service elsewhere, the grand prince was able to choose among them, and the *mestnichestvo* was not allowed to determine membership. Ivan III gave some preference to the princes for the higher duma rank, but he also increased the proportion of *okol'nich'i*, the lower rank, in the total membership. Vasili III, on the contrary, decreased this proportion and enlarged the Duma from ten to fifteen members, the size it retained during the minority of Ivan IV.

Ivan gradually yet drastically changed the Duma in size and in nature. During his reign about 40 per cent of the members were princes, but Ivan stressed the point that they were servitor princes and applied to all ranks indiscriminately the word *rab*, "slave," and the even more degrading synonym *kholop*. He increased the membership until in 1564 it reached forty-seven, and thus he reduced the stature of the individual members and the intimacy of the group. He further undermined what little cohesion the Duma possessed as the institutional organ of the high aristocracy by introducing, beginning in 1553, a growing number of men who were neither princes nor of old boyar families. Mostly administrators, *d'iaki*, these were "small men" having no claim by birth to their positions but owing them solely to Ivan. With them he felt safer and less suspicious than with the boyars. More accustomed to independence of judgment, the latter were more likely to disagree with him and thus, to Ivan's mind, to question his position as the autocrat responsible to God. In 1564 he created for his small men a third duma rank, that of *dumnyi dvoriane*, but he did not attempt to overwhelm the higher ranks with them.*

Like the old *veche*, the Boyar Duma embodied no principle of representation, but unlike the *veche*, it was not a decision-making body, except when the grand prince left it in charge of affairs during his absence. When the grand prince was away from Moscow the Duma prefaced the following formula to its actions: "By direction of the sovereign the boyars have decided. . . ." Sometimes such decisions were later sanctioned by the grand prince, and sometimes written into the law-books without his approval being expressed. In his presence the formula was, "The sovereign has directed and the boyars have decided. . . ." In the code of 1550 (Article 98) it was provided that new laws would be enacted only "by announcement [*doklad*] of the sovereign and the decision of all the boyars." In this Sergeevich saw an attempt to make the youthful Ivan simply the chairman of the Boyar Duma, and certain passages in Ivan's letters indicate he thought (or pretended to think) that such an attempt had been made.[2] D'iakonov, on the other hand, finding instances before 1550 and also late in Ivan's reign in which this same formula was used, concluded that it had no special significance.[3] In any event it appears that, even in the reign of Ivan, the boyars of the Duma regularly participated in the legislative and decision-making process in an advisory capacity and as regents. The basis of that participation was not clearly formulated, however, and genuine differences of opinion about it were possible.

Soon after taking personal control of the government at the age of sixteen Ivan is said to have called a meeting of clergy and nobility to be held on the Red Square on Easter morning 1550 which undoubtedly

---

* At that time they numbered only five while there were thirty-three boyars and nine *okol'nich'i* in the Duma. This account is based on A. A. Zimin, "Sostav Boiarskoi Dumy v XV–XVI vekakh," *Arkheograficheskii ezhegodnik za 1957 god*, ed. M. N. Tikhomirov (Moscow, 1958), pp. 41–87. The most thorough study of the Duma is V. O. Kliuchevskii, *Boiarskaia Duma drevnei Rusi* (4th ed.; Moscow, 1910).

attracted many ordinary inhabitants of Moscow and which has come to be called the first zemski sobor. Not much is known of this meeting, but it is reported that Ivan appealed for help from the metropolitan, attacked the boyars for their misgovernment, and promised the people in Old Testament style, "I, even I, will be unto you a judge and a defender. Yea, I will root out iniquity, and recover of the robbers the spoil." [4]

Yet Ivan did not declare war upon the *mestnichestvo*—knowing it to be a divisive rather than a cementing force among the nobility—nor upon the boyars. He called for peace and unity. In the church council of the following year, controlled by the Josephites, unity prevailed even when the now autonomous Muscovite church deviated from the canons of the Greeks. For ten comparatively quiet years two "small men," Alexis Adashev and the priest Sylvester (supposed compiler of the book of popular wisdom, the *Domostroi*), were Ivan's closest advisers.

This new institution, the zemski sobor, which Ivan assembled again in 1566, had some viability, as will be seen. It reflected the growing centralization of government in Moscow and the dependence of the tsar upon larger numbers of officials, as well as his desire to free himself from the Boyar Duma. For the sobors were not representative bodies but were primarily assemblies of officials, coming together, mostly by personal invitation although some members may have been elected by corporate bodies of merchants or provincial nobility, to give advice and to receive instructions which, in their administrative capacities, they were to execute. Aside from the clergy and nobility only merchants economically or fiscally important were included, and even these came from only a few cities. The assembly had neither fixed periods for its meetings nor independent status nor any definite powers. As Kliuchevski described it, "The idea in Moscow of the sixteenth century was that a nation had no right to appoint exponents of its will, since there already existed aboriginal and suitable authorities for the purpose—namely, authorities appointed of God in the shape of the Government and its agents." [5] Yet since the zemski sobor was more broadly based than any other institution, it came at times to speak for the nation.*

* The thesis has been advanced that the zemski sobor was patterned after the Senate as part of a conscious effort to imitate Byzantine institutions. The use of the word *synklete* for the Boyar Duma, however, argues against this view. See

Besides this institution, and new collections of sacred and secular law, Ivan introduced the printing press into Muscovy and made other attempts toward the modernization of the country. It was in his reign that Muscovite policy began to be shaped by an awareness of the value of European secular learning and technology. This awareness was matched by a realization in Ivan's Western neighbors that their first line of defense against Muscovy lay in her backwardness, and they therefore refused to supply her with goods that would contribute to her military strength. About 1547 Ivan tried to employ and bring to Moscow a group of Western artisans and scholars. Through a Saxon, Hans Schlitte, some 120 "doctors, masters of arts, and men of learning, bell-founders, miners, goldsmiths, apothecaries, paper-makers, master builders, printers, and similar craftsmen" [6] were assembled at Lübeck, but this Hanse town, fearing a modernized Muscovite giant, arrested Schlitte and dispersed his troop. Released, he continued his efforts, but in vain; this path being barred, Ivan turned to more forceful methods. His attack upon the Livonian knights was aimed toward an opening upon the Baltic Sea, the "window to the West" which Peter the Great was to achieve.

While he thus moved toward the West in some ways, in one of his important measures Ivan appears to be going backwards in history, extending feudalism at a time when the West had largely abandoned it. By a ukase of 1556 he made the services required from the nobility proportional to the amount of land they held. In so doing he made no distinction between holders of *votchiny*, from whom service had been voluntary, and holders of *pomest'ia* and *kormleniia*, whose tenures had always been conditional upon service.

The Tsar and Grand Prince Ivan Vasil'evich of all Rus', with his retinue [lit., brothers] and boyars, has decided concerning *kormlenie* and service for all people. . . . It is the pious tsar's custom that the source of his great wisdom should be the fear of the Lord and that he keep himself clean before God in everything; setting aside all royal amusements, he tries in everything to act according to Christ's will and to guard the tsardom

---

G. I. Bratianu, "Les assemblées d'états en Europe orientale au moyen âge et l'influence du régime politique byzantin," *Actes du VIeme Congrès International des Études Byzantines*, I (Paris, 1950), 35–56, and G. Stökl, "Russland," in Helen M. Cam, Antonio Margongiu, and Günther Stökl, "Recent Work and Present Views on the Origins and Development of Representative Assemblies," *Relazioni* of the Tenth International Congress of Historical Science, I (Firenze, 1955), 94–98.

committed to him and to establish fitting justice and to defend it against all heterodox, Mohammedans and Latins. . . . The sovereign also commanded them to measure the land in the *pomest'e* estates and to allot to each [servant] his due and to divide the remainder among those not having [land]; and from the *votchina* and *pomest'e* estates to establish the appointed service of one man fully armed and mounted for each 100 quarters [approx. 135 acres] of good land.[7]

The deterioration of the old "free servants" was legally complete. Service to the tsar became obligatory for all ranks of the nobility—and this just when the energy released by the decline of feudal obligations was carrying western Europe to unprecedented heights of artistic and scientific achievement. Within a century, as will be seen, the remaining vestiges of the peasants' freedom to change landlords were also eliminated and compulsory service became universal from the top of Muscovite society to the bottom.

To these developments some significant characteristics of later Russian political life may, in part, be traced. The expectation that all persons of rank would enter the princely, later the public, service (or that of the church) meant the presence in the government of many who lacked ability, with resulting inefficiencies; but more important, the absence of free persons of ability outside the government retarded private enterprise in economic and cultural fields. Service to the tsar placed governmental employment on a subjective, personal basis that greatly encouraged obsequiousness and narrowed the channels for statesmanship so that, in spite of the enormous area and wide variety of the country, and in spite of Ivan's and later Catherine II's efforts to improve local government, the administration remained centralized and local initiative was actively discouraged. Bureaucracy, built upon military service, which had long been a way of life for many families, became the only available pattern of response to all public problems.

The death of Ivan's first wife in 1560 marked the turning point of his reign. He became suspicious that his closest advisers had caused her demise. Adashev and Sylvester were exiled. Ivan's aggressive nature, his distaste for advice, and his accumulated antagonisms were now unleashed. By some it is believed that he lost his mental balance and subsequently indulged in pointless murders. Other students remember his experiences with the boyars in the impressionable years before his coronation, his criticism of them at the zemski sobor of 1550, and their defections at the time of Ivan's illness in 1553, when many of them had shown reluctance to swear allegiance to his infant son, and believe that his entire reign was an attack upon them as a class. As an additional motive, the Marxist historians credit him with supporting the lower classes against their exploiters.

It is true that, with his sense of the dramatic, Ivan played upon popular hatred for the aristocrats, and it is also true that his reign shows remarkable consistency throughout. But it is not clear that his policies were aimed at the destruction of the boyar class, or even at their elimination from positions of influence. Few boyars' names appear among the thousands whom he executed. The boyars were, in fact, administratively necessary to him. But the *udel* psychology of brotherly equality was in conflict with all Ivan's theories of government as well as with his suspicious and violent temperament. It was, moreover, in conflict with the concept of the grand principality as a private *votchina* (above, pages 62–64). This psychology survived especially among those princes, like the Kurbskis, who were descended from the senior branches of the Riurikides (the Moscow branch was geneologically quite junior), and among those, like the Shuiskis, who resented the gathering by Moscow of the other *udely*, some of which had also been grand principalities. It was this psychology that Ivan determined to eradicate by subjecting everyone, including his closest relatives, to obedience. Such subjection required the completion of the work begun by Vasili II: the elimination of any independent bases of power upon which others might mount effective resistance to his will. Muscovy must be, as his ancestors had aimed to make it, his private estate. Ivan even adopted the old formula of the landowner, and applied it to everyone: "We are free to reward our slaves [*kholopei*], and we are also free to punish them." The basis of aristocracy must be service, not the holdings of land that some princes retained in their *udely* and *votchiny*.

To this end he conceived the *oprichnina*, the thousand (later five thousand) horsemen dressed as monks, with dogs' heads and brooms tied to their saddles, who executed without question Ivan's most ruthless commands. Toward their support he reassigned almost half the land of Muscovy, transferring the previous holders to new lands elsewhere as his grandfather had done (above, page 65). By this technique he uprooted many boyars from their ancestral estates, weakening their economic positions, reducing their personal followings, and loosening their connections with the past. The nation was thus divided into two parts, necessitating two separate administrative machines, the new *oprichnina* as well as the old officials. In the new machine the offices were less subject to the *mestnichestvo* and Ivan was freer to appoint "small men." Yet the *oprichnina* was not directed against the boyars as a class. Those among them who chose to be submissive enough were permitted to join its ranks and to retain their lands. When, after some twelve years of their depredations, Ivan tired of his "monks" and combined the two administrations, all the boyars had endured intensive lessons in submission. Ivan had even submitted himself, setting a Mongol prince upon the throne of Vladimir and for over a year pretending homage to him. How effectively the *udel* psychology had been exorcised, however, his successors would discover.

Against Ivan's claim to unlimited authority the boyars had three choices: submission, departure, or death. The deterioration of the old right of free departure has already been noted. While legally the right remained, in Ivan's time there were no independent parts of Rus' united by bonds of brotherly friendship as there had been in the *udel* period, and the practical basis of free departure was gone. Not all the *udely* had been "gathered"; some were held by Lithuania and Poland, but these were foreign states in a sense in which the old *udely* had never been. Yet even these had once been included by treaty in the old departure system, and a number of boyars preferred to leave Muscovy rather than submit to Ivan. Some lost their lives in the attempt.

Among those who escaped the most famous was Andrei Kurbski, one of the senior Riurikides who had been a close friend of Ivan's and had served him well until a military defeat in 1564 caused him to fear the tsar's wrath. Well received by King Sigismund Augustus of Poland and Lithuania, Kurbski carried on from there a vitriolic correspondence with Ivan and wrote a *History of the Grand Prince of Moscow*.* These works, with Ivan's replies, constitute the best statements of the two positions, the aristocrat versus the autocrat, although neither author displays systematic thought.

In Kurbski's writing one does not find, as might be expected, a defense of the right of departure: this he assumed without apology. One finds instead attacks on Ivan for dereliction in the duties of a prince. Kurbski had been a student of the Sorski school and tended to apply its rigorous morality. He may have acted on a customary right,

* *Prince A. M. Kurbsky's History of Ivan IV*, ed. and trans. J. L. I. Fennell (Cambridge, 1965).

but he wrote always in terms of duties: Ivan had a duty to take the advice of the boyars, to render informed judgments, and to respect ancient property holdings.

Behind this approach lay a deep conviction of the power and value of reason, and especially of collective thought, the advice of councillors—even "the holy angels are governed by counsel and intelligence." Like Sorski, Kurbski believed that the human mind was one of God's finest gifts, a tool for salvation both here and hereafter. In one of his letters to Ivan, after sending him a long translation from Cicero, he expostulated:

Behold, O tsar, with attentiveness: as the pagan philosophers, according to the law of nature, attained such truth and understanding, with wondrous wisdom . . . , for this reason then did God grant them to rule the whole universe; but we call ourselves Christians, and not only do we attain the truth of the Scribes and the Pharisees, but also [the truth] of those who live by the law of nature! O woe unto us! What answer [can] we give to our Christ at the judgment? And whereby shall we justify ourselves? [8]

Having both the old and the new revelations, as well as natural reason, it was the duty of Christians to use them. Kurbski saw Ivan's new conception of autocracy as a surrender of the tsar's rational faculty to the domination of his arbitrary will. From this excess of willfulness flowed three deleterious results. In the first place, the tsar refused to accept counsel from others and therefore acted unwisely on his own limited resources.

The tsar, if he is [to be] respected by the tsardom, since he did not receive certain gifts from God, must seek good and beneficial advice not only from his counsellors but from men of the people; because the gift of intellect [dukha] is given not according to external riches nor by strength of kingdom, but according to spiritual justice. [9]

Second, Ivan's suspicious nature, acting without advice, caused him to destroy "the strong in Israel" and to confiscate their property. In this connection Kurbski speaks always of counsellors and generals, of state servants and not simply of aristocrats. And in the third place, Ivan's attitude cut him off from those "who tell you the truth without shame" and left him prey to "most foul parasites and adulators." He and his people were thus the victims of self-reinforcing and self-perpetuating error.

To such suggestions Ivan replied with contempt: "How, pray, can a man be called autocrat if he himself does not govern?" [10] Like Kurbski, he had great respect for reason, but always his own, not that of others.* Autocracy, he insisted, required the absence not only of restraints but even of advice:

We have reached the grade of the age of Christ's fulfilment [i.e., 33 years], and, apart from the mercy of God and of the most pure Mother of God and of all the saints, we ask for no teaching from men, for it is not befitting, when ruling a multitude of people, to ask for understanding from others. [11]

Kurbski's idea of cooperation with counsellors he ridiculed as rule by a group:

See you then that the rule of many . . . will still be like unto the folly of women, if they are not under one authority. For just as a woman cannot make up her mind—now she [decides] one way, now another—so is the rule of many in the kingdom: one man desires one thing, another desires another. Therefore are the desires and the minds of many like unto the folly of women. [12]

Ivan then accused Kurbski of plotting against the throne from the beginning. "You took counsel with the priest [Sylvester] that I should be sovereign only in word, but that in deed you and the priest should be sovereign: for this reason have all these things come to pass." [13] The evidence of this he professed to find in Article 98 of the Code of 1550, which, he said, was intended to strip him of power, "to be held in honour only by virtue of his presidency [of the Boyar Duma] and for the sake of the renown of the kingdom." Having later discovered this betrayal by his friends, Ivan determined to trust no one and to assert his autocracy.

Is this then the sign of "leprous conscience" to hold my kingdom in my hand and not to let my servants rule? And is it "contrary to reason" not to wish to be possessed and ruled [*obladannomu i ovladennomu*] by my own servants? And is this "illustrious Orthodoxy"—to be possessed and ordered about by my own slaves [*raby*]? [14]

Kurbski disdained to rebut Ivan's charge of conspiracy. Instead he explained the change in Ivan on other grounds, as the result of the words of a serpent, the embittered ex-bishop Vassian Toporkov,

* He was greatly irritated by an accusation by Kurbski that he acted "contrary to reason," and repeatedly tried to refute it. Our MSS of Kurbski's letter, all corrupt, do not preserve this charge.

93

whom Ivan had asked, "How should one rule well and have in obedience one's great and powerful [men]?" Vassian had replied, "If thou wilt be an autocrat, keep not a single [counsellor] wiser than thyself, for thou art better than anyone; thus thou shalt be firm in thy kingdom, and shalt have everything in thy hands. If thou shalt have wiser [men] near thee, by necessity thou shalt be obedient to them." *[15] The reply, Kurbski avowed, should have been, "The tsar himself should be like the head, and love his wise counsellors as his limbs." This would accord Ivan much more than a "presidency."

Although less conservative than Bersen-Beklemishev, Kurbski reflected, in his views of the central government, the old *udel* concept of cooperative rule. Yet in his manner of governing his own domain he was autocratic, insisting upon independence in judging his subordinates.† This inconsistency of the small autocrat objecting to the larger autocrat, objecting, one might say, not to autocracy as such but to unwise autocracy, lies near the heart of the weakness of Kurbski as a political thinker. It accounts in part, since he was not alone in that weakness, for the failure of Ivan's opponents.

Yet Kurbski was not simply an anachronism, a voice from the past. He expressed, rather, a different compromise between the old customs and the new problems, a compromise in a more aristocratic pattern. He had supported the "small men" Adashev and Sylvester, and not the *mestnichestvo*, recognizing that Ivan's growing empire needed competent men wherever they could be found. He may have been in sympathy with the creation of the zemski sobor, as his phrase "men of the people," quoted above, would imply.‡ Perhaps realistically, he considered competence more prevalent among the nobility than elsewhere. It

---

* Toporkov was a Josephite and therefore an advocate of autocracy. Kurbski was present at this interview and his account has the ring of truth; but this occurred in 1553, so Ivan clearly did not act on the advice until years later. Moreover, it is doubtful that a man of Ivan's egotism would have thought others wiser than himself.

† Solov'ev reports that the Polish king, having given Kurbski an estate at Kovel, sent an agent to investigate complaints against his arbitrary administration. Kurbski's constable informed this emissary, "My lord rules over the land and over the subjects of Kovel; therefore he is free to punish them at will, and neither the king nor anyone else need concern himself about it" (Sergei M. Solov'ev, *Istoriia Rossii*, VII [St. Petersburg, 1896], 499).

‡ V. O. Kliuchevski so interprets him, although there is little evidence for or against that view (*A History of Russia*, trans. C. J. Hogarth, II [London, 1912], 68).

is likely also that he thought of the Code of 1550 as a formal acceptance by Ivan of the old pattern of consultation with the Boyar Duma, perhaps as the conversion of a custom into a legal right. However, it is doubtful that, to his mind, Article 98 was a provision for a Duma veto over the tsar's decisions, and even more doubtful that, as Ivan charged, it relegated the tsar to the role of a chairman.

For Kurbski admitted that the tsar's power came from God, and he was as insistent as Ivan himself upon the tsar's duty to rule according to God's laws. He saw the tsar, and not the Duma, as the "head" of the body politic. Moreover, he recognized that times had changed and that some remolding of institutions was necessary. Just as Ivan tried repeatedly to end his isolation from Europe, so Kurbski tried, even in exile, by his writing and translating to spread some enlightenment and Western culture in Muscovy. Thus a broad area of agreement between the former friends served to render more poignant the differences that divided them. Both Kurbski and Ivan had made adjustments to the changes expansion had brought to Muscovy. The aristocratic solution advanced by Kurbski was quite different from that of Ivan. He emphasized the public, political nature of government, the importance of tradition, and the proper utilization of the available intellectual resources. Ivan, on the other hand, stressed the private aspect of Muscovy as his personal demesne, his own unlimited sovereignty, and the proper attitude of submissiveness in his subjects. A careful appraisal of Kurbski's position indicates that the development of autocracy was not the only solution then available for the government of Russia.

CHAPTER IX

From Riurikides to Romanovs

HAVING killed his eldest son, and having little respect for his second, Fedor, Ivan asked the Duma to choose a successor. None dared be nominated or nominate anyone except Fedor, so Ivan named him. The custom of succession by the eldest surviving son, initiated by Vasili I and reinforced by his father's will, had become strong enough to offset the mental deficiencies of Fedor, but perhaps not strong enough to give him sufficient claim to the throne. After Ivan's death a third zemski sobor appears to have been convened,* therefore, which confirmed his title—heredity, the tsar's will, election, and divine inspiration thus all coinciding.

The actual administration, however, passed into the hands of Ivan's favorite, the boyar Boris Godunov.† As an indication of the heritage left by Ivan as well as of the government of Boris the words of the English emissary, Giles Fletcher, are trenchant. Visiting Moscow in 1588 (and not being well received) he wrote:

The manner of the government is much after the Turkish fashion: which they seeme to imitate as neare as the countrie, and reach of their capacities

---

*This sobor is listed by Mikhail D'iakonov, *Skizzen zur Gesellschafts—und Staatsordnung des Alten Russlands*, trans. Eugen Goluboff (Breslau, 1931), p. 407.

† Godunov was probably descended from a Tatar noble who entered Muscovite service in the fourteenth century, although this traditional view is disputed (see S. B. Veselovski, "Iz istorii drevnerusskogo zemlevlodeniia," *Istoricheskie zapiski,* XVIII [1946], 56–91). Ivan had chosen Boris's sister as a wife for Fedor in 1580, and shortly before his death named a council of five guardians for Fedor, including Boris and Nikita Romanovich (brother of Ivan's first wife and grandfather of the future tsar Mikhail Romanov). Nikita obligingly died the following year, and the others were outmaneuvered and eliminated by Boris, who with his sister's help could manipulate the tsar.

in pollitique affayres, will give them leave to doo. The state and forme of their government is plaine tyrannicall, as applying all to the behoofe of the prince, and that after a most open and barbarous manner. . . .[1]

Yet, an enigmatic man, Boris caused to be cast the largest bell the world has ever seen, a symbol of liberty from the days of the early *veche*. He anticipated Peter the Great by a hundred years in importing foreign teachers on a large scale, and in sending native youths abroad to study, but at the same time he attempted by ukase to restrict the peasants' traditional right to change landlords, helping thus to establish serfdom.

In the religious sphere Godunov took the initiative in a long overdue reform of some future significance for Moscow, the elevation of the metropolitanate to a patriarchate. Since Moscow had become the third Rome, as was thought, it deserved *de jure* as well as *de facto* independence. After protracted negotiations with the Orthodox patriarchs, Boris and Fedor were paid a visit by Patriarch Jeremiah of Constantinople, who, finding himself in difficulties with the sultan, appears to have thought it expedient to journey to Moscow in 1588. At first they tried to persuade him to transfer his seat to Christian soil, but the suspicious Boris would not have him permanently at Moscow, and offered the old capital, Vladimir, instead. When Jeremiah refused this provincial exile they asked, or perhaps demanded, that he create a new patriarchate. To this he agreed. The existing metropolitan, Job, was elected, by "permission" of God, by the "will" of the tsar, and by the "blessing" of Jeremiah, and was elevated with appropriate ceremony.[2] In this ceremony the crosier was handed to Job by Fedor, not by Jeremiah, a symbolism indicative of the secular supremacy prevalent in Moscow. But would the ruler of the third Rome assert the primacy of his patriarch over the others, whose sees, after all, were ruled by infidels?

When Jeremiah returned to Constantinople, out of Boris' reach, he convoked a general council to confirm what had been done in Moscow. This council, giving its approval, dispatched a letter "declaring synodically that the newly-created patriarch of Moscow, the lord Job, is to be named patriarch, and to be reckoned with the other patriarchs, and to have his place and commemoration after the patriarch of Jerusalem [that is, at the end of the list]. . . . And he is to treat and regard as his chief [*archon; nachalo*] the apostolical chair of Constantinople, as do also the other patriarchs." [3] To which the tsar (not the patriarch) replied:

To the Most Holy Pastor of God, Jeremiah, Teacher of the Command-
ments of Orthodoxy . . . it has been here synodically ordained that thou
shouldest be named the first . . . and next to thee the patriarch of Alexandria, and then the patriarch of the royal city of Moscow, the capital of our
vast dominions, and after him the patriarchs of Antioch and Jerusalem.[4]

It thus appears that either complete agreement had not been reached
with Jeremiah, or else that he was unable to sway the other patriarchs
to accept the Muscovite position. In any case the Muscovites had so
long been in fact independent that they did not hesitate to disagree
with a synod at Constantinople, but they had no intention of entering
into the sort of dispute with Constantinople for first place which had
divided Rome from the ecumene. The tsar already had political primacy, and by taking the initiative in securing *de jure* independence for
his church he had cut it off from outside support, and thus had made it
more dependent on the secular power than before.

With the death of Fedor in 1598 the reigning branch of the Riurikides came to an end. The precedent of the acclamation of Fedor by a
zemski sobor, however, had already pointed the way for the solution of
this difficulty, and the position that Boris Godunov had occupied in the
last years of Ivan and those of Fedor, plus the power he actually held,
made him the leading candidate in the sobor. But hardly the only one.
The boyar jealousies and ambitions, quelled at the beginning of Fedor's
reign, flared up anew. The unpolished manner and methods of Boris,
which had appealed to Ivan, were uncongenial to the boyars, and his
elevation would do violence to the thought patterns of *mestnichestvo*.
He was accused of bribing the sobor, and there was also a rumor that
he had paved his way to the throne by the murder of Fedor's half-
brother, Dmitri. On the other hand, the remaining Riurikides were not
united and were opposed by the strong Romanov faction. The patriarch, Job, remembering his own elevation ten years before, mar-
shalled the hierarchy in favor of Boris, and the tsarina (Boris' sister), to
whom Fedor had tried to leave the throne, appealed to the sobor on
Boris' behalf. His election and continuation in power at least produced
a respite in the grim power struggle then in progress. It was only by his
ability that he maintained his grip upon the scepter until 1605.

Following Boris' reign ensued a period known as the Time of Troubles, characterized by the struggle for the throne, by efforts of the
boyars to recover the status they had lost under Ivan IV, and by efforts

of the "small men," since grown great in service, to defend their positions. This period did not produce the political literature that the comparable civil war in England stimulated. The publicist tradition and the widespread public press were both lacking; the issues were not sharply differentiated; and the struggle was one of personality as much as of policy. Some of the public documents, however, display the currents of thought. Old conceptions of justice and of property, long submerged under Ivan's autocracy, reappeared in the coronation oath exacted from Tsar Vasili Shuiski (1606):

I, the great sovereign, [obligate myself] not to sentence any man to death without having judged him with my boyars in a true court, and not to take his *votchina*, houses, or chattels from his brothers or wife or children if they were not of the same mind with him; and also among merchants and tradespeople, if, after judgment and investigation, any of them should be deserving of death, not to take houses or shops or goods from the wives and children left behind if they had no part in the guilt of the condemned.[5]

The special mention of merchants, for whom the promise of fair trial is implied but not expressed, indicates that the "any man" of the first clause applied only to the nobility. More comprehensive and more clearly indicative of the boyar viewpoint were the terms of the treaty of 1610, drawn up by the boyars with King Sigismund of Poland in their negotiations for the election of his son as tsar. It provided for the obligatory consultation for which Kurbski had contended and seemingly went further, requiring the tsar to do nothing with which the Duma disagreed. Among other restrictions the boyars insisted:

And when Prince Vladislav, the son of Sigismund, is sovereign of the Russian state he shall honor and adorn according to previous custom the holy churches in Moscow and in all the cities and towns in the whole Muscovite state . . . and the bishops, priests, and other ranks, and all orthodox Christians shall be in the orthodox Christian faith of the Greek law as previously . . . ; however, in the capital city, Moscow, there might be one Roman church for the Poles and Lithuanians residing with His Grace the Lord Prince. . . . And without [Vladislav] having investigated the guilt and having deliberated with all the boyars, nobody will be punished, nor honor taken from anybody, nor anybody sent to prison, nor *pomest'ia*, *votchiny*, and houses taken away. . . . And all that the sovereign does he will do by the decision [*prygovor*] and counsel of the boyars and the entire Duma; and without counsel and a decision he shall not conclude such affairs. . . . His Sovereign Grace will command that the state revenues be collected as previously, as in the time of former great sovereigns; and beyond the previous customs he will not add anything without having consulted the boyars.[6]

No provision was made for the zemski sobor, however, and therein the boyars displayed their shortsightedness, as events swiftly proved.

One conviction was general: the new tsar should not have the unlimited power that Ivan Grozny had wielded. In the sixty-odd years of its tradition the zemski sobor also had grown to feel itself strong enough, when it could agree, not only to choose a tsar but also to stipulate conditions of his tenure. Especially did this appear feasible when stalemate among the major contenders permitted the election (1613) of Mikhail Romanov, a tractable young man from a relatively new family without power of his own on which to base resistance. What conditions, then, were imposed on Mikhail? We do not know. Nor can we be sure that any were exacted, although there is some evidence to that effect.* For perhaps understandable reasons no document that would settle the matter has been forthcoming from the official archives. In its absence the actual practices of Mikhail's reign may be adduced, and outstanding among them were the participation in the government of the patriarch and of the zemski sobor, the organ of the lesser nobility.

The patriarch, Filaret, was the actual as well as the spiritual father of Tsar Mikhail, and a powerful personality whom Boris Godunov had forced into monk's attire in order to eliminate him as a contender for the throne. Upon becoming patriarch in 1619, Filaret, like the tsar, was called "great sovereign." Until his death in 1633 he rather than the tsar was the real ruler.† No Byzantine *symphonia* had ever worked in closer

---

* A historian of the succeeding reign, Grigori Kotoshikhin, stated that Mikhail's son, Alexis, was the first tsar on whom no conditions were imposed; the Swedish ambassador, Philip J. T. von Stralenberg, who visited Russia in the 1730's, laid it down quite confidently that Mikhail had to agree, "I. To maintain and protect the Religion of the Country. II. To forget and forgive all that had happened to His Father, and not to think farther on any Personal Enmity whatsoever. III. To make no new Laws, nor to alter the old ones. In high and weighty Causes, not to judge for Himself, but according to the Law, by ordinary and usual Process. IV. To make no Peace, nor War, with His Neighbors, of His own Head. V. To resign His Estates to His Family, or to incorporate them with those belonging to the Crown, as a Proof of His Justice, and to avoid all Manner of Process with private Persons" (*A Historico-Geographical Description of the North and Eastern Parts of Europe and Asia* [London, 1738], p. 217).

† See J. L. H. Keep, "The Régime of Filaret (1619–1633)," *Slavonic and East European Review*, XXXVIII (June 1960), 334–360.

harmony, yet theirs was a personal and practical rather than a formal and theoretical relationship. Only when another such personality, Patriarch Nikon, later sought to duplicate the relationship did the theoretical implications assume importance.

The position of the zemski sobors is deserving of more thorough analysis, for in the reign of Mikhail they were repeatedly called into session. No important decision was taken without consultation with a sobor. This was the closest that Muscovy ever came to the establishment of parliamentary government.* Yet if, in England before the seventeenth century, there were parliaments, meeting at the king's call, but not yet a Parliament, in Moscow the zemski sobors never achieved this regular status.

It has already been noted that the sobors were composed largely of officials, coming together to give advice, to elect tsars, and to receive instructions which, as local or central administrators, they were expected to carry out. These features remained essentially unchanged in the seventeenth-century sobors, although the aristocratic element was perhaps slightly less predominant than formerly. Behind this administrative composition lay a number of considerations, some shared with Western parliamentary bodies and some peculiar to Muscovy.

First, the character of the zemski sobors reflected the virtual absence in the population of any class independent of the tsar. "Each class was under an obligation either to *defend* the State or to *work* for it (i. e., to support those who defended it). Commanders, soldiers, and workers there were, but no citizens," Kliuchevski tells us.[7] As *votchinnik* of the whole of Muscovy, Ivan IV had effectively eliminated other property holdings which, as *udely* and *votchiny*, had to a degree been independent, so that the privileges of the nobility were more clearly than ever based not upon their properties but upon their state service. The interest of the lesser nobility lay in preserving this requirement of service as against any restoration of independent property.

* Choice of the word *sobor*, which has a religious connotation, rather than *sobranie*, used in referring to European parliaments, indicates that from the beginning a distinction from Western institutions was intended.
The most detailed study in a Western language is that of Félix de Rocca, *Les assemblées politiques dans la Russie ancienne: Les Zemskié Sobors* (Paris, 1899). See also Günther Stökl, "Russland," in H. M. Cam, A. Margongiu, and G. Stökl, "Recent Work and Present Views on the Origins and Development of Representative Assemblies," *Relazioni* of the Tenth International Congress of Historical Science, I (Firenze, 1955), 94–98, and J. L. H. Keep, "The Decline of the Zemsky Sobor," *Slavonic and East European Review*, XXXVI (Dec. 1957), 100–122.

With service as a justification, the formerly free peasants had in fact, if not yet in law, been bound to their lords. The commercial people of the cities were fiscal agents of the tsar, and the clergy, being dependent upon the state, were committed to service in a very real sense. There was, consequently, no economic foundation for an independent power which might exercise a will of its own, no need for systematic representation of such wills, and no need for their measurement either in terms of proportional membership in the sobor or of formal voting machinery. The tsar consulted the opinions of the assembly, not its will. Even on the occasions when it acted as an electoral body it was not able to alter this characteristic.

Second, in consulting the sobor the tsar was seeking superior wisdom, not public opinion, and this consideration influenced the composition of the membership. The issue or questions to be decided determined the groups from whom advice would be sought. For this reason many sorts of sobors were held. From consideration of military or religious matters merchants might be excluded; on the other hand separate sobors of merchants were at times held to consider commercial problems. The high clergy met in sobors to decide religious questions and, in fact, their supposed susceptibility to divine inspiration coupled with their special knowledge of the Scriptures made the clergy desirable members of any assembly, even one called for a military decision. The boyars also, respected for their wisdom, participated at times in church sobors, the Stoglav synod of 1551, for example. Less fortunate were the provincial nobility who might be excluded because of the delays involved in their arrival or for other reasons. In the absence of provincials, however, the gathering was not accepted as a zemski sobor. The word *zemski* was, therefore, an essential qualifying adjective used when the subject of the assembly was of general import and requiring, at least in the seventeenth century, that all ranks of officials be included and that some should come from places other than Moscow. The search for the wise decision was from the Time of Troubles thus conditioned by a belief, never well defined, that distant parts of the country should participate. Clearly it was not thought that all ranks and areas were entitled to opinions on all subjects, but rather that valuable advice might be had from those qualified by experience in special fields and that the opinions of distant communities might be different and useful. At times groups in the sobor declined to state opinions on certain questions, pleading lack of the necessary qualifications. On the other hand an opinion was not disqualified by belonging only to a minority; even single individuals might occasionally present separate advice to the tsar.

Third, the zemski sobor was an organ of the central government, serving its ends and not the interests of local areas or separate classes or ranks of the population. To be sure, petitions were frequently brought along by the delegates, but these did not form the basis of any general discussion, investigation, or advice apart from the problems posed by the tsar. Far from regarding the assembly as an instrument for their use, and demanding or desiring representation therein, the local communities frequently sought to avoid the sending of delegates. As de Rocca summarized it, "The Muscovite representatives . . . came to the assembly to discharge a duty and not to exercise a right." [8]

Fourth, an essential feature of the membership of a sobor was their individual and collective responsibility for carrying out the decisions made by the tsar after hearing the sobor's advice. At the end of proceedings an oath was taken (by the clergy an affirmation) to uphold these decisions, and as officials and public servants the members returned to their posts to implement it. From this feature several effects devolved. (1) Although differences of opinion might be voiced during the advising process, no dissent was possible from the final conclusions since they were decisions of the tsar and dissent amounted to rebellion. (2) Only those who occupied positions enabling them to execute the decisions of the sobor were invited or were eligible for membership. (3) Conversely, corporate groups choosing delegates to the sobor agreed in advance to accept them on their return as administrative officials. Elections, therefore, were not usually necessary: those already in office simply went. (4) The identification by the government of the possessors of wisdom with its own officers was inherently, and became openly, a denial of the validity and even the legitimacy of any opinion not emanating from official circles.

With these characteristics in mind one can hardly be surprised at the failure of the zemski sobors to develop into a permanent parliament. Too many circumstances and too many conceptions barred their path. Yet their activities, both their deeds and their omissions, were indicative of the aspects of Muscovite political thought which brought about their decline. They sought the restoration of hereditary monarchy, restrained perhaps by moral, but not by legal, forces. Lacking in internal cohesiveness and in a sense of any purpose separate from that of the tsar, the sobors did more to restore the prestige of autocracy than they did to change its nature.

By the time Mikhail was elected, assemblies calling themselves zemski sobors had already elected Fedor, Boris Godunov, Vasili Shuiski, and the Pole, Vladislav, but the bloodshed and anarchy of the Time of Troubles were a discouraging introduction to the practice of election. So far were they from attempting to make the office of tsar elective that, trying to restore the *status quo ante*, they justified the selection of Mikhail by his being a cousin of the last tsar of the old dynasty, and proceeded to take oaths of allegiance both to him and to his children.* Nor did they insist upon the publication of a coronation manifesto, which might have contained limitations on the tsar's powers as Shuiski's had done, or upon any similar constitutional document. To their descendants they left only a tradition of frequent sobors and no legal monument, like the English Magna Carta, from which strength might later be drawn.

It was not easy for an elected monarch to maintain a claim to Muscovy as his *votchina*, as the later Riurikides had done, and this claim was not voiced. On the other hand the sobor did not undertake to revise the tsar's relation to the land. The officials meeting in Moscow, somewhat like modern bureaucrats, thought in terms of improving their positions against fellow-officials rather than in terms of redefining the position or the power of their chief. Thus Sergeevich attributed the decline of the zemski sobors to manipulations by the Duma boyars who did not enjoy sharing their influence with the provincials. In any event Mikhail died in 1645 and did not attempt to transmit his power by testament, but left matters in the hands of the sobor, which dutifully elected his son, Alexis, aged sixteen. In his turn Alexis also refrained from bequeathing the throne, although he did formally present his eldest son, Fedor, to the nation as his presumptive successor. In the third generation, however, a Romanov tsar, Peter, seized the formula of Ivan III, "To whom I will I shall give the princedom"; but even then, although the zemski sobor was dead, Peter thought an elaborate justification necessary.

The sobor's most serious omission, perhaps, was the failure to exact any charter of limitations or immunities at the time of the election of

* Through the inveterate use of patronymic second names Mikhail could easily be mistaken for the son of Tsar Fedor. His father's secular name was Fedor also, thence Mikhail Fedorovich. The last name, Romanov, was not usually added.

Alexis. The ghosts of the Time of Troubles had been well laid, the zemski sobors had accumulated more experience, and the new tsar was so young that such a project would have been relatively easy to accomplish. It is not adequate as an explanation to say, as the Slavophils were later to do, that the Muscovites were not legalistic, drawing their conceptions not from Rome but from the integrated, harmonious patterns of Byzantium, for in those days they were using formal documents for everything from interprincely treaties to the contract of landlord with tenant farmer. The key lay rather in the relations of the boyars of the Duma to the other members of the zemski sobors, in which can be detected not only the hauteur of the higher aristocrat but also something of the disdain of the policy maker for the executive, of the courtier for the bureaucrat. From the collapse of their prestige following the failure of their attempt to seat Vladislav of Poland on the throne the boyars recovered but slowly, so that any formal limitation of the tsar's power in 1645 would have accrued not to the Duma but to the zemski sobors, perpetuating their participation in policy formation. This the boyars were strong enough to prevent although they were not able to secure limitations upon the autocracy in their own favor. The weight of tradition and of those who, by conviction or by subservience, actively supported the autocrat contributed to this result, but it was caused equally by the stalemate of mutual jealousies and disunion. Subdued by Ivan and again by Boris, and further weakened by the Time of Troubles, the boyars modified the ideas of cooperative rule of Kurbski and of the *udel* period, lost their intransigence toward the tsar, and sought through influence over him to exclude the lower ranks from the advisory function. A century later, in another clear opportunity to limit the autocracy at the accession of Anna, this same conflict of higher and lower aristocrats, by then much more open and bitter, would again protect the autocrat.

CHAPTER X

The Patriarch and the Tsar

IN contrast to contemporary England, where rising political forces converged against the king, in Muscovy under Alexis the political forces sought rather to win the tsar's support, enabling him to utilize their differences for his own advantage. Autocracy was accepted and the struggles went on at a lower level, between secular and clerical aristocrats and between the higher and the lesser ranks. Both the autocrat and the boyars grew in strength, but although the lower nobility continued to be important in administration, zemski sobors ceased to be called. During the first eight years of Alexis' reign five such meetings were held, but in the remaining twenty-three years not one. The Duma doubled in size, compared with that under Godunov, thus increasing the store of wisdom within it and absorbing the stronger of its opponents from the zemski sobor. A *modus vivendi* of tsar and boyars had been achieved: he accepted them as advisers and frequently followed their advice; they encouraged him to do without the sobor, and thus promoted autocracy.

One of the early fruits of the renewed cooperation between tsar and boyars was the development of the most comprehensive code of laws Russia had yet seen, the *Ulozhenie* of 1649. The preamble indicates, somewhat ambiguously, the nature of this cooperation, the relative positions of the Duma and the zemski sobor, here called the General Council (*Obshchii Soviet*), and the received sources of the law:

In the year 7156 [1648], the 16th day of July, the Sovereign Tsar and Grand Prince, Aleksei Mikhailovich, autocrat of all Russia, being in the twentieth year of his age and in the third year of ruling his God-protected country, conferred with his Father and Interceder before God, Most Holy Joseph,

Patriarch of Moscow and all Russia, as well as with the metropolitans, archbishops, bishops, and the whole Holy Sobor, and discussed with His Majesty's boyars, *okol'nichi* * and [other] Duma members as to the following: to copy the articles written in the rules of the Holy Apostles and Holy Fathers or in the civil statutes of the Greek Emperors which are suitable for the affairs of the state and the country; also, to collect the edicts and boyars' decisions concerning various affairs of the state and the country, which were issued by the former Great Sovereign Tsars . . . ; and to collate such edicts and boyars' decisions with the old judicial codes. And where some articles [situations] were not provided for in the judicial codes of the former Sovereigns or in the boyars' decisions rendered in the past years, the General Council to write and formulate such articles in accordance with His Majesty's order, so that citizens of the Moscow state of all ranks, from the highest to the lowest, have equal [*rovna*] justice and trial in all cases. His Majesty the Tsar and Grand Prince of all Russia, Aleksei Mikhailovich, commanded the boyars Prince Nikita Ivanovich Odoevskoi [and] Prince Semen Vasil'evich Prozorovskoi, *okol'nich* Prince Fedor Fedorovich Volkonskoi, and *d'iaki* Gavrila Leont'ev and Fedor Griboedov, to collect all this and prepare a report.

For the purpose of accomplishing this great undertaking of the Sovereign and the country, the Sovereign conferred with his Father and Interceder before God, Most Holy Joseph, Patriarch of Moscow and all Russia; and the boyars resolved to select from among the Moscow gentry . . . two men from each rank, and to take two men from among the gentry and junior boyars [boyars' sons] of each big town except Novgorod [and] from among the citizens of Novgorod one man from each section [see above, p. 5], one man from each smaller town, three men from among the great merchants, two men from the merchants' guild and two men from the drapers' guild, one man from the artisans' guild [*lit.:* black hundred], one from each merchant settlement,—all of them good and wise men, in order that this great undertaking of the Sovereign and the country be confirmed. . . .[1]

Thus the canon law continued in part to be integrated into the civil code, and old rules borrowed from other nations as well as Muscovite precedents continued to be preferred to the positive enactment of new law. Yet the *Ulozhenie* did contain a number of new laws usually reflecting the interests of the boyars and detracting from those of the church. The advisory participation of the clergy is apparent, and they, along with all the boyars and *okol'nichi*, sat with the "selected" repre-

---

* The rank next below that of boyar.

sentatives of the other ranks (excluding, of course, peasants both free and serf) in the ratifying council. Clerical influence, however, was at a low ebb, as will shortly be seen. The lower secular ranks likewise, whether hand picked or not, apparently accepted the "report" of Odoevskoi and his colleagues.

From other parts of the code it is apparent that by "equal justice and trial" the usual differentiation of duties and rights according to rank and status was not disturbed, and no new egalitarian tendency was implied. Each rank was equally entitled to its customary position and privileges, and within each rank individuals were to be treated equally.

Appropriate for the peasants was serfdom, and by this code they legally lost any right to change landlords that they may still, by staying out of debt, have retained. The attachment of the formerly free tiller to the soil, which had begun with the Mongol census, was thus completed, and approved by a zemski sobor. There were differences, however, from European serfdom. The Russian serf, like the American slave, could be sold without land; it is, therefore, more accurate to say that he was attached not to the soil but to the person of the landlord. Nor was he so attached in return for the use of the landlord's land. The long experience of temporary possession under the *kormlenie* and *pomest'e* systems of tenure, coupled with the shifts of the days of Ivan IV, had impressed upon the peasants the fact that the landlord did not really own the land. Peasant adages quoted by Kliuchevski from the sixteenth century confirm this: "What though the land be of our holding, it yet doth belong unto the Tsar," and the like. Service, in the mind of the serf, could not be given for the use of the land to anyone save the tsar, since the land belonged to the tsar. Just as the landlord had been given the use of the land, so service was given to him to support him while he, in turn, served the tsar. Serfdom was, therefore, from the peasant's point of view, tightly linked to the state service of the nobility. The stage was set for violent reaction should the latter be abolished and not the former, as Catherine II was to learn in the eighteenth century.

Another aim of the boyars, accomplished in the code of 1649, was the restriction of the privileges and immunities so long enjoyed by the church. The prevalent practice of entrance into a monastery in old age (considered conducive to salvation), coupled with the jurisdiction of the clergy over estates left by such monks and nuns, meant not only great accumulations of property in religious hands, comparable to that in medieval Europe, but also irritating interference by the church in the distribution among lay heirs of any property left them by these aged novices. This growth of church estates also brought peasants resident thereon under clerical control, removing them from the rolls of secular taxpayers (until 1584), boyars' tenants, and military recruits. Upon this complex of problems, grown more acute in the century and a half since the debate between Sorski and Volotski, the boyars and Alexis made a twofold attack.

In the first place, a new secular office was created to exercise some of the old clerical jurisdiction (Chapter 13, Article 1):

His Majesty the Tsar and Grand Prince of all Russia, Aleksei Mikhailovich, upon petition by [the secular and commercial ranks], has ordered that from now on a Department for Monasteries shall be organized separately and that all cases in which plaintiffs present their complaints against metropolitans, archbishops, bishops, their officials and servants, [their] junior boyars and their peasants, monasteries, archimandrites, hegumens, persons in charge of monasterial supplies, treasurers, ordinary monks and monasterial servants and peasants, priests and parochial church officials, shall be tried by the Department for Monasteries.

From these new arrangements the patriarch and his immediate servants were in part exempted, but all religious establishments and lower clergy were included.

In the second place, the granting of lands to the church or to any of its officers, including the patriarch, repeatedly forbidden since 1573 with little effect, was again prohibited and the rule reinforced with a mandatory recapture clause (Chapter 17, Article 42). Relatives of grantors could redeem such properties "in accordance with the former code" in spite of provisions in some of Mikhail's grants; and if no relative wished to redeem, "then the *votchina* shall be taken by the Sovereign and the money for it given to the monastery from His Majesty's treasury according to the *Ulozhenie*, one half ruble for one quarter [*chetvert:* about 1.35 acres], but the estate may not be held by the monastery." Further, the patriarch, metropolitans, archbishops, and bishops were forbidden to "buy, accept as a mortgage, or hold for a monastery a *votchina* that was inherited, granted for services or bought, and may, in no manner, take it for the promise of saying prayers for one's soul. No such *votchina* shall be registered by the Land Office in the name of the patriarch, metropolitan, archbishop, or bishop, and no holder of a *votchina* shall give it to a monastery." Lands could be sold and thus gifts to the church could still be made; but in a country where capital had not widely accumulated this new rule substantially decreased the flow of wealth to the church. The participation of the clergy in the making of these new restrictions and their acceptance of them are indicative of the decline of their influence as a result of a century and a half of the Josephite policy. The submissiveness of Volotski had been learned much better than his defense and use of the canon law.

As if to meet the challenge of these secular enactments, the Russian church at this time produced one of its most remarkable statesmen, Nikita Minin, known as Nikon (1605–1681).* Born a peasant near Nizhni-Novgorod, he attained by ability and perseverance a religious education, a reputation for unusual spiritual gifts, and by the time he was thirty-eight, the headship of a monastery. In 1646 he was presented to young Tsar Alexis, upon whom he made a very deep impression. With the tsar's help Nikon rose within six years through the metropolitanate of Novgorod to the patriarchate.

One of the qualities which most pleased Alexis was Nikon's capacity for leadership in the church reform movement which Alexis was sponsoring and upon which they were in close agreement. Through lack of scholarship over the centuries, various errors had crept into the texts and rituals of the Russian church against which spasmodic corrective efforts, such as those of Maxim the Greek, had always been handicapped by conservatism and lethargy. Patriarch Filaret, before Nikon, had wished to change this situation and had gathered a group of scholars, whose aim was to promote moral and spiritual purity through study of the apostles and early fathers and to encourage the printing of religious books, but who, like their mentor, were wary of Western contamination. Under Alexis, however, the cultural superiority of Kiev contributed new members to the group, who brought with them a more tolerant attitude toward modern, philosophic, and even Western, religious ideas.

For the older members of the group, led by the archpriest Avvakum, the stigma of the Florentine Union still attached to the Greek church, so that the modern Greeks were not to be trusted, but the ancient

---

* Many of the documents relating to Nikon's work and his trial, and to earlier Russian church history, are translated in *The Patriarch and the Tsar*, ed. and trans. William Palmer, (London, 1871–1876), I–III. See also Anton V. Kartashev, *Ocherki po istorii Russkoi tserkvi*, II (Paris, 1959), 119–230.

Greek fathers were the source of spiritual light which would reawaken the Russian church to the purity of its early saints. As Avvakum said:

You who cultivate philosophy, dialectic, and rhetoric, see your masters' end: in this world no glory, and their memory still pollutes the atmosphere. But a few fishermen have captured the universe. . . . So superior is the virtue of faith and simplicity, or rather of divine wisdom, to philosophy and rhetoric and exterior wisdom! . . . Simplicity in Christ with charity edifies; reasoning with eloquence vaunts.[2]

For Alexis and Nikon, on the other hand, the important thing was purity of revealed knowledge, which they identified with ecumenical uniformity with the other Orthodox churches. They also hoped to attain a position of respect in religious thought commensurate with Moscow's position as the political center of Orthodoxy.

Their agreement on this enhanced the tsar's regard for Nikon; yet the expressed aims of the two may have concealed divergent motivations. Alexis, a religious man, wanted to fulfill well his duties as the successor of Constantine and Justinian, to bring spiritual harmony to the entire ecumene. He may also have had in mind the corollary: to extend his influence outside his realm, to further the messianism of the Third Rome concept. Nikon, as a churchman, could see another advantage in such harmony: it would be a substitute for the severed link with Constantinople from which the old metropolitans had drawn support in their rare disputes with the secular power. If the uniformity of the Russian church with the other Orthodox churches could be established and maintained, the tsar could never weaken the position of the church without violating that uniformity or without obtaining the approval of prelates seated beyond his political power.

Nikon did not anticipate such difficulties from Alexis, over whom his personal influence was so great, but his attachment to the tsar in itself evidences his awareness of where the power in the Muscovite church was located. He depended much upon the tsar's friendship for the implementation of his ideas of reform within the church and also for the redress of secular inroads upon the church—which he saw as the essence of the boyars' policy. Upon that friendship he based a master stroke in 1652: he declined to accept the patriarchate. After repeated entreaties by Alexis, Nikon stood before him and the assembled boyars and clergy in the Uspenski Cathedral and pronounced the conditions of his acceptance:

If, most religious tsar and honorable boyars and all-holy synod and all Christian people, it pleases you that our humility should be your patriarch, give me your word and make a vow in this holy apostolic cathedral church, before our Lord and Savior, Jesus Christ, and before the holy gospel and before the most holy Mother of God and before His holy angels and all the saints, to keep Christ's evangelical dogmas and the rules of the holy apostles and of the holy fathers, and the laws of the pious [Greek] emperors, intact. If you also promise sincerely to obey us, as your superior and pastor and most esteemed [? *krasneishago*] father, in all that I shall make known to you of God's dogmas and of the laws, for the sake of this, for your desire and for your petition, I cannot refuse this great archbishopric.[3]

And such was his magnetism that all bowed to his will.

These words make it clear that, as head of the church, Nikon planned to use the ecumenical concept of the reform not only to attain doctrinal and ritual purity but also for the protection of church interests. Even as metropolitan of Novgorod he had been able to persuade the tsar to restore, in that metropolis, some of the judicial authority taken from the church by the code of 1649; now he proposed, through the printing of church books, to build a bastion around clerical prerogatives throughout the land. His predecessor, the traditional patriarch Joseph, had started the printing of an edition of the canon law, the *Kormchaia kniga*, which had not previously been printed at Moscow. This was now halted and superseded by a Nikonian version, to which were prefaced several additional documents including the induction ceremonies for Patriarch Filaret and a new translation of the famous Donation of Constantine, already long discredited in western Europe. (The Donation, to be sure, spoke of the Pope but, following the Greeks, the Muscovites reasoned that, although the church of Rome had deserted its heritage, the grant of Constantine had been to the whole church.) The strong statements of clerical immunity and jurisdiction included in the latter, Nikon believed, gave earlier and more general support to the Russian church than even the statute of Vladimir.

It is to be noted that these charters, supposedly granted by earlier secular rulers from the throne now occupied by Alexis, Nikon did not consider to be revocable by later rulers. They were not so much acts of the rulers' wills as revelations through them of the divine will, and the longer they had been permitted to endure, the more certainly did they enjoy divine approval. To him, therefore, their authority was vastly greater than that of the *Ulozhenie*.

In similar fashion Nikon included among the canons Justinian's Sixth Novel, the preamble to the *Ecloga* (quoted in part above), parts of the *Epanagoge* on the dignities and powers of the emperor and patriarch, and the documents of the creation of the Moscow patriarchate—all indicating his vision of the reproduction in Russia of the *symphonia* of church and state prevailing at Byzantium in its classical age.

Yet in these efforts Nikon lacked the subtlety of Volotski. He accomplished much, but not without great conflict and destruction. In its ecumenical emphasis his textual and ritual reform offended Avvakum and the more national segment of the clergy, who preferred their comfortable old errors to the dangers of the Latin heresy, influences of which they suspected in Nikon's scholarship. The doctrine of the Third Rome had long been developing in the direction of a purely national church; Nikon undertook to reverse this trend, to use the doctrine dynamically to strengthen the bonds of the ecumene. Thus the conservative, isolationist, ritualistic strain of the Josephites came face to face with the worldly, administrative strain. Neither Avvakum nor Nikon was a spiritual descendant of Sorski, and neither could see virtue in tolerance. The result was the Raskol, the great schism, which never healed.

Avvakum was driven into exile and later was condemned by the synod of 1666, which also deposed Nikon. But it was not for the schism nor yet for the reforms that Nikon was deposed; in fact he was supported in his reforms by almost all of the hierarchy. It was in his efforts to protect the church from secular encroachments that he overreached himself, going from a defensive position to one almost actively belligerent. Admitting no conflict between the administrative and fiscal needs of the state and the time-honored jurisdiction and privileges of the church, he saw the new laws as the work of boyar avarice. His interpretation of the *symphonia* also irritated the boyars, and their enmity and influence on the tsar eventually brought him down.

Leaning upon the precedent of Tsar Mikhail and the tsar's father Filaret, Nikon assumed, with Alexis' tacit consent, the tsar's title of *veliki gosudar*, great sovereign, and with the title he tried also to take the role that Filaret had played. He used his administrative talents and the confidence of the tsar to insert himself into secular affairs. In his preface to the missal printed in 1655 he repeatedly linked himself with the tsar in a *dvoitsa*, a pair, a duality.[4] From this he apparently deduced that, in the absence of one great sovereign, the other could exercise the powers of both, except that the tsar, of course, could not administer sacraments.

But Nikon was better as a lawyer than as a psychologist. The boyars had recovered their confidence considerably since the days when Filaret had been a great sovereign. By the code of 1649 they had thought to end for good the state-within-a-state resulting from the clerical immunities; now they saw their handiwork being undermined by this exalted peasant who had hypnotized the tsar. Especially while Alexis was away with the armies, leaving civil affairs in Nikon's hands, did his imperious manner toward the boyars rub salt into the injury which his rank gave to their aristocratic pride.

The objections of the boyars and those of some churchmen who found Nikon's ecclesiastical administration oppressive, coupled with the growing self-reliance that military experience had given Alexis, wrought a change in the tsar's attitude toward his patriarch. In 1658 he decided to deflate Nikon gently. After an unpleasant exchange he sent the trusted Prince Romodanovski to tell him no longer to call himself *veliki gosudar*. "We have only one great sovereign, the tsar. . . . The tsar's majesty honored thee as a father and pastor, but thou hast not understood this."[5] But Nikon was proud: he renounced the patriarchate and retired into the Voskresenski Monastery.

For eight years, before final action was taken to resolve the anomalous situation, he had leisure there to mature his political philosophy. What he wrote was colored, of course, by special pleading, but its content is important as a final extreme statement of an old current of thought, exemplified by the metropolitan Alexis and seen again in his later successor Philip's refusal to bless Ivan IV. These prelates took seriously the mission of the church to guide the secular ruler and insisted upon independence in the execution of its mission. A similar attitude of independence in the boyars had been the target of Ivan's exertions; now when it became articulate in the church it was again anathema to the autocracy. Nikon's thought and action, showing the patriarch to be a potentially difficult if not dangerous participant in power, eventually led under Peter I to the abolition of the patriarchate.

Nikon had set himself to defend the church against secular encroachments, but in so doing he was betrayed by ambition into an attempt to find in *symphonia* the clerical authority of a Gregory I if not the supremacy of an Innocent III. *Symphonia*, indeed, had never meant a separation or mutual isolation of church and state, and Nikon, having experience with and a taste for participation in secular government, was not satisfied with clerical independence. His often reiterated concept of a *dvoitsa* was deeply rooted in his thinking, and in it he went further than Gregory had gone. He convinced himself that the dual nature of man required him to be ruled by a dyarchy, that the patriarch should share the secular power on his own terms. Repeating the old Byzantine formula distinguishing secular and spiritual spheres, he went on, "However, the bishop has a certain right in the secular jurisdiction, for its better direction, and in suitable matters: but the Tsar has none whatever in ecclesiastical and spiritual administrations." [6] Moreover, in delimiting the spiritual realm Nikon tended to apply the reasoning that a secular grant was an expression of the will of God. Property and persons given to the church were given to God, by God's will, and could not again be reclaimed by the secular power. So all church lands and also the jurisdictions named in the canons were among things spiritual. Any legislation to the contrary was blasphemous, in particular the *Ulozhenie* of 1649. Supposedly a collection of earlier laws and canons, Nikon saw this code as "all newly written, foreign to orthodoxy and to the holy apostles and to the canon laws of the holy fathers and to the civil laws of the orthodox Greek emperors." [7] This exaggerated description appears almost to equate "newly written" with "foreign to orthodoxy," and thus to deny to the tsar a power to legislate, even in the secular realm, in any manner deviating from the canons or the Greek civil codes.

From his retreat Nikon conducted an elaborate and acrimonious debate with the tsar and his boyar advisers. The boyars denied categorically his prescriptive interpretation of grants made to the church. One of their leaders, Semen Streshnev, attempted to use the patriarch's own documents against him, averring that he had held his power from the tsar. "He [Alexis] made a grant to him of all the privileges which Constantine the Great, out of his great respect for the Roman Pope Sylvester, had given to that Pope." [8] This meant, of course, that what one tsar had given another could give and could take back, that the position of the church in Muscovy depended not upon the canon law but upon the will of the tsar. Thus the boyars defended the provisions of their *Ulozhenie* as derived from the authority of the tsar. The code itself, sanctioned though it was by a zemski sobor, they did not think strong enough to stand alone.

To this argument the patriarch replied contemptuously:

Hast thou not learned . . . that the highest authority of the priesthood is not received from Tsars, but, contrariwise, it is by the priesthood that rulers are anointed to the empire? Therefore it is abundantly plain that priesthood is a very much greater thing than royalty.[9]

This claim to clerical superiority, once made, was elaborated.

Royalty, it is true, was given from God to the world; but it was given in his wrath. . . . But to us even he himself who wears the diadem is under the duty of offering gifts, and obedience in all things, as the Lord has commanded. . . . But thou . . . wouldest bring us down to submit ourselves to kings.[10]

Along this road Nikon moved step by step until he came to assert a power to excommunicate the tsar if he "does not what is proper for him to do in obedience to the laws of God."[11] The walls of the Voskresenski isolated Nikon from Russian reality in more ways than one, but he never attempted to exercise that power.

Yet, similar as these statements are to the claims of Rome five hundred years earlier, their counterparts could be found in the East. Peter's "We ought to obey God rather than men" (Acts 5:29) was followed also by the patriarch Nicholas the Mystic of Constantinople, for example, who wrote to Pope Anastasius III, in 912, "If the emperor, inspired by the devil, gives an order contrary to divine law, no one is obliged to obey him. . . . Any subject can rise up against any administrative act contrary to the law and even against the emperor, if he is ruled by his passions."[12] Nicholas, moreover, had himself applied this doctrine against Emperor Leo VI.

After two local church councils, whose jurisdiction over him Nikon denied, Alexis finally called together in 1666 a great synod which included, in addition to the Muscovites, the patriarchs of Alexandria and Antioch and other high Orthodox clergy from abroad. The prosecution was led by a glib and sycophantic but well-educated Greek, Paisius Ligarides, formerly metropolitan of Gaza in Palestine, whom Nikon himself had earlier invited to Moscow. Among his many charges against Nikon the first two, and most weighty, were "that he described the most excellent and most orthodox tsar as an *apostate* and a tyrant in his letters which he sent to the four patriarchs," and "that he declared that the whole of the most splendid *synklete* [the Boyar Duma] *latinized*, and had run on the rocks of heretical doctrines . . . slandering his own flock." [13] On both these counts the proud prelate was condemned. In denouncing Nikon's attitude the synod not only disavowed as uncanonical any claim to spiritual superiority but went out of its way to impress upon the tsar the freedom of his secular powers. Paisius quoted Justinian's One-hundred-fifth Novel which says, without his embellishments, "The Emperor, however, is not subject to the rules which We have just formulated, for God has made the laws themselves subject to his control by giving him to men as an incarnate law." [14] From this and other authorities he deduced, apparently with general assent, that "the king on earth, then, is not circumscribed by the written laws, as being most self-sufficient, and not to be ruled by any." [15]

To the tenor of these conclusions, however, two Russian metropolitans raised a revealing objection:

And though . . . we put up with and dissemble the greater part of the wrongs from the boyars, yet we shrink with trembling at the thought that the evil must go on and become worse when it shall be determined and made a fixed principle that the State is supreme over the Church. And though we have no suspicion in our minds that we shall in any degree be wronged or hurt in this most happy time of the thrice-happy government of our heaven-defended and glorious and victorious emperor, our sovereign, the sovereign Alexis Michaelovich—Almighty God forbid that we should ever conceive such a thought!—we nevertheless fear for the future. . . .[16]

They expressed fear of the boyars, but their cringing before the tsar shows that extension of his autocracy into church affairs in support of the boyars' policies lay at the root of their apprehensions. Supremacy of the state, they feared, would soon strip the church of the protective covering of the canons. The two bishops recanted, but they were none the less disciplined by the synod, being accused of contumacy toward the patriarchs and the synod and of refusing to trust the tsar.

The synod, however, subservient to the tsar as it was, did not undo Nikon's work. It degraded the unbending cleric, but it also continued his defense of the church. The protest of the two bishops was not entirely fruitless. The canon law was reaffirmed above both the secular law and the tsar. The immunity of church property was maintained, and clerical participation in the suits and trials of church people was reestablished in the spirit of Vladimir's statute. The general result was a compromise between the position of Nikon and that of the boyars, and much closer than either to the old pattern of Joseph Volotski.

By the end of the long reign of Alexis, therefore, it may be considered that the autocracy had recovered much of the power and prestige it had lost during the troubled period of transition from the Riurikides to the Romanovs. By contrast, the struggles between the boyars and Nikon, and between each of these and the lesser nobility, had weakened both the aristocracy and the church without much initiative from the throne. The zemski sobors had been effectively discontinued, leaving behind, in spite of their role as creator of the new dynasty, no document which might be embarrassing to later claimants of absolute power. The boyars had become reconciled to a position of subordinate cooperation with the tsar. Their situation was superficially similar to that which had prevailed under Ivan III, but now it was little buttressed by the *udel* psychology which had strengthened Bersen-Beklemeshev and Kurbski. They were not able to protect their *Ulozhenie* when Alexis chose to give lands to the church, thus clearly establishing the principle that the tsar was above the law. The same generation that, in England, permanently established the supremacy of Parliament reaffirmed in Muscovy the supremacy of the tsar.

The church, a third source of potential restraint upon autocracy, had apparently defended its jurisdiction, but in fact it had lost ground in several directions. By reaching for ecumenical unity it had lost even the national unity it possessed, greatly reducing its prestige through recriminations of its two hostile camps. By overplaying its hand against the secular power it had stimulated the open affirmation of its subordinate position in secular affairs; the challenge by a second sovereign had served to clarify the supremacy, even within the church, of the first, the tsar. Finally, by interpreting the canons through its synods, the church reduced the importance of its personal head: it made clear the dispensability of the patriarch.

The reaffirmation of old norms after a period of strife and experimentation did not, however, imply universal approval of them. Two extremely potent and revolutionary forces were developing, needing only the human instruments to exert their influences. Beneath the surface of official Russia the dissatisfactions of the peasants, aggravated by the code of 1649, were reaching the boiling point. In Stenka Razin they found a leader for the first widespread revolt which, crushed with much bloodshed, made him a popular hero, the subject of many folk tales and songs, and an inspiration for those who tried later to emulate him. The second force, a dissatisfaction born of the realization that Russia lagged behind western Europe, both institutionally and technologically, was, on the contrary, felt only in the higher circles. Of this force the tsar Peter was to make himself the exponent.

PART FOUR

The Impact of the West

(1682–1825)

CHAPTER XI

Revolution from Above: Peter and Anna

PETER THE GREAT (r. 1682–1725) has long been, with considerable justice, the symbol, both in Russia and outside, of the modernization and Westernization of his country—the "democratic tsar" who abandoned regal ceremony and caroused with the people, the "crowned revolutionary" who gave color to the hope that reform would come from the throne. As such he has been both worshiped and anathematized. The symbol becomes a myth, however, if it is thought either that modernization began with Peter or that all Peter's aims were modern.

I

It has already been noted that the line of reformers and Westernizers stretches back through Nikon, Ivan IV, and Volotski to the first Vladimir and beyond, but better perspective upon Peter's attitude toward reform can be obtained by a look at the ideas of a contemporary whom Peter sent into exile. This was Vasili Golitsyn, a prince of Lithuanian ancestry who had served as chief minister for the regent Sophia, Peter's half sister, who ruled in his youth.

The dynamic and ambitious Sophia was interested in reform, and Golitsyn had proposed a broad scheme of modernization based upon the emancipation of the serfs with the lands they tilled. They would also be freed from conscription, but in lieu of service they would be taxed and the taxes used to pay the service nobility, who would compose a professional army of high standards and who would thus be compensated for the loss of their serfs and lands. Golitsyn also wanted the village industries replaced with large factories so that the self-sufficiency of household economy would yield to extensive commercial exchange, and he wanted the steppes to be colonized. Foreign intercourse should be encouraged, and the sons of the service nobility sent abroad to be educated. He capped his ideas with a plea, then unusual even in western Europe, for full freedom of religion.

In these proposals military reform, although not neglected, was obviously not the only motivating consideration. It was to be founded upon, and integrated with, quite revolutionary economic and social changes. To Golitsyn and other well-educated men of similar views the conflict between Sophia and Peter was a matter of protecting the opportunity for such reforms against a youngster already showing his military inclinations. They did not see in him, nor he in them, a kindred soul, and it was over the opposition of such men as Golitsyn that Peter came to power. Were they, then, wrong in their estimation of the young monarch?

Peter was a physical giant, with a will and a temper to match, who lacked the patience of his father, Alexis. He was thus temperamentally attuned to violence and revolution rather than to administration or reform, and this temperament forced the pace of change in Russia as did no other before Lenin's.

In his decisions there was a mixture of whim and calculation which at times made violence a political instrument but which also at times enabled him to turn the need for reform into an occasion for the increase of his own power. Peter is best understood in terms of the long struggle of the princes to subjugate Russia, to eliminate all rivals of their personal power. As Ivan III had extirpated the *veche* of Novgorod and broken the grip of the Mongols, as Ivan IV had cowed the aristocracy by confiscating their lands, so Peter harnessed the nobles to his chariot, defeated his foreign opponents, and destroyed the vestigial independence of the church. Since the positions of the zemski sobors and the Boyar Duma under his grandfather and father had depended upon mutual jealousies and upon the personalities of those tsars, and not upon any basic changes in political ideas, there were no legal barriers to prevent the powerful new personality upon the throne from seizing the autocracy of Ivan IV. Its reestablishment by Peter was much easier than its first achievement. With him autocracy approached modern totalitarianism; even the sphere of personal habits was invaded by the will of the tsar in his decrees on European dress and on shaving.

All his reforms were instrumental to these autocratic ends. They were, therefore, opposed not only by those, such as the Raskolniki, who objected to his Western orientation but also by those who disliked his narrow practical approach and by those who objected to his tyrannical methods and motives. The defection of Mazepa, hetman of the Ukrainian Cossacks and the only popularly elected leader in Russia, was not only an attempt to restore Ukrainian independence but also a protest against Peter's arbitrary power. And there were many who objected.

It was in his first battles with the Turks (and not in his childhood visits to the German suburb of Moscow, as has been claimed) that Peter seems to have discovered the necessity to modernize Russia, as the military rather than commerical nature of his modernization attests. He built factories, but for army and naval supplies; he sent young men to school in Europe, but to study subjects, not only practical rather than cultural, but even practical in the immediate military sense.

Yet the effects of Peter's reforms were not the same as their aims, even though the distortions of his aims were to some extent reflected in the results. For example, he wanted factories capable of supplying his armies and fleets, and he stimulated them with subsidies and governmental contracts. After Peter's time these factories continued slowly to expand, but the pattern of dependence upon the government was firmly established. By the 1880's Plekhanov was able to find in the industrial workers an adequate foundation for the Marxist movement in Russia, but the development of an independent capitalism, such as had withstood Marxism in western Europe, was greatly retarded. As another example, Peter's conscript students went to schools that were not circumscribed by his military interests. They did study military mathematics and naval architecture, but perforce they encountered new cultural and intellectual horizons, and while many were little affected and some became dilettantes, a few labored seriously and also gathered for themselves and their children libraries of foreign books. Thus were laid the bases of a secular intelligentsia in Russia not confined to military interests.

This intelligentsia, with its noble birth, its foreign dress and manners, its habitual employment of French, and its service in the new "foreign" capital of St. Petersburg, grew with each generation more remote from the Russian people, and Westernization did not spread downwards. In these hands the government, too, became more remote from the people. Peter came down from his throne to soil his hands in work and play, but the enterprises for which he increased taxes by 250 per cent were beyond the ken of the Russians in their self-sufficient villages. At the same time the service nobility was separated by new chasms of education and language from any comprehension of the peasants. The removal of the capital from its historical site at Moscow to the less central and more artificial St. Petersburg, symbolic of the transition from Muscovy to Imperial Russia, was as much psychological as material.

Upon the structure as well as the location of the government Peter impressed his will. His changes tended to be improvisations, however, not like the elaborate schemes later so carefully prepared for Alexander I. In 1711, hurrying to the wars, he established a Senate of nobles to act as regent in his absence—an organ that lasted some two hundred years. In 1715 he reorganized the heterogeneous bureaus of his government, the *prikazi*, as "colleges" with group responsibility, most of them subordinate to the Senate. In both these structures the same principle is evident: the avoidance of individual power other than his own in favor of collective. There were to be no other lions, even under the throne.

More carefully planned was his *Order of Ranks*, decreed in 1722, which made the privileges of the various ranks depend not upon ancestry but upon level of service. It classified into fourteen ranks all civil, military, and other positions, and opened them to commoners as well as nobles, foreigners as well as Russians. This reaffirmed the nobility's obligation of service, and at the same time opened to foreigners and commoners a path, through such service, to the privileges previously enjoyed only by the old nobility. Still, like so much in Peter's reforms which seems radically new, this decree was much influenced by old ways of thinking. Not only did it have precedents, in Ivan Grozny's compulsory service ukase of 1556 and in his use of "small men," but it was also by no means an affirmation of new democratic principles. Rank by service clearly contradicted rank by birth; yet Peter's effort was not to disestablish hereditary nobility, but rather to extend its advantages to the newcomers. The order went on: "All servants, Russian or foreign, who are or actually were in the first eight grades [from the top] will have their legitimate children and descendants in time eternal honored in all dignities and advantages equally with the better older nobility, even if they were of lower birth." [1]

This meant that the descendants of both new and old nobility were permitted, and required, to enter the tsar's service at the fourteenth, the lowest, rank. By time and merit they might advance in precedence and advantages; but whether they advanced or not they retained the basic privileges of aristocracy: they remained tax exempt and they could own serfs.

Two other, perhaps unforeseen, results followed. For one thing, the Germans who came to Russia in considerable numbers were educated and diligent, and they achieved great favor, especially in the army, thus helping to divorce the government from the Russian people. For another, commoners of ability, otherwise free from the obligation of service, were seduced by government employment away from independent private activities, and the people thus lost many of their leaders.

Certainly the system prevailing before, the *mestnichestvo*, by which administrative posts were distributed in conformity to birth and without regard to real qualifications, had broken down, even the patriarch execrating it as "God-detested, enmity-creating, brother-hating, and love-repelling." By rather general agreement, the records on which it was based had been burned in 1682. But the new system adopted to replace it still bore clearly the mark of subordination to an autocratic will. The *mestnichestvo* had given men claims to high offices, however poorly grounded, independent of the tsar's will. The *Order of Ranks* gave them only the fourteenth rank, while anything above this depended directly upon the tsar.

II

These motivations were even clearer in Peter's suppression of the patriarchate. Alexis' difficulties with Nikon had shown that an independent patriarchate could be a serious obstacle to a smoothly running autocracy, and following a personal difference with the patriarch Adrian, Peter resolved to leave the office vacant when Adrian conveniently died in 1700. His first solution for the headless church was twofold: he revived the Monastery Prikaz for administrative purposes; for ceremonial purposes he gave custody of the patriarchal dignity (but little power) to one of the metropolitans, as had been done before in clerical interregna. His choice for this honor is revealing. He named Stefan Iavorski, whom he had brought from Kiev and who had no following among the Moscow clergy—a choice which prevented the church from presenting a united opposition to Peter's policies and which thus reduced its prestige among the people as well.

Iavorski, however, disliked his role and Peter's church policy. An educated and urbane monk, he, like Golitsyn, saw in Peter an excrescence of arbitrary power. For years he praised the tsar, as his position required, but always for qualities Peter obviously did not possess. Eventually he wrote a tract, *The Rock of Faith*, ostensibly against the Protestants, which Peter refused to see published for the good reason that it was really an attack on his policies, as the title hints. In it he said:

We respect the authority of the tsar as given by God, but not in such affairs [the definition of dogma]. For the construction of the church and the limits and rules of church offices, also proper to faith, God entrusted to the apostles and their successors. . . . Christ did not entrust his church to Tiberius Caesar, but to the apostle Peter and in Peter's person to all the apostles. . . . In truth tsars are guardians of the laws of God and church but not determiners or establishers of rules and articles proper to faith.[2]

Seeing this attitude in his favored bishop, Peter drew again on Kiev, and this time secured an adequately opportunistic cleric, young Feofan Prokopovich, whom he caused to be installed as bishop of Pskov in 1718. Well educated in the West, versed in Hobbes and in Pufendorf, Prokopovich could and did find a theoretical justification whenever the tsar needed one. He thus became the tsar's amanuensis and the author of the decree creating the Clerical College, Peter's second solution of the church problem, which soon became known as the Holy Synod, and to which was soon added a lay chairman, the Procurator.*

Prokopovich went to the crux of things when he said:

* In this statute were spelled out the arguments for collective administrative bodies, which had also influenced the tsar in creating the Senate and the other colleges: (1) "Truth is more clearly discover'd" by a group than by an individual; (2) the power of execution is greater "because the decree of an assembly inclines men more to belief and submission"; (3) this is especially true when the college is directly under the "grand monarch," eliminating the suspicion of a vested interest; (4) business is not delayed by the absence of the chief administrator; (5) there is no room for favoritism, fraud, or bribery, "especially . . . if the persons are of a different order"; (6) fear of "the resentment of the great and powerful" does not prevent "righteous judgement"; (7) a "single spiritual ruler" causes tumults and

Many think that not all people are bound to obey the authorities, that some are excepted, that is, the priests and the monks. This is a thorn, this is poison of asps, this is a Popish spirit, which I know not how has caught hold of us. The clergy are a separate class within the state, but not a separate state within the state.[3]

Peter's ukase read, ". . . having taken upon Us the care of the regulation of the clergy, and spiritual order," and preferring a collegial administration, "because, this is too weighty a charge for any single person to whom the supreme power is not hereditary, We appoint a spiritual college." And the oath required of members included this: "I acknowledge upon oath, that the monarch of all Russia himself, our most gracious sovereign, is the supreme judge of this spiritual college." [4]

Extreme as these statements seem, the priesthood itself was not claimed by Peter as Leo III had claimed it. It was over organizational, administrative questions and not over substantive, theological ones that the tsar's authority was asserted—a distinction that had prevailed in Byzantium over Leo's view. Asked if he intended to unite the Russian and Latin churches, Peter replied, "Ecclesiastical matters belong not to me but to the clergy," since church union involved questions of doctrine.[5] Yet the destruction of its traditional head was a severe blow, making the church legally a department of the tsar's government. To the Raskolniki this proved that Peter was the Antichrist; but the official church, like the synod that deposed Nikon, sought safety in subservience.

As in ecclesiastical matters, so in temporal the tsar's will was unchecked. His *Articles of War* described him thus: "His Majesty is a sovereign monarch whom no one on earth may call to account for his actions, but who has power and authority to govern his realm and lands, as a Christian sovereign, according to his own will and judgment" (Article 20).

When Peter decided to deny the succession to his son Alexis, Proko-

---

sedition, "for the ignorant vulgar people do not consider how far the spiritual power is removed from, and inferior to the regal, but . . . consider such a ruler as a second sovereign, equal in power to the king himself"; (8) a patriarch is "unwilling to be try'd by his peers"; and (9) the college is "a school of spiritual improvement" for its members in "spiritual polity" (*The Present State and Regulations of the Church of Russia,* ed. and trans. Thomas Consett, I [London, 1729], 15–22).

povich wrote his *Right of the Monarchal Will* (1722), which Shcher-batov later called "a monument of flattery and monkish servility before the arbitrariness of the ruler." [6] Although limited considerably by the special purpose for which it was produced, this short work, based largely upon Hobbes and Pufendorf, is the best general statement of the political ideas both of Prokopovich and of his master.* Paying lip service to the social contract theory, then in vogue in the West, the author promised that from such "true interpretations of popular will we will also shed much light on the free or unfree will of monarchs in the designation of their successors." Yet he did not derive the powers of the tsar from the nature of the contract, but rather the nature of the contract from the powers in fact held by the tsar. "It is not possible to interpret popular will other than from the appearance and form of the monarchy itself; it should be understood that whatever the monarchy is, such also is the people's will, having been at the basis of that monarchy." [7] Against any agreement really limiting the monarch's power he presented not argument but simply disdain.

He interpreted the original contract as an expression, not only of the will of the people, but also of the will of God (as became a church-man), without noticing, apparently, how close he thus came to saying that the will of the people is the will of God. The bent of his mind precluded any democratic consequences that might flow from that coincidence of wills. The people had no authority over God's will, and therefore they remained powerless to revise that ancient agreement: "Although the people should want to rescind their will . . . they still cannot rescind the will of God, which put the people's will in motion and acted together with it." By their one act of will they had divested themselves forever and in everything of any subsequent will. In all of Russia no one save the tsar, then, could have a will, and no representation of the public in the government was needed, nor was the government in any sense responsible to the public. "And so each autocratic sovereign is not obliged to preserve man's law and consequently for violation of man's law he is not judged; the precepts of God he must preserve, but for violation of them he answers only to God Himself and cannot be judged by men." This tone indicates how congenial Prokopovich found Peter's rule: he enunciated not a threat of divine

* His "Sermon on Royal Authority and Honor," also valuable, is translated in *Russian Intellectual History, an Anthology,* ed. Marc Raeff (New York, 1966), pp. 14–30.

judgment, nor even a pious admonition to rule justly, but clearly an exemption from any responsibility to terrestrial beings, thus supporting complete autocracy.[8]

III

Between the reigns of Peter I and Catherine II (between 1725 and 1762) came a pretorian period when the palace guard, on five separate occasions, took a hand in the making or unmaking of autocrats, and when the nobility again, as in 1613, had a fine chance to limit the autocracy. They made their strongest bid following the sudden death of Peter II (r. 1727–1730) on the eve of his wedding.*

The prime mover in this episode was Prince Dmitri Golitsyn, first cousin of Vasili Golitsyn, who was discussed above, and the last effective spokesman of the ancient aristocracy before it became submerged in the new service nobility brought forward by the *Order of Ranks* of 1722. Western educated, he was well qualified for his role both by study and by diversified experience under Peter the Great. As governor of Kiev he had engaged the scholars of that intellectual center to provide translations of leading works on political philosophy, including those of Machiavelli, Grotius, Pufendorf, Locke, and Thomasius. Both before and after the Swedish reform of 1720 he studied the constitutional arrangements of that country, then at the height of its prestige.

Golitsyn was one of the *verkhovniki*, the handful of highest nobles who had obtained control of the Supreme Secret Soviet, a group which had been set above the Senate in 1726. In a secret conclave on the night after Peter's death he persuaded his colleagues to offer the throne to Anna Ivanovna (r. 1730–1740) of Courland, a niece of Peter I. Also, since several other claimants stood ahead of her and she could not without the Soviet expect to succeed, he persuaded them to impose conditions upon the offer.

Golitsyn had objected not so much to the content of Peter's reforms

---

* On these events and ideas see Walther Recke, "Die Verfassungspläne der russischen Oligarchen im Jahre 1730 und die Thronbesteigung der Kaiserin Anna Ivanovna," *Zeitschrift für osteuropäische Geschichte*, II (1911–1912), 11–64, 161–203, and D. A. Korsakov, *Votsarenie imperatritsy Anny Ioannovny* (Kazan, 1880). Several of the documents are translated in Marc Raeff, *Plans for Political Reform in Imperial Russia, 1730–1905* (Englewood Cliffs, N.J., 1966), pp. 41–52.

as to the arbitrary and single-handed manner of their conception. He now hoped to restore something of the pre-Petrine cooperation of sovereign and boyars in decision-making by formally requiring the approval of the Soviet for certain acts. Anna was, therefore, asked to sign these conditions:

We [*sic*] promise herewith most strongly that my chief care and endeavor will be not only the preservation but the utmost and greatest possible propagation of our Greek orthodox faith; also, upon receipt of the Russian crown, not to enter into wedlock throughout my whole life, and not to designate a successor either during my life or after it [by testament]; also we promise that, since the integrity and the welfare of every state is made of good counsel, we shall always maintain the already-established Supreme Secret Soviet composed of eight persons, and without its consent,

(1) will not engage in war with anyone;

(2) will not conclude peace;

(3) will not burden our loyal subjects with any [new] taxes;

(4) will not grant ranks higher than that of colonel in civil service, in the army or in the navy, nor assign anyone to important affairs, and the guards and other regiments will be under the jurisdiction of the Supreme Secret Soviet;

(5) will not deprive the nobility of life, property or honor without trial;

(6) will not grant estates and villages;

(7) will not promote either Russians or foreigners to offices at court;

(8) will not use state revenues for [personal] expenses, and will continually maintain all my loyal subjects in my good graces; and if I do not carry out everything according to my promise, then I shall be deprived of the Russian throne.[9]

The historians have shown that these provisions were, in part, borrowed from those adopted in Sweden in 1720 and from earlier Swedish laws.[10] It is instructive to notice how much they resemble the restrictions imposed upon Vladislav of Poland in 1610 in favor of the Boyar Duma (above, page 99). The *verkhovniki*, smaller in numbers than the Duma in 1610, or even in the great days of Ivan III, nevertheless thought of themselves as the heirs to the Duma tradition; and, seeing how easily it had lost ground under such men as Ivan IV and Peter, they wanted legal and moral guarantees from Anna of their collective role as consultants to the crown. More than that: they wanted written guarantees that on certain points their advice would be followed, and that they would be able to control the pretorian guards.

They did not, however, appear to desire any major changes in the machinery or powers of government.* Their aim was not to abolish absolutism but to assure their own participation in it; their document contained limitations upon Anna alone, but none upon Anna acting with the Supreme Soviet. And there was nothing of representation, of popular rights, nor of emancipation for the serfs.

Nor was there satisfaction for the other ranks of the nobility, and therein lay Golitsyn's defeat. In presenting the conditions to Anna the *verkhovniki* led her to think that they came from the whole nobility, and said nothing to the lesser nobles about them in hopes that the conditions would be taken as Anna's own idea, freely granted. "And thus these men have deceived the Tsarina in Courland in the name of the people, and the people in Moscow in the name of the Tsarina," as Prokopovich summed it up.[11] However, large numbers of both provincial and Petersburg nobles were gathered in Moscow for the tsar's wedding and had to be informed of the new political arrangements. When Golitsyn read Anna's acceptance of the conditions to the Generality (the first four ranks) he sensed their dissatisfaction and thought it necessary to ask them to prepare their own ideas as to the form of the new government. Later, finding that they wished to suppress the Soviet, he called upon the remaining ranks of the nobility to prepare another plan. He hoped thus to find support, or at least to divide the opposition; what had begun as a secret conspiracy was forced to seek a broader basis.

IV

In the clamor of majority and minority proposals that soon resounded, one voice, speaking for the Generality, showed some analytical power. Vasili Tatishchev, a conservative historian, supporter of Peter's reforms, and student of Western political philosophers, well illustrated the aims and confusions of contemporary Russian political thinking. He asked four preliminary questions:

(1) On the death of a sovereign without heir, who has the authority to rule the people?

* It has been suggested that Golitsyn planned to present an additional implementing document later. On this disputed point see Recke, "Die Verfassungspläne," pp. 161–183.

(2) Who, in such a case, can change any inveterate law or custom and begin a new one?

(3) If we need to change the autocratic ancient government, then first should be considered: which [form of government], for the condition of the people and the circumstances, is the best?

(4) By whom and in what manner is that [new] institution to be established? [12]

On the first he argued that, since the oath of allegiance was to the tsar alone, any delegation of power by him must end at his death, and "there remain people in their previous status, altogether equal." But to avoid lacunae in administration, "the general public [*obshchenarodie*] grant them [the old administrators] only such authority as they had before by previous laws, and without specific designation from the people no one can demand more."

On the second, "it is clear that the power of law-giving is bestowed only on the sovereign himself," and no laws are issued without his confirmation. "When there is no sovereign his permission and confirmation also do not exist, and in his name nothing can be promulgated; consequently, no one can change any law or arrangement unless the general public consents."

On the third. For a change of government there is no need nor any advantage, but rather great harm. . . . Great and vast nations . . . cannot be governed by certain of the above [forms of government], especially where the people are insufficiently enlightened and preserve the laws out of fear rather than good morals or understanding of [public] benefit and harm. In such it is none other than autocracy or absolute monarchy that is necessary. . . . Democracy can never be used, for the great expanse of the state precludes this. Events have taught us that aristocracy is harmful enough. . . . And by this any reasonable person can see well enough that autocratic government is more beneficial than all others here, and that others are dangerous.[13]

This negative answer precluding a direct reply to his fourth question, Tatishchev instead described the proposals of his group. "Something for the aid of Her Highness" was needed, because, "being a female, she is unsuited to so many labors since her knowledge of laws is insufficient." They proposed, "after adequate discussion lasting for three days," to establish a Senate of twenty-one persons "including the present members of the Supreme Soviet," and another body of one hundred divided into three rotating groups sitting for four-month periods. These two bodies would fill their own vacancies and help to elect other high administrators.[14]

This mixture of vague and medieval concepts rested in part on the contract thinking of Pufendorf.* The death of the ruler ended the governmental contract, but the underlying social contract remained; so the nobility retained their special position as "natural leaders," representatives, in the medieval sense, of the nation, each able to speak for his serfs. Thus, clear distinctions were blended with old ideas of consensus and tacit consent. That such representatives could impose conditions in a new governmental contract Tatishchev was not sure; that they should do so he was even less sure. For him the important task was to limit or dilute the power of the Supreme Soviet, not that of the new empress.

In his plan the lower ranks of nobles fared little better than in that of Golitsyn. He was interested in administrative machinery, not in the representation of opinions from outside the bureaucracy nor in the protection of individual rights, even for the nobility. He suggested a bureaucratic complex of governmental organs (without the Soviet) which would perpetuate themselves by co-option and would prepare legislation for the approval of the sovereign without consulting most of the nobility.

The lesser nobles, in their turn, insisted upon having their elected representatives in the higher organs, a minority wishing to extend the elective principle to the Senate and to Peter's administrative colleges. Although they talked of the English form of government, they showed little comprehension of the principles or techniques by which it had been built. Their plan carried 743 signatures, including those of many who had also signed Tatishchev's project. This overlapping is evidence both of a scarcity of matured conviction on constitutional matters and of a widespread primary desire to thwart the *verkhovniki*. Although revival of the zemski sobors was not proposed, their basic concept, the search for wisdom, still dominated political thought. The groups differed mainly as to the ranks of nobility they thought promising for such a search. With all groups the aim was participation in power, not limitation of it.

It was evident that the *verkhovniki* regarded all this activity as advice which they could take or leave, and they made very inadequate concessions to the lesser nobility. Suspicion of their motives on the

* See Samuel Pufendorf, *Of the Law of Nature and Nations*, Bk. 7, Chap. 5, sec. 22, and Chap. 7, secs. 7–9.

parts of both the service nobility and those members of the old aristocracy whom they failed to invite to share in their deliberations, coupled
with divisions and intrigue within the Soviet, undermined their authority. When they did seek to compromise with the "constitutionalists"
against the autocratic group it was too late. Perhaps they trusted Anna
to keep her promises.

She, indeed, reaffirmed her agreement upon arrival at Moscow, but
two weeks later she received delegations of the several factions in a
palace surrounded by guards led by a trusted relative. Tatishchev read
a petition from the Generality asking her to join with them and the
lower nobility to study proposals for the form of government. The
verkhovniki objected to this; a recess was granted for the redrafting of
the petition, during which the situation became clearer; and the new
draft read:

Humbly we present ourselves before Your Imperial Majesty to give proof
of our gratitude, and with the greatest veneration beg Your Imperial
Majesty to deign to accept the sovereignty as it was held by your predecessors, and to annul the conditions sent to Your Imperial Majesty by the
Supreme Soviet, which Your Imperial Majesty signed.[15]

With the guards at her side, Anna asked the advice of the Soviet, but it
remained silent; she then tore up the conditions.

In Golitsyn the old line of political thought expressed by Bersen
and Kurbski, who had sought to defend ancient customs and privileges
of the old nobility against the encroachments of autocracy, met the
new line of the modern reformers, who would restrict the autocracy
and the old nobility in the interest of new classes rising from below. An
incorrigible aristocrat, he was unable to reconcile these two lines,
seeing in the service nobility neither a prescriptive right to participate
in high policy nor a promise to contribute wisdom to its formulation.
Badly gauging the forces of his time, he based his attempt too nar-
rowly, and the other ranks, as represented in Tatishchev, still saw as
their main enemy the great boyar families rather than the autocrat. The
autocracy survived, less by its own initiative than through the obsoles-
cence of its old enemies and the immaturity of its new ones.

CHAPTER XII

The Enlightenment: Catherine and Her Critics

ALTHOUGH, as the events of 1730 had shown, the nobles were unable to wrest power from the autocrat by their own efforts, they were destined in the next generation to enjoy a breath of freedom decreed from above, a voluntary relaxation of its grip by an autocracy which had learned that it could depend upon the support of the nobles—at least as long as they remained divided among themselves. In 1762 Tsar Peter III issued a decree releasing the nobility from the obligation to serve the state, an obligation which it had borne for centuries. For the first time a class was created that neither served nor paid taxes. Yet this breath of freedom contributed strongly to the estrangement of the Russian people from their government.

The peasants, as has been seen, connected their own service to the nobility with the latter's service to the state: they served their lords because the tsar needed the lords and had no money with which to pay them. With this simple logic they saw their society integrated and saw their own place in it. Therefore, with this integration ended, the peasants were convinced that they too should be freed, or rather, that they had been freed but that the nobles had suppressed half of the tsar's decree. The religious Russian peasant could not believe that the tsar, whom he had been taught to regard as Christ's vicegerent, the guardian of justice on earth, would free only the nobles. The new situation thus seemed to confirm the ancient myth that the nobles were their only enemies, oppressing them and hiding the truth from the tsar. The following twelve years saw peasant uprisings on an unprecedented scale, culminating in the one led by Emelian Pugachev, who for a time held a third of Russia.*

This profoundly unsettling decree had hardly been issued when the palace guards deposed and killed Peter and proclaimed as empress his German wife Catherine. She it was who had to ride the gathering storm.

I

The reign of Catherine II (r. 1762–1796), known as the Great, brought, in addition to wars, insurrections, and three partitions of Poland, substantial intellectual achievements stimulated partly by her sponsorship of the western Enlightenment. Correspondent of Voltaire and friend of Diderot, she had a fair store of political ideas gleaned from reading the political classics from Plato and Cicero to Beccaria and the Encyclopedists, particularly Montesquieu. It is customary to consider that, so far as a monarch could, she shared the attitudes of the more liberal of these writers—at least until revolt within Russia and revolution in France produced in her a negative response of fear and conservatism. There is, however, little evidence to support such a judgment.

Of her conservatism there need be no doubt:

Everything which is established and ordered in the world today is established and ordered by experience, which demands that everything be based on precedent, and not on arbitrary will. If it were otherwise, it would be worse, for the better is an enemy of what is good today, and it is better to hold fast to what is known than to lay out a path to what is unknown.[1]

She wrote this in 1790, but that she had long held such views is clear from her statement in 1767 that "a Monarchy is destroyed, when the

---

* The focus of this insurrection against the nobility is illustrated by the manifesto (1773) of Pugachev, who capitalized on the peasants' faith in the tsar: "I am Peter III, your lawful Emperor; my wife swayed to the side of the nobility, and I swore . . . *to exterminate them to the last man*. The noblemen persuaded her to give all of you into slavery, but I opposed this, and they became indignant against me, sent murderers, but God saved me" (quoted by Edward J. Geary and Pierre C. Oustinoff, eds., in their Introduction to Denis Diderot, *Observations sur l'Instruction de Sa Majesté Impériale aux députés pour la confection des lois*, I [New York, 1953], xlvi).

Sovereign imagines, that he displays his Power more by *changing* the Order of Things, than by adhering to it." [2]

In substantiation of her liberalism are usually cited the great Commission for a new code of laws which she assembled in 1767, and the *Instruction* that she composed to guide it. In this somewhat lengthy document the influences of Montesquieu and Beccaria are quite evident, as she freely admitted. Yet it is equally evident that, with support drawn from Montesquieu, Catherine was basically an autocrat and intended to remain so. For the great Frenchman, himself less liberal than the other *philosophes*, had written in his *Ésprit des Lois* (Book 8, Chapter 19), "A large empire presupposes a despotic authority in him who governs," and it was with these, his opinions on the influences of environment and geographical expanse on government, that Catherine was impressed. Russia, she said, extended across 32 degrees of latitude and 165 of longitude; therefore

the Sovereign is absolute; for there is no other Authority but that which centers in his single Person, that can act with a Vigour proportionate to the Extent of such a vast Dominion. The extent of the Dominion requires an absolute Power to be vested in that Person who rules over it. It is expedient so to be, that the quick Dispatch of Affairs, sent from distant Parts, might make ample Amends for the Delay occasioned by the great Distance of the Places. Every other Form of Government whatsoever would not only have been prejudicial to Russia, but would even have proved its entire Ruin.*[3]

For Montesquieu's more significant defense of liberty she had no appreciation. She quoted his two ambiguous statements (Book 11, Chapter 3), "Liberty can only consist in doing that which every One ought to do, and not to be constrained to do that which One ought not to do," and "Liberty is the Right of doing whatsoever the Laws allow," but his idea of preserving freedom by dividing power was foreign to her.[4] In her opinion, "in the very Nature of the Thing the Sovereign is the Source of all imperial and civil Power," and "a Society of Citizens, as well as every Thing else, requires a certain fixed Order: There ought to be *some to govern*, and *others to obey*." [5] Perhaps she, like many after her, did not understand the main point of Montesquieu's theory

---

* It is probable that she brought Montesquieu's views to the throne with her. In February 1764 she told the Procurator-General of the Senate, "The Russian empire is so vast that any form of government other than the autocratic must be injurious to it" (Russkoe Istoricheskoe Obshchestvo, *Sbornik*, VII [St. Petersburg, 1871], 347).

of the separation of powers—that each great function of government must have an independent foundation, that their combination in the same hands is tyranny. In any event she did not accept it. She disbanded the codifying Commission in 1768, its task unfinished.

True, she talked much of a government of laws, and thereby gave an impetus to this idea in Russia; yet in her mind law was an instrument by which she would govern, never a force above her, under which and according to which she *must* govern. At the inception of her reign, Count N. I. Panin, combining the ideas of Dmitri Golitsyn with the bureaucracy of Tatishchev, presented her with a proposal for a Permanent Imperial Soviet and almost secured its adoption until she learned that it was planned as a legal restriction upon her own powers. Again, a year later, she decided to confiscate some church lands which Peter I had taxed but which even he had not taken; how liberal her bishops thought her is indicated by the fact that only one of them dared oppose. The synod degraded him for this defense of the church, and Catherine cast him into prison. It may be concluded that neither a new idea (French or Russian) nor a traditional mode of thought was tolerable if it tended to restrict her autocracy.

Diderot, whom she persuaded to visit Russia, told her plainly, "All arbitrary government is bad; I do not except the arbitrary government of a master who is good, resolute, just, and enlightened." [6] Too polite to criticize his hostess directly, he wrote some extensive *Observations* on her *Instruction* but kept them from her until he died years later. These show how far her thinking was, even in 1767, from that of the Encyclopedists, and her reaction to the *Observations*, when at last she read them, shows how little she believed her thinking had changed. In 1785 she wrote to Baron Grimm of Diderot's criticism:

That piece is pure prattle. . . . Now I maintain that my *Instruction* has been not only good but even excellent and well applied to the circumstances, because, in the eighteen years that it has existed, not only has it not done harm, but what is more all the good that was accomplished, and that everyone acknowledges, was done by the principles established by that *Instruction*.[7]

The French Revolution itself only confirmed and emboldened her in autocracy.

Abroad, and to a degree among the nobility at home, however, Catherine retained a reputation for reform. She devolved certain functions upon provincial and local governments (at the expense of rather chaotic disorganization of the central administration) and in 1785 granted to the nobles a charter confirming their exemption from service and from taxation and giving them exclusive authority to choose representatives to manage local administration. Their controls over the peasantry were strengthened and serfdom was extended to the Ukraine, where it had not been before. This was not to be the last time that the government of Russia, while professing to follow an advanced Western philosophy, moved backwards in terms of the trends in the West.

Yet, as in the case of Peter I, the results of Catherine's efforts were not identical with her aims. The Enlightenment was a powerful leaven, and her sponsorship of it hardly enabled her to control it. Those manifestations of it against which she set her face were as important for the future of Russia as were those on which she smiled, and perhaps even more beneficent.

With all its weaknesses Catherine's *Instruction* reinforced the hope for reform from above and disseminated more widely the ideal of a reign of law. If she understood law as a means of administration, others before long would see it as a restraint upon administration and upon the autocracy. Catherine was no liberal but she was urbane, and during her reign the intellectual currents in Russia both broadened and deepened. The publication of books and journals increased prodigiously. In contrast with the drunken stupor, imbecility, and madness of preceding and succeeding reigns, hers has gathered in retrospect a respectability almost amounting to a golden age.

II

Among her contemporaries, however, not only the Encyclopedists were disappointed. Her Russian critics appeared from both the right and the left. Of the former the strongest example was Mikhail Shcherbatov (1733–1790), a descendant of Riurik and, like Tatishchev, a conservative historian. Released from military service by the decree of 1762, he subsequently held several civil offices, reaching the Senate in 1779. He was sent by the nobility of Iaroslavl, the old seat of the Kurbskis, to serve on Catherine's Commission, where he opposed both the extinction of serfdom itself and the extension of serf-holding outside the ranks of the nobility.

In his youth Shcherbatov had been attracted by the Enlightenment, under its influence writing and translating a number of works. Indeed, he never entirely abandoned rationalism nor succeeded in reconciling it with his preference for traditional ways. This conflict in his thought was most evident in his efforts to interpret the reforms of Peter I. Admiration for Peter permeates his utopian novel, *A Voyage to the Land of Ophir* (1784), in which he idealized what he thought Peter should have established.* The result was static perfection, a society ordered in detail, once and for all, by the will of the tsar. Yet he was clear that Peter had made errors, of both commission and omission. The creative power of rationalism and of the monarch's will, therefore, needed to be tempered with respect for tradition and for enlightened opinion. In his best-known work, *The Corruption of Morals in Russia* (1788), he traced the sad state of contemporary affairs back to the autocratic manner in which Peter had instituted his reforms.†

Shcherbatov was unconvinced by Montesquieu's advocacy of despotism for large states, and held that republican government could compensate for the time lost in deliberation by the greater wisdom and temperance of its decisions and by the greater diligence of the rulers, diligence induced by the pressure of public opinion. He hardly wanted a Russian republic, but against Catherine's defense of autocracy he argued, in the spirit of the old Duma boyars, that a ruler, "not giving account to anyone in his affairs, is easily thrown into passions and does not listen to those who, by contradiction, direct him on the true course, but to those who, with dishonorable flattery, have stolen their way into his affection." [8] In his essay "On Legislation" he discussed the traditional three forms of government, indicating that in fact all governments were mixed. He then went on:

Having thus described the various types of government, I shall proceed to autocracy or despotism. One cannot call this a government, nor place it with the others, for it is nothing more than an abuse of monarchial power, because a monarchy must have its fundamental laws and preserve every-

---

* On this novel see N. D. Chechulin, *Russkii sotsial'nyi roman XVIII veka:* ("*Puteshestvie v zemliu Ofirskuiu g. S., shvetskago dvorianina*"—*sochinenie kniazia M. M. Shcherbatova*) (St. Petersburg, 1900).

† His estimate of Catherine, as well as his own prudent character, is indicated by his refraining from publishing these literary efforts. The *Corruption* itself circulated only in manuscript until 1858, when Herzen printed it in the safety of London.

thing that is well established, but autocracy, following only its own dictates, breaks all laws at will. A monarchy, by established law, preserves the life, honor, possessions, and peace of its citizens; but an autocracy sees nothing in this, spills in streams the blood of its best subjects, does not preserve their honor, does not consider the tenderness of their hearts, deprives [them] of possessions at will and disrupts all parts of life and the peace of each citizen for, indeed, how can anyone be at peace where nothing is protected by established laws? [9]

In an autocracy "intellect is extinguished" lest the bases of society in mutual rights be investigated to the autocrat's disadvantage. The autocrat envies men of merit; "despot promotes despot and the state is filled with them." Such a system, he concluded, "cannot exist among an educated people." [10]

"The Russian Empire," however, he said ambiguously, "has a monarchial government, as Her Highness in her *Instruction* explained."

Because the monarch is not a *votchinnik* but a governor and protector of his state, there must be certain fundamental laws which do not restrain the power of the monarch in everything beneficial to the state but which would sometimes limit his disorderly desires, which redound in great part to his own detriment.

Most essential among such laws were, he thought: (1) "an unchanging foundation and regulation for the order of succession to the throne"; (2) preservation of the established religion "and the adherence of the sovereign to it and to civil laws," plus toleration for "foreign" religions "wherever it need be extended"; (3) a fixed order in the establishment of legislative changes; (4) a right of self defense, with counsel, in criminal cases, and a right of appeal; and (5) "the right to a title of nobility, by various ranks." [11]

Like Kurbski, Shcherbatov believed that the effective participation of the aristocracy in the government was essential for the success of monarchy. The Roman Empire, he said, had fallen only after the decline in the Senate's power, "when the emperors' power became unlimited and instead of wise counsel they began to follow the advice of flatterers." In his mind noble rank was still connected with service to the state, although he rationalized the hereditary, nonserving nobility as justified by the service rendered by its ancestors. Yet, unlike Kurbski, he saw the most effective restraint on arbitrary power not in "wise counsel" but in law.

For Shcherbatov the regularity and dependability of public order was a measure of the public welfare, and he opposed the disturbance thereof by the arbitrary action of an individual will, whether that will belonged to the tsar or to the landlord who, at his caprice, could exile his serf to Siberia. Like Burke, he lacked confidence in rapid change because he lacked confidence in the results of individual reason. Only the deeply rooted and slowly ripened ideas of the community were, to him, dependable in politics.

III

Criticism of a very different sort appeared from the left, from Alexander Radishchev (1749–1802), a man more Westernized, more emancipated both from his Russian background and from the perversions of the official Westernism at Catherine's court. In sharp contrast to the attitude of Shcherbatov was his radical optimism, for he believed that "in order to govern the multitude it is sensible to assume that the worst citizens are better than they really are." [12]

Catherine had sent him, as a promising page, to the University of Leipzig in 1766. There he studied law under Karl Hommel, a follower of Beccaria. Under young Ernst Platner he read Locke and Priestley and also absorbed the radical philosophy emanating from France. Returning to Russia after five years, he occupied a few minor governmental posts with growing frustration. He finally gave vent to his feelings and opinions in a *Journey from Petersburg to Moscow,* a group of essays, stories, and poems published in 1790. By then, however, events in Paris had frightened conservatives everywhere, and Radishchev was condemned to death. The Empress read his book and found him "filled and infected with French errors," but she commuted his sentence to ten years in exile.

At her death he was permitted to return to his estate, and her grandson Alexander I recalled him to St. Petersburg in 1801, appointing him to his new Codification Commission under the chairmanship of Count Zavadovski. In a fever of activity to do something for Russia after thirty wasted years, and sharing the optimism of the new reign, Radishchev quickly produced a number of memoranda and draft proposals to implement Alexander's supposed liberalism, including a "Project of a

Civil Code" and contributions to a "Charter for the Russian People" to be read at the coronation.*

The "Project," the most substantial of these, shows that Radishchev, unlike Catherine, had digested his theoretical sources. He gave to the doctrines of natural law a practical and contextual embodiment that was his own. Influenced by the French utilitarians, he asked what incentive men had to leave the unlimited freedom and complete equality of the state of nature, and answered, "Reason says, one's own welfare; the heart says, one's own welfare; uncorrupted civil law says, one's own welfare." With this motive behind the social compact, which must be accepted by all, "if they all set limits to their freedom and a regulation over their actions, then all, from the mother's womb equal in natural freedom, must be equal under those restrictions." [13]

From this equality he did not, as did his contemporary, Jefferson, tacitly exclude the slaves. His work is filled with loathing for the institution of serfdom and with hatred for the class structure that supported it. He saw clearly the interdependence of the parts of the Russian system of social control. In places in the *Journey* he seemed to give the tsars credit for trying to resist the enserfment of their people and to cast the blame wholly on the nobility. But in his "Ode to Freedom," written in the early 1780's under the inspiration of the American Revolution and also printed in large part in the *Journey* (at the town of Tver, the ancient enemy of Moscow), the tsar himself is the villain, "of all villains most violent."

We look upon vast areas where a tarnished throne upholds slavery, [where], in peace and quiet, sacred and political superstition, supporting each other, jointly oppress society. The one strives to enchain reason; the other hastens to stifle will—for the general benefit, they say.[14]

Radishchev was not irreligious, but to him there was little connection between the state church and religion.

He early deduced from the social contract the idea that the ruler, by acts of injustice, became liable to punishment in the same manner as any law-breaker: "The injustice of the sovereign gives the people, who are his judges, the same or an even greater right over him than the law

---

* On this charter see p. 149. The authorship is uncertain; Radishchev's draft may have been toned down by Alexander Vorontsov, who presented it to the tsar. See Georg Sacke, *Graf A. Voroncov, A. N. Radiščev und der "Gnadenbrief für das russische Volk"* (Emsdetten, n.d. [1938?]).

gives him to judge criminals." [15] Even when the ruler was not at fault, Radishchev also deduced, he was obligated to protect the citizens and in certain circumstances to compensate them for injuries inflicted by others.

The law is merely the confirmation of what Nature bestowed on man. From this it follows that as a man on entering society yields to it some portion of his rights, then it is obligated to compensate him for them. Consequently every man living in society is entitled to demand from it defence and protection. [16]

He then went on to reassert a concept once widely held which modern governments have conveniently neglected: "Compensation for harm is a consequence of the original social pact, and if the guilty party be brought by punishment into a state of being unable to make reparation for the damage he has caused, then society as a whole is under an obligation to do so." [17] The citizen under the compact should never suffer injury without just compensation; the guilty party should compensate, but if he be unable society should do it.

In such statements Radishchev displayed a doctrinaire confidence in reason and in legal remedies that was quite oblivious to the scepticism that, for half a century, had depreciated social contract thinking in western Europe. In the conditions of Russia, however, such confidence was still pertinent. From his position on the Codification Commission he tried to implement his ideas, working for months at top speed. So dedicated was he that Zavadovski became worried about his "enthusiastic" ideas and threatened him with a return to Siberia.

Radishchev had high hopes for Alexander's reforms. The first of them, the organization of the ministries and the new statute for the Senate, came on September 8, 1802; three days later Radishchev poisoned himself. Was it fear, or overwork, or disappointment?

CHAPTER XIII

Promise and Denouement: Alexander and His Aides

ELEVATED to the throne at twenty-three by the murder of Tsar Paul, his sadistic father, Alexander I (r. 1801–1825) stimulated a tide of optimism by declaring in his accession manifesto that he would rule "after the laws and heart of our grandmother, Catherine the Great." His education had been a special concern of the old Empress', and for eleven years he had been tutored by the Swiss republican, La Harpe. His initial expressions and activities nurtured expectations that, after the erratic and suspicious whims of Paul, he would revive not only the laws of Catherine but also the energetic reforming tendencies of her earlier years.*

I

Alexander started off by calling home four of his closest friends, several of whom had fled abroad during Paul's reign, and forming them into an unofficial committee to work out plans for reform. They were the Polish Prince Adam Czartoryski, whose interests lay in diplomacy

---

* Yet even in this honeymoon of his reign Alexander did not inspire universal confidence. His minister in London, S. R. Vorontsov, wrote to his son Mikhail, "Because the present sovereign is good, the nation believes itself really free, without thinking that the same man can change in character or be succeeded by another tyrant. The present condition of the country is only a suspension of tyranny, and our compatriots are like Roman slaves during the Saturnalia, after which they relapse into their usual slavery" (*Arkhiv kniazia Vorontsova*, ed. Peter I. Bartenev, XVII [Moscow, 1880], 6). Catherine too had toyed with reform.

and an independent Poland; Count Paul A. Stroganov, an extremely wealthy man who had been a librarian of the Jacobin Club in Paris in 1790; Nikolai N. Novosiltsev, a clever and energetic cousin of Stroganov's; and Count Victor P. Kochubey, who had been brought up in England. All young, between five and ten years older than Alexander, they had been stimulated by the ferment of the French Revolution, but none of them was radical enough to insist upon either republicanism or equality. From June 1801 to May 1802 they met about once a week with Alexander for after-dinner talks that ranged from immediate personality problems of daily administration to general principles of government.*

Stroganov, who kept notes in French on their proceedings, summarized their plan of action in a preliminary note to Alexander thus:

If I have correctly understood the idea of Your Majesty, this principle could be stated thus: the governmental reform must be the work of the Emperor and no one who will not have his special trust in this matter must know that such a thing is being considered, and no indication whatsoever must create the suspicion that His Majesty would approve a thing of this kind.

We have then gone on to another principle: to understand that the reform ought to begin with the various branches of the administration, but that the drawing up of a constitution in the proper sense of the word should be no more than an adjunct to it, or, as it were, its sequel.

Your Majesty has told me concerning this matter that indeed it was only necessary that a good administration at the beginning, inspiring public confidence, become the earnest of the benevolence of an institution so necessary, so beautiful, but simultaneously so difficult to establish well, and prone to become dangerous through the manner of its introduction. It seems to me that, in explaining yourself thus, Your Majesty wants a moderate [*douce*] liberty and the inviolability of property—fruits of an administration reformed and regulated according to the true principles of national prosperity—to prepare, by means of their healthy influence, [the people's] minds to accept without danger, and with pleasure, a law which guarantees the bases of general happiness against arbitrary change.[1]

The committee was caught by its own timidity on the horns of two

* Several documents from Alexander's reign, including some from this committee, the "Charter for the Russian People," and drafts by Speranski and Novosiltsev, are translated (in part) in Marc Raeff, *Plans for Political Reform in Imperial Russia, 1730–1905* (Englewood Cliffs, N.J., 1966), pp. 75–120.

separate dilemmas, and with neither of them did it make much progress. In the first place, ideas for the amelioration of the chief sickness of the society, the persistence of serfdom, were regarded as both dangerous and unkind because of the deep ignorance and untrained helplessness of the serfs; at the same time, serfdom stifled the initiative which could have produced the economic surplus to support a school system and the teachers necessary to operate it. The serfs could thus not be freed with their primitive understanding of society, but teachers were not available to enlighten them. Even more basic was the second dilemma: the first step on any road to freedom for Russia was the limitation of the absolute power of the monarch, but Alexander and his friends feared that any such limitation would serve to restrict his freedom to effect reforms. The reforms had to be accomplished before the power to reform was relinquished; yet all reforms remained illusory so long as arbitrary power stood above them.

The caution which led the committee to work in strictest secrecy (because of "the facility with which all these heads could catch fire at the slightest sign of such a project") also gripped their theoretical work. As Stroganov said, "Anything which can change the direction of the general spirit is very dangerous, because it must be done well or things must be left on their old foundations." [2] A good illustration of this conservatism occurred when elder statesman Alexander Vorontsov presented the "Charter for the Russian People" mentioned above, intended as a coronation manifesto. In ideas closely akin to Shcherbatov, Vorontsov had toned down the "enthusiastic" version prepared by Radishchev so that Catherine's charter for the nobility was reaffirmed and serfdom untouched; but even so the "Charter" was too radical for the young men around the tsar. It contained some fine sentiments like "Peoples are not made for sovereigns, but sovereigns themselves are established by Providence for the benefit and welfare of peoples," [3] and some judicial provisions based on the English *habeas corpus*. When these latter came up for consideration, Stroganov recorded, "Novosiltsov observed that before adopting them one should calculate carefully if it would ever be necessary to withdraw them, for it would be better in that case not to adopt them. His Majesty said that that was exactly the observation he had already made to Count Vorontsov." [4] They were, of course, not adopted.

The popularity which the theories of Montesquieu had gained under

Catherine caused general approbation, both in the committee and outside, for the doctrine of the separation of powers; but since, in its
essence, this would require a power or powers independent of the tsar,
it was always conceived by the tsar's advisers as being applicable only
to levels of power once or twice removed from the highest, and thus
tended to mean a separation of functions rather than of powers. In this
form it could be used for the clarification of duties among administrative organs, but no progress could be made toward checking or balanc-
ing the imperial power.

Another of Montesquieu's ideas, his connection of political institutions with influences of the soil and climate, gave the Russians a
respectable explanation for their differences from the rest of the world
and, what was more, encouraged them to retain these differences.
Among Alexander's closest advisers, therefore, coupled with a desire to
profit from the experiences of western Europe with various types of
governmental machinery, was a certain fascination with the "national
spirit" of Russia and a determination that their reforms should not do
violence to that spirit. "Here," Stroganov wrote,

are the rules which should underlie this plan. . . . The general principles
which govern men's actions are, after all, identical; yet in the various
nations they undergo various modifications according to climate, prejudices,
etc. The form of the administration should conform to these various
modifications, and consequently, what suits one people may very well not
suit another. Hence, the prime basis on which the committee should establish itself is the understanding of the true spirit of the nation, which should
serve it as a guide in all its operations.[5]

From the high hopes of Alexander's early months some concrete
administrative improvements emerged. Over the surviving Colleges of
Peter were placed single administrators (although without well-defined
authority). The functions of the Senate were clarified and it was
declared to have the right to protest against ukases of the tsar. It is
indicative both of the imperfection of Alexander's constitutional conceptions and of the tenacity of his hold upon absolute power that, on
the first occasion of the exercise of this right by the Senate (on a
relatively trivial matter), and in spite of the fact that under the rules
the Senate had to accept the ukase if its protest failed to move the tsar,
Alexander informed the Senate that its right to protest applied only to
old ukases, not to new ones.

II

With this declaration the new emperor's honeymoon was over. The realities of Napoleon's Europe increasingly absorbed attention, and the war of 1805–1807, followed by the Tilsit peace, ushered in new conditions of cooperation with Napoleon in the "continental system." With them came new men around the tsar, in particular Mikhail Speranski (1772–1839).

Another example of a man of lowly origins who rose to dizzy heights in tsarist Russia, Speranski, like Nikon, started his climb in the church. Son of a village priest, he was sent in 1784 to the Alexander Nevski Monastery in St. Petersburg, which operated a respected school. A dozen years later the quality of his public sermons had earned him posts first as tutor and then as secretary with the influential Kurakin family. When, on the death of Catherine, Prince Alexis Kurakin became Proc-urator General, Speranski decided to leave the monastery and follow him into the government. From this point his unusual administrative talents carried him upward as high officials vied for his services. He did some drafting for the unofficial committee, and in 1803 he presented to Kochubey an original memorandum on the general reorganization of the government.

At that time he was pessimistic about the immediate prospects. The reign of law seemed to him the prime aim of reform; but,

in the present order of things we do not find even the first elements unavoidably necessary to the composition of a monarchial government. Indeed, how can a monarchial administration be founded . . . in a country where half the population is found in complete slavery, where this slavery is linked with almost all parts of the political structure and with the military system and where this military system is necessary because of the extent of the borders and the political situation? How can a monarchial adminis-tration be founded without a constitution and without codes? How can there be established a constitution and codes without the separation of the legislative power from the executive power? How can the legislative power be separated without an independent branch constituting it and without general opinion supporting it? How can the general opinion be formulated, a popular spirit created, without a free press? How can a free press be introduced or permitted without education? How can true ministerial responsibility be established where it answers to nobody and where both the answerer and the questioner constitute one person and one side? [6]

It being impossible to establish a "true monarchial administration," he proposed to move slowly toward it through institutions that, although "arranged on the present autocratic constitution of the state without any division of the legislative power from the executive power," would adapt the national spirit to more modern government. The most promising means to that end he saw in the development of public opinion through giving publicity to the actions of the government.

This is not a mere ceremony but one element of constitutional monarchy that now may be achieved. It acquaints the people with the government, engenders public opinion, enlightens the lower executives, prepares people for public affairs, places ministers under the judgment of the general reason.[7]

How the autocracy would be adapted to cope with an informed public opinion he did not make clear.

His "monarchial administration" or "constitutional monarchy," however, was not limited monarchy in the Western sense. The monarch should act through and by means of the law although he was not under the law, and Speranski persuaded himself that the capricious and arbitrary features would thereby be eliminated from government. Perhaps the churchman in him reminded him that God's government of the universe was neither limited nor capricious.

Inherent in this and all his subsequent work was an organic view of society. As he expressed it much later, "Social life is not the result of need, a creation of man and his reason; it is a basic part of the general establishment of God for the raising of man to highest perfection." [8] This view, usually conducive to conservatism in Burke, Spengler, and others, tended in Speranski to mean that the autocrat was not free to cease to be an autocrat because his position was a part of the social organism. Since autocracy corresponded to the condition of the people, any constitution for Russia must conform to the position of the tsar and consequently must not accord the people any rights or status that would derogate from his position. Speranski qualified this circular reasoning by suggesting some institutions that would gradually "adapt the popular spirit," but because he never escaped from this thinking he always conceived a constitution to be primarily an expression or description of the nation's organic social unity rather than an instrument for the protection of rights or for the construction or limitation of governmental powers.

When Alexander went to Erfurt in 1808 to negotiate with Napoleon, he took Speranski with him. Contact with a dynamic emperor who had codified the laws of France and rearranged her government may have encouraged Speranski to take a more optimistic view of Russian possibilities. In any event, when Alexander asked him for a new reorganization plan he produced in 1809 a comprehensive system, laid out in a theoretical analysis and built up in Montesquieu's three branches through four governmental levels—local, regional, provincial, and imperial.

The plan was based on a somewhat mystical conception that the three powers of government are found in each individual in the state of nature and can, in society, be united to different degrees (*stepeni*). Complete fusion would mean tyranny; union into three conjoined branches leaves room for civil rights. These branches, or forces as he calls them, in conjunction "produce the sovereign power and its political rights," while in "their condition of individual separation" they "give birth to the rights of citizens."

Indeed, civil rights in their essence are none other than these same political rights, but acting separately and individually for each. This divided activity of theirs cannot have any firmness if it does not presuppose their other united activity. From this it follows that true civil rights must be based on political rights, exactly as civil law in general cannot be firm without political law.[9]

It is not entirely clear what Speranski meant by this, but it seems that civil rights, for him, were a service function of the sovereign rather than anything inherent in the citizen that could be defended against the sovereign.

He argued that "it is impossible to base a government on law if one sovereign power both composes and executes the law," and he claimed that his plan consisted "not in hiding autocracy in external forms only, but in limiting it by the internal and substantial force of institutions." Yet his practical proposals failed to solve the dilemma of the indivisible autocrat. The so-called "legislative" branch he apparently regarded only as a repository of, and a training school for, public opinion.* He gave it consultative and petitioning functions in the style of a zemski

* In this he anticipated the Slavophils (see Chap. XVII).

sobor, but neither initiative nor confirmatory powers (like those of the French *parlements*) in legislation. In its structure he displayed his conservatism by carrying indirect election to a bureaucratic extreme: the voters were to elect only local (*volost*) dumas, these dumas then electing regional (*okrug*) dumas, these, provincial (*guberniia*) dumas, and these, finally, at least nominating an imperial duma. The real power of legislation, as well as the power of execution (through appointees at the various governmental levels), he left in the hands of the tsar and his ministers. In the judicial branch he suggested "jurymen," to be elected at the three lower levels by the dumas, for the determination of matters of fact, and the conversion of the existing Senate into a high court. At the imperial level, then, the three branches were headed, respectively, by the advisory imperial duma, the ministries, and a judicial Senate; but this apparent trichotomy of governmental powers was confronted with the indivisible unity of the tsar. Recognizing this, and frankly abandoning Montesquieu's precepts, Speranski left to the autocrat the appointment of all three. Moreover, as an ingrained bureaucrat, he crowned his structure with an Imperial Council (*Gosudarstvennyi Soviet*), which he described as "a body in which all actions, legislative, judicial and executive, are united in their principal relations and, thus, approach the sovereign power and devolve from it." [10]

A similar alteration of the theory of the separation of powers into a theory of the separation of functions, with all power devolving from a monarch, was taking place at this time in France, also under the influence of one-man rule. In 1818 Benjamin Constant, the leading theorist of liberal monarchy, distinguished the "royal power" from the executive and placed it above the legislative, executive, and judicial powers on the ground that a means was necessary for the resolution of deadlocks between or among them. "It must stand outside," he said, "it must be neutral in some manner, so that it can act wherever its action is necessary, and so that it is preservative and reparative without being hostile." [11] The practical compromise to which the tsar's advisers had been led by the hard fact of autocracy was thus confirmed at the fountainhead of advanced political thought, and Constant enjoyed high prestige in Russia.

Like others before and after it, this plan of 1809 failed of adoption, but an apparently mutilated version fell into the hands of the Decembrists, and Speranski's ideas circulated widely. In practice Speranski secured some reforms in the civil service and the creation of an Imperial Soviet. Working thus directly under the tsar he was no longer a servant of the nobility but a target of their envy. His reforms, including a ukase requiring a university diploma or the passing of an examination by all collegiate assessors (the eighth rank) and councillors of state (the fifth), roused the anger of the bureaucrats, and their opposition systematically undermined his influence. He was named Imperial Secretary in 1810, but by 1812 the tsar was persuaded to exile him.

With the fall of Speranski, Novosiltsev became Alexander's chief constitutional draftsman, producing in 1820 the last and most symmetrical of the long series of never quite satisfactory constitutions. The descriptive nature of its treatment of the tsar is apparent:

> Art. 10. The present constitution, which we grant to our dear and faithful subjects, determines the principle and the manner of exercise of the Sovereignty.
> Art. 11. The Sovereignty is indivisible; it resides in the person of the Monarch.
> Art. 12. The Sovereign is the sole source of all the civil, political, legislative, and military powers of the empire. He exercises, in all its fullness, the executive power. All executive, administrative, and judicial authority can issue only from him.[12]

In the production of this document Novosiltsev scoured the numerous constitutions of western Europe and America, and drew upon the accepted theorists. The influence of Constant is most evident.

Thus, for nineteen years, before reaction became all-pervasive at the Russian court, this constitutional activity continued, always in secret, with how much sincerity and how much cynicism can only be guessed.

III

Among the critics of Alexander's reorganizing activities none expressed himself more clearly than Nikolai Karamzin (1766–1826), another conservative historian. His multivolumed *History of the Russian State* (1816–1826), for which he is best known, was a romantic saga of fluctuations between anarchy and order, between the evil forces of democracy and localism, exemplified in the *veche* and the *udel* princes, and the good forces of autocracy and centralization, to which he thought the Mongols had contributed substantially.*

* In French as *Histoire de l'empire de Russie*, trans. St.-Thomas and Jauffret (Paris, 1819–1826).

Having chafed for ten years under reforms and rumors of reforms, Karamzin finally set forth his political ideas in a *Memoir on Ancient and Modern Russia* presented to the tsar in 1811 and circulated in manuscript during the 1830's.* Convinced that "we require more preservative than creative wisdom," he felt that "the reforms accomplished so far give us no reason to believe that future reforms will prove useful; we anticipate them more with dread than with hope, for it is dangerous to tamper with ancient political structures." Alexander's legislators showed "excessive reverence for political forms," whereas "what matters is not forms, but men." Worried lest there be real fire behind the smoke of constitution making, he presented his inverted version of limited autocracy:

If Alexander, inspired by generous hatred for the abuses of autocracy, should lift a pen and prescribe himself laws other than those of God and of his conscience, then the true, virtuous citizen of Russia would presume to stop his hand, and to say: "Sire! you exceed the limits of your authority. Russia, taught by long disasters, vested before the holy altar the power of autocracy in your ancestor, asking him that he rule her supremely, indivisibly. This covenant is the foundation of your authority, you have no other. You may do everything, but you may not limit your authority by law!" [13]

Yet autocracy, "the Palladium of Russia," had its own rules, the first of which was that the position of the autocrat is defensible only in proportion to his virtue. He criticized Ivan IV for never learning this.[14] Moreover, laws, such as those of Peter I, circumscribing "the innocent inclinations and tastes of our domestic life," are beyond the power of autocracy. "In this realm, the sovereign may equitably act only by example, not by decree." The failure of the ruler to "fulfill his sacred obligation . . . breaks the ancient covenant between authority and obedience," and reduces the nation to "the chaos of private natural law." [15]

By this, of course, Karamzin did not mean to justify revolution. Like a medieval churchman he saw an "evil autocrat" as "the scourge of heavenly wrath." Looking back at the French Revolution in 1802, he believed it had "clarified our ideas."

We saw that . . . the institutions of antiquity are endowed with a magic power, which no power of the intellect is capable of replacing; that the

---

* In English in *Karamzin's Memoir on Ancient and Modern Russia*, ed. and trans. Richard Pipes (Cambridge, Mass., 1959), with good Introduction.

correction of the defects found in civil societies must be left to the force of time, and to the good will of legitimate governments.[16]

By 1810 he believed that the Revolution had "cured Europe of the dreams of civil freedom and equality." [17]

Thus, in official circles, the reactionaries criticized the conservative reformers, and Alexander moved gradually to the right while those who desired basic changes were driven underground. These men, themselves already conservative by the standards of western Europe, will appear in the next chapter as the Decembrists.

Speranski himself was recalled to membership in the Imperial Soviet in 1821, raising false hopes that Alexander had recovered his reforming mood. From 1825 until its completion in 1833 he worked on one of his early projects, the codification of the laws. His great *Complete Collection of Laws*, reprinting everything from early times to the death of Alexander, was, if not a model of historical scholarship, a worthy monument of his organizational and administrative skill.

Two years later he was made legal tutor to the crown prince who became Alexander II, the "tsar-liberator." In this capacity he tried to impart to his pupil some general principles of government. Despite his exile and the fate of his plans, he retained his belief in the efficacy of enlightened despotism. Following Constant, he imagined that the tsar could be an impartial arbiter above the conflicts of political forces.* The tsar's power must be based on justice, and "because justice itself is unbounded, so the authority based on it also is unbounded." He argued that "fundamental laws" exist in every state; they underlie the constitution, and "can act even without being written." A charter, therefore, was unnecessary. The goal of the state lay not in the "material advantages of certain classes," but rather "in all people gradually moving

---

* It is possible, but not probable, that Speranski may have seen in Constant's theory of "royal power" a solution to the problem of the tsar's unlimited power different from that of Montesquieu. Since there was still no independent foundation upon which to rest a power that could challenge the tsar, there was no real basis for the system of checks and balances. If, however, the tsar could be persuaded to stand apart from the daily routine, as an impartial arbiter, intervening only when the regular organs of government failed, he might, as improved efficiency and clarification of functions reduced the frequency of failure, gradually be exalted, so to speak, right out of the government. This solution, while unrealistic to Western minds, had already been the means whereby the great powers of the Mohammedan caliph and the Japanese emperor had passed in practice to the sultans and the shoguns, leaving the former ruler in each case as much a figurehead as the British king became through the operation of constitutional limitations.

toward good, toward moral perfection." The former was a matter of interests that could be weighed by reason; the latter was a matter of conscience, not amenable to rational calculation. Although of lowly origin, Speranski defended for the aristocracy both a right to property and a right to participate in the government, while "for the people only the first is necessary." He disparaged elections, democracy, and independent legislative bodies, which, he said, "bred new desires, and, without providing any material blessing, have strengthened the dreaming of freedom." [18]

There is no way to estimate what influence Speranski may have had on the crown prince, but it was clearly a conservative one. Nicholas I would have tolerated no other.

In Speranski were combined three types of thought that were shortly to be differentiated among three mutually hostile groups. In his desire for the rule of law, his dynamic efforts at reform, and his interests in sciences and languages, he thought like the later Westerners. In his moralizing and mysticism, his organic conception of the state, his faith in public opinion, and his admiration for Schelling, he anticipated the Slavophils. And in his confidence in administrative solutions to all problems, his preference for centralization, and his bureaucratic isolation from society, he was at one with the official nationalists. His mind was analytical but not deep, mystical but not insightful, yet he stood above his generation of Russians and gave his country a strong stimulus toward modernization.

From the time of Catherine increasing numbers of the intelligentsia looked for guidance to the experience of western Europe, and ideas current in the West exerted, with decreasing delay, their influences in Russia. But the service classes, to whom intellectual pursuits were so long confined, acted with bureaucratic insight as selective filters, admitting to Russia conservative ideas more readily than radical ones. As theorists of the social contract Hobbes and Pufendorf were preferred to Althusius and Locke; in jurisprudence, Montesquieu and Beccaria to Helvetius and Bentham; in philosophy, Voltaire and Diderot to Hume and Rousseau. Even from a single thinker the more unsettling concepts were handicapped, distorted, or filtered out entirely. The Enlightenment, which in France mounted through a crescendo of social criticism to the Revolution, was diverted by the artistry of Catherine and Alexander into the twin channels of mild administrative reform and legal entrenchment of the autocracy.

CHAPTER XIV

Revolution from Below: The Decembrists

SCEPTICISM of Alexander spread as his reign advanced and reform became submerged in the Napoleonic wars. Especially as mysticism engrossed the tsar after 1820 did conservatism and reaction settle upon Russia and despair upon those who had retained faith in Alexander's promises.

At the same time, by taking many impressionistic young Russians to Paris in pursuit of the retreating French armies, the wars of Napoleon made the Russians more conscious than ever of their institutional backwardness. These observers were not infected so much with Jacobin ideas of the 1790's or with contemporary French radicalism as with the contrast between the autocracy and repression of their homeland and the constitutional monarchy and liberalism of the Bourbon restoration. As one of them (Pestel) later explained:

The restoration of the House of Bourbon on the throne of France, and my subsequent meditations on that event, I can call an epoch in my political opinions and conceptions and in my viewpoint, for I then began to perceive that most of the basic principles introduced by the Revolution had been preserved and recognized as beneficial under the restored monarchy, although everybody was opposed to the Revolution and I myself had always been opposed to it. From this consideration arose the opinion that, apparently, revolution is not as bad as they pretend, and it can even be very useful; I have been strengthened in this opinion by this other consideration, that the nations which have not had a revolution continue to be deprived of such advantages and institutions.[1]

I

Considering themselves good patriots, a number of guard officers returned to St. Petersburg and formed in 1816 an association, necessarily secret, to expedite such reforms as the tsar had hinted at in his youth and as he had recently mentioned in his speech at the opening of the Diet under the constitution he had just conferred upon Poland. This group, later known as the Decembrists from the date of their eventual revolt, wished to see Russia catch up with the political progress of the West. Being convinced that Alexander was moving too slowly, if at all, they undertook to act not through him but against him and to bring limited monarchy, or even a republic, into existence by their own resources.

Nearly all high aristocrats and too much influenced by the successes of the guards during the eighteenth century, they excluded from their arsenal the weapon of a mass uprising and thought in terms of an almost bloodless victory either through a palace revolution or through their strategic positions as troop commanders. "Our revolution will be similar to the Spanish revolution of 1820," another of them (Bestuzhev-Riumin) boasted. "It will not cost a single drop of blood, for it will be executed by the army alone, without the assistance of the people." [2] Even in propaganda among their own soldiers their efforts were both rare and clumsy. Although for a time beginning in 1821, under the influence of Mikhail Murav'ev, some members engaged in "educational work," they were opposed in this by the more conspiratorial members, the later Marxist combination of legal with illegal work not being developed.

Even as conspirators, however, they displayed a certain ineptness which prevented them from preparing, in the nine years of their activities, either an integrated organization or a coordinated plan for the seizure of power. They attempted through conferences to harmonize their objectives and to consolidate their membership, yet their ranks continued to include some who hoped to achieve their ends by convincing the tsar, and others who hoped to exterminate the Romanov dynasty. As time went by, military transfers separated the leaders, and difficulties of communication combined with differences of opinion to engender misunderstanding and mistrust.

II

Among the many shades of Decembrist thought two seem most characteristic and most completely developed, those of Nikita Murav'ev and Paul Pestel. The northern wing of the secret society, centering at St. Petersburg, was led from 1822 until early in 1825 by Murav'ev (not to be confused with other members of the family also involved), one of the original organizers of the movement. In the southern wing the most dynamic of the conspirators, Pestel, was the prime mover.

Already acquainted with French revolutionary ideas through his tutor, Murav'ev had fought his way to Paris before he was twenty and returned with a determination to win a constitution for Russia. He soon discovered that most of his comrades wanted less radical reforms than he, and he tried to preserve cohesion by pursuing an acceptable minimum program, whereas Pestel, even more radical, attempted to bend the wills of the others to his own pattern. When Pestel, on a visit to the capital in 1820, asked the northern group to agree to the republican form of government and, if necessary, regicide, Murav'ev was among his supporters. This episode frightened some of the participants, and when a small group of the more conservative conspirators met in Moscow the following January they decided to pretend to dissolve the society. Their ostensible aim was to free the movement of spies, but it is illustrative of the society's internal dissensions that neither Murav'ev nor Pestel was informed that the dissolution was intended as a sham. These tactics failed, however, and both men, each in his own region, soon succeeded in reviving the organization. Nevertheless the experience convinced Murav'ev of the impossibility of obtaining solid support for a radical program, and he became one of the most stubborn opponents of Pestel's extreme methods. When, therefore, in an attempt to unify the aims of the northern group, he undertook to draft a constitution for Russia, it represented not his personal goals but his judgments of the most practical compromises with his fellows.

The project of regicide was repeatedly discussed without being generally accepted, and on this rock the abstract preference for a republic foundered. Murav'ev proposed a constitutional monarchy, in federal form, in many ways similar to the plans drawn up by the tsar's advisers.* Like them he used as models the documents of western Europe and America, and such similarities were to be expected. His attitude toward the tsar, however, made his constitution fundamentally different. Although Stroganov and Speranski wrote of the people as the basis of society, in practice they accepted the sovereignty of the tsar. Murav'ev, not depending as they did on approval from the throne, clearly stated instead the sovereignty of the people and relegated the tsar to a circumscribed constitutional position as the chief executive. Another basic difference between Murav'ev and the tsar's advisers lay in his attitude toward serfdom: in the spirit of French liberalism he provided for its complete abolition.

At this point, however, the economic background of the Decembrists asserted itself and in the spirit of his landowning colleagues Murav'ev gave the former serfs no land except their garden plots. This background is evident also in his heavy property qualifications both for voting and for office holding, although he provided for equality before the law and for the formal abolition of nobility. In effect he agreed with Speranski: civil rights were necessary for all, but political rights only for the wealthy. In his constitution he stated:

Communal owners [former serfs] do not have the right each personally to participate in the election of the mayor (*tysiatski*), of national representatives or of other officials, but the whole community, in a meeting, has the right to name one elector from each 500 male inhabitants; and these electors named by communal owners vote equally with citizens, as agents of the whole community.[3]

The "citizens" themselves he divided frankly into four classes having respectively 30,000, 15,000, 2,000, and 500 rubles sterling of immovable property or twice those amounts of movable property, thus discriminating against commercial wealth and denying citizenship to those having less property. Only those in the first class could be elected as mayors, state councilmen, governors, or members of the Supreme Duma, while those in the fourth class could be jurors and could cast ballots—rights denied to noncitizens except as communal electors.†[4]

* There is some evidence that he remained personally a republican (see Anatole G. Mazour, *The First Russian Revolution, 1825* [Berkeley, 1937], p. 87).

† Not all manuscripts include the 500 rubles among the qualifications for citizenship, which may indicate disagreement within the northern group (see *Dekabristy: Otryvki iz istochnikov,* ed. Iuri G. Oksman [Moscow, 1926], p. 237).

Murav'ev has been much criticized for these property qualifications. Although they might have meant oligarchy for Russia, it should be recalled that in those days the world had few advocates of manhood suffrage and also that elsewhere, once voting has been established, the qualifications have in practice been gradually relaxed. The criticism remains valid, however, since these qualifications were extreme even by contemporary standards, and they serve to demonstrate how far these revolutionaries were from being Jacobins.

American readers of this document are frequently amazed at how closely it follows, in places, the provisions and even the order of ideas in their own constitution. Murav'ev's federalism, based on Montesquieu's reasoning, was the most genuine that Russia had seen.

Nonpopulous nations ordinarily fall prey to neighbors, and do not enjoy independence. Populous nations enjoy external independence but usually suffer from internal persecution, and in the hands of a despot are instruments of persecution and the ruin of neighboring nations. The expanse of territory, a large army, prevent some from being free; those who do not have these difficulties suffer from their impotence. A *federal* or *union government* alone has resolved this problem, has satisfied all conditions and reconciled the *greatness of a nation with the freedom of citizens.*[5]

Created thus by his national constitution, the thirteen states (*derzhavy*) and two provinces into which he divided Russia lacked the independence of previously existing organisms, such as the states that formed the American union, but each was provided with a legislative body expected to express local peculiarities. Previous attempts at federalism like those of Speranski (if his can be so called) and Novosiltsev had been handicapped by the unity of an autocratic tsar. Novosiltsev had tried to surmount the difficulty by placing the tsar at the head not only of the central government but also of each of the lieutenancies (a revealing name), or provinces. In Murav'ev's system, with the tsar reduced to the stature of a chief executive, the problem was much easier. In another way also Murav'ev's federalism was more real than Novosiltsev's: for the latter, federalism had been a means toward greater uniformity, toward the reduction of the local autonomy enjoyed by Finland and Poland, whereas for Murav'ev it meant recognition of such local differences.

III

If Murav'ev's constitution seems much like those that were prepared for the tsar himself, the same cannot be said of the work of Pestel, who brought into the underground movement considerably more radicalism and greater definiteness of purpose. German by ancestry and education, and variously interpreted as a Napoleon or a communist, he had more advanced ideas than his generation of Russians, including his fellow conspirators. He had made an intensive study of Western theory and practice, and he displayed greater originality than any of his contemporaries in adapting this knowledge to Russian reality. Yet with this clarity and originality he combined an inflexible personality; he saw in his own opinions the quality of mathematical correctness and, therefore, defended them stubbornly—to the detriment of his colleagues' confidence in him.

On several major points Pestel differed sharply with the St. Petersburg conspirators. In the early years, while he had been stationed there, he too had accepted their goal of constitutional monarchy; later, however, he became an advocate of a "lost brigade" that would sacrifice itself to extinguish all possible claimants to the throne, as a necessary preparation for a firmly founded republic. After his arrest he explained his conversion to republicanism as stemming from the reading of the works of Destutt de Tracy and accounts of growth and prosperity in the United States, as well as from the study of Greek and Roman history. He continued:

The history of Novgorod the Great also strengthened me in the republican frame of mind. I found that in France and England constitutions are only veils, in no way prohibiting the ministry in England and the king in France from doing everything that they wish, and in this respect I preferred autocracy to such a constitution, for in an autocratic government, I reasoned, the unlimitedness of power is openly visible to all, while in constitutional monarchies there also exists unlimitedness, although it acts more slowly, but as a consequence it cannot correct anything harmful so quickly. As concerns two Houses [of Parliament], they exist only as a veil.

It seemed to me that the major trend of the present century is the struggle between the popular masses and aristocracy of any kind, whether based on riches or on inherited rights. I judged that these aristocracies are making themselves stronger than the monarch himself, as in England, and that they are the major obstacle to national prosperity and in addition can be eliminated only by a republican form of state.[6]

Another matter which divided the conspirators, and which led some of the northern members to suspect Pestel of Napoleonic ambition, was his conviction of the necessity for a lengthy transition period with a dictatorship patterned on the French Directory of 1795. This idea immediately brings to mind the "dictatorship of the proletariat" by which Lenin later planned to bridge a similar transition from capitalism to socialism; but whereas Lenin, following Marx, thought primarily, before the seizure of power at least, of a class weapon against counter-revolution, Pestel saw his "provisional supreme government" as a machine which would construct the new republic. He therefore wrote a book of instructions for its guidance, borrowing the old title of Iaroslav's code of laws, *Russkaia Pravda—Russian Justice*. In its preface, doubting Murav'ev's plan for an immediately elected *veche* to proclaim a new constitution and write a new code, he explained:

All the events that have occurred in Europe in the last half century demonstrate that nations carried away with the possibilities of sudden action, and repudiating gradualness in introducing governmental reorganization, have fallen into most terrible calamities and again were subjected to the yoke of absolutism and lawlessness.[7]

The size of the country and the great number of needed changes required, in his opinion, "a multitude of preparatory and transitional measures" that could be carried out only by a new provisional government. This government could not be representative because "the bases of a representative supreme system do not exist in Russia." Yet a guarantee was needed that the government would "act only for the welfare of Russia and for every possible improvement." The publication of *Russian Justice*, "in the form of an instruction to the Supreme Government," would, he believed, provide such a guarantee.[8] This work was not conceived as a blueprint either for the future government or for the provisional one, but rather as an exposition of principles that the latter should follow and that public opinion could use as a measure of its performance.

A third major difference between Pestel and the men of the north lay in the attention that he gave to the social and economic needs of Russia. Seeing the twin sources of her poverty and backwardness in the aristocracy and the autocracy, he hoped to destroy both, root and branch. "The rich will always exist and this is very good, but it is not necessary to add to riches still other political rights and privileges to the exclusion of the poor." The provisional government must, therefore, establish a representative system in which the voters could disregard "every shadow of the aristocratic order," whether based on birth or on wealth. It followed that "the institution of classes must immediately be destroyed, that all people in the state must belong only to one class, [the class] called citizens, and that all citizens in the state must have the same rights and all be equal before the law." [9]

From the nobility he wished to take not only their serfs and their privileges but also, gradually, most of their land. His solution to the land problem, which shows the influence of the Western socialism of Robert Owen and Saint-Simon, he presented in a detail indicative of the importance he attached to it.

Like Locke, he began with basic principles, but he found contradictory two theories that Locke had tried to reconcile—one, that God had given the earth to men in common to nourish them, and that, therefore, no man could be excluded from the soil, and the other, that labor is the source of property, so that he who tills the land has an exclusive right of ownership of it. To Pestel both theories had merit and both had weaknesses. They must be properly combined.

Having established the possibility for each man to enjoy the necessities of life, without subjecting himself for their acquisition to dependence on others, [but] only then, there should be given a guarantee of and complete freedom in acquisition and preservation of wealth.[10]

This could be done by "dividing the lands of each *volost*, by types, into two halves." One half would be owned in common, could neither be sold nor mortgaged, and would provide the necessities of life for all. The other half would be owned by individuals (or by the Treasury pending private purchase), with full freedom to buy and sell, and would provide wealth as a reward for extra effort.[11] The development of a proletariat like that of the urbanized West would be permanently avoided, since wages could never fall below the level at which the workmen would prefer to return to the soil, for every Russian was always entitled to his share of the public land.*

* By these principles, the provision of necessities for all people, which always came first with Pestel, might, as population increased, require more than half of the land, and common land might intrude upon private land.

Seemingly the most radical and schematic of his proposals, this plan rested, none the less, upon an ancient Russian agricultural practice which, on many estates, divided the land into a part that the serfs tilled for the landlord and another that they tilled for themselves.

If at first glance the introduction of such an arrangement seems to present great difficulties, it should be remembered that this arrangement could meet great obstacles in any other state, but not in Russia, where popular ideas lean very much towards it and where from ancient times one has been accustomed to a similar division of land into two parts.[12]

Moreover, the common ownership and annual redistributions included in his plan were already in operation in the peasant community, the mir or *obshchina*, in which both Westerners and Slavophils were later to see such virtue, but which Pestel considered too small a unit. By linking existing village practices with his ideals of social justice he laid the foundation for the radical tradition of idealization of the peasant and his mir, and for the later doctrine of Russia's peculiar path to socialism.

Yet Pestel was no physiocrat, no Jefferson hating the cities as festering sores on the body politic:

Factories open a new source of wealth independent of land ownership, a source of wealth which makes the artist a citizen of the world and spreads the spirit of independence and freedom. An agricultural economy, on the contrary, imposes the most exacting principles of private property and inequality and protects slavery.[13]

Following Adam Smith and his school, he hoped to achieve a diversified economy through *laissez faire*.[14]

His suggestions on serfdom also contain an economic element, and in addition give an indication of how he expected the provisional government to proceed. Finding serfdom "a shameful thing, against humanity, against natural law, against the holy Christian faith," he was emphatic that "slavery must be decisively destroyed and the nobility must immutably, eternally renounce the infamous privilege of owning other people"; yet he did not, as Murav'ev did, insist upon immediate abolition. Proceeding gradually and cautiously, the provisional government "must call for projects from assemblies of literate nobles and take measures accordingly," being guided by these three rules:

(1) liberation of the peasants from slavery must not deprive the nobles of the income received from their estates; (2) this liberation must not bring

agitation and disorders to the state, for which reason the supreme government is obliged to use merciless severity against any disturbers of the peace; (3) this liberation must bring the peasants a better position than at present, and not grant them sham freedom.[15]

In this a certain modesty is apparent in Pestel's character. He did not believe that he had all problems solved or that a *coup d'état* would solve them. Even his provisional dictatorship might not be adequate, and the old search for wisdom led him, much as he disliked them, to the nobility.*

Modesty also lies behind the absence from the *Russian Justice* of a structural pattern for the future republican government. Pestel had ideas on the subject but he apparently never thought them final enough to complete that section of the book. He was persuaded to dictate them in 1825 to representatives of the United Slavs, a less aristocratic secret society for whose support he was negotiating, and from that skeleton account, which leaves many things unclear, it seems that he advocated three major organs of government: (1) a National *Veche*, a unicameral legislature, popularly elected for five year terms, one fifth of the members being replaced each year in the manner of the rotation in the United States Senate; (2) a Directorate (*Derzhavnaia Duma*), an executive of five members, similarly rotating, elected by the National *Veche* from candidates proposed by the provinces; and (3) a Supreme Sobor of 120 members similarly nominated and elected, but for life terms, having "supreme guardian powers." This last body, which he had adopted from Destutt de Tracy, was not a third judicial branch but was intended to check the other two.† Its members, called boyars, were excluded from other governmental posts, and were asked to pass upon all laws of the National *Veche*, but not as a second chamber: "The Sobor does not consider the substance of the matter, but only examines the form so that it is completely legal." [16]

* When emancipation was finally undertaken, under Alexander II, assemblies and committees of provincial nobles were asked to present proposals and to consider the program proposed by the bureaucracy.

† Antoine Destutt de Tracy saw the French Senate of 1799 as the prototype of his "conservative body" although other examples were numerous, reaching back to the "nocturnal council" of Plato's *Laws* (Bk. 12) and the more ancient tribunal of the Areopagus. He, however, hedged the body about with restrictions that Pestel did not copy: it could suspend a law only if the law was challenged by the executive, or an executive act only when challenged by the legislature, and such suspensions were subject to a type of popular referendum (*A Commentary and Review of Montesquieu's Spirit of Laws* [Philadelphia, 1811], pp. 136–140).

There was in Pestel an element of the censorious, which caused him to include this Supreme Sobor in his scheme, and which also appeared in his prohibiting private societies with definite objectives and in his defense of a secret police for their detection. He reasoned that if such societies were open and aboveboard they were useless, "because they can concern themselves only with subjects which enter into the sphere of action of the government"; on the other hand, if secret, they were harmful, for *"Russian Justice* not only does not compel the hiding of anything good and useful, but on the contrary even provides all means for its introduction and promulgation by legal order and invites each and all benevolently and amicably to announce such matters and items." [17] So stunted was the development of private initiative in Russia and so customary the dependence upon central governmental action, supported by the political police, that even the most adamant enemies of the existing government still thought in those terms.

As has been said, these ideas remained largely individual, the Decembrists as a whole never agreeing upon either methods or aims. Nevertheless, the end of Alexander's reign in November 1825, while his brothers, Constantine and Nicholas, each bowed to the other, seemed to them too good an opportunity to be missed—especially in view of the uncertainty of the succession. But the confident audacity that might have meant success was replaced at the critical juncture by an atmosphere of pessimism. The poet Ryleev, then leader of the northern wing, expressed it well: "I am certain that we will perish, but the example will remain. Let us offer ourselves as a holocaust for the future liberty of the fatherland." [18] In the south the atmosphere was even worse: betrayal brought police scrutiny, and on December 13 Pestel was arrested. On the fourteenth, the day set for the oath to Nicholas, most of the conspirators in St. Petersburg came with their troops to the Senate Square, insisting upon Constantine. Their elected commander, Prince Trubetskoi, failed to appear, however, and they huddled without leadership until the cannon of Nicholas dispersed them.

This pitiful showing in action was not permitted to end their influence. By pursuing them with a fanatical inquisition (teaching Russia how to conduct a sham trial), by hanging five of them (including Pestel and Ryleev), and by exiling more than a hundred to Siberia, Nicholas despoiled Russia of a generation of its most energetic and public-spirited citizens and set the reactionary tone of his thirty-year reign. At the same time he enormously magnified the importance of the

Decembrists, gave the inspiration of martyrdom to all future Russian radicals, and set an indestructible barrier between the government and the rising generation of intellectuals. The new tsar had interrogated the conspirators personally, but how little he understood is shown by his manifesto of July 13, 1826:

> The thundercloud of revolt rose upon the horizon only to cause the design of rebellion to be extinguished forever. This design was in harmony neither with the character nor with the feelings of the Russian nation. Entertained by a handful of vile criminals, it infected their immediate associates . . . but in the course of ten years of criminal efforts it never penetrated, it never could penetrate, any farther. The heart of Russia has ever been, and will ever be, inaccessible to its poison. . . .
>
> It is not by means of insolent and impracticable projects, which are ever destructive, but it is from above, that national institutions are gradually improved, defects remedied, and abuses reformed.[19]

On the contrary the era of radicalism was only beginning, and the "vile criminals" came to be idealized far beyond their not inconsiderable merits. The reasons for their failure were not assessed equally by all, but their ideas and their methods were diligently studied by succeeding generations of revolutionaries who sought to avoid their errors. Their narrow base, their discounting of the masses as a possible political force, was abandoned in favor of the opposite extreme, and their successors came to expect more sympathy and support than the people were prepared to give—a tendency which plagued the radical movement until Trotsky and then Lenin reverted to another narrow base. Similarly, their unresolved divergences of viewpoint, the retention in their ranks of irreconcilable opinions, may account in part for the vehemence of doctrinal controversy which has characterized Russian radicalism. Even their Draconian punishment, an enduring example of the inhumanity of the autocracy, contributed to the conviction of some that inhuman means were justified in a war against the government and thus to the prominence of terrorism.

PART FIVE

The Roads to 1917

CHAPTER XV

The Official Ideology

THE sparks of rebellion struck by the Decembrists having been stamped out with gallows and exile, Russia settled down to the censorship and repression that characterized the reign of Nicholas. Untrained for the throne, and having a pedestrian yet conscientious military mind, the new tsar saw as his primary duty a defense of his nation against the subversive democratic notions that had caused and were still causing so much trouble in western Europe.

The regime of Nicholas was the result of his own narrow interests and military education, but it was also a part of the general reaction to the French revolution and Napoleon, prolonged and intensified against the Decembrists. The universal intellectual community, in which Catherine and Alexander had dabbled, was replaced by romantic nationalism, strengthened and rendered complacent by the victory over Napoleon. Both at home and abroad the answer to revolution was believed to be repression—repression not only of subversive activities but also of ideas. This meant egregious proliferation of censorship and the secret police, and tight control of education.

I

In 1833 Nicholas appointed as Minister of Education the scholarly Count Sergei Uvarov (1786–1855), who held that office for sixteen years and who distilled the essence of the regime into a three-word formula that was widely circulated and came to incorporate the whole atmosphere and policy of official Russia: Orthodoxy, Autocracy, Nationality. In his first instruction to the officials and educators under him he wrote:

Our general duty consists in this, that public education, in harmony with the high purpose of the August Sovereign, be conducted in the united spirit of Orthodoxy, Autocracy and nationality (*narodnost*). I am sure that each professor and tutor, permeated with the same sentiment of devotion to the Throne and the Fatherland, will exert every effort to make himself a worthy instrument of the government.[1]

These terms were almost indefinable, but in describing them all the resources of the obsequious and patriotic imagination could be displayed.

The supporters of Nicholas joined the three concepts tightly together. The popular journalist Faddei Bulgarin found the hand of Providence behind the creation of autocracy by Vladimir and Iaroslav, and saw the introduction of Orthodox Christianity as the essential step in the creation of the Russian state and nationality by those early autocrats. From the beginning the three elements had been joined. What gravitation is for the planet, he effused, Orthodoxy and autocracy are for Russia: nothing else could hold the vast nation together. The literary historian Stepan Shevyrev believed that these elements were characteristic of human nature itself in Russia: "With the name of the Russian people I indivisibly unite two ideas: unconditional submissiveness to the Church and the same devotion and obedience to the sovereign." All approved aspects of the social order were said to be interrelated and were conservatively defended by their beneficiaries with the help of this troika of terms.[2]

The most ingenuity was displayed in explaining the nature and necessity of autocracy. This was done in no defensive spirit of apology but with pride and complacency. Several of these explanations had religious bases. Uvarov believed that the fall of man through Adam's sin was the "key to all history," and that the resulting wickedness of men required authoritarian rule. The novelist Nikolai Gogol repeated the ancient idea that the tsar is the image of God on earth. The poet Vasili Zhukovski refined these concepts; for him the autocracy was the highest level of human power, "the final link between the power of man and the power of God." For Gogol, it was necessary that the tsar be above the law, since law was harsh and inflexible. "Supreme grace, softening the law, is necessary, and it can come to men only in the form of absolute power. A state without an absolute monarch is an automaton." The supreme power, according to General Iakov Rostovtsev, was "the conscience of society," and its dictates should be morally as binding as the dictates of an individual's conscience. The people's will, on the other hand, was an anarchistic element in society, involving "an unavoidable struggle of different wills" and a threat to the moral order. To "protect society from destruction" some other force was necessary —the autocracy. Other arguments were derived from history. It was widely held, on the basis of Karamzin's *History* and other studies, that the founding and unification of the state would have been impossible without autocracy. Similarly, on the basis of the reigns of Peter I, Catherine II, and Alexander I, it was held that the preservation and advancement of Russia required absolute power.* The vast size of the country, as Catherine had learned from Montesquieu, made it so.[3]

These doctrines of Orthodoxy, Autocracy, and Nationality showed clearly the effects of the absence of a separation of church and state. As a recent student of the official ideology has remarked:

It is not difficult to understand why the appeal to "Orthodoxy" in the doctrine of Official Nationality has frequently been considered a gigantic fraud. Religion was used to preach obedience to the emperor, the officer, and the landlord. The government which taught meekness and charity distinguished itself by despotism and brutality. Even the Church was effectively controlled by the state and generally did its bidding.[4]

Yet these doctrines were embraced both by sycophants and by sincere believers, and they continued to influence public policy until the end of the autocracy.

They were, moreover, too subtle to bear monolithic interpretation, and it is necessary to see them as flexible and developing in spite of the rigidity of their exponents.

II

Unlike most of Nicholas' minions, Uvarov was not simply a reactionary, fighting the tide of change. He wanted to develop a national

---

* This opinion implied a corollary that made the official ideology ambivalent in its assessment of the Russian people. On the one hand, it stressed their virtues, their uniqueness, their power, and their special destiny. On the other, to prove autocracy necessary, it said that they were sinful like all mankind, that they could be governed only with the stick, and that they were "low, horrid and beastly" (N. P. Barsukov, *Zhizn i trudy M. P. Pogodina*, II [St. Petersburg, 1889], 17). Pogodin expressed both views; cf. *Rechi*, in his *Sochineniia*, III (Moscow, 1872), 388.

culture. At his appointment to the Ministry of Education he was already enjoying an enviable reputation as a classical scholar and had been since 1818 president of the Imperial Academy of Sciences. He combined adequate conservatism and obsequiousness with a conscientious commitment to his own substantial conception of Russia's role in world history.

Standing geographically between East and West, Russia was destined, he believed, not only to absorb the best of both worlds, rejecting the bad, but also to create a new, different, and higher culture of her own. He wished

to abolish the contradiction between European civilization and our needs, to relieve the younger generation of its harmful and ill-conceived taste for the superficial and the foreign, to implant in young minds a salutary respect for the national being and a deep conviction that only an adaptation of universal civilization to our national existence, to our *narodnost,* can bring advantageous results to each and all.[5]

The chief difficulty he saw as the reconciliation of old and new conceptions, "but *narodnost* implies neither a halt nor a march to the rear, and does not at all require the immobility of thought."

It did, however, require that thought be directed by the government. Like Nicholas, Uvarov was a statist by nature. Those in authority were better equipped than the general public, in his opinion, to decide what was best for Russia.

If escape from the darkness of churlish ignorance and the farthest possible advance toward the light of knowledge is necessary *for the individual,* then the solicitous participation of the government in this matter is necessary *for the public.* Only the government has all means necessary to know both the extent of world-wide progress in enlightenment and the actual needs of the Fatherland.[6]

The government was thus in a position to develop a system of education that was proper for the country, facilitating "for everyone" the acquisition of "useful" knowledge (almost, but not quite, in the narrow practical sense encouraged by Peter I) while at the same time guaranteeing that the movement of new ideas did not deviate from the prescribed channels of Orthodoxy and the existing institutions or lead to criticism of the Establishment. The freely inquiring and creative mind was not among Uvarov's objectives. All the forces of the nation should be enlivened, but always "within the limits of order and security." Independence for educational institutions, or for individual professors, was wasteful and dangerous.

Since the government knew best, the public should not participate in the decision-making process. Not only did the government claim a monopoly in policy making, but comment on policy after it was made, even favorable comment, was frowned on. After 1830 criticism, even indirect, of the acts and decisions of the government, "or of the established authorities at whatever rank," was forbidden. "Neither praise nor blame," Nicholas himself wrote, "is compatible with the dignity of the government or with the order that fortunately exists among us; one should obey and keep one's reflections to one's self." [7]

Uvarov seems to have thought of himself as an exalted pedagogue commissioned to educate Russia in his own special way. She was, as he saw her, still young and innocent with no taste, as yet, for the political tempests and tumults, renovations and revolutions of the West.

It is necessary to prolong her youth and, in the meantime, to educate her. That is my political system. . . . My work is not only to watch over education, but to preserve the spirit of this generation. If I am able to turn Russia aside for fifty years from that which the theories are preparing for her, then I fulfill my duty and I die content. That is my theory.[8]

During his tenure tutors were put into uniform and all private instruction was brought under government license. Educational policy was also used to keep the people in their proper places, to prevent, so far as possible, the development of declassed individuals (*rasnochintsy*), such over-educated plebeians as Pogodin and Belinski. "Diversity in the needs of the various estates of people and different conditions inevitably lead to appropriate delimitation of subjects of study among them." [9] Lip service was given to the ideal of a system of education that would provide each man with the knowledge needed for his station in life, but the maintenance of class lines seemed more important than the development of the nation's intellectual resources.

As might be expected, in the secret discussions on the emancipation of the serfs, a subject on which Nicholas was equivocal, Uvarov's weight was always thrown against it. "Political religion," he said, "has its inviolable dogmas, just like Christian religion; for us they are: autocracy and serfdom." The two were inextricably bound together, in his opinion, and would stand or fall together. The gentry would require some compensation if the serfs were freed, and they would seek it at the expense of the power of the autocrat. Serfdom was "a tree that has spread its roots widely: it shelters both the Church and the Throne." [10]

Even so, however, Uvarov was not reactionary enough. He wanted obedient citizens, but he also wanted them educated and able to create within the limits he imposed. Nicholas, on the other hand, was satisfied with obedience alone.

III

A distinction is needed, in analyzing the proponents of the official ideology, between those, such as Uvarov, who placed greater stress on the dynasty, the autocracy, the government and its objectives, and those, on the other hand, who stressed *narodnost*, the special qualities and mission of the Russian nation. To the former, Orthodoxy and Nationality in the official formula tended to be subordinate to Autocracy. In their conceptions of nationality, the special characteristic of the Russian people thought most praiseworthy was submissiveness to authority. For the latter, nationality tended to be the primary member of the troika. They were much impressed by the nation's past, as presented in the histories of Shcherbatov and Karamzin. They never went so far as the Slavophils to discount the autocracy, but they frequently set the national interest, as they conceived it, ahead of the tsar's policy, as, for example, in the support of Pan-Slavism. The former were concentrated in St. Petersburg, were usually high officials, and included many, such as the Baltic Germans, who could not share the enthusiasm of the Great Russian nationalists. The latter were centered in Moscow and were mostly university professors, students, and journalists of less exalted ancestry.

The most typical example of this nationalistic type of thought was that of Mikhail Pogodin (1800–1875), who was born a serf and rose, by a combination of luck and ability, to be a professor at Moscow University. His studies in early Russian history earned him membership in the Academy of Sciences, and his journal, *The Muscovite*, brought him a large popular audience. He had great vigor, of both person and pen, and strong convictions, but he was naïve and suffered from an overbearing, tactless personality that cost him his professorship. He resigned it in a temper in 1844, expecting to be recalled, but he never was.

His heroes were Peter I and Karamzin. His adulation of the former was quite obsessional, but he criticized the latter for being insufficiently philosophical in his approach to history. From Herder and Schelling, probably indirectly through his friends, he had come to understand history as a predetermined organic unfolding and fulfillment of God's purposes. Like other organic processes, it proceeded from small beginnings by fixed principles. The job of the historian, therefore, was to discover the principles implicit in his materials.

In Russian the same word, *nachalo*, means both a principle and a source or beginning, and in his search for the principles of Russian history Pogodin went back to the beginning, to the *Primary Chronicle*. There he found the story of the invitation to Riurik (above, page 4), and from it he built his conception of the Russian state. Never doubting this doubtful tale, he based on it the most sweeping deductions. The Varangians had come to Rus' peacefully, not as conquerors, and this basic fact, he believed, showed conclusively the fundamental dissimilarity of the Slavs from the western Europeans in nature, and was the key to the great differences in their histories. For the states of the West were built by conquest and subjection, with physical and legal force; conflicts and antagonisms were built into them at the beginning and their history clearly disclosed such principles. The history and institutions of Russia, on the other hand, had evolved organically and peacefully from the indigenous population. Over the centuries this difference had been reinforced by others, so that there could be no doubt that the destiny of Russia was different from that of the West. Russia could absorb Western knowledge and technology without fear; her civilization would necessarily remain unique.

Uvarov's Orthodoxy, Autocracy, and Nationality well summarized that civilization and Pogodin endorsed it enthusiastically. Unlike his student Konstantin Aksakov and the other Slavophils, he did not interpret the government of the Varangian princes as being separate from the Slavic community. The government was an organic part of the nation. The tsar was the patriarch of his people, and Pogodin frequently expressed legal relationships in family terms, as the old interprincely treaties had done.

There it is, I shall add here, the secret of Russian history, the secret which not a single Western sage is able to comprehend. Russian history always depicts Russia as a single family in which the Sovereign is the father and the subjects the children. The father retains complete power over the children while he leaves to them full freedom. Between the father and the children there can be no suspicion, no treason. Their fate, their fortune, and their tranquility they have in common. This is true of the whole state, but also in its parts a reflection of the same law is noticed: the military commander must be the father of his soldiers, the landlord, father of his peasants. . . .[11]

It was easy for Pogodin to be an apologist for Nicholas and for Alexander II, therefore, when they, like Peter I, provided leadership for the nation. Yet in his mind the nation came first, and he was prepared to differ with the government when the interests of Russia seemed to him to demand it.

One such issue was serfdom. His own origin, coupled with his reading of history, made him an advocate of emancipation throughout the reign of Nicholas and thereafter. Less impressed than Karamzin with the role of the aristocracy in history, he thought that class distinctions and antagonisms like those of the West were not natural in Russia, and he tended, like Nicholas, to think of only one class under the tsar. Uvarov was wrong, he believed, to worry about the gentry's claims in the event of emancipation. The danger to autocracy lay elsewhere—in the injustice against which the serfs themselves might rise again as they had under Catherine. Besides, serfdom limited the resources of talent on which the state could draw. Peter had expanded these resources with his *Order of Ranks,* and his work should be extended.

A second and related point, if hardly an issue, was that of the role of public opinion. As a writer and publisher he occasionally felt the pressure of the censorship, but, more important, he thought of the ideas of the people as a part of the organic life of the nation. "Every supreme authority, even the wisest, will become still wiser through the voice of the entire people." The tsar, advised and supported by a zemski sobor, would be strengthened, not weakened, thereby.[12]

A third matter, on which Pogodin's emphasis on nationality caused him to differ with Uvarov and other dynastic supporters of the autocracy, was the policy of Russification of the other ethnic groups of the empire. He interpreted *narodnost* in terms of the Great Russian ethnic group, whereas at court the Baltic Germans were very highly regarded. Iuri Samarin, another of his Slavophil students, newly arrived in the Petersburg bureaucracy, wrote a detailed indictment of the privileges and methods of the Baltic barons, and was reprimanded for his pains by the tsar in person. Yet Pogodin was undeterred from much more extreme views. As a historian he knew that the Teutons had pushed the Slavs out of much territory. "The Slavs have lost the Oder, the Vistula, the Pregel, even the Memel; it is necessary, therefore, to secure in good time the Dvina. . . . It is necessary to Russify the Letts and the Ests at any price, and as quickly as possible." [13] Russification was thus in part a defensive policy, but it was also an expression of notions of racial superiority that easily led to expansionistic views. In his mind the colored races were inferior, so "let Europeans sit down on the thrones of the Ashantis, the Burmese, the Chinese, the Japanese, and let them introduce European usages. Then the destiny of those countries will be decided. And why should this not be done? . . . The happiness of the human race depends on it." [14] He was thus an early advocate of the imperialistic policies that led to the war with Japan.

Pogodin was an expansionist also in Europe. The authority of the empire over non-Slavic peoples was adequate ground for their Russification, and the ethnic proximity of the southern and western Slavs was justification for the extension of the authority of the empire. So again he went beyond official policy in political Pan-Slavism. Quite early he entertained wild ideas of the extension of Russia's boundaries, thinking her armies invincible and even welcoming the conflicts that would be necessary. With age and disillusionment, however, his program shrank to the creation of an ill-defined confederation. Religious differences among the Slavs he deplored and discounted, and the strife with the Poles he explained as due to the non-Slavic character of the Polish nobility. Nicholas, throughout his reign, strove to retain the friendship of Germany and Austria as his brother had done, but to Pogodin the Germanic and Hungarian peoples were the arch enemies of the Slavs, and ultimately, in the Balkan rivalries, the government came to his opinion. Thus the Pan-Slavic movement, of which he was an early exponent, contributed to the origin of the First World War and to the utter destruction of the dynasty.

Pogodin anticipated the Slavophils in his admiration for Russian national characteristics and in his Pan-Slavism. During the reign of Nicholas he was ahead of the government in seeking to end serfdom and in advocating chauvinistic policies. He thus helped to turn the thinking of subsequent reigns into new channels, both good and bad. He felt personally involved in the decisions of the government in a way that the Slavophils did not, and he was vexed and impatient with the cautious policies of Nicholas. As the repressions increased after the

European revolutions of 1848 he accused the bureaucracy of trying to make Russia "a graveyard, rotting and stinking, both physically and morally." Firm supporter though he was, he had lost sympathy with much that Nicholas stood for, and he rejoiced with the nation as Alexander II reversed the worst trends.

IV

The early years of the reign of Alexander II, like those of Alexander I and Catherine II, were years of planning for reform. The defeats of the Crimean War had demonstrated beyond all doubt the bankruptcy of Nicholas' system. Great optimism prevailed among the intelligentsia and only gradually crumbled into disillusionment as reforms were delayed, as defects were detected in the plans, and as the reformers were replaced with reactionaries. Yet, in spite of all disappointments, the "great reforms" were carried out. The judicial system was reconstructed, local government was changed, and, most important, serfdom was abolished.

Alexander himself deserves considerable credit, particularly for the emancipation, for he took the initiative ahead of his bureaucrats and protected the legislation in its final stages against the amendments of the conservatives. But his motives were not of the highest. He simply believed that it was impossible to maintain the status quo and that it was better to abolish serfdom from above than to wait for it to be overthrown from below. He collected a group of conscientious men who labored long and diligently on the details of the decrees, but none of them breathed the fire of righteous indignation as Radishchev had done. They were not guided by the natural-law doctrine of man's inalienable right to personal liberty. They shared, instead, a paternalistic attitude of protecting the security and welfare of the whole society—peasants, landowners, and the government. Whenever the welfare of the peasants or the security of the state seemed in conflict with individual freedom, freedom was restricted. The peasants remained bound to their communes by collective responsibility for taxes and fees for the redemption of their lands, enforced by a system of passports. They were required in many cases to redeem their allotted lands by continuing to work for their former owners, and in order to protect them from the landowners, they were locally organized in a way that subordinated them to the police and the bureaucracy.

As a result, the promulgation of the emancipation in February 1861 brought not great public elation but very general dissatisfaction. Then, as Alexander's reforming zeal wore away and the regime became increasingly repressive, the pendulum of public opinion swung from hope to despair and the revolutionaries set themselves to kill him. Yet throughout his reign he was able to draw to his support men of strong and independent minds. This was particularly evident among the Slavophils of what might be termed the second magnitude.

It will be noted in Chapter XVII that the leading Slavophils were not sympathetic toward the government, remaining aloof from it as a coercive monstrosity created from the misguided mind of Peter I. Their followers, however, while retaining their strong belief in Orthodoxy, Autocracy, and Nationality (as they understood those concepts), their hatred of serfdom, their tenet of an advisory role for public opinion, and their generally conservative, nonpolitical views, were close enough to the official ideology to be attracted when an opportunity came to participate in the preparation of reforms. Along with some of the liberals, such as Prince Eugene Obolenski, they became the first of the opposition groups to be drawn into the orbit of the government. The bureaucracy, after all, was the only avenue of effective influence on public policy, and these men sincerely desired to contribute what they could to their country. Iuri Samarin was one of the earliest and most energetic architects of the peasant reform. His faith in the power of autocracy to do good and his scepticism of the motives of the landed gentry were reflected in the final decrees. Prince Vladimir Cherkasski, although sceptical toward the autocracy, the bureaucracy, the gentry, and the people, nevertheless was a key participant with Samarin in giving shape to an emancipation with land. These men never lost their attitude of independence toward the government, but the opinions they arrived at so individualistically were frequently also those of the government. This was especially notable in Ivan Aksakov in contrast to the critical attitude that his brother Konstantin, whom he survived by twenty-six years, had always maintained. Ivan supported the official church's persecutions of the Raskolniki, the policy of Russification of the minorities, and the war in 1877 against Turkey. After Alexander was assassinated in 1881 he made a notable address in which he described the tsar as the father, leader, and sole representative of his people, and equated terroristic nihilism with anarchism, constitutionalism, liberalism, and Westernism.[15] It was easier thereafter for Slavophils to make their peace with the bureaucracy.

It has been seen that Pogodin was able to accept some Slavophil ideas, while still supporting the official ideology. So too were these Slavophil supporters of the government, and gradually there took place an amalgamation of some elements of the two streams of thought. The meaning of *narodnost* was modified from the old official emphasis on submissiveness so that it included more open discussion of public affairs, some popular participation in local government, and the freedom of the serfs, as well as Pan-Slavism and Russification—all ideas that the later Slavophils could support. As soon as the autocracy began to invite participation by the public in the planning of reforms, it appeared to approximate the Slavophil ideal of government: concentrated executive authority guided by public opinion. The heirs of Peter came more and more to be also the heirs of Mikhail and the Riurikides, if not of the ancient *veche*. And in religious thought as well, where the early Slavophils had searched for truth as a criterion for the reform of the existing church, their followers sought, instead, to achieve organic unity, harmony, and strength (which they had also desired) by voluntary adherence to the visible Orthodox Church as itself the standard of truth. The natural harmony of church and state, the old *symphonia*, another ideal of the early Slavophils, became to their successors as to Pogodin an acceptance of the official state church, and therefore of the uncanonical reforms of Peter I.

At the end of that line of development stood Pobedonostsev, for a quarter of a century the most influential man in Russia.

V

Of a priestly and academic family, Konstantin Pobedonostsev (1827–1907) was born in Moscow and later taught at Moscow University, but he studied law in St. Petersburg and spent most of his life there, thus personally linking the "capital of the Slavophils" with the capital of the bureaucracy. He earned a reputation as a legal scholar with a three-volume work on Russian civil law, and helped with the judicial reform of 1864. He gained an appointment as one of the tutors to the tsar's eldest son, who died in 1865, and then to his second son, who became Alexander III, over whom frankness and an unusual lack of personal ambition won him extraordinary influence.

Even under Alexander II his advancement was rapid. As the tsar's thirst for reform was quenched, the temperament of the crown prince's tutor kept pace. He was appointed to the Imperial Soviet in 1872 and as Procurator (secular head) of the Holy Synod in 1880, a post he held until 1905. His influence was not dominant, however, until in 1881 the bomb of Grinevitski precipitated his imperial pupil to the throne.

It happened that Alexander II had just approved a program, proposed by Loris-Melikov, that would permit some advisory participation in the government by invited exponents of public opinion—to some, a promising reversal of the reactionary trend. To the chagrin of the close collaborators of the dead tsar, Pobedonostsev persuaded Alexander III to reject all such programs in his accession manifesto:

In the midst of our profound sadness we hear God's voice which commands us to enter upon the task of government with courage, to put trust in divine Providence, in the efficacy and the truth of absolute power, which we are called upon to exercise for the good of the people and to guard against all encroachment. Let the hearts of our faithful subjects, dejected by the horrible shock, recover hence their courage, [and let] all those who love their native land and the representatives of hereditary power lift up their heads! [16]

Thus the hopes of the bureaucrats around Alexander II, as well as those of the terrorists of The People's Will who had killed him, were dashed on a rock that was to prove more reactionary than Nicholas I.

His long association with royalty had congealed in Pobedonostsev's mind a conviction that the preservation of the absolute monarchy was both the last hope of Russia and his own mission in life. Thus, the concessions to the public on which Loris-Melikov had been working, while far from the constitutional monarchy that some defenders of tsarism would picture them, seemed to Pobedonostsev dangerous enough and so became his first target. Within fifteen months he had brought about their rescission and the downfall of their major protagonists. The reactionary character of the new reign became apparent, and although Pobedonostsev's opinions did not always prevail with the tsar, he continued to stand, a dark shadow behind the throne, earning an international reputation as the prime mover of the policies of Russification, clerical control of education, compulsory conversion to Orthodoxy, and the persecution of all dissenters. Though his aims were narrow, his abilities were great, as is attested by the survival of his power, only slightly impaired, for years after the accession of Nicholas II.

His policies were not the expressions of blind reaction. Like Machiavelli and Burke, he had seen enough of politics in high places to dispel any illusions about the natural goodness of men or the reliability of their mental processes. To the restlessness of the ancient Greek mind he traced the rationalism of western Europe, and to the latter, all the strife of classes and nations which had exhausted Europe's cultural advance. Even the fairest political flowers of that civilization—such as freedom of religion and of the press, parliamentary government, and the sovereignty of the people—he believed to be disruptive delusions of reason, fundamentally irreconcilable both with human nature and with true religion. It was madness to think of importing them into Holy Russia, where the symbolism and pageantry of Orthodoxy produced a much higher degree of order and contentment. Reason was a source, not a solvent, of problems, both for the nation and for the individual.

The principle of popular sovereignty he thought to be "among the falsest of political principles." From it was derived the theory of "parliamentarism," which he expounded to show the impossibility of conforming to it in practice. The old Burkean ideals of representation had been abandoned "under the influence of that fatal delusion about the great value of public opinion, as enlightened by the periodical Press." Thenceforth it was necessary, according to the theory, for the representative and the minister to "abdicate their personalities," to understand precisely the will of the majority who elected them, and to execute that will conscientiously—without regard to their own interests and opinions. In practice, however, even this perverted ideal of a specific party mandate broke down under the influence of organized minorities and the undesirable personality traits favored by the elective process. Instead, even in the classic countries of parliamentary government,

the elections in no way express the will of the electors. The popular representatives are in no way restricted by the opinions of their constituents, but are guided by their own views and considerations, modified by the tactics of their opponents. In reality, ministers are autocratic, and they rule, rather than are ruled by, Parliament. They attain power, and lose power, not by virtue of the will of the people, but through immense personal influence, or the influence of a strong party. . . . The people loses all importance for its representative, until the time arrives when it is to be played upon again; then false and flattering and lying phrases are lavished as before; some are suborned by bribery, others terrified by threats—the long chain of manoeuvres spun which forms an invariable factor of Parliamentarism.[17]

The root concept from which all Pobedonostsev's ideas on public policy were derived was that of the organic interdependence of the state and the church. "However powerful the State may be, its power is based alone upon identity of religious profession with the people; the faith of the people sustains it; when discord once appears to weaken this identity, its foundations are sapped, its power dissolves away." [18] The truths of religion being known and unchanging, the state must, to preserve itself, enforce general conformity to them. Institutions being well adjusted to such truths, the state must be wary of all changes that might subject these adjustments to strain. Moreover, the state should actively promote the Orthodox faith and protect the people against secularism in education, to save their souls and to strengthen its own position.

As lay head of the Synod, the religious group that Peter I had created to replace the patriarch, Pobedonostsev integrated its management so thoroughly into the government that it was in practice a ministry for church affairs. He attacked the doctrine of the separation of church and state as an expression of "religious indifferentism" or even contempt for religion. This doctrine, he believed, had long been a source of conflict in the West because no sincere church could agree to it.

Thus the free State may decree that the free Church concerns it not; but the free Church, if it be truly founded on faith, will not accept this proposition, and will not endure indifferent relations to the free State. The Church cannot abdicate its influence on civil and social life . . . nor can such relations be tolerated if the Church is not to abjure its duties and abandon its divine mission. . . . The position in any case is an abnormal one, which must lead either to the predominance of the Church over the apparently dominant State, or to revolution.*[19]

Denying in his administration as in his writing both the possibility and the value of separation, he succeeded in adjusting political and religious

* He pointed to the growing strength of the Roman Catholic Church in the United States as an illustration of his thesis.

policy so completely, each to the other, that in the popular imagination Orthodoxy became a part of autocracy, and all the shortcomings of the latter were reflected upon the Church. While both stood they might support each other, but when revolution overcame the one, the other not only had little independent strength to resist but had, through Pobedonostsev's policies, become widely identified as a bulwark of the political regime.

VI

If Pobedonostsev represented the more religious and reactionary aspect of the official ideology toward the end of the autocracy, Count Sergei Witte (1849–1915) as clearly represented its more practical and optimistic aspect. Indeed, Witte is usually adduced by those who wish to show how rapidly Russia was becoming free and modern before the revolutionaries spoiled it all.

Although of Baltic German ancestry, Witte was born and grew up in Tiflis, where his father and maternal grandfather were colonial administrators, and in Odessa, where he studied mathematics at the university. He was not broadly cultured in the German tradition, but this handicap, which he felt keenly, was offset by his ability and high family connections. He began his career in 1871 as a railway administrator, and from a solid base in that important industry, under both public and private ownership, he rose to be Minister of Finance from 1892 to 1903 and Premier in 1905 to cope with the revolution.

His power was greatest as Minister of Finance; in this position he did much to promote the industrialization of Russia by such methods as raising import duties, introducing the gold standard, borrowing capital abroad, and building railroads, including the trans-Siberian. It is not necessary to describe or evaluate the "Witte system" but rather to look at the ideas and attitudes from which it arose.

Because he worked hand in glove with the capitalists and financial manipulators it is frequently thought that Witte believed in free-enterprise economics and the virtues of individual initiative. His commitment, however, was not to capitalism but to industrialization, and this as a means not to the welfare of the people but to the preservation of the autocratic system against foreign pressures and the threat of revolution.

In his early writings, in spite of his administrative experience, he took a shallow moralistic approach to economic problems. The teachings of Christianity should, he thought, enable the upper classes to set an example of thrift, industry, and social justice. As for the people, "A wide distribution of property is the best guarantee against militant socialism." [20]

By 1885, in an article in the Slavophil journal *Rus'*, his later views began to emerge, still mixed with religious notions. He criticized Adam Smith as a prime source of Western economic errors. "This remarkable thinker considered wealth from an entirely abstract point of view, without regard to the people for whom wealth is produced." Like most of the intelligentsia, he sharply attacked the evils that the industrial revolution had brought to the West. He wrote of "factory automatons, unhappy slaves of capital and of the machine," yet he thought Russia had already embarked upon the course of industrialization. The problem, as he saw it, was to prevent this development from disrupting the traditional way of life. Already a centralizer, he believed this prevention to be a responsibility of the government. "The government should especially insist upon the satisfaction of the spiritual needs of the workers" by requiring time off for church ceremonies and the like, which he thought would keep their minds free from Western materialistic and socialistic ideas. [21]

Witte's mature views, however, were more dynamically paternalistic. They were derived from the German economist Friedrich List, on whom he published a book in 1889. List is well known as an advocate of protective tariffs as a means of developing industry in agricultural countries. His *National System of Political Economy* (1841) presented a series of stages of development and stressed the political dangers of economic backwardness. He criticized the materialism and "disorganizing individualism" of the classical economists, who did not "show how to bring into activity and to give value to the natural power at the disposition of a whole people, how to conduct a poor or feeble nation to prosperity and power." He argued that, in the current period, the nation and not the firm was the significant economic unit—a line of thought that led him to the conclusion that planned cooperation among producers within a nation, and not unregulated competition, was the path to economic progress.

Individuals would be in vain laborious, economical, ingenious, enterprising, intelligent, and moral, without a national unity, without a division of labor and a co-operation of productive power. A nation cannot otherwise attain to a high degree of prosperity and power, nor maintain itself in the permanent possession of its intellectual, social, and material riches.[22]

He also emphasized the social, political, and environmental peculiarities that differentiated nations and conditioned their development.

To Witte, List's reasoning was most convincing. It pointed up the predicament of Russia, an agricultural country confronted with industrialized enemies. National survival required that it too industrialize, and he set himself, in spite of great opposition from the agrarian interests, to bring it about. In his first budget report he restated the responsibility of the government to direct the national economy: "In the conceptions of the Russian people, from time immemorial, the conviction is profoundly rooted that to the Tsarist Power belongs the initiative in everything touching the welfare and the needs of the people." He therefore proposed to "give reasonable assistance to the development of the productive forces of the country" and to kindle "a healthy spirit of enterprise." [23] Clearly he had no objection, as had many intellectuals, to capitalistic initiative, but his attitude was ambivalent. He wanted to stimulate business initiative among the people, but he also led them with an energetic bureaucratic paternalism. Like Uvarov in regard to education, he did not believe that the people could develop the economy without government participation. Aiming at a well-integrated system of private and public enterprises, he used public funds to build, buy, and operate banks, railroads, mines, and factories.*

He was even more sceptical toward local initiative in government. From his youth he had a strong emotional attachment for the autocracy, and as a bureaucrat he believed strongly in centralization. Throughout Russian history, he thought, the central government had taken the lead in progressive reforms. Yet he professed great respect for public opinion, which government could disregard only at its peril. All revolutions, he said, are the result of failure of the government to satisfy in time the needs and demands of the people. He held, as the Slavophils

---

* Theodore H. Von Laue, a close student of Witte, sees his system as suffering from "a profound contradiction" because, "while he tried his best to recreate the conditions of Western capitalism in Russia, he made the capitalists the servants of the state" (*Sergei Witte and the Industrialization of Russia* [New York, 1963], pp. 303–305). It was, however, a political system, and not an economic ideology, that interested Witte and that he tried to save. He bought railways until, by the close of his ministry, the government owned almost three quarters of the total.

had done, that freedom of thought, speech, and social initiative would strengthen the autocracy. He thought, however, of the public's ideas being filtered through St. Petersburg, and not of local autonomy.

One reason for Witte's attitude, of course, was that local spokesmen were generally agrarian critics of his high tariff policy, which raised their costs substantially. As his attention was finally drawn by crop shortages to the perennial backwardness of agriculture, he began to see more clearly than the Slavophil or the socialist defenders of the rural commune (or the Marxists later, it might be added) the inherent contradiction between the conception of "national coöperation of productive powers" directed from the center by the autocracy and the conception of a nation of farmers freely cooperating through their communes (or collective farms). He preferred the former, and desired to convert the communal lands into individually owned farms, but was unable to secure this change.* Again his motives were mixed. He wished to free the energetic kulaks from the weight of their less ambitious neighbors, but perhaps even more he wished to increase the exportable surplus of grain.

Witte had no doctrinaire belief in private enterprise and no desire to Westernize Russia. He did not see industrialization as requiring, or even leading to, any drastic remolding of political institutions on Western models. Pobedonostsev, whose insight was much deeper, believed industry itself to be subversive of the old way of life and for that reason opposed Witte with all his strength. The two men, nevertheless, had great personal respect for each other and important areas of agreement. Both were conservatives. Both were devoted to Russia and its stratified social order, to Orthodoxy and the use of religion for social purposes, and to the autocracy and its preservation. Their differences were over means, not ends. Witte believed that the old could be protected only by a specific admixture of the new, namely, industrial power. Pobedonostsev, on the contrary, thought this unnecessary and dangerous; he preferred to rely on repression and obscurantism. These contradictory views illustrate the immobilizing differences within the government and the partial disintegration of the official ideology.

This ideology, with roots in the whole history of government in Russia, maintained remarkable continuity for nearly a century, down

* Stolypin achieved such a law in 1906, making it easy for a peasant to leave his commune and acquire a private title to his allotted lands. In ten years of its operation, however, less than a quarter of the peasants did so.

to 1917. Witte still took seriously Uvarov's Orthodoxy, Autocracy, and Nationality. The idea of autocracy, derived from both the Mongols and the Byzantines, had been adopted as the culmination of the élitist attitudes of the Riurikides, who had separated themselves from the people by their title of "prince," and who had destroyed the *veche* in order to eliminate the voice of the people from the government. Once this separation had been accomplished with the help of the boyars and the church, and the Mongols expelled, both the nobility and the clergy were brought to heel by Ivan's *oprichnina* and Peter's *Order of Ranks* and church statute. The Establishment thus created resembled a foreign force occupying a conquered country, continually using French to emphasize its distance from the people it ruled. On this whole course of development the marks of the Byzantine heritage of conservatism, exclusiveness, and the political uses of religion are prominent. They are typified by the twofold significance of the word Orthodoxy in Uvarov's formula. It stressed, on the one hand, the complete and final truth that supposedly underlay the society, that made change unnecessary and undesirable, and that gave a conservative, defensive quality to policy in general, from Uvarov's desire to hold back the tide to Witte's insistence on industrialization to prevent defeat. On the other hand, it displayed the symbiotic relations of church and state that justified, for example, the persecution of the schismatic sects and clerical control of elementary education, designed to produce loyal subjects, not thinking individuals. The third member of the trinity, *narodnost*, covered the national peculiarities and backwardness on which the regime rested. It was not intended to readmit the voices of the people into the governing process, yet unwittingly it gave an entree to unexpected forces. An emphasis on nationality easily led to chauvinism, Pan-Slavism, and imperialism, policies that were not conservative but dangerous, involving the nation in wars and opening the door to revolution. The ban on the expression of public opinion was lifted, in part, but no duty to seek or to be guided by the people's will was ever admitted, nor did the government ever relax its view that the autocrat and his bureaucracy must make all final decisions.

The government was not an "enlightened despotism"; knowledge was neither respected nor encouraged, and the universities were always suspect. It was not a matter of *noblesse oblige*, or even of paternalism, for little was done for the people, and that little, as in the case of the emancipation, was done in defense of privilege and not in pursuit of justice. As at Byzantium, value was placed on conservation, not on construction. For these defensive purposes the police and the censors seemed more reliable than the thinkers, and the autocracy never again reached even Uvarov's level of original thought.

It is phenomenal that a government adhering to such ideas should have lasted so long. In the perspective of this background attention can now be turned to the other, the opposing, currents of thought.

CHAPTER XVI

The Westerners

MUCH as Nicholas desired to eradicate the germs of Western thought, he could not do so. Too many books had been brought home by the traveling scholars of Peter and Catherine, and too many had been printed in Russia under Catherine and Alexander; too many men had been personally to the West as soldiers, and too many émigrés had come to Russia as tutors; and the dramas of the invasion of Napoleon and the trial of the Decembrists had stimulated too many people too deeply. The release of the nobility in 1762 from the necessity to serve the government had produced a cultural pattern by which they served a sort of apprenticeship in army or civil service and then, still young, retired in comfortable leisure to individual pursuits, sometimes intellectual. The foundation of several new universities to supplement that of Moscow, itself dating only from 1755, and the establishment of a number of periodicals, in spite of the censorship, provided employment outside the routines of administration for a growing intelligentsia, including a few members of nonnoble families. Moreover, these universities had attracted a number of professors from Germany who expounded the German idealists, particularly Schelling, Fichte, and Hegel, and thus introduced stimulating and conflicting currents into a mental atmosphere previously dominated by the French philosophers. The conditions were present, in short, which had been largely absent on previous occasions of crisis, and which were needed for an extensive development of Russian political thought.

I

The intelligentsia, aloof from the government by choice and from the people by education, looked about for a rationale, for a compass to guide their thoughts and actions. Some found it in the achievements of the West and the great task of importing and adapting them to Russia, while others found it in the peculiarities that set Russia apart from the West and in the task of developing these into a new civilization better than, as well as different from, all others. From these divergent orientations arose the two main schools of nineteenth-century thought, the Westerners and the Slavophils.

Easily distinguished thus in general terms, these schools were quite complex beneath the surface, having many points in common in spite of their basic disagreements, and also having important points of difference among the members of each. Both schools were broadly cultural, philosophic, and religious, as well as political, and both had roots deep in the history of Russia. Becoming consciously differentiated in the 1830's and 1840's, they gradually lost their cohesion during the remainder of the century.

Behind the Slavophils lay the anti-Catholicism of the twelfth-century monk who compiled the *Primary Chronicle*, the traditional thinking which created the *mestnichestvo*, the uncompromising self-reliance of Nil Sorski and of Kurbski, the conservatism of the Raskolniki who had resisted both Nikon and Peter, Shcherbatov's admiration for pre-Petrine institutions, Radishchev's confidence in public opinion and a free press, and the organic conception of society articulated by Speranski. Behind the Westerners stood Vladimir's acceptance of a new religion from the center of foreign culture, the princes' long series of foreign wives culminating in Catherine II, the opposition of Sorski and Nikon to ritualism and obscurantism in religion, Ivan's drive toward the Baltic and Peter's achievement of it, as well as his general Western orientation, Catherine's Enlightenment and Radishchev's impatience with her progress, and, most immediately, the Decembrists. From these diverse elements the Slavophils, looking to the past for the roots of Russia's uniqueness, distilled a generally conservative attitude that attributed any deficiencies of the society to ill-conceived reforms that had not evolved organically from the spirit of the people. The Westerners, on the contrary, decried the backwardness of their country, the inadequacy and slowness of reform, the unhealthy propping of outmoded institutions: they thought themselves progressives. Both were opposed to the "official nationalism" of Nicholas and of the bureaucracy as typified in Uvarov's formula, Orthodoxy, Autocracy, and Nationality.

In the contrast between Shcherbatov and Radishchev the conflict of these two schools was foreshadowed, but neither of these men clearly formulated the alternative paths of Russian development. In them, and in the following generation of Alexander's reign, admiration for Russia was blended with admiration for the West, both among the tsar's advisers and among the Decembrists. A similar blending can be seen in the writings of Peter Chaadaev (1794–1856), who belonged to the same generation.

II

A grandson of Shcherbatov, Chaadaev early lost his parents, but was given an excellent education by an aunt and an uncle, both Shcherbatovs, and entered the University of Moscow at fifteen. In his third year, however, he dropped his books to help repel Napoleon from his native city, and he served with distinction until 1821. In that year he is said to have snubbed the tsar by declining to become his personal adjutant. He then resigned from the army and immersed himself in the study of mysticism. Two years later, his health breaking, he departed for western Europe, where he stayed until 1826, forming during this time a lasting friendship with Schelling. This trip may have saved him in more ways than one, for he was a close friend of several of the leading Decembrists, and only his long absence from the country cleared him. Arrested and released upon his return to Moscow, he again secluded himself, formulating his religious and philosophical opinions under the influences of the German mystics Jung-Stilling and Eckarthausen and of the French Catholics Bonald, Ballanche, Chateaubriand, and Maistre. These opinions he set forth in a series of lengthy letters, written in 1829 and passed around among his friends for years thereafter.

In 1836 with his permission one of these letters was printed in the magazine of the Moscow Schellingians, *The Telescope*. The resulting public uproar undoubtedly surprised the author, the editor, and the censor who had approved it. Herzen, who read it while in exile in Viatka, called it "a shot resounding in the dark night, a death cry, a signal, a call for help, a herald of the dawn or a sign that dawn would never break," and concluded, "in any case one had to wake up." [1] The intelligentsia was shocked into self-consciousness by Chaadaev's black picture of Russia—past, present, and future—and excited clamor arose from both friends and enemies, ranging from enthusiasm in the radicals to indignation in the conservatives. The tsar pronounced him a raving lunatic, thus exempting him, being mad, from official punishment. For a year and more he was examined daily by a doctor, and even thereafter the publication of his writings was banned. The last effective voice in Russia of the generation of the Decembrists was thus silenced. Until his death in 1856 Chaadaev moved through the philosophic salons of Moscow, "an incarnate veto, a living protest," as Herzen described him. Among his friends of the new generation were the founders of the Slavophil movement, Ivan and Peter Kireevski, Alexis Khomiakov, and Konstantin and Ivan Aksakov, as well as the Westerners, Alexander Herzen and Timothy Granovski.

In his theories, as in his friendships, he reached across the then widening chasm separating these two schools of thought. No one was more aware than he of the differences between Russian and Western development, but unlike the Slavophils he did not find the major advantages on the side of Russia, and unlike the later Westerners he did not see Europe as a source from which to borrow, but rather as a school from which to learn. Through his absorption in religion he had an affinity for the former school, but his negation of the Russian heritage definitely excluded him from its ranks.

We [Russians], who have come into this world like illegitimate children, without ties to those who have preceded us on earth, we carry in our hearts nothing of the teachings that preceded our own existence. . . . There is with us no deep-seated development, no natural progress. . . . Recluses in the world, we have given it nothing, we have taught it nothing; we have not poured a single idea into the mass of human ideas; we have contributed in no respect to the progress of the human mind, and we have distorted all that has come to our understanding.[2]

Chaadaev's condemnation of Russia was based on his philosophy of history. The path of historical development, he believed, lay through the mutual interchange of ideas on the widest possible scale, which meant that isolation, whether that of individualism or that of nationalism, must retard progress. In the West the Roman church had provided unity and stimulated interchange, while the Russian church had held its people apart from the great stream of progress, stunting their development.

The church of Rome, however, had lost its unifying power, and Chaadaev saw clearly that the advance of the West had been obstructed by internal conflicts. As he grew older he became convinced that Russia's failure to follow Europe into that predicament, her freedom from those conflicts, her intellectual virginity, would make it possible for her to lead Europe to a solution. His became a voice of stimulation and of encouragement. "I hold the inmost conviction that we are called upon to solve most of the problems of the social order, to perfect most of the ideas that have arisen in the old societies, to pronounce upon the most momentous questions that trouble the human species." [3] Thus, more clearly than in Speranski, was sounded the messianic note that, taken up by the Slavophils, led so easily to political Pan-Slavism.

Moreover, in Chaadaev's opinion, the accomplishment of Russia's mission was facilitated by the autocracy. "It is enough that a supreme will among us speak out in order that all opinions be effaced, that all beliefs yield, that all minds be opened to the new thought offered them. . . . Formed, moulded, created by our sovereigns and by our climate, it is only by dint of submission that we have become a great people." [4] He thus expressed a hope for reform from above, a faith in the tsar that characterized most of the early Westerners—even Herzen—and made them distinctly less revolutionary than the Decembrists.

III

Lacking the aristocratic poise of Chaadaev, another social critic, Vissarion Belinski (1811–1848), a man of lowly origin, spent his short life passionately struggling with the problems that Chaadaev had raised about the condition of Russian culture and its relation to the West. Writing as a literary critic on *The Telescope, The Moscow Observer, National Notes,* and *The Contemporary,* he shaped the pattern of literary criticism as a method of analysis and criticism of society itself not otherwise permitted by the censorship. At the same time, by judging literary works in terms of their social orientation, he began the tradition of Russian criticism that still demands that writers be conscious of the social impact of their works.

At first a Schellingian of the Stankevich circle,* Belinski was led by Katkov and Bakunin to a superficial acceptance of Hegel's formula, "the rational is real, and the real is rational." From 1837 to 1840 he was carried away by this mystery, writing of the word "tsar" as "a marvelous fusion of the consciousness of the Russian people," a necessity of history.

In the tsar is our *freedom*, because from him will emerge our new civilization, our enlightenment, just as it is from him that we draw our life. . . . Unconditional submission to tsarist authority is not only useful and necessary for us, but it is the highest poetry of our lives—our nationality.[5]

Yet he was too sensitive to Russian realities to think them rational for long. Influenced by Herzen and by Feuerbach, he turned to socialism and materialism and attacked all those, like his former idol, Gogol, who defended in literature the existing conditions.

I am now at a new extreme, which is the idea of *socialism*, that has become for me the idea of ideas, . . . the alpha and omega of belief and knowledge. . . . There is no object more noble and lofty than to contribute towards its progress and development. But it is absurd to imagine that this could happen by itself, with the aid of time, without violent changes, without bloodshed. Men are so insensate that they must forcibly be led to happiness.[6]

Supremely endowed with social conscience, and unencumbered with the mysticism of Chaadaev, Belinski shook his generation of intellectuals persistently, orienting many of them toward Western ideas of progress and human dignity and sharpening the conflict between Westerners and Slavophils. His temperament was not one to construct theories, but his example of vehement concern for the downtrodden exerted lasting influence. Among the more theoretical Westerners who admired and followed him, none did more to shape nineteenth-century thought than the two who will be considered in detail—Herzen and Chernyshevski.

* On these philosophic groups see Edward J. Brown, *Stankevich and His Moscow Circle, 1830–1840* (Stanford, 1966).

IV

In the crowd that attended the mass of thanksgiving in the Kremlin for the coronation of Nicholas I was a boy of fourteen, Alexander Herzen (1812–1870). He later wrote in his memoirs that he had been thinking of the five Decembrists, "the murdered men," and that he then and there vowed to devote his life to their cause, "to the struggle with that throne, that altar, and those cannon."

The favored, though illegitimate, son of a very wealthy and Voltairean aristocrat, Herzen absorbed the beginnings of a good education from his father's and his uncle's libraries and knew three languages before he entered the University of Moscow in 1829. There he became the center of a circle of young radicals more interested in politics than were those who formed the famous philosophic circle around Stankevich. Like the latter they were influenced by the writings of Schelling, but they preferred Rousseau and the French socialists. Their enthusiasm for these subversive subjects, expressed in song, earned them arrest in 1834; and Herzen spent five years in exile in various uninspiring towns of European Russia, reading books of French and German philosophy sent by his friends, working as a government clerk, and beginning the writing career in which he gradually made his name.

He then entered the bureaucracy at the center, in St. Petersburg, but his critical tongue and pen brought him exile again, this time to Novgorod. In 1842 he was permitted to return to Moscow, where he continued to write for the leading journals until the death of his father left him a wealthy man and he determined to fight the regime of Nicholas from the freedom of western Europe. In January 1847 with a caravan of family and retainers he left Moscow; his destination was Paris, still viewed in Russia as the capital of revolution.

Quickly disillusioned by the shopkeeping atmosphere of the Paris of M. Guizot, "the unclean worship of material gain and tranquility," he went briefly to Italy, but he soon returned to observe at first hand the events following the February 1848 revolution. Paris was more alive than he had thought, but the uprising of June and the sight of the bourgeoisie again in bloody triumph turned him permanently against violent revolutions. This reaction, so different from those of Bakunin and Marx, was for years somewhat obscured by his enthusiasm for revolutionary objectives, but it ultimately separated him both from his friend Bakunin and from the younger representatives of the Russian revolution.

These experiences in Paris forced him to reassess democracy and republicanism, but they confirmed him in his inclination toward socialism. He saw that the erection of a supreme parliament, even by manhood suffrage as in the short-lived Second Republic, was not only an inadequate solution to the problems of society but even a counterfeit solution, a crushing of the individual into fixed political patterns that gave him only an illusion of freedom. "The free man can no more give up his sovereignty than his breathing; nor can he be a slave to his vote. Representation is also a monarchy, a hypocritical monarchy." [7] In Europe, the revolutions of the past had made real advancements, but they had left too much of the old centralization of authority.

The State, based upon the Roman idea of the absorption of the individual by society, of the sanctification of accidental and monopolized property, of a religion consecrating the most absolute dualism (even in the revolutionary formula, *God and the people*), can offer nothing to the Future but its carcase.[8]

Political revolution, therefore, was insufficient; it was necessary to go deeper.

Socialism takes the Republic as a path that must be traversed; the political, representative Republic is the transition between monarchy and socialism. The Republic has an ideal, has aspirations, but it is not an actuality as long as it restricts itself to the *representation* of the sovereignty of the people. Under the most favorable conditions it can be freer than a constitutional monarchy, but it can not be entirely free so long as it accepts as unalterable the bases of the existing historical social order. . . . Economic questions are extremely important, but they form only one side of the whole outlook which strives, along with the abolition of the misuse of property, to destroy on the same principle everything monarchial and religious in the courts, in government, in all social organization, and especially in the family, in the home, in conduct, and in morality.[9]

Because they shared such views Herzen much admired Blanqui and Proudhon. Like Bakunin, he formed a friendship with Proudhon and was strongly influenced by him. He supported Proudhon financially and contributed to his journals. But the Europeans in general, he suspected, had already invested so much in their revolutions that they were morally committed to the partial solutions they had won and unable to abandon these in a bid for the thorough-going solution—socialism.

Christianity has grown shallow and quietened down into the calm stony haven of the Reformation; the Revolution too has grown shallow, and sunk into the calm sandy haven of liberalism. Protestantism, a religion austere in trifles, has found the secret of reconciling the Church, which despises earthly goods, with the supremacy of commerce and profit. Liberalism, austere in political trifles, has learned even more artfully to unite a continual protest against the government with a continual submission to it.[10]

The Russians, on the contrary, as Chaadaev had said, were unencumbered by the past, were free to make the bid. "Socialism, which so definitively, so profoundly divides Europe into two enemy camps, is it not accepted by the Slavophils as by us? . . . Socialism appears to us to be the most natural syllogism of philosophy, the application of logic to the state." [11] The social question and the Russian question, therefore, were but one, and Europe might well fear Russia as she feared socialism.

The Russian question is the western side, the negative proof, the new apparition of the barbarians, scenting the death-agony, screaming their *memento mori* in the ears of the old world, and ready to put it out of the way if it will not die of its own accord. Indeed, if revolutionary socialism will not come to a conclusion with society in its decline, then Russia will make an end of it instead.[12]

Thus Herzen, the most clear-sighted of the Westerners, shared, at times, the messianic dream.

When his associations and activities were reported to St. Petersburg, the tsar demanded that Herzen return to Russia, but he rejected this demand. He was able to rescue his fortune from the confiscating grasp of Nicholas, but only with the help of James Rothschild. A part of this money Herzen dispensed to wandering radicals who appealed to him, including Bakunin, but the most effective use he made of it was the establishment in London of the first free Russian press.

In 1855, when Alexander II came to the throne, a new day seemed to dawn for Russians at home and abroad. As with Alexander I, his early actions removed some of the worst features of the preceding reign. The repression under Nicholas gave place to the hope for reform, and Herzen believed that an uncensored journal might exert influence upon the new course of events. In August appeared the first issue of the *Polar Star,* named for the old journal of the Decembrist, Ryleev, and carrying on its cover pictures of the five who were executed to inaugurate the reign of Nicholas. It proved a bit ponderous for Herzen's volatile pen, however, and two years later, with the collaboration of Ogarev, a cheaper, more frequent paper, the *Bell* (*Kolokol*), also began to be smuggled into Russia. Starved for uncensored news and comment, both liberals and radicals supported the *Bell* widely with subscriptions and with reports of events, even from within the tsar's ministries. Herzen's opinions were frequently addressed to and read by Alexander himself—and not always with disapproval, since the *Bell* rang praises for the tsar whenever he showed tendencies toward reform. The bureaucracy was its *bête noire.*

Herzen's program was short: liberation of the serfs with land, abolition of corporal punishment, and freedom of the press. For liberation even the tsar was ready, being convinced that "it would be better to abolish serfdom from above than wait till it will begin to liberate itself from below." Herzen became ecstatic when the decision for emancipation was announced in 1858 and the first of his goals seemed within sight. He saw the tsar as the only political force available for reform, and his confidence in Alexander led him to attack his fellow Westerner, Chernyshevski, who showed signs of disillusionment with the new reign. In 1859 Chernyshevski made his only trip abroad to see Herzen and to attempt to coordinate their policies, but neither would abandon his position, and in 1860 Chernyshevski lashed out with "Russia has been ruined for a hundred years by believing in the good intentions of her Tsars." To this attack, printed anonymously in the *Bell,* Herzen replied that he would not call for rebellion "so long as there remains one vestige of reasonable hope for a solution." Paris in the spring and summer of 1848 was still before his eyes.

In the atmosphere of expectation and of trepidation that accompanied the liberation of the serfs in 1861, the university students engaged in demonstrations against repressive educational policies, which caused the authorities to expel hundreds of young men. This gave Herzen the occasion to enunciate his most influential slogan—"To the people!" The debate concerning the means and conditions of the emancipation had focused attention upon the near-helpless ignorance of the masses of peasants and had aroused in many intellectuals a recognition of the need, perhaps the duty, to give these people knowledge as well as freedom. To this vague consciousness Herzen added a concrete proposal:

Where shall you go, youths, from whom knowledge has been shut off? Shall I tell you where? Give ear, for even darkness does not prevent you from listening,—from all corners of our enormous land, from the Don and the Ural, from the Volga and the Dnieper, a moan is growing, a grumbling is rising,—this is the first roar of the sea-billow, which begins to rage, pregnant with storm, after a long and tiresome calm. *V narod!* To the people!—that is your place, O exiles of knowledge. Prove . . . that out of you will emerge not clerks, but soldiers, not mercenaries, but soldiers of the Russian people! [13]

Thus was stimulated the first wave of *narodniki,** intellectuals who went to share the life of the peasants, hoping to teach them not only something of the medicine and science then so popular in the universities but also something of Western ideas of freedom and social order. Misunderstood, discouraged, many of them betrayed by the peasants and turned over to the police, the *narodniki* grew in numbers through the ensuing years and will be discussed more fully in Chapter XIX.

In 1861 occurred also the first of the riots in Poland that culminated in the widespread insurrection of 1863, which led to the collapse of the *Bell.* Herzen supported the independence movement and attacked Alexander II, but in this he ran afoul of a great wave of patriotism that swept over Russia, impelled by a threat of French intervention, making the *Bell* sound like treason rather than freedom. Liberal support was withdrawn while, at the same time, his differences with Bakunin and Chernyshevski and his scepticism toward revolution were too much for the extremists. The circulation of the *Bell* was decimated. This was, however, only the culmination of Herzen's separation from his former supporters, right and left. The liberal Westerners, such as Chicherin, Granovski, and Kavelin, rejected socialism and became reconciled, through the study of history, to the autocracy of Alexander. The radicals, on the other hand, obstructed reform, according to Herzen, by offending society and by demanding too much. He denounced the extremism and nihilism of Chernyshevski's journal, the *Contemporary,* and Pisarev's *Russian Word.*

"Violence," he believed, "can be used only to destroy, to clear the

* This word itself, from *narod* (people), was not used until about 1870.

ground—nothing more. By the terror *à la* Peter the Great the social revolution will not go beyond the compulsory equality of Gracchus Baboeuf." Much thought, planning, and organization were necessary before the destruction of the old order, for if the new order were not "sufficiently ready to be completed in being realized," the old, bourgeois world would revive. The pace of the revolution must be adjusted to the growth of men's understanding, and "knowledge and understanding will not be gained by a *coup d'état*, nor by a *coup de tête*." [14]

Herzen believed that he had adapted to that pace, but others believed that he had adapted, instead, to the "calm sandy haven" of liberalism. Russian radical thought had moved beyond him toward terrorism; the émigrés at Geneva, to which he moved his press in 1865, rejected his leadership and denounced him in terms of increasing rancor. He lived to stigmatize the new generation of warriors against the tsar's throne, altar, and cannon as "this syphilis of our revolutionary lusts."

To them, as to Bakunin, it seemed that Herzen had moved far to the right. A wealthy man, growing old—what would be more natural? It should be remembered, however, that in 1848 he had not mounted the barricades, and also that in the 1860's he had not abandoned socialism. In his memoirs he wrote, "One thing we have discovered for certain, and it will not be rooted out of the consciousness of the coming generations; that is: that the *free and rational development of Russian national existence is at one with the ideas of Western Socialism*." [15]

He was sure that Russia would never accept a solution to the problem of political liberty which did not also attack the problem of economic distribution more effectively than had Western capitalism. One of the most individualistic and most Western of the Russians, he none the less emphatically rejected the individualistic economics of the West. Yet he was too individualistic to seek socialism through the organization of labor. An enemy of Marx, he had no more faith in the proletariat than in the bourgeoisie. On the other hand he had too little confidence in human nature to accept the anarchism of Bakunin. Having a keen eye for the weaknesses of all dogmas, he was stronger as a critic than as a builder. The greater freedom of western Europe, together with its science and technology, he hoped to import into Russia, but like Chernyshevski, he hoped also that the mir and the artel would enable Russia to avoid capitalism. Even so he saw more clearly than the Slavophils or Chernyshevski the static and uneconomic aspects of the mir. It was this acute perceptiveness that seemed always to deny him the enthusiasm for immediate answers which might have made him a leader of men.

V

While Herzen rose and then declined in the esteem of the revolutionaries, his younger contemporary in radical journalism achieved, partly through martyrdom, a prestige that has not yet faded. Lacking Herzen's great literary talent and without his freedom from censorship, Nikolai Chernyshevski (1828–1889) yet managed, by combining ideas imported from the West with attitudes closely attuned to his environment, to form the dominant strain of thought among Westerners in the 1860's and '70's. From this strain Russian Marxism itself may be regarded as a development.

Herzen and Bakunin represented the radical nobility whereas Chernyshevski sprang, like Belinski, from the lower classes. This difference of origin, more than differences of ideas, accounts for their mutual suspicion and lack of understanding. Herzen, unlike Bakunin, never became *déclassé*.

Tutored at home in Saratov by his father, an Orthodox clergyman, Chernyshevski left the local theological seminary after one year and was admitted to the University of St. Petersburg because of his wide knowledge and command of ancient and modern languages. There his studies in philology and literature did not completely absorb his energies. Through contact with the circle of I. I. Vvedenski he also turned to the forbidden books of the French socialists and the German philosophers, and to the writings of Belinski, who had shown how literary criticism could be used for social ends. From the university he emerged in 1851 with an official degree and an interest in political and social questions which, interacting with his religious background, became a dedication.

After teaching for two years in Saratov he returned to the university for graduate study. He wrote and defended before a large audience a thesis on "The Aesthetic Relations of Art and Reality," which showed strong influences of Belinski and of the German materialist, Feuerbach. His ideas offended the Orthodox, however, and his degree was withheld by the Minister of Education. Three years later a change of ministers brought him the degree, but by that time he was connected with the influential monthly, the *Contemporary*, and no longer wanted the university position for which he had been preparing. Taking up the pen of Belinski, who had died at thirty-seven, he soon raised the journal to new heights of popularity.

From 1854 until his exile ten years later he exerted, within the restrictions of the censorship, an increasingly effective force on behalf of freedom, particularly for the emancipation of the serfs and of women. Recognized as a leader of the radicals, he was an object of police attention in the days of dissatisfaction following the freeing of the peasants, and after the great fire of 1862 in St. Petersburg he was arrested and accused of writing an inflammatory proclamation. The proof of his guilt remains doubtful, since he carefully avoided direct involvement in conspiratorial circles, and the severity of the punishment earned him sympathy in many quarters. He spent two years in the Peter-Paul fortress; from there he was sent to the mines of Siberia for seven years, and thence to permanent exile near the Arctic Circle. The organization of terrorists called The People's Will tried repeatedly to rescue him and in negotiations with the government made his freedom a condition of peace for the coronation of Alexander III. This agreement was violated by the government, but in 1883 he was moved to relatively comfortable Astrakhan, still under surveillance, where he remained until a few months before his death in 1889. During this exile he wrote little of importance, yet his earlier works, coupled with the circumstance of his trial and the persistence of his punishment, made him an inspiring symbol to the opponents of the autocracy.

His most influential work, written during his stay in the Peter-Paul fortress, was the very popular novel, *What Is to Be Done?* Appearing just when Turgenev's *Fathers and Children* was causing a clamor about nihilism, this book presented the "nihilists" in a very different light, as platonic, peaceful servants of the underprivileged. It painted an optimistic picture of what could be achieved in Russia, not by terror, but by cooperation, by education, and by enlightened self-interest. It became a bible for two generations of *narodniki*, guiding them along the paths of Fourier, Louis Blanc, and Robert Owen.

He was also influenced by Hegel, whom he thought to have discovered the key to the general process of history, which Chernyshevski stated as an "axiom": "In its form, the higher stage of development is similar to the beginning from which it sprang." [16] As examples of this he mentioned such things as the similarity of the steel suspension bridge to the primitive bridge of vines, but the most significant application he made of it was to the peasant commune. The commune was not, as the Slavophils thought, a peculiar product of the Slavic genius, but none the less it gave the Russians a great advantage over Europe in the attainment of socialism, for they alone had retained the primitive collective form until the higher yet similar form, the socialist, had come into sight. The cycle of social organization was again approaching collective forms, and the commune had already conditioned the peasants to common ownership of land. If it could be converted to modern socialism, many of the hardships of the intervening stages of capitalism could be skipped.

It is sometimes said that Marx learned Russian so he could read Chernyshevski. That his opinions regarding Russia were influenced by Chernyshevski's theory of the peasant commune is attested in Marx's letters more than once.* Marx's admiration, shared by Plekhanov and Lenin, has preserved the fame of Chernyshevski even in the Soviet period. Though clearly no Marxist, he is approved because of his materialism, his stress upon economic matters, and his militant assurance that the lower classes must work out their own salvation.

Chernyshevski probably read the *Communist Manifesto*, translated by Bakunin in Herzen's *Bell*, and perhaps other works of Marx, including *Capital*, which was sent to him in Siberia, but we have no record of his opinion of Marx. Between them there were substantial areas both of agreement and of disagreement, illustrated by the theory of the commune just described. Although Marx and Engels conditionally accepted it, this theory had to be set aside by later, more consistent Marxists, for it ran counter to Marx's preference for proletarians over peasants and counter to his normal historical pattern of progress from feudalism to capitalism to socialism.

Chernyshevski based his economics not on Marx, whose *Capital* did not appear until 1867, but on Mill, whose *Principles of Political Economy* he translated with extensive commentary in 1860. Mill had not yet abandoned the wages-fund theory and he provided, therefore, a most scientific and respectable demonstration of the necessity for poverty under capitalism. The publication of this translation was an important

* See, for example, Karl Marx and Friedrich Engels, *Selected Correspondence* (Moscow, n.d.), pp. 293, 311, 377. Marx called him "a great Russian scholar and critic."

element in the consolidation, among Slavophils and Westerners alike, of opposition to the development of capitalism in Russia.

In the 1860's Chernyshevski's confidence that the capitalistic stage could be avoided was the basis of his popularity and influence. His essays and his novel provided theoretical justification for this confidence and also a detailed plan of action for the eager young men and women who wished to obey Herzen's call, "To the people!" Moreover, he provided for his theories an aura of natural science, then enjoying high prestige, while at the same time he spiked the reactionary guns of the Slavophils by turning the supposedly ancient institution they so much admired, the commune, into the fulcrum of revolutionary social change, guaranteed to preserve Russia from the proletarian horrors of capitalism.

During the period of preparation for the emancipation both Chernyshevski and Herzen welcomed the tsar's declaration of his intention to free the serfs; both campaigned for emancipation with land; both advocated preservation of the commune as a means to circumvent capitalism on the way to socialism. Each criticized the role taken by the liberals, but where Herzen thought them mistaken and naïve, Chernyshevski applied a class analysis and saw them as sinister enemies of the peasants. Like Marx, he had faith in neither the intention nor the ability of the upper classes to achieve reforms advantageous to the lower classes. Nor did Chernyshevski share with Herzen and the Slavophils the hope that the commune would lead Europe to socialism; to him, Europe was not so moribund as Herzen thought, and was moving toward socialism quite independently of Russia.

More complex than most of the *narodniki*, he had no desire, in avoiding capitalism, to avoid industrial development. *What Is To Be Done?* has an urban, not a rural, setting. Like Marx he saw in the evolution of the tools of production the fundamental dynamic force of social progress and the basis of the antagonisms of classes. The division of labor, he believed, had an "inevitable tendency" to decrease wages, since it required less skill and training of the workman, and also a tendency to restrict and distort the worker's mental and physical development. Yet proper organization of industry would take advantage of the lower training requirement by putting "one man to work alternately at a multitude of varied fractional operations." At the same time, "changes in the qualities of labor are evoked by changes in the character of the productive processes." Slave labor is incompatible with complicated and delicate tools, so industrial labor must be free. But freedom is not enough when the size of factories grows beyond the power of the owners to observe the employees, for they will waste their time unless they are given an incentive to conscientious labor.

It is already necessary that the reward for labor consist in the product of the labor itself and not in any wages, because no wages here can sufficiently reward conscientious labor, and to distinguish conscientious labor from unconscientious becomes less and less possible for anyone except the toiler himself.[17]

Chernyshevski's materialism, elaborated with much circumlocution in the essay "The Anthropological Principle in Philosophy" (1860), was also important in preparing the ground for the seeds of Marxism.* He had borrowed it, without deep study, from Feuerbach, but by setting it in effective contrast to the spiritual and religious emphasis of the Slavophils he attracted to it many who were dissatisfied with Orthodoxy and inclined toward secular thought. Moreover, the trend among Westerners away from German idealism, somewhat superficially begun by Belinski's reaction against Hegel as a defender of the status quo, was thus reinforced and given a materialistic bias through Feuerbach's much more thorough criticism of Hegel's system. Feuerbach had already influenced Bakunin, Belinski, and Herzen; now he was presented as "the later development of science in Germany," draped in the mantle of Chernyshevski's prestige, and through him connected with socialism. Marx, who also built on Feuerbach, could stand in Russia on this foundation.

Materialism, however, unqualified as are some of his statements of it, did not make Chernyshevski a determinist and did not blind him to the power and importance of personality. In *What Is To Be Done?* he sketched a hero, Rakhmetov, who towered above his other characters, a man "of a very rare species." Then he explained:

Had I not shown Rakhmetov's figure, the majority of my readers would have lost their senses of proportion in regard to the main characters of my story. . . . But those people who are completely described, you can reach unto, if you want to work over your self-development. Whoever is lower

---

* Due to the censorship Chernyshevski frequently could not say explicitly what he meant. It is necessary to extract and deduce his meaning, to read between his lines.

than they are is low. Lift yourselves up, my friends; lift yourselves up! It is not very hard. Go out into the free, white world! . . . Read . . . observe . . . think . . . desire to be happy! . . . Oh, what an enjoyment there is for a fully developed man! [18]

This volitional element was so strong among the *narodniki* that it carried over into Russian Marxism and was defended by Plekhanov and Lenin in their protracted controversy against the "Economists," who discounted political activity in favor of a deterministic interpretation of Marxian economics (page 299). In Chernyshevski this element was expressed as an ideal of individual dedication to the cause of the people in an ascetic sense that was foreign to Herzen. There was much of the puritan in Chernyshevski, and it led him both to stress the opportunity and need for individual effort and to establish as his ethical criterion the contribution of the individual to the development of society.

From Herzen and Chernyshevski the Western current of thought flowed in several different channels to the present time. It was blended in varying proportions with Slavophilism and the official ideology. From the beginning various personalities among the Westerners responded differently to the flow of ideas and events, at home and abroad, and gradually the reformers and the revolutionaries parted company, developing Western thought along the divergent lines of liberalism and socialism.

The early Westerners, who became self-consciously so in conflict with the Slavophils, were never blind worshipers of the West. They wanted to remake Russia, not on a Western model, but by combining the best features of Europe, such as political and civil liberties under limited and responsible government, with those parts of their own heritage that they admired, such as the peasant commune. They were acutely aware of many aspects of European life that they hoped Russia could avoid while adopting others, although they may have been less aware than their opponents of the connections among these aspects that might make their hopes unattainable. The flower of personal freedom, so striking by contrast with tsarist oppression, they wanted to transplant, but they did not believe that the soil of capitalism or the cultivation of parliamentary institutions were necessary to its viability. Their liberal followers were willing, in order to have the flower, to take the soil and the cultivation as well; some of them, in fact, came to see merit in both. The socialists, on the other hand, put economic and social problems ahead of political freedom and fought the growth of capitalism as diligently as they did the autocracy.

This vigorously reiterated theme of anticapitalism, so widely shared, indicates that the Westerners, in spite of their philosophic materialism, held humanistic values higher than the material achievements of the West. They learned from Western critics of the West as much as from its institutions. This theme and its humanistic basis need to be remembered for an understanding of the Westernized officials, such as Witte, as well as of the revolutionaries, including the Marxists.

CHAPTER XVII

The Slavophils

OFTEN presented as an indigenous pattern of thought peculiar to Russia, Slavophilism becomes more readily understandable if viewed instead as a part of the great philosophical reaction against the devastating rationalism of Hume, Voltaire, and the French Revolution. Its elements—its admiration for ideals (even when plainly contradicted by realities), its opposition to materialism and its tendency toward mysticism, its emphasis upon religion and its attempt to submerge reason in it, its loyalty to autocracy even though in constant conflict with it—in short, its inconsistencies and irrationalities, then are more understandable. The most fruitful segment of that reaction, German idealism, attained in Friedrich von Schelling a form of religious mysticism adaptable to Russian Orthodoxy, and beginning with the professors of science in the universities, his system gradually captivated many Russians. It thus formed the principal connecting link by which the conservative thought of the West spread to Russia and reinforced opposition there to the importation of innovations from the West.

I

Generally from rural backgrounds, centered in the salons of Moscow and hating St. Petersburg, the Slavophils gradually polarized themselves against the Westerners, many of whom were personal friends, in the 1830's and 1840's. The founders of the school, Alexis Khomiakov and Ivan Kireevski, attracted a close group of disciples including Peter Kireevski, Iuri Samarin, Konstantin and Ivan Aksakov, and Alexander Koshelev. They all died between 1856 and 1886, and with them the movement, strictly interpreted, terminated; yet by that time its influence had ramified widely, some of their ideas, but not all, being taken up in government circles, among liberal critics of the government, and even among the anarchists and revolutionaries. The distortion of their views into political Pan-Slavism, particularly by Nikolai Danilevski, contributed to unrest in eastern Europe, and other individual figures, such as Fedor Dostoevski, the grim Konstantin Leont'ev, and the even darker Konstantin Pobedonostsev, developed aspects of their thought.

Their most substantial theoretical work lay in the deepening of the meaning and understanding of Russian nationality and its relation to Orthodoxy. In the practical realm, they contributed vigorously to the abolition of serfdom. "It is a disgrace, a thing incomprehensible," as Koshelev said, "to be able to call oneself a Christian and to hold one's brothers and sisters in slavery. . . . The suppression of serfdom must be based, above all, on the Christian doctrine of brotherhood." [1]

For the Slavophils generally, as in connection with serfdom, religion formed the central element of thought, even of political thought. It was important not only for individual salvation but also socially, as the cohesive and enlightening force, the moral consensus, that gave unity to the nation. This required an idealization of the Russian church that soon replaced its divided and bureaucratic reality in their minds, and the process of idealization was extended to the peasant (as the most religious of men), to his rural commune, and to the whole of pre-Petrine Christian Russia, although some went further than others in this process.

Their admiration for the past, interpreted, as in part it was intended, as criticism of the present, brought down on the Slavophils the ire of the government, and in spite of their professions of loyalty and their proximity to Uvarov's Orthodoxy, Autocracy, and Nationality, they and their publications were pursued as vigorously as were the Westerners. To them, the contemporary ills of Russia were all traceable to Peter I, who had introduced Western errors wholesale, including the Roman and Western idea of coercive government where previously the people had been ruled by consensus. They emphatically rejected majority rule, however, as being merely another form of coercion, a Western materialistic form, and with it they rejected the idea of parliamentary government and all other formal, constitutional limitations of the tsar's power. On the contrary, they believed the autocracy to be unlimited and legitimate, based on the choice of Mikhail Romanov by consensus of the people. The autocracy, before Peter, had been an organic expression of national unity, and this they wanted to recover. Yet the tsar and his bureaucrats were far from infallible, so the Slavophils believed that the government should be open to advice from the public. The zemski sobors had been called, in Khomiakov's opinion, to seek the advice of the public, and similarly sound advice could now be obtained simply by relaxing the censorship. In this they were lineal descendants of Kurbski, looking back nostalgically to Ivan III and his "passion for advice."

They looked to moral but not legal restraints upon the autocracy, and this attitude amounted to a rejection of political reform, except in the emancipation, in favor of internal moral and religious revival. "Political protestants," such as the communists and socialists, had confused the life of society in the state with the external form of the state, Khomiakov held, and imagined that social problems could be solved by a new form, different from the old but in essence equally external. Instead, the aim should be to redirect the education of society away from politics and toward self-conscious understanding of its own weaknesses: "The root and principle of the work is religion, and only the open, conscious, and complete triumph of Orthodoxy will open the way to the possibility of other developments." [2]

II

The Slavophils were not simple religious reactionaries, trying to recover a pre-Petrine Arcadia. They were highly educated, several of them holding advanced degrees, and they were well acquainted, through study and travel, with western Europe. Alexis Khomiakov (1804–1860), for example, educated at home and at the University of Moscow, had lived for eighteen months in Paris, had traveled widely, and knew many languages, ancient and modern. Independently wealthy, quite religious, yet much given to laughter, he spent his life in study, writing, managing his estates, and above all in intellectual conversation, at which he excelled.

Khomiakov built his system not on Russian history but on a Western theory of knowledge and a theory of world history based thereon. For the former he drew on Schelling and Maistre, and perhaps on Jacobi, and insisted that the knowledge accessible to the intellect is only a part of knowledge, that faith can grasp parts that the intellect cannot reach.

I have given the name of faith to that faculty of the mind that perceives the data of reality in order to transmit them to the analysis and knowledge of the intellect. . . . In that domain, which precedes logical knowledge and fills the living consciousness, not requiring proofs or demonstrations, man is conscious of what belongs to the world of his thought and what to the exterior world.[3]

Intellect is analytical and deals with exterior features; faith is synthetic and deals with interior qualities. Intellect is directed toward concepts, the abstract formal relations of phenomena; but the aim of knowledge is the whole of life itself, which requires the whole being to grasp it. Moreover, the participation of the moral powers of the whole soul in the cognitive process is guaranteed only when the act of cognition is shared in love. Knowledge must, therefore, be collective within the communion of love that is the church.

A one-sided faith in logical knowledge kills true reason and leads to the self-condemnation of logical reasoning, as we have seen by the whole history of Western civilization; but an absence or vagueness of logical knowledge in historical development takes away from life and from the convictions their rational consistency and solidity.[4]

Connected with these two aspects of knowledge were two great historical orientations or tendencies that Khomiakov distinguished as the Cushite and the Iranian, names derived from the locales from which they spread, Iran and ancient Ethiopia (the Biblical Cush). His basis of distinction was not primarily geographical or racial but religious and philosophical: determinism versus freedom. The Cushites, he said, thought in physical terms, of a world generated by necessity from sexual unions of gods and goddesses, and governed by laws of cause and effect. They depended upon the intellect and its utilitarian grasp of the material world, and upon the force of external authority. By these means they achieved marvels of architecture, mathematics, and organization, but they neglected the other source of knowledge, the faith that was the basis of freedom. The Iranians, on the contrary, explained the universe not by generation but as the free creation of God, containing, moreover, elements of creative freedom and moral responsibility in which mankind participated. They combined faith with intellect and understood the reconciliation of man's freedom with submission to

God through love, and also the internal acceptance of social authority through love in the family and in all free societies.

The Cushite tendency had culminated in the administrative, material, and legal achievements of the Roman Empire, while the Iranian orientation was especially characteristic of the Slavs and had also been preserved among the ancient Hebrews. Over the centuries and millenia, the races, religions, and philosophies that carried these conflicting tendencies had become mixed and none remained pure. In general, however, western Europe had become deterministic under the strong influence of Rome, while Russia had absorbed freedom both from its Iranian heritage and from Orthodox Christianity.

It was thus as a strategy in the great world struggle of freedom against determinism, both temporal and spiritual, that Khomiakov opposed the Westernization of Russia.

In the West, Christianity itself had been distorted through the organization of the church as a state, a denial of love, depending on the externals of ritual, hierarchy, and authority. "A worldly state had replaced the Church of Christ. The unique and living law of unity in God was replaced by partial laws marked by utilitarianism and juridical relations. Rationalism developed under the form of authoritative decisions." [5] The Roman Church then, by the adoption of the new dogma, the word *filioque* in the creed (page 35 n), cut itself off from the community of love, the universal church, which was a precondition of true knowledge, and gave itself up to rationalism. Next, just as the Latins had sacrificed liberty and the internal unity of love for the external unity of organization, the Protestants sacrificed the remaining unity for liberty. But, since their liberty was not based on love, it was an external freedom from restraint, and it soon permeated Western society with protests and revolutions against all kinds of restraints. [6]

In Russia, on the other hand, Orthodoxy was characterized by "the law of love."

Love is not a solitary aspiration: it requires, it finds, it produces echoes and a communion, and in those responses and that communion it grows, acquires strength, perfects itself. Thus the communion of love is not only useful but quite indispensable for the attainment of truth, and the comprehension of truth depends on it and is impossible without it. Inaccessible to individual thought, truth is accessible only by the union of thoughts bound together by love. [7]

Liberty as well as truth was based on love, and, since love implied more than one person, no individual alone could be completely free, completely a man; so individualism—Western or any other—was contrary to Orthodoxy and to human nature.[8]

The attempts of Peter and his successors to impose external, authoritative, administrative power tended to undermine the communion of love. They had always been contrary to the spirit of the people and had led to the estrangement of the government from the people. While the aristocracy had followed Peter on his erroneous path, the people had preserved the purity of their traditions through two institutions, the church and the commune. Khomiakov's idealized picture of the church bore little resemblance to reality, but he saw it as a repository of inner, spiritual freedom and love. The mir, too, he idealized: "the *obshchina* is the only civil institution that has survived all Russian history. Take it away and nothing remains; develop it, however, and the whole civil order can be developed from it." It was a guarantee against poverty and the growth of a proletariat. Further, it was a school for the peasantry superior to any formal education:

To hear continually talk of the work done in common, then to take part in it; to hear from childhood justice and punishment meted out; to see how human egotism develops when constantly face to face with moral thought of the general interest, of the conscience, of the customs, of the faith, and submits itself to these high principles—that is truly moral education, that is civilization in the broad sense, that is the development not only of morality but also of the mind.

The commune was held together by the unity of love, as was evident in its customary Slavic method of decision by consensus, which Khomiakov contrasted with decision by majority, imported from Germany, "as if wisdom and justice belonged to the greater number." [9]

To retain and strengthen the commune in the elimination of serfdom was highly important, and this, Khomiakov believed, required that the serfs retain the land they had tilled. To justify this he analyzed the concept of property. Private property rights, he argued, were never absolute; society always retained an overriding claim: "all private ownership is more or less a usufruct, differing only in degree." In Russia, both the ownership and the usufruct had been recognized as hereditary. The lands of the nobility, owned vis-à-vis other nobles, were held only by right of usufruct in relation to the state. Similarly, the right of the peasants to their lands, "in relation to us, is a hereditary right of usufruct; indeed, it differs from our own only in degree, and not in its essential character." [10]

III

Another of Chaadaev's younger friends who were spurred to self-consciousness in 1836 by his philosophic letter, and who then undertook the defense of Russian tradition, was Ivan Kireevski (1806–1856) who, with Khomiakov, prepared the philosophic foundations of the Slavophil group. In him, as clearly as in Chaadaev, can be seen the close connections between the early Slavophils and the Westerners.

Of a highly cultured gentry family, familiar with western Europe yet conservative and religious, Kireevski was educated at home and appointed at eighteen to the Archives in Moscow, a center for young intellectuals. In 1830, impelled by the prevailing interest in German idealism, he went to sit at the feet of both Schelling and Hegel. He was disappointed with both, yet his enthusiasm for the West survived. In 1832 he undertook to publish a periodical which he named *The European*, "because I propose to fill it with articles more concerned with Europe than with Russia." After two issues, however, it was suppressed.

His admiration for the philosophy of Schelling also remained. When, in 1834, he married a woman whom he discovered to be too pious for his sophisticated religious taste, he turned to the reading of Schelling with her as a means of reconciliation. She surprised him by insisting that all this philosophy she had previously discovered in the works of the church fathers. Thus challenged, Kireevski began to read the Eastern fathers himself, and from that contact with the roots of the Russian faith his later philosophy evolved. It should not be overlooked, however, that he drew from this reading, not a system of thought, but rather a basis for a special application of Schelling's system to Russia. The German's struggles with the Ego, the Non-Ego, and the Absolute were sufficiently similar to some of the Byzantine fathers' struggles with the trinity to convince Kireevski that he saw in the latter, and therefore in the early Russian church, an even purer form of the latest wisdom advanced by Western philosophy.

By this means he was able to formulate a comprehensive answer to Chaadaev's indictment. All the failures and deficiencies of Russia were really evidences of her rejection of an overweening rationalism; all her differences from the West were proofs of the higher morality of her civilization, enlightened as it was by a deeper understanding of the Christian faith.

In Kireevski's opinion, the differences between Russian traditions of government and those of the West were the result of old differences of temperament between Greece and Rome. The Athenian emphasis on harmony and balance, integration and organic development, had led in Christian times to a unified, mystic religion and to government by consensus. The legalistic logic of Rome, on the other hand, had produced authority, sovereignty, Catholicism, and individualism. Moreover, the greater ignorance of the people of the West in early times had exposed them to "the irresistible influence of the remaining traces of paganism which communicated to their thinking the rationalistic character of Roman external-logical abstraction and by this deviation of reason obliged them to seek the external unity of the Church instead of spiritual unity." From this ignorance, and from the papal love for power, had come the *filioque*, "this first triumph of rationalism over faith," and the uncanonical supremacy of the popes. Such ignorance, he said, "excommunicates people from the vital community of minds by which the truth is maintained." Meanwhile, the East had understood that, in the struggle against paganism, Christianity must not concede reason to the enemy, must not stand aside from it, but must subject external reason to divine truth, which "must, in the general consciousness, stand above other truths as a dominating element, permeating the whole expanse of civilization, supported for each private person by the concordance of social culture." [11]

To the medieval Schoolmen, Aristotle had been *the* philosopher, so Kireevski attacked him as a source of the rationalism of the West:

The system of Aristotle tore apart the wholeness of intellectual awareness and turned the root of the internal convictions of man away from moral and aesthetic understanding towards the abstract consciousness of rationalistic intellect. The instruments by which it discerned truth were confined to the logical activity of the mind and to passive observation of the external world. . . . And actually the philosophy of Aristotle was destructive to the moral worth of man. Having undermined all convictions standing above rationalistic logic, it destroyed also all incentives able to raise man above his personal interests.[12]

The Greek theologians, who knew Aristotle better than did the Latins, preferred Plato because he "represents more wholeness in intellectual movement, more warmth and harmony in the speculative activity of the mind." For, according to Kireevski, "the Orthodox believer knows that for the whole truth the wholeness of reason is necessary." This meant that, in seeking truth, Eastern thinkers "seek inner wholeness of reason" and "the correctness of the internal state of the thinking spirit," whereas Western thinkers are more concerned about "the external connection of ideas." The West had applied itself to the reconciliation of reason with divine revelation, using reason as its method. It had thereby introduced into religious thought a solvent that had destroyed faith. The East, on the contrary, had never separated revelation from reason, had never believed them separable. The Russians, therefore, had escaped all the agonizing consequences of that separation and should continue diligently to preserve their wholesome heritage, to purify it of recent contaminations, and to resist the influence of the heretical and chaotic West.[13]

Kireevski attempted to show how these philosophic and religious differences had worked out in government and politics. Rationalism in the West led to individualism and class antagonisms, as exemplified by the knight in his stony castle exploiting the peasants of the surrounding countryside. Social cohesion was attained only formally, through law and force, and social development was possible only through revolution. In Russia, by contrast, there were no castles, and social cohesion was attained not by formalism and force but by the natural harmony of the communes blending into the great general unity of the whole Russian land under the grand prince. Law was not invented by jurisconsults nor enacted by legislative assemblies, but "customarily only written down on paper after it had already been formed spontaneously in the conceptions of the people, and little by little, compelled by the necessity of things, had entered into popular morals and popular existence." In a society so organically evolved, "the law of revolutions, instead of being a condition of life's improvements, is for it a condition of ruin and death, for its development can be accomplished only harmoniously and imperceptibly by the law of natural growth in continued common accord." [14]

In this neat contrast, built though it was on some legitimate cultural differences, Kireevski stood on somewhat shaky historical and even shakier philosophical ground. The spirit of free inquiry so characteristic of the Athens of Socrates, then as always corrosive of ancient faith, had exalted reason as high as ever Rome could do. The authority of the Byzantine emperor, touching both secular and religious spheres, which the tsars had endeavored to imitate, had never been matched in the West. The elements common to the heritages of the eastern and the western Romans, such as classical art and philosophy, Roman law and government, and a thousand years of unified Christianity, were at least as important as the differentiating elements. To all such links between Greece and Rome the Westerners could appeal, but all these had to be discounted by the Slavophils. Thus Kireevski and Khomiakov began a process of selective integration or exclusion of those facts and ideas that fit or did not fit a *Weltanschauung* they held (logically, given their premises) more by faith than by reason—a process with inherent inconsistencies leading inexorably to the obscurantism of Pobedonostsev.

IV

Less philosophical than his older colleagues, but more directly political, was Konstantin Aksakov (1817–1860), eldest son of the writer, Sergei Aksakov. So close and congenial was the home atmosphere on his father's estates and in Moscow that Konstantin never left it, except for a brief trip to Germany in 1838, as long as his father lived; and so close were their personal relations that he faded and died within a year of his father's death. This environment caused a quality of arrested development in his thought, a tenacity of opinion, a narrowness and intolerance that irritated even his friends. He was, nevertheless, well educated and widely respected for his outspoken honesty.

His political views were all derived from his interpretation of history. A member of the Stankevich circle, he wrote for the master's degree a thesis on Lomonosov under the domination of Hegelian dialectics, from which he interpreted Russian history as a progression from the particular to the universal. He saw Peter I as the antithesis, the great negative force that had been necessary before the narrow, exclusive nationalism of Russia, which feared the West, could be elevated into a new, open, tolerant nationalism able to accept the West without fear, and thus to participate in the universal. Peter had brought slavish imitation of foreign ways and the negation of native life, but the people, other than the gentry, had remained aloof from his reforms and had thus preserved their traditions.

Aksakov had hardly finished his thesis in 1844 when he began to change this interpretation. As the spell of Hegel lost its grip upon him, he saw less necessity for an antithesis, for Peter's reforms. Moreover, pre-Petrine Russia seemed to him less particular, less exclusive and afraid. Muscovy, he now believed, had accepted from the West what it found useful; with Peter, however, this process became a misguided, compulsive denial of everything Russian. Yet the aloofness of the people from Peter's westernization remained a key element in his analysis. In fact, it became the basis for his hope for the regeneration of Russia and for his positions on public policy.

Our past is not gone; it follows us. The Rus' of the past even now lives with the simple people and is preserved in them. . . . It is thought that we want to return to the old forms of life. No, I say to that, . . . not to the forms that ancient Russian life took, but to the spirit and to the life and . . . to the bases of our existence.[15]

The life of the people was expressed most fully in the peasant commune, which he idealized as a communal principle of voluntary consensus, and from which he believed the *veche* and the zemski sobor had naturally evolved. In his view, however, these institutions were not organs of government. They were organs of opinion, by which the people made their views and wishes known to the princes and the tsars, to whom they had voluntarily granted the powers of government. The people, Aksakov held, had invited Riurik to rule them, and similarly had chosen Mikhail, without imposing any limitations on their power, but always considering them as agents external to the life of the community. A distinction had prevailed throughout history, therefore—the distinction between the community of the Russian land and its agent, the state. The state, made necessary by man's sinful nature, required compulsion, but within the community, guided by his moral attributes, man could be free. The Slavic genius had understood that these two should be kept separate. If, through democracy or aristocracy, the community undertook to participate in government, its voluntary unity would be lost—or, at best, replaced by a coercive unity. Monarchy, therefore, was the only form of government that left the people free—free from the taint of participation in compulsion and free to live the moral life of the community. Moreover, monarchy should be unlimited, for any limitation would require popular participation and would thus violate the essential distinction.

Aksakov had arrived at a defense of autocracy, but his antagonism toward the state was worthy of an anarchist. As an external authority, the state tended, he believed, to weaken and replace the internal authority of the moral law, to substitute institutions for principles. No matter how liberal or democratic, "the State is the principle of slavery, of external compulsion." It is not a free embodiment of man's internal world, but something shaped and established.

The more developed the State, the more forcefully do institutions replace the inner world of the individual, and the more profoundly and tightly does it grip society even though it appears to conform to all of society's demands. . . . If state liberalism goes so far that every person becomes an official, his own policeman, then the State finally kills the living principle in the individual. Leading thinkers of the West begin to recognize that the lie inheres not in this or that form of the State, but in the State itself as an idea, a principle, . . . that the State, as State, is a lie.[16]

Such ideas made him an enemy of all political reforms that tended to increase the interrelations of the people with the government. He was sure that the people had no desire to hold power and that the government showed a basic misunderstanding in trying to defend itself against them. "In its essence the national principle is antirevolutionary and conservative," and there had never been a single uprising demanding political rights for the people. "The Russian people are a nonpolitical people," lacking even a germ of the love of power, he wrote to the new tsar Alexander II in 1855. "Long ago Russia could have had a constitution . . . but the Russian people do not wish to rule." [17]

It was not, however, without cause that his writings had been proscribed under Nicholas I, for he regarded the tsar not as sovereign but as the people's agent, legally unlimited but morally bound to heed their opinions and wishes. As expressed in his most famous formula, "to the tsar—the power of government; to the people—the power of opinion," this view was an extension to a broader basis of Kurbski's idea that the tsar is obliged to seek advice. Instead, the government cut itself off from the people; it refused to consult a zemski sobor and even used censorship to prevent other expressions of the people's views. The salutary distinction between state and community had, therefore, become a gulf of incomprehension across which neither side understood the other. The only justification for the absolute monarchy was thus undermined and the bases of stability exposed to revolution.

This critical attitude was displayed most thoroughly in Aksakov's writings on the abolition of serfdom. Like the other Slavophils, he argued that the serfs must be freed with land, both for justice and because the peasants believed the use of the land to be theirs. Going further than Khomiakov and Kireevski, he held that alodial tenure had never been recognized in Russia, that the land had always belonged to the people collectively, not as property but as an object of use. It had been administered by their agent, the state, through its agents, the landlords, who enjoyed only *pomest'e* tenure (page 88), not full ownership.

The meaning of the landlords was not the meaning of owners; inheritability and free disposition of estates . . . were the hereditary transmission of their relation to the land, of their right to utilize the land. . . . The rights of the *votchinnik* were restricted by the rights of the commune to the land from which it could not be expelled.[18]

The landlords were only administrators; the peasant reform must not give them the people's land.

Like the other Slavophils, Aksakov thought it essential to preserve the customs of the village commune. He objected strenuously to proposals that seemed to him designed to make the commune a part of the administrative machinery of the state. He conceded the need for proposed assemblies at the *volost* level, in addition to the communes, but he insisted that they should be organs of opinion based on the communal principle for communication with the government, not administrative organs designed by the government with prescribed rules. "Different rules and forms of meetings, with a majority and with a president having two votes"—this was a parody and abuse of the people and their mir. Even more insulting and vicious, in his opinion, was the plan to impose the rule of decision by majority vote. This he termed a "complete violation of the whole essence of the Russian communal principle," which called for decision by consensus.

Clearly, the majority principle is a principle according to which consent is not necessary; it is a coercive principle, conquering only by physical superiority: those who are more overpower those who are fewer. Unanimity is difficult; however, every moral eminence is difficult. . . . Moreover, the nation that has fixed in its life the principle of the commune and of unanimity attains it with incomparably greater ease than those that recognize the prerogative of the majority as right and law. . . .

The peasants had mastered this great secret of achieving agreement, and it must not be taken from them. "The very essence of Russian history is thus consultation." To impose majority rule on the commune would be to destroy "the very basis of our life, to kill our Russian freedom." [19]

These criticisms had little or no effect on the government's course of action. They serve most clearly to illustrate the impotence of the Moscow Slavophils' approach, of their rejection of political methods in their effort to influence the formal government by informal moral suasion. Had the government shared their ideals, they might have succeeded; their methods might be effective within a consensus, but they were not effective in achieving a consensus.

V

In its second generation Slavophilism lost the cohesion of elements that had made it a respectably coherent philosophy. As Masaryk saw it:

In these subsequent developments the philosophy of history becomes more and more conspicuously replaced by a superficial interest in current politics; the philosophy of religion is overshadowed by official clericalism; and endeavours towards religious development are overcast by the Russifying ecclesiastical policy of the holy synod. . . . In like manner, in the theoretical and philosophical field, Kireevskii's broad religious and historical program narrows into the program of Uvarov; and after 1863, subsequent to the Polish rising, the victory of Uvarov over Kireevskii is decisive.[20]

Yet the vigor of the movement was far from exhausted. On the one hand, it contributed arguments to those Westerners who, like Herzen and Chernyshevski, wished to avoid capitalism, and its admiration for the peasant and his mir became an important part of the doctrines of the *narodniki*. On the other hand, Kireevski's vigorous denial of the West and his confidence in the mission of Russia were strains of thought leading in Ivan Aksakov, Nikolai Danilevski, and others to cultural and political Pan-Slavism. His idealization of the unity of the

Eastern Church became in Konstantin Leont'ev a driving, authoritarian imperialism hoping to recreate the Byzantine Empire.*

In direct conflict with the Westerners, particularly with the active revolutionaries, Slavophilism also continued to develop in the hands of Fedor Dostoevski (1821–1881) in the area where religion, psychology, and politics meet. The great novelist did little strictly political writing, and that of poor quality, beating the drums of Pan-Slavism. In his novels, however, Dostoevski probed the psychological depths of certain problems, such as liberty and security, stability and change, that are basic to political thought. He thus gave to Slavophil ideas a currency, both in and outside Russia, that without his literary genius they would never have attained.

Dostoevski, son of a doctor so tyrannous that his serfs finally murdered him, joined the Petrashevski circle and was arrested with them in 1849 and sentenced to fourteen years labor and military service in Siberia. There is little evidence that he was very radical even before his arrest, but any such tendencies he may have had did not survive the prison at Omsk. During his exile he found much comfort in the New Testament. In his search for social solutions he turned his back upon the youthful follies that had brought him to such distress and with the Slavophils found in the unspoiled peasant the repository of the highest spiritual values.

In him the intellectual and religious messianism of Chaadaev and Kireevski became assimilated to the Pan-Slavism of Danilevski.

The Slavophile doctrine, in addition to that assimilation of the Slavs under the rule of Russia, signifies and comprises a spiritual union of all those who believe that our great Russia, at the head of the united Slavs, will utter to the world, to the whole of European mankind and to civilization, her new, sane and as yet unheard-of word. That word will be uttered for the good and genuine unification of mankind as a whole in a new, brotherly, universal union whose inception is derived from the Slavic genius, pre-eminently from the spirit of the great Russian people. . . . Now, I belong to this group of the convinced and the believing.[21]

---

* The earlier doctrines also were refined and restated still later by the "Neo-Slavophils," including Khomiakov's son Dmitri and Sergei Sharapov (see A. Gratieux, *Le mouvement Slavophile à la veille de la révolution: Dmitri A. Khomiakov* [Paris, 1953], and Sharapov, *Samoderzhavie i samoupravlenie* [Berlin, 1899]).

The Orthodox Church, as a cohesive force, as an expression of the unity of the nation, was not restricted within the bounds of Russia; and even non-Orthodox Slavs shared many elements of a common heritage. Yet he was doubtful that the other Slavs would appreciate the role of Russia in the coming union, and therefore was careful to deny that world union required any territorial expansion by Russia.

The Possessed (1872), based on the episode of the jesuitical and murderous Nechaev (page 251), he wrote as a contribution to the protection of Russia against the Westernized radicals, but he grossly distorted the picture by interpreting Nechaev as typical of the whole revolutionary movement. The probing of human consciousness and motivations, rather than the polemical content of his work, retained Dostoevski's paramount interest, and he had an artistic sympathy for characters whose views he most disliked. The introspective quality of his mind he applied to analyzing the psychology of the revolutionaries. His conclusion was that he who deserted the traditional faith for the false gods of materialism and socialism lost thereby all feeling for human dignity, all sense of the spiritual worth of man, and, far from building a heaven here on earth, would be driven by his own sense of futility to murder or suicide or both. In his analyses of freedom he distinguished sharply man's internal liberty from his external, social opportunities, and saw with the clarity of religious conservatism that anyone who would undertake to rearrange society would necessarily try to improve upon God's handiwork. These analyses brought him close to modern existentialism and currently are receiving much attention in both popular and scholarly journals.*

During his last years Dostoevski worked intermittently upon *The Brothers Karamazov* (1881), the unfinished masterpiece in which, in the legend of the Grand Inquisitor, both his art and his philosophy were brought to the highest pinnacle.† This story, recounted by the lost soul, Ivan Karamazov, deals with the basic question of man's capacity for freedom. The Inquisitor denies this capacity, and Dostoevski, carried away like Milton in *Paradise Lost* by the strength of the arch villain he has created, states the case for authoritarian

---

* A few of these articles are included in the bibliography.

† This was the period of his Saturday evenings with Pobedonostsev, and the latter's religious views may have influenced the novel in places (Jacqueline de Proyart, "Pobedonoscev et Dostoevskij: une amitié littéraire," *Revue des études slaves*, XXXVIII [1961], 151–163).

government with a power almost belying the author's disagreement. He also contrasts, by implication, two views of man—one, attributed to the West (specifically to the Roman church), that men "are weak, vicious, miserable nonentities born wicked and rebellious," the other, his interpretation of the Orthodox or Slavophil view, that they are meek, patient, and long-suffering, but wise and free. He sees the problem of freedom in the burden of responsibility it entails and the tendency of men to turn from it in search of security.* "There are three powers," the Inquisitor explains, "three unique forces upon earth, capable of conquering forever by charming the conscience of these weak rebels—men—for their own good; and these forces are miracle, mystery and authority." [22] All three must be rejected, Dostoevski says, if man is to be free, but in asking man to reject them Jesus had *seemed* to act "as if there were no love for him in Thine heart, for Thou hast demanded of him more than he could ever give." "Miracle" he interprets as catering to men's baser needs. Acutely aware of human suffering as a theological and as a psychological problem, Dostoevski believes it an essential concomitant of freedom and is convinced that all efforts to deal with it as a social problem are made at the expense of liberty in the external sense and in direct denial of the internal liberty on which, in his opinion, Christianity is based. He thus sets spiritual freedom in sharp contradiction to the material progress and utilitarianism of the West, suggesting that pursuit of Western values in Russia would undermine the purity of her religion.

The Slavophils' rejection of the material civilization of the West has become in him a contradiction between temporal and spiritual salvation. As in Malthusian economics, a foundation is laid for the acceptance of the status quo, for the justification of an existent evil. At the same time, he recognizes that, for both good and ill, the revolutionaries too have suffered in the wilderness. Their alliance with the devil is stated most emphatically, but the positive case for freedom is not: with great artistry the reader's knowledge of the New Testament is used to supply, in rebuttal, a quietistic faith impervious alike to autocracy and to materialism.

Like the ideas of the New England Transcendentalists, to which they were related, the concepts of the Slavophils were inadequate as

---

* On this problem see Erich Fromm, *Escape from Freedom* (New York, 1941).

political tenets and subject to grave distortion. They were, nonetheless, healthy and timely reminders that the past of Russia neither could nor should be cast off like a worn garment in favor of the latest fashion from the West, and that the government itself was not the sole custodian and interpreter of that past. The Westerners, of course, admitted that the institutions of the West had not conducted Europe to utopia. They saw especially the injustices of Western economic arrangements, but the Slavophils were much more clearly aware that the external progress of the West had brought no comparable internal, moral, or spiritual progress. Their critique of the West, therefore, was more penetrating than that of the Westerners and contributed substantially to Russia's resistance of the temptation to borrow governmental institutions as Japan was to do.

The chimerical and self-contradictory qualities of Slavophil thought are patent. These men thought the West to be decadent and fundamentally misguided in religion and philosophy, yet they derived their basic notions from the West. They believed in the superiority of autocracy yet they wanted the tsar to act as an agent of the people. They admired local autonomy in the peasant commune yet they defended autocracy, which is necessarily centralized. They insisted upon freedom of opinion and of expression yet they denied the validity of individual thought and held only community opinion to be true. They thought the Russian people to be apolitical yet these men wanted to influence the course of political events. They extolled custom over positive legislation yet they hated Aristotle, the great defender of custom. They thought freedom possible only under an autocrat. Such a list of seemingly irreconcilable positions could be extended to great length.

Yet Slavophil political thought, more reactionary than conservative, was psychologically appealing to the nationalistic, to the introspective, to the defensive, and to the religious. In the West itself similar amalgams of mysticism and history had, and still have, wide appeal and influence, as the procession of thinkers from Rousseau and Herder to Alfred Rosenberg and Arnold J. Toynbee attests. Even in a country subject to an indictment like Chaadaev's there were many who preferred to look backward rather than westward for guidance to the future. Some of the country's best minds were numbered among the Slavophils, and the national peculiarities they stressed have endured to make their mark even on so secular and materialistic a movement as Russian Marxism.

CHAPTER XVIII

The Anarchists

AS Western and native ideas increasingly agitated the growing intelligentsia, the autocracy continued, as has been seen, to claim a monopoly of political wisdom and to consider itself above public opinion. It thereby gave a strong stimulus to the philosophic rejection of government—that is, to anarchism. The concept of society without government had deep historical roots in Russia, and it still has a place in Soviet political thought.

I

Anarchism has had a variety of formulations in different civilizations. Among the ancient Greeks, the Cynics, with their individual self-sufficiency and their utter contempt for social organization, were early proponents of a form of anarchism. At Rome, the Stoic Seneca made it a feature of his "golden age," in which men had dwelt before the discovery of private property compelled then to resort to government. The early Christian idea of a religion above the state was potentially anarchistic, and was so viewed by the Romans. There are elements of this doctrine in many writings, medieval and modern, but it is to William Godwin that credit is usually given for laying, in his *Enquiry Concerning Political Justice* (1793), the philosophical foundations of modern anarchism. Godwin's ideas belonged to the same trend of emphasis on personal liberty that found expression in the *laissez faire* economic doctrines of Adam Smith and the utilitarian ethics of Jeremy Bentham. He simply carried further their faith in rationality: just as economic prosperity could be expected to result from the exclusion of the state from the economic realm, so could general prosperity and happiness be expected to result from the exclusion of the state from all realms; that is, from the abolition of the state. To Godwin, there was an "invisible hand," so to speak, that would cause each individual to work toward the greatest good for all, in the absence of all governmental interference.

Among nineteenth-century radicals, however, it was not Godwin but Pierre Joseph Proudhon who caught their imagination. Godwin was too individualistic and too patient to appeal to the most ardent spirits, while the Frenchman was an active revolutionary. He went to the heart of matters with his famous formula, "Property is theft," and stressed the collective and cooperative nature of man and of the ideal society.

Anarchism in Russia, therefore, was in part derived from the West, especially from Proudhon, but there were also many native historical antecedents. One such root may be discerned in the old freedom of the boyars, until the fifteenth century, to desert their prince and take their allegiance elsewhere without forfeiting their estates (page 20). Another can be found among the religious sectarians, such as the Trans-Volga Elders of the sixteenth century, the Old Believers, or Raskolniki, numerous since the seventeenth, and the later Dukhobors. A third lay in the repudiation of both landlord and tsar that recruited and maintained the Cossacks. Still a fourth was the tradition of peasant revolts, usually attended by fire and murder, the most widespread of which was led by Pugachev against the Empress Catherine in 1773. And finally, and most important as a contributing stimulus, was the radical separation, which has been mentioned (page 126), of the government from the people.

These were, however, largely expressions of an intuitive conviction of traditional freedoms, in the manner of British regard for "the ancient rights of Englishmen." Russian anarchism had not yet developed a philosophical foundation; it tended to be particular and negative rather than general and constructive.

II

Mikhail Bakunin (1814–1876), Russia's first major exponent of anarchism as a political philosophy, shared these tendencies toward the negative and the particular and labored with difficulty to overcome them. A large and powerful bulk of a man, he possessed almost boundless energy and expended it wantonly in active revolutionary endeavors in many countries, yet in spite of his own undisciplined personality he gave to anarchism an almost systematic program.

Drawing on the spirit of Pugachev and the logic of Hegel, he argued that democracy must create a new world through revolutionary demolition of the old. He voiced a doctrine of pandestruction in his most famous sentence: "The urge for destruction is at the same time a creative passion." * He called for ruthless and violent smashing of old institutions, to be followed, not by individual autarchy, but by spontaneous community cooperation and the federation of communities, in which a man would obey only his own convictions. More a doer than a thinker, ready always to abandon his pen for the barricades, he was still the chief theoretical opponent of Karl Marx in the first International.

Bakunin was the eldest son in an old but not wealthy *d'iaki* family of eleven children. After a brief taste of military life, ending in a violent dispute with a general, he decided to prepare at a German university for a professorship at Moscow. His father opposed this plan and, having no funds, Bakunin stayed in Moscow. He moved in intellectual circles, both Slavophil and Westerner, debating German philosophy with Stankevich, Belinski, Chaadaev, the Aksakovs, and Herzen. At first a disciple of Fichte, he grew toward Hegel, and then, like Marx, toward Feuerbach and the Left Hegelians. Finally in 1840, on Herzen's money, he went to the University of Berlin, but three semesters, including some lectures by Schelling, were enough to cause him to abandon the idea of becoming a professor. He threw his energies, instead, into the radical movement; he traveled around western Europe, making speeches, writing articles, and meeting such revolutionary leaders as Weitling, Marx, Engels, and Proudhon.

To Proudhon, a self-taught workman, he introduced the doctrines of Hegel, and from him in exchange Bakunin absorbed the idea of a federated society without the state. His debt to the French anarchist is, therefore, very great. His opinions were evolving rapidly, finding

---

* "Die Reaction in Deutschland," *Deutsche Jahrbücher für Wissenschaft und Kunst*, nos. 247–251 (Oct. 17–21, 1842), signed Jules Elysard. Thomas G. Masaryk, analyzing it at length, said, "it is the best that Bakunin ever wrote, and furnishes a genuinely philosophical program of democracy" (*The Spirit of Russia*, I [London, 1919], 436–445).

the communisms of Weitling and Marx attractive but only Proudhon's anarchism and atheism sufficiently libertarian.

His thinking in this period centered around the idea of the revolutionary liberation of the various Slavic peoples and their federation into one great nation. He participated in the abortive insurrection of June 1848 in Prague and another in Dresden in May 1849. He was captured, condemned to death in Saxony and in Austria, extradited to Russia, imprisoned for eight years, and then exiled to Siberia. Escaping in 1861, he came to London and joined his friend Herzen, eager to take up the fight where he had left it. With Herzen, then at the peak of his influence, he supported the activities of the Poles that led to the uprising of 1863. He soon learned, however, that the nobility directing the uprising had no intention of redistributing land to the peasants. This so disgusted Bakunin that he withdrew his support and washed his hands of all Slavic nationalist movements.

His thinking now came to its final focus, and from that time forward he worked for a spontaneous international uprising that would eliminate all states and usher in a peaceful anarchist federation. His anarchism, in contrast to that of Max Stirner and other individualists, included very widespread organization, but no coercion, no state.

The state, as he saw it, implied "violence, oppression, exploitation, injustice, established as a system. . . . The State is the negation of humanity. It is so in two ways: as the opposite of human liberty and human justice (internally), and as the violent disruption of the solidarity of the human race (externally)." The state implied other states, and, "since every State regards itself as an absolute end" and its own existence as the highest law, it followed that as long as the state exists wars cannot cease.[1]

All coercive political authority, therefore, no matter how directly and democratically derived from the people, Bakunin rejected. He did not, however, reject authority as such. He insisted that it be based on scientific or practical knowledge of the physical world, and that it be imposed on one, not by the will of the scientist or practitioner or "by any extrinsic will whatever, divine or human, collective or individual," but by one's own reason. "Therefore there is no fixed and constant authority, but a continual exchange of mutual, temporary, and, above all, voluntary authority and subordination."[2]

Following Proudhon, he developed this basic concept of voluntary authority into a comprehensive system of social organization.

Other than the Mazzinian system, which is that of the Republic as a State, there is no other system but that of the Republic as a commune, the Republic as a federation, a socialist and truly people's Republic—that of Anarchy. That is the politics of the social revolution, which aims at the abolition of the State, and the economic and altogether free organization of the people, an organization from below upward, by means of a federation.[3]

The basic unit of his structure was "the commune, absolutely autonomous, represented always by the majority of the adult inhabitants, men and women equally." This was a very different unit from the mir, for Bakunin did not share the *narodnik* faith in the peasant commune as Russia's special base for socialism. Above such communes he envisioned provinces, nations, and an international organization, each created by the free federation of the autonomous units next below it.

Each commune will have the incontestable right to create, independently of all superior sanction, its own laws and its own constitution. But, to enter into the provincial federation and to be an integral part of a province, it will have to make its particular charter conform absolutely to the fundamental principles of the provincial constitution and have it sanctioned by the parliament of that province.[4]

Thus, the paraphernalia of government—constitutions, laws, officials, parliaments, tribunals, etc.—were not eliminated from Bakunin's system. How, then, did it differ from the state? By being completely voluntary at all levels, was Bakunin's answer—"liberty, in a word, never pressure or violence from the provincial power, for even truth and justice, violently imposed, become iniquity and falsehood." The final sanction was always exclusion from the community, never coercion, but the implications of this Bakunin left inadequately examined.

Another important characteristic of Bakunin's anarchism was the importance he attached to destruction of the church and of the belief in God. All religions, he argued, "were created by the credulous fancy of men who had not attained the full development and full possession of their faculties." Heaven is a mirage in which man "exalted by ignorance and faith, discovers his own image, but enlarged and reversed." With revealed religion comes revealers, messiahs, and priests, and these, once recognized as God's representatives, must "necessarily exercise absolute power," since against the reason and justice of God no human reason and justice can hold. Men thus become slaves of the church and the church-supported state.

For, if God is, he is necessarily the eternal, supreme, absolute master, and, if such a master exists, man is a slave; now, if he is a slave, neither justice, nor equality, nor fraternity, nor prosperity are possible for him. . . . A jealous lover of human liberty, and deeming it the absolute condition of all that we admire and respect in humanity, I reverse the phrase of Voltaire, and say that, *if God really existed, it would be necessary to abolish him.*[5]

No other idea or institution, he thought, had such power to enslave men's minds, and therefore men.

Whatever the merits of these constructive and destructive notions, it is not by them that Bakunin is most widely known, but by virtue of his collision with Marx in the International Workingmen's Association. Until that time the distinction between anarchists and socialists was not so clearly drawn, and Bakunin thought of himself as both; thereafter, to the followers of Marx and Engels, the "authoritarian communists" as he called them, the anarchists were more hated than the capitalists. Marx finally succeeded in expelling Bakunin from the International in 1872, but that organization never recovered from their conflict.

The struggle with Marx was both personal and ideological. The rebellious Russian aristocrat-turned-plebean could not endure the intellectual arrogance of the renegade German bourgeois. Yet Bakunin had great respect for Marx. He translated the *Communist Manifesto* into Russian, referred to *Capital* as a magnificent work, and began translating it also. He saw, however, that within the International Marx wished to build a tightly disciplined proletarian party that could be used to capture political power and to turn the state against the old ruling classes in the "dictatorship of the proletariat." Neither this means nor this end appealed to Bakunin. Discipline meant authority and the denial of freedom, while the "dictatorship of the proletariat" was only another name for the state.

The Marxists . . . console themselves with the thought that this dictatorship will be only temporary and of brief duration. They say that the only care and aim of this government will be to educate and uplift the people—economically and politically—to such an extent that no government will be necessary, and that the State, having lost its political character, that is, its character of rule and domination, will turn all by itself into an altogether free organization of economic interests and communes. . . .

Our polemic had the effect of making them realize that freedom or Anarchism, that is, the free organization of workers from below upward, is the ultimate aim of social development, and that every State, their own people's State included, is a yoke, which means that it begets despotism on one hand and slavery on the other.[6]

The state should be destroyed, not captured, and this should be accomplished by voluntary, spontaneous cooperation of communes of workers and peasants.

Bakunin saw, too, that Marx's economic analysis, strong as it was, had led him away from the poor and the downtrodden in general and toward a special and relatively prosperous group, the factory workers, as the base for the revolution. This upper layer Bakunin distrusted; it was too deeply penetrated with bourgeois aspirations. Yet this "layer of semi-bourgeois workers" was precisely the class the Marxians "want to use to constitute their fourth governing class," and Bakunin thought it quite capable of forming one. "It can be said that this layer is the least socialist, the most individualist, in all the proletariat." [7]

Unlike Marx, Bakunin had great respect for the peasantry as a revolutionary force. As toilers they had common interests with the proletariat, but as landowners they feared socialist redistributions of property. The urban proletariat, he thought, must take the lead in the revolution and also reassure and stimulate the peasants, not impose its urban solutions upon them. For this purpose, in view of the peasants' illiteracy and suspicion, he advocated the method of "propaganda by the deed." Even so he rejected individual terrorism, although he spoke of it with understanding and sympathy.

Yet it was Marx and not Bakunin who believed the peasant commune to be a potential revolutionary instrument in Russia. Bakunin, with fewer illusions about the mir than even Herzen, denounced it for many faults and failures, including "the cruel and systematic oppression that the *mir* exercises on every individual who dares to manifest the least feeling of independence." He went on to ask why, in ten centuries of its existence, the mir "had been able to produce only the most abominable and odious slavery; only the degradation of woman and unconsciousness or even absolute denial of her rights and honor." *[8]

The influence of Bakunin's personality and of his ideas, ill digested as many of them were, was felt more strongly in Russia and in the Latin countries than in northern Europe. The syndicalists borrowed heavily

* Bakunin's respect for women contrasted sharply with the attitude of Proudhon and contributed to his popularity among the numerous female revolutionists in the Russian movement.

from him, and various secret societies found him more congenial than Marx. He was active among the young Russian revolutionists in Zurich, and thus his ideas, reflecting as they did his Russian experiences, were transmitted more easily than were those of Marx to the *narodniki*, and thence to the subsequent groups and movements. As before in the International, so again in Russia the Marxists have had to reckon with the strength of Bakunin's appeal.

III

Of a temperament as restless if not as active as Bakunin's, Count Leo Tolstoi (1828–1910) became the father of a very different kind of anarchism. Both men seethed with indignation at social injustice, and they saw injustice in many of the same institutions. They both judged man and society to be naturally moral when not perverted by government. But where Bakunin attacked government with violence, Tolstoi made nonviolence the cornerstone of his thinking, and where Bakunin made the destruction of religion a prime objective, Tolstoi founded his system upon it.

Tolstoi grew up with little discipline as an orphan among French tutors and religious female relatives. Two experiences that did much to shape his mind were a brief encounter with the University of Kazan and the Crimean War. At the university he was introduced to the writings of Rousseau, a strong and lasting influence that turned him toward the natural and against the conventional forever. In the war he beheld the blood and futility of the siege of Sevastopol, which raised insistent questions of the morality and utility of violence.

A happy marriage in 1862 brought him some fifteen years of peace, the period of his literary triumphs, *War and Peace* and *Anna Karenina*. By the end of the 70's, however, his intense interest in moral questions dominated him and didactic and critical writing took precedence over his fiction. He visited the slums of Moscow to acquaint himself with urban poverty and resolved to avoid the exploitation of others, going to the lengths of renouncing his property and copyrights (turning them over to his wife) and making his own shoes and clothes.

The reading of Henry George supplied him with a solution to the land question, which had replaced serfdom as the great national problem; yet the single tax was based on governmental power and therefore was only a palliative, in Tolstoi's opinion, and not the great moral cure that George thought. For a more general solution he turned to the Bible. He read it, however, as philosophy, not as divine revelation. By his rejection of authoritative interpretations he separated himself from the Orthodox Church while at the same time he accepted very literally the words of Jesus. He hardly accepted those of his followers, however. Paul in particular, Tolstoi believed, had made a fundamental mistake by trying to reconcile the teachings of Jesus with the old rules of the Hebrews, an error that had perverted all subsequent Christianity. Tolstoi's personal understanding of Jesus, especially as an advocate of nonviolence, became thenceforth the basis of his anarchism.

Among the Dukhobors, a schismatic sect in the Caucasus, Tolstoi found many of his moral opinions already in practice, such as the rejection of violence and of ritual and the acceptance of brotherhood and of productive labor. The persecution of this sect by the government confirmed his hatred for political authority and stimulated him to devote the receipts from his novel, *Resurrection*, toward their emigration to Canada. This earned world-wide publicity for their cause and some sympathy for his position against violence, but it brought him also formal excommunication from the church, by order of Pobedonostsev.*

During the Crimean campaign Tolstoi had recorded in his diary the idea of "the founding of a new religion corresponding to the present development of mankind: the religion of Christ, but purged of dogmas and mysticism—a practical religion, not promising future bliss, but giving bliss on earth." [9] This idea, reminiscent of Auguste Comte and later somewhat modified, contributed the inner discipline of his outwardly erratic life. Stripping the New Testament of its mysteries with the rationalism of a Voltaire, he was overwhelmed by the practical value of the suggestions for conduct that remained. Happiness in this

---

* Masaryk noticed similarities between these two: "Both men manifested the same aversion to civilization, science, and philosophy; to both, religion seemed the alpha and omega of endeavour. Tolstoi's estimate of parliament, democracy, and many other institutions, was closely akin to that of Pobědonoscev" (*Spirit of Russia*, II, 205). He was aware, of course, that the two were poles apart. Pobedonostsev stressed the mystery in religion while Tolstoi desired religion to be rational and practical. Pobedonostsev hardly shared Tolstoi's antagonism to government, to violence, to private property in land, or to the church, nor could he claim or inspire the moral elevation and deep human sympathy that gave Tolstoi his strength.

world, he became convinced, could come only through the utter suppression of selfishness within the individual and the devotion of his energies to the welfare of others—in a word, through love, not an anemic general love of mankind, but a concrete serving of one's neighbor.

In this conviction, as in other Russian ideas, Eastern and Western elements were united; Tolstoi stood somewhere between the optimistic formula, "Live for others!," advanced by Comte, an apostle of progress, and the pessimistic Hindu pursuit of contentment through the suppression of desire. Happiness required a discounting of the world's values, a losing of the world—not in order to gain heaven, as the primitive Christians had thought, but in order to gain satisfaction with life here, a concept akin to the religions of India. Happiness, moreover, especially required the denial of the use of violence in the promotion or defense of any values, even in defense of life itself, which made the teachings of Tolstoi congenial to Gandhi.*

Political anarchism was a corollary. Service to one's neighbor must never violate the neighbor's will: persuasion but never compulsion. Government, however, no matter what its form or its foundation, was essentially coercive. If consensus was present there was no need for government; if it was not, then government was a means for forcing some people to obey the will of others, always an immoral, degrading enterprise. To Tolstoi—and this was one of the weaknesses of his position—it made little difference whether the forcing was accomplished by a tyrant's whim or under the rule of law.

The essence of legislation does not lie in the subject or object, in rights or in the idea of the domination of the collective will of the people, or in other such indefinite and confused conditions; but it lies in the fact that people who wield organized violence have the power to compel others to obey them.[10]

Freedom under law was a contradiction in terms; it was, indeed, a formula for slavery. In this rejection of coercion Tolstoi's ideas coin-

* On Tolstoi's interest in Eastern religion and philosophy, and their influences upon him, see Paul I. Birukov, *Tolstoi und der Orient* (Zürich, 1925), and Derk Bodde, *Tolstoy and China* (Princeton, 1950). The direct influence of Tolstoi on Gandhi during his formative years is well known. As late as 1942 Gandhi wrote of Tolstoi as "a teacher who furnished a reasoned basis for my non-violence" (Mohandas K. Gandhi, *Non-Violence in Peace and War*, I [Ahmedabad, 1942], 413).

cided with Bakunin's, although his anarchism was not derived from Bakunin.

Tolstoi was especially incensed by violence used in the protection of private property. "Things really produced by a man's own labour, and that he needs, are always defended by custom, by public opinion, by feelings of justice and reciprocity, and they do not need to be protected by violence." But vast holdings of land or productive goods that are needed by the people are so contrary to the people's natural sense of justice that they must be defended by laws, police, courts, prisons, and other instruments of governmental violence. Such tactics, in his opinion, instead of inculcating respect for property, tended to undermine the people's "natural consciousness of justice in the matter of using articles—that is, the natural and innate right of property." The violent defense of injustice thus weakened the moral fiber of society.[11]

Unlike Bakunin, Tolstoi was willing to depend for the initiation of his new regime upon peaceful individual withdrawal of support from the existing governments, as Thoreau had done. This could be achieved gradually, he believed, if each person would himself do three things. First, he should take no part, willingly or unwillingly, in any governmental activity, refusing to be a soldier, juryman, representative, or other official. Second, he should pay no taxes, directly or indirectly, and accept no salary or other benefit, nor use any governmental institution supported by taxes. Third, he should not "appeal to governmental violence for the protection of his own possessions in land or in other things, nor to defend him and his near ones; but should only possess land and all products of his own or other people's toil in so far as others do not claim them from him."[12]

Less Westernized than Bakunin, he also had less to say about a new social order, although he shared Bakunin's confidence in the spontaneous abilities of men. Expressing a vehement moral revulsion against the tsar's government and his church, Tolstoi was equally revolted by the tactics and goals of the revolutionaries. "Attempts to abolish violence by violence neither have in the past nor, evidently, can in the future emancipate people from violence nor, consequently, from slavery."[13] He offered, instead, the primitive and peaceful life of the countryside, where agents of government rarely appeared and where custom and personal acquaintance rather than formal and legal rules controlled the relations among men.

Such a primitive life, however, was sharply in conflict with modern technological civilization. Although influential in the East, Tolstoi's theories have made little headway either in Russia or in the West. Lenin characterized them as reactionary and utopian, the product of a "crazy landlord obsessed with Christ"; yet he believed that Tolstoi accurately reflected the peasantry's opinions on land ownership and was "the spokesman for that vast mass of the Russian people which *already* hates the masters of present-day society, but has *not yet* realized the necessity of waging a consistent, uncompromising fight to a finish against them." [14] In the West too, while he remains a major prophet to the pacifists, his doctrines have usually been viewed as utopian and "oriental." At the same time, as with Dostoevski, his stature as an artist has made his work as a thinker a subject of perennial attention. Many who do not accept his extreme conclusions do accept his indictment of violence. To an imponderable degree Tolstoi has contributed to the strengthening of world public opinion, which no longer stands helpless before governmental violence.

IV

As Bakunin represents the atheistic and violent strain of anarchism and Tolstoi the religious and nonviolent strain, so Prince Peter Kropotkin (1842–1921) represents the moderate, evolutionary strain based on his characteristic concept, mutual aid. On theoretical ground as well as in practice he stood between the other two, and he was more convincing than either, largely because his scientific temperament, training, and experience enabled him to bring the resources of zoology, anthropology, and history to bear upon the theory and practice of anarchism.

A descendant of the Riurikide princes of Smolensk, Kropotkin was reared largely by his father's serfs after his mother's death in 1846, and he tended from that time to identify with the poorer people. He was conventional enough, however, to endure the Corps of Pages and to emerge at the top of his class. This earned him a year in close personal attendance upon Alexander II, which gave him an insight into autocracy that no other revolutionary had. From this taste of court life he retreated to Siberia, where he rapidly acquired a reputation as an explorer and geographer, and went on to contribute ideas regarding the orography of Asia, the extent of glaciation, and the continuing dessication of the Eurasian continent.

In 1871, without abandoning his profession, he became a *narodnik*, in response, perhaps, to the suppression of the Paris Commune, for he went to Switzerland, the center of the ex-Communards, to study the revolutionary movement. He never met Bakunin, but he investigated both wings of the International and returned to Russia already an anarchist. For two years he worked with the Chaikovski circle, teaching secret workers' classes in St. Petersburg. Arrested, he made a spectacular escape in 1876 and fled abroad, where he remained, agitating and writing, until 1917. He lost influence among anarchists in 1914 by supporting the Allied war effort, but he refused Kerenski's invitation to join his government and he played no part in the revolution.

Kropotkin grew to manhood just as Darwin's work began to make its impact. In his Siberian explorations he searched for evidence of the competitive struggle for existence among individuals of the same species, but found, on the contrary, evidence of advantage for survival among those species practicing cooperation rather than competition. From these and other studies his whole system of thought took on an evolutionary character based on the fundamental concept of mutual aid.

Darwin himself had noticed the advantages of cooperation * but he had emphasized the role of competition, and his followers, particularly Huxley and Spencer, so exaggerated competition as to distort the meaning of evolution. Against them Kropotkin wrote *Mutual Aid* (1902), displaying the significant role of cooperation in the development of animal species, including man. "The fittest are thus the most sociable animals, and sociability appears as the chief factor of evolution, both directly, by securing the well-being of the species while diminishing the waste of energy, and indirectly, by favouring the growth of intelligence." [15]

He continued this line of analysis into historic times, finding a cycle repeated in each great civilization. "In every case, the first phase of the evolution has been the primitive tribe, passing on into a village commune, then into that of the free city, and finally dying out when it reached the phase of the State." [16] The main point of his indictment of the state was that it retarded and stopped the development of human

* See Charles Darwin, *The Descent of Man*, Chap. 4.

life by destroying the prime factor of evolutionary progress, the creative freedom and initiative of mutual agreement and cooperation among men. For such freedom, in his opinion, provided the strongest stimulation to achievement, while compulsion, whether physical, legal, or economic, always reduced and deteriorated men's performances. The free cities of the late Middle Ages illustrated this, he thought, being the high point of freedom and creativity in European civilization before the state was able to erode the spirit of the people. But Kropotkin was always optimistic; this time the state would not destroy civilization because at last its nature was understood and the revolution would destroy it instead.

He criticized all those, including the socialists, who wanted to use the state, even temporarily, in the form of a revolutionary government or a dictatorship of the proletariat. Its evils were not, as they thought, due to the state being controlled by the exploiters. It had been developed through evolution for a certain purpose, "to hinder union among men, to obstruct the development of local initiative, to crush existing liberties and prevent their restoration." Like any other organ so developed, it could not be used for an opposite purpose. Kropotkin conceived revolution as a somewhat gradual popular upheaval following no blueprint; the people must have their hands free, and the initiative must never pass from them. "To allow any government to be established, a strong and recognized power, is to paralyse the work of the revolution at once." The "elaboration of new social forms" to meet the variety of conditions resulting from the abolition of private property would require not a government but "the collective suppleness of mind of the whole people." [17]

In Kropotkin's mind, as in that of Marx, the path he wanted history to take seemed inevitable. Already, he found, the state's claim to a monopoly of initiative * had broken down and many things were being done by free agreement among the people. Such evolutionary changes, however, were not enough, and he expected also revolution. His optimistic confidence in the people and his sense of history led him to believe that this revolution could not stop at half measures.†

* It is doubtful that Western states ever asserted that claim as effectively as did the tsar, and Kropotkin was misled by his Western evidence, seeing a weakening of the state where he should have seen a difference between Russia and the West, and possibly some change in Russia.

† Similar traits led Trotsky later to believe that the Marxist minimum program would be swept aside by the momentum of the revolution, and that a workers' government would be established even by a minority.

All is interdependent in a civilized society; it is impossible to reform any one thing without altering the whole. Therefore, on the day we strike at private property, under any one of its forms, territorial or industrial, we shall be obliged to attack them all. The very success of the Revolution will demand it.

Every society which has abolished private property will be forced, we maintain, to organize itself on the lines of Communistic Anarchy. Anarchy leads to Communism, and Communism to Anarchy, both alike being expressions of the predominant tendency in modern societies, the pursuit of equality.[18]

Revolution would not come simultaneously nor in the same way in all countries; it was neither desirable nor possible to wait until revolution "is ripe in all civilized countries." * Nor would it come to all parts of a single country at one time. He therefore gave considerable attention to the means, especially the economic means, by which a revolutionary city (he expected the cities to take the lead, and mentioned Paris, Vienna, Brussels, and Berlin as most likely) might maintain itself in a hostile environment.

This economic interest, while it hardly made him an economist, enabled him to integrate many economic matters into his system of thought.

He attacked the economists for their attention to production, whereas human needs should be the starting point of economics. Starting with production, the economists saw man as a tool and admired the division of labor, but Kropotkin, in the spirit of Chernyshevski and William Morris, objected to its effect on the producer. Excessive specialization stunted the development of the individual and perpetuated inequality and class distinctions. It did worse, in his opinion; it stunted the development of humanity, since only the healthy individual of well-rounded experience could achieve the creative potential that carries the species forward. He therefore advocated the learning of both mental and manual skills and the combination of industry with agriculture in garden cities.

Other forms of specialization, such as centralization of industry and international specialization of products, admired from the viewpoint of production, Kropotkin saw as methods of capitalist exploitation. He

* He thus anticipated by twenty-odd years the "law of uneven development" of the revolution, attributed to Lenin, on which Stalin based his socialism in one country. Bakunin had opened the door to this line of thought by seeing that the forms of revolution would differ in different countries.

also saw evidence of a historical trend away from specialization. Machine industry, once a monopoly of Britain, was spreading over the globe. The great steam engine, the hub of the huge factory, was being replaced by the electric motor, which, Kropotkin was one of the first to point out, could be used to encourage small village industries.

He also attacked the socialists who wanted to end capitalist rule but who "intend nevertheless to retain two institutions which are the very basis of this rule—Representative Government and the Wages System." The socialists called for common ownership only of the means of production, but Kropotkin rejected this distinction: all consumer goods also must be common property.

The means of production being the collective work of humanity, the product should be the collective property of the race. Individual appropriation is neither just nor serviceable. All belongs to all. All things are for all men, since all men have need of them, since all men have worked in the measure of their strength to produce them, and since it is not possible to evaluate every one's part in the production of the world's wealth.[19]

Distribution of the output of agriculture and industry must be according to need, not according to individual contribution, for three reasons. First, distribution on the basis of contribution was impossible because the contribution of each man could not be measured separately. It could not be measured because the interrelations of modern productive processes are entirely too complex, and because all such processes use the common heritage of nature, knowledge, inventions, or capital. Second, such a scheme of distribution was undesirable because it would entail a wage system. No matter how it might be disguised in labor tickets or hour currency, a wage concept would perpetuate inequality and exploitation. And third, even if these difficulties could be overcome with acceptable justice, such a plan of distribution would still be undesirable because the ethics of anarchism are not satisfied with justice but must go beyond it into generosity, beyond a niggardly calculation of a man's deserts to a meeting of his needs. "If each man practiced merely the equity of a trader, taking care all day long not to give others anything more than he was receiving from them, society would die of it." [20] Only the complete freedom of the individual to take from the common stores of goods all that he needed, without regard to the work he may have done, would satisfy Kropotkin.

Yet he did not think of this system of anarchist communism as one among several alternatives available to men. On the contrary he believed that he was describing the inescapable implications of the natural and universal human feeling of community solidarity that had been instilled in men by the evolutionary process. This feeling had helped man to develop his mental powers and to survive, and it still prevailed where, as in the family, it was not perverted by capitalism and the state. It was this feeling, he thought, that made anarchist communism inevitable.

Russian anarchism thus included a variety of temperaments and differences—even contradictory differences—of thought. To Bakunin and Kropotkin the overthrow of the state by violence was essential, but to Tolstoi the avoidance of violence was more important than the elimination of the state. Bakunin saw man as Prometheus, defying the gods; to the others, man was not so entirely free—he had a place in a larger system, the system of God for Tolstoi and the system of nature for Kropotkin. Many such distinctions are apparent.

Yet these differences are minor in comparison with the views they held in common. They shared inordinate confidence in men and their cooperation, but perhaps too little in men who held power. They wanted to build their new societies from the bottom, from the individual and the commune, and not from the top, as most socialists did, with a revolutionary government. They were vehemently opposed to coercion, exploitation, and inequality in both the political and the economic realms. Each had a sensitive social conscience and high moral ideals, and each found private property and the state, not only in practice but in essence, irreconcilable with those ideals. They were aristocrats and strongly individualistic, yet they subordinated individualism to the solidarity of the group and of the race.

This element of individualism has always hampered the anarchists in their efforts to influence revolutionary situations. As Kropotkin's analysis of evolution would suggest, the superior unity of the socialists has given them an advantage in the current struggle. But anarchists do not measure their success by their attainment of power. The strength of syndicalism in the 1917 revolution, the frantic response of the Bolsheviks against the Kronstadt uprising, and the persistence among the Marxists of the doctrine of the "withering away of the state," are all tributes to the appeal of anarchist ideas.

CHAPTER XIX

The *Narodniki*

THE word "populist," accepted as translating the Russian *"narodnik,"* hardly conveys the content of the latter and carries unwanted connotations. The populisms of America and Russia did have features in common, but perhaps they had more differences, only some of which were results of the different political and economic conditions of the two countries. It may, in fact, be best to set aside the American parallel, to think of Russian populism as a special type of socialism, and to remember the *narodniki*'s own phrase for themselves: "friends of the people." For the Russian movement was not a movement *of* the people, but almost purely of the urban intelligentsia on behalf of the people, primarily the peasants. It drew upon the other movements, Westerner, Slavophil, and anarchist, as well as upon European socialism. And its goal was always a socialist society, with or without the state.

Socialism, as a system of thought originating in intellectual circles, encounters the problem of how to reach and activate the ordinary people whenever it undertakes to become a mass movement. This involves also the problem of the proper relationship of the socialist intellectuals to the industrial workers and peasants. These problems have great practical as well as doctrinal import, since they bear upon the issues of legal versus illegal methods, propaganda and education versus organization, leadership and discipline versus the spontaneity of the masses, and the priorities among political and economic goals.

In Russia these problems assumed prime importance because of three circumstances that differentiated her from western Europe. Two of these were matters of degree: the overwhelming illiteracy and rural life of the masses, which made a wider chasm between them and the urban intelligentsia, and the more repressive attitude of the government, which regarded all attempts to bridge that chasm as subversive. The third was the existence of the artel and the mir, which led to the belief that, unlike the Europeans, the Russian people were already socialist. These and other circumstances gave rise to doctrines of Russian "exceptionalism" and to a special form of the problem of the relationship of the intellectuals to the people: should the intellectuals themselves undertake to carry out the revolution for the people, with or without the help of the masses, or should they educate and help the people in their own search for justice and in their spontaneous uprisings?

I

Among the members of the socialist circles of the early 1860's these alternative roles were neither differentiated nor thought of as mutually conflicting. As experience increased with the passing years, however, some with faith in the people tended to emphasize propaganda aimed at the stimulation of a mass movement for socialism, while others having greater faith in the intelligentsia tended to stress militant organization for the immediate conquest of political power as a precondition for economic and social reform. The former, the distinctively *narodnik* orientation, saw the mir as an institution making possible a peculiarly Russian path to socialism. The latter, less patient, drew more from the European revolutionary movement and were especially inspired by the Jacobin tradition of Robespierre and Barbès.

The emerging differences of opinion were well illustrated by the contrast between two clandestine proclamations that appeared in St. Petersburg.* A manifesto *To the Young Generation,* written by Chernyshevski's friends, the writers Nikolai Shelgunov and Mikhail Mikhailov, and printed but not approved by Herzen, was distributed in 1861. Combining Slavophil and Western ideas, it was a description and analysis of the situation, not an appeal for revolution.

We are a backward people and in this lies our salvation. We must thank fate that we have not lived the life of Europe. Its misfortunes and its hopeless situation are a lesson for us. We do not want its proletariat, its

---

* These proclamations are analyzed and quoted at some length in Franco Venturi, *Roots of Revolution,* trans. Francis Haskell (London, 1960), pp. 247–249, 291–299.

aristocracy, its governmental principles, its imperial power. . . . We have no political past. We are bound by no tradition whatever.[1]

But its positive program called for such Western institutions as republican government, free elections, and free speech, as well as for the collective possession of all land. The manifesto ended with great optimism regarding "the party of the people made up of the young generation of all classes," but it also displayed great patience, being content with urging the youth to "get ready . . . form groups . . . look for leaders."

A year later, in a manifesto *Young Russia*, Peter Zaichnevski said boldly that Russia was ripe for "a revolution, a bloody and pitiless revolution, a revolution that must radically change everything, all the bases of contemporary society without exception." He was more specific in demanding a federal "Social and Democratic Republic" with regional autonomy and even national self-determination for each region. But he expected a transition period of continued centralization during which the revolutionary party would have to rule the country and destroy the reactionaries through a dictatorship. It would "be more consistent than . . . the great terrorists of '92," and would "not be frightened if, to overthrow the present order, it has to spill three times more blood than the Jacobins of the 1790's." [2] Zaichnevski wanted to use political weapons in the tradition of the French Convention, but his aim, like that of Shelgunov and Mikhailov, was not so much liberty and democracy as peasant socialism based on the mir.

Young Russia was criticized by Herzen, by Chernyshevski, and by Bakunin for its confidence in the capabilities of revolutionary government. Its author was guilty, according to Bakunin, of "a mad and really doctrinaire scorn for the people"; and Herzen argued that "decentralization is the first condition for our revolution, which comes from the land, from the fields, from the countryside. . . . Preach to the people neither Feuerbach nor Babeuf, but an understandable religion of the land, and be ready." [3]

Similar differences of view were also embraced at this time in the first widespread clandestine organization since 1825: Land and Liberty. Supported by Herzen but inspired more by Chernyshevski, it was a loose collaboration of local groups, mostly of students, sharing only very general ideas. Rejecting reform, they hoped for peasant revolution but failed to bridge the gulf between themselves and the peasants. They tried to support the Polish uprising of 1863 and the organization was destroyed in the process.

As the reactionary tendencies of Alexander II hardened, so too did the tactics and the determination of the tsar's young enemies. Underground activity increased in extent and in sophistication, and with it the influence of the Jacobin trend. In 1864 a more extreme type of organization was created at Moscow by Nikolai Ishutin which undertook to combine educational and propaganda work with terrorism. Ishutin thought that peasant revolution was imminent and wanted to touch it off by the assassination of Alexander before his reforms turned Russia away from its natural socialist development, based on the mir, into the path of Western capitalism. A special disciplined corps of terrorists within the organization was to control it and also infiltrate and control other organizations. Dmitri Karakozov, who decided to shoot the tsar in 1866, was a member of this organization but acted without its approval and carelessly brought about its destruction.

Russian Jacobinism reached a peak in Sergei Nechaev (1847–1882), a dedicated and completely jesuitical revolutionary who was influenced both by Babeuf and by Bakunin. Convinced that the peasants would revolt in February 1870,* he undertook to lead the uprising by means of an organization more rigidly disciplined than that of Ishutin. With Bakunin he issued in 1869 a *Revolutionary Catechism*, which described the revolutionary as a "lost man" always ready to die or to kill for the revolution, whose only thought and purpose was merciless destruction. The organization was to be decentralized and all members were required to work among the people, but the uprising must be aimed against the state itself.

Practicing what he preached, in November of that year Nechaev and three members of his organization killed a fourth, whom he charged with being a traitor. Going abroad, he showed his independence of Bakunin by arguing openly that the central committee must have absolute authority and exercise it during and even after the revolution. When the details of the murder became known the dangers of his doctrines to the revolutionary movement were apparent to all. He was disowned by the whole movement, including Bakunin who, while still recognizing his dedication, denounced his Machiavellian attitude in manipulating the revolution through a small group of conspirators.

* The date, under the emancipation statutes, when peasant tenure of certain lands would be revised.

These organizations, like the earlier proclamations, were amalgams of irreconcilable elements—Slavophil and Western ideas, conspiracy and propaganda, violent and pacific approaches, and political and social aims. Only gradually during the 1870's were the conflicting elements partially differentiated in the discussions of theory among Bakunin, the anarchist, Lavrov, the gradualist, and Tkachev, the Jacobin.

II

Coming from the wealthy nobility, Peter Lavrov (1823–1900) spent his early and middle life in the army, teaching mathematics in the artillery college, yet he was associated with the revolutionaries enough to be arrested in 1866, after Karakozov's shot at the tsar. He spent four years in exile in northern Russia and then escaped in time to work for the Paris Commune of 1871. From 1873 to 1876 he edited at Zurich and London the journal *Vpered!* (*Forward!*), which in some ways replaced Herzen's *Bell*. His popularity declined thereafter but he continued to write and publish extensively both in Europe and, under pseudonyms, in Russia.

Lavrov possessed the temperament of a scholar, not that of an organizer or a leader. He saw the *narodniki* as educators of the people in a careful and gradual building of the forces of social justice. He had read widely in European history and social thought, and his works, mostly intended for publication under the censorship, were leisurely theoretical studies unrelieved by any felicity of style. The extent of his influence is debated, yet clearly some of his ideas had wide appeal while others provoked sharp criticism from divergent sources.

His most important work, the *Historical Letters,* was written during his exile. In it he attempted to combine the positivism of Comte with the moral imperative of Kant. By stressing the role of the individual and the great cost to the many by which the few have advanced in civilization, he touched responsive chords among the "repentant nobles" and provided a rationale for the *narodniki* of the 1870's who wanted to pay their debt to the people and most of whom, after the Nechaev affair, rejected Jacobinism.

The book is a treatise on the theory and practice of progress, which is defined as "the physical, intellectual and moral development of the individual; the achievement of truth and justice in social forms." [4]

Lavrov struggles with the problem of free will and determinism, so important to the *narodniki* who wanted to change things. He rejects both idealism and materialism as metaphysical dogmas and deals only with phenomena, all of which, including psychic phenomena, he believes to be determined by the laws of nature. However, since the individual does not know the forces that determine his actions, he retains an illusory consciousness of freedom. This consciousness is an extremely important phenomenon generated by the evolutionary process because it makes possible the application of critical thought to the existing situation, which is the primary requisite for progress.

The actions of critical individuals, therefore, have been the means by which the prehistoric era of the rule of custom was modified into the current historical era dominated by individual interests. Critical thought, however, has shown the disadvantages of selfishness and has developed a sense of justice. Progress consists in the growth and spread of solidarity among men. Those individuals who have attained this level of understanding are uncomfortable when they are not following the dictates of their own conscience, and they are thus obliged to push mankind forward into a new era of social solidarity dominated by moral conviction. Kant's categorical imperative thus becomes a product of evolution and an instrument for further progress.[5]

There was also an anarchistic element in Lavrov's theory of progress, derived mainly from Proudhon. Without actually embracing the old contract theory of the origin of the state, Lavrov stressed the voluntary nature of agreements and the coercive aspect of the state as a force by which some people compel others to do things to which they have not agreed.

It [society] possesses a *juridical* bond if the coercive force that sees to the execution of a contract belongs to persons who are not parties to the contract. It becomes *political* when, in the midst of society itself, a power is formed that obliges the members of society to execute the contract. A political society becomes a *state* when it makes the contract, which is obligatory for those members who concluded it, equally obligatory for those whose consent has never been asked or who have consented only from fear of personal injury if they resist.[6]

By its nature, therefore, the state violates the moral conscience of those who disagree, and stands in the way of progress toward the era of moral conviction. Already, however, there are signs of its decline.

Through federalism and local autonomy differences of opinion can be accommodated.* As the state becomes more democratic a larger portion of the people do agree, and fewer are forced to act against their convictions.

The ideal of the state is a society in which all the members consider the law as a reciprocal contract consciously accepted by all, subject to modification by the general consent of the contracting parties, and obligatory only for those who have consented to it, precisely because they have consented to it and are, in case of violation, liable for a penalty.[7]

If all could always agree, no coercion, hence no state, would be needed, but at their current stage of development men sometimes act "under the influence of animal impulses, of routine, or of the passions," and other men then need the protection of the state against them. Lavrov hoped for a minimal government, not for anarchy.[8]

With all his patience and gradualism Lavrov still thought that the tenacity of the old regime would make social progress impossible, in most cases, without revolution. Yet his experience with the Paris Commune † and his study of the French Revolution impressed upon him the futility of revolution without adequate preparation. He wanted thorough planning of the new society and much educational work and propaganda among the intelligentsia and the people. He stressed also the value of organization: "Isolated individuals are weak, no matter how strong and sincere their conviction; only a collective force can have historical importance. . . . Thus, a clearly understood plan for the active utilization of an organized social force, without which future progress cannot be accomplished, is indispensable." [9] Lavrov was, however, strongly opposed to conspiratorial methods, as Herzen had been.

These views, expressed in *Forward!*, brought him into conflict with Bakunin and with Tkachev. From Russia itself, even so patient a *narodnik* as Chaikovski objected that Lavrov's advocacy of education was operating to weaken the movement "to the people" by keeping the students at their studies. Thus, like Herzen a dozen years before, Lavrov lost the respect of the more active revolutionaries.

* Lavrov pointed to the United States as an illustration, but thought it still too centralized.

† Like Marx, Lavrov saw the Commune as a "new kind of state." He was influenced by Marx and by Chernyshevski to stress the role of economic forces in politics, but he differed from Marx in rejecting materialism and in emphasizing the power of ideas and the role of the intelligentsia.

III

At the opposite extreme of populist thought from Lavrov's gradualism and faith in the people stood Peter Tkachev (1844–1886), the leading Russian exponent of revolution by minority conspiracy. His ideas were very close to those of August Blanqui although he seems to have arrived at them independently.*

Coming from the poorer gentry, Tkachev absorbed his earliest political ideas from Chernyshevski's *Contemporary* and was active in the underground movement from his student days in 1861. He was fairly close to Nechaev but was not implicated in the murder mentioned above, since he had been arrested eight months earlier. He was sentenced among Nechaev's followers but managed to escape to the West in 1873. For a time he tried to cooperate with Bakunin; then he tried to organize the active revolutionaries around a journal, *Nabat* (*The Tocsin*), which he edited at Geneva from 1875 to 1880. Its circulation was small, since it was intended for the professional revolutionaries, so Tkachev also wrote under pseudonyms in both legal and illegal journals.

Like Lavrov, Tkachev was a student of the French Revolution, but from it he drew very different conclusions. Where Lavrov saw the failure of the revolution as a result of inadequate preparation among the people, Tkachev was impressed with the importance of holding state power and with the fact that it had been held by a minority composed of dedicated revolutionaries. He concluded that the preparation of the people for a social revolution was impossible while all the institutions of political and economic power and of education were held by the enemy, and that, since a mass movement could not be organized, the revolution must be accomplished by a conspiracy of professionals. Furthermore, since control of political power was so crucial to success, a political revolution must precede social and economic revolution.

Tkachev was thus among the first to anticipate the failure of the *narodniki* in going to the people. He interpreted this failure as evidence of the futility of propaganda among the people and as a wasteful effort to promote social ends without first capturing political power. He

* This is the conclusion of Franco Venturi, the best informed student of this period (see his *Roots of Revolution*, p. 403).

advocated instead a return to the methods of the 1860's, to conspiracy aimed at the destruction of the tsarist power.

A violent revolution is possible only when the minority does not want to wait for the majority itself to become conscious of its needs, and when it resolves, so to say, to impose this consciousness upon the majority, when it strives to bring the people's vague but ever-present sense of dissatisfaction with their situation to an explosion.[10]

To achieve this a centralized, disciplined organization was necessary; a federation of independent groups would not be enough.

The ultimate aim of the revolution, however, was not political; it was the establishment of complete equality among men in society. This had been the aim of the French Revolution, in Tkachev's opinion, and the victory of the bourgeoisie over Babeuf's conspiracy of the equals had left the revolution unfinished. The French had gained some *liberté* but no *égalité* and no *fraternité*. Tkachev reached beyond Babeuf to the earlier, more utopian notions of absolute equality:

This equality must not be confused with political and legal or even economic equality; this is an organic, physiological equality conditioned by the same upbringing and community conditions of life. . . . This is the final and only possible goal of human society; this is the supreme criterion of the historical and social process. Everything that brings society nearer to this goal is progressive; all that diverts it is regressive.[11]

Early in his career Tkachev was very interested in economic influences in history. He was one of the first, after Bakunin, to introduce the ideas of Marx to the Russians, but he adopted only a few of them as his own. He rejected all attempts, whether by Comte, Spencer, Lavrov, or Marx, to discover necessary patterns of historical development; to him the freedom of the will was no illusion. "The laws that govern society . . . are always the product of society itself, i.e. the product of human will and human calculation. They are born and die with society." [12] Yet he saw clearly that, following the reforms of Alexander II, the institutions of capitalism were invading the countryside, and that, barring revolution, the peasant commune would be destroyed. Plekhanov and the Marxists were later to welcome these developments as necessary steps toward a proletarian revolution, but as a *narodnik* Tkachev wanted to save the commune, the institution that made the peasants "communist by instinct, by tradition."

Tkachev had a unique sense of the urgency of revolution. The motto

of *The Tocsin* was "Now, or in the remote future, maybe never."
Socialism could be easily achieved before capitalism developed, he
believed; if it were not done soon the growth of the economic power
of the bourgeoisie would make it much more difficult if not impossible.
As private property grew, the socialist psychology of the peasants
would fade; the intellectuals now turning to the people would be
absorbed in capitalistic jobs and lost to the revolution; the machinery
of oppression would be greatly improved and strengthened.

Thus, with us at this moment all the conditions already exist for the
formation, on the one hand, of a very strong conservative class of peasant
landowners and farmers; and on the other, of a moneyed, commercial,
industrial, capitalistic bourgeoisie. As these classes take shape and grow
stronger, the situation of the people will inevitably grow worse, and the
chances for the success of a violent revolution will grow more and more
problematical. That is why we cannot wait. . . . Now circumstances are
for us; in ten or twenty years they will be against us.[13]

If time were wasted in trying to educate and propagandize the masses,
Russia would follow the path of western Europe; her great opportunity would be lost and social justice would be long and needlessly
delayed.

In an *Open Letter to Friedrich Engels* (1874) on the differences
between Russian and Western circumstances he said:

The position of our country is quite unique; it has nothing in common with
the position of any country in western Europe. The means that they have
adopted recently to carry on the struggle are, to say the least, wholly useless
for us. . . . We have no urban proletariat, that indeed is true; but on the
other hand we have no bourgeoisie. Between the oppressed people and the
despotism of the state that crushes them, we have no middle class; our
workers will have to fight only against *political power—the power of
capital* with us is still in embryo.[14]

Tkachev deduced that Russia could lead the way to socialism. Her
people were "communist by instinct" and, as Bakunin had said, always
ready for revolution, so, in spite of their backwardness, they were
"much nearer to socialism than the peoples of the West." But he
completely rejected the idea that they could initiate and carry out their
own liberation. "Taken as a whole the people does not and cannot
believe in its own strength; therefore, on its own initiative, it never
begins nor can begin to fight against the poverty that surrounds it."[15]

Besides, misplaced expectations of this kind tended to encourage inactivity among the revolutionaries. It was necessary that the revolution be started by a minority and that it then earn majority support. A conspiracy of dedicated revolutionaries must seize power; and in Russia that should not be too difficult, for the state was, so to speak, "hanging in the air."

Our state gives the impression of strength only from a distance. In reality its strength is only apparent and imaginary. It has no roots in the economic life of the people; it does not embody the interests of any estate. It oppresses alike all classes of society and is equally hated by all.[16]

A dictatorship must be established and the old institutions destroyed; that would be the first phase of the revolution. The dictatorship must then educate and inform the people, and carry out the constructive phase of social, economic, and political reorganization, which would include the elimination of the dictatorship. Thus in the end, like Lavrov, he expected the substantial minimization if not the elimination of the state, another point where he was influenced by the anarchists.

Yet he was quite critical of anarchism. He thought the anarchists inconsistent if they used organization as a means to revolution, because all organization is authoritarian and therefore against anarchist principles. On the other hand, if the anarchists depended on spontaneous mass uprisings, these are always local and uncoordinated and likely to be suppressed by the central power. Besides, even if anarchy were achieved, he argued, it would only open the flood gates of selfishness unless complete equality among men already existed, and this could be established only by an extended period of dictatorship. Even so, Tkachev was closer to Bakunin's point of view than to that of Lavrov, whom he accused of delaying the revolution and of holding an unrealistic Slavophil view of the peasants and of their communes.

Most of the socialists and all of the anarchists strenuously objected to Tkachev's ideas, primarily on three grounds. They accused him of separating the revolution from the people, of putting political revolution ahead of socialism, and of wanting to perpetuate state power. They feared that the ruling minority of successful revolutionaries would never relinquish power, that they would become corrupted and forget the ultimate aims of the revolution. Against such objections Tkachev denied that power always corrupts * and insisted that the ruling elite would not come exclusively from the upper classes, but would include men from working-class origins.

It is impossible to say to what extent Tkachev's ideas influenced The People's Will organization (page 261), but it is clear that he anticipated very closely the course of events in October 1917. The willful seizure of political power at the center by a well-organized conspiracy of professional revolutionaries, without waiting for mass support over the whole country or for the development of capitalism to produce a majority of proletarians in the population, was closer to the pattern of Tkachev or of Blanqui than to that of Marx and Engels. Yet Tkachev has never been accepted officially as a forerunner of Bolshevism.† He was too much like Blanqui, against whose followers in the International Marx and Engels had to struggle, and Engels had written against him. So also had Plekhanov, who needed to distinguish and defend his own moderate wing of Land and Liberty against The People's Will, and who tried to identify Tkachev as the intellectual father of that group even though he, Tkachev, was always unenthusiastic about terrorism. The problem for Russian Marxism, nevertheless, was to escape the opprobrium of wanting an extended and "inevitable" period of capitalism, which could be done by adapting some of Tkachev's ideas. As will be seen, Trotsky in 1905 and Lenin in 1917 made the adaptations.

IV

While Bakunin, Lavrov, and Tkachev in Europe were expounding alternative lines of action, the *narodniki* in Russia were trying various combinations of these and others. From 1869 the group known as the Chaikovskists gathered in secret around Nikolai Chaikovski and Mark Natanson. In repudiation of Nechaev's Jacobinism and in suspicion of the political goals of the liberals, they abandoned politics and launched a "book campaign" on social and economic subjects aimed at the

---

* He cited Cromwell, Washington, and Robespierre, among others, in proof of this thesis.

† In non-Bolshevik circles the similarity has been noted (see, for example, Nicholas Berdiaev, *The Origin of Russian Communism,* trans. R. M. French [London, 1937], pp. 80–85).

peasants through the textile workers of St. Petersburg, who returned to the farms each summer. Most of the Chaikovskists were followers of Chernyshevski and Lavrov although some, including Kropotkin, adhered to Bakunin's anarchism.

Also in the Lavrov current of thought, always strongly motivated by ethical and humanistic aims, was the subtle mind of Nikolai K. Mikhailovski (1842–1904), the best known and respected of the legal populists (those who remained in Russia where they were subject to censorship and police rules). Earlier than most populists he became aware of the growth of capitalism under the aegis of the government as a threat to the commune, to the artel, and to the prospects for socialism, and like Tkachev he strongly wished to forestall it. He too saw this threat behind the constitutional demands of the liberals, and he repudiated what he called "a damned landowners' constitution." He had little faith in the masses and few illusions about revolution as a method, but he thought the Chaikovskists went too far in leaving the political arena to the liberals, and he helped to keep political objectives alive in a largely social and economic movement.

One of Alexander II's reactionary measures, intended to prevent the spread of Western ideas, was the recall of students who had gone abroad to study. These and other young men and women, remembering Herzen's "To the people!," became new and much larger waves of *narodniki*, especially in the "mad summer" of 1874. Most of them aimed to educate, help, and minister to the peasants or factory workers, and only a few hoped to stir up an insurrection, but by 1877 several hundred of them had been imprisoned or exiled. Thus again, as with the Decembrists, the government depleted the supply of educated and civic-minded citizens, discouraging the peaceful propagandists among them and encouraging the terrorists.

This experience turned a number of young people away from the peasants, toward the factory workers and toward Marxism, but a larger number of the survivors attributed their failure to inadequate organization and preparation. They revived the secret society Land and Liberty in 1876 and tried to orient it toward what they believed the peasants already understood and wanted. Soon, however, under the spur of their own frustrations and of Tkachev's sense of urgency, they evolved its program rapidly in the direction of immediate political revolution. The peasants' aims might be limited to a redistribution of land and self-government in the mir, but the threatening development of capitalism would make such aims visionary unless forestalled by a change in the government. To some of its members, however, this evolution toward political objectives was a heresy amounting to the abandonment of socialism, and on this argument the society divided.

The small moderate wing, led by Plekhanov, who was still following Lavrov and Chernyshevski, was called Black Redistribution (*Chernyi Peredel*) from the peasants' desire for land. It favored a patient struggle for socialism through the artel and the mir, and less emphasis on politics and terrorism. As an organization it was short lived, but its moderation fed into the Marxist movement and into legal populism.

The larger, frankly terrorist wing, The People's Will, was led by an Executive Committee sparked by Andrei Zheliabov. He had drawn an opposite conclusion from going "to the people," the conclusion that propaganda could not be carried on without some improvement in political freedom. With this group Mikhailovski collaborated; he wrote under pseudonyms in their illegal journal, *Narodnaia Volia*, and was a strong influence in turning them toward constructive political objectives as distinguished from exclusive concentration on terrorism. As Lev Tikhomirov (1850–1923), their leading theorist, summed up Zheliabov's views:

The social-revolutionary party does not have as its goal political reforms. These things ought to be exclusively incumbent upon those people who call themselves liberals. But in Russia these people are utterly impotent, and whatever the reasons, they are proving incapable of giving Russia free institutions and guarantees for individual rights. Yet these institutions are so indispensable that without them activity is impossible. Therefore the Russian social-revolutionary party is compelled to take on itself the responsibility of demolishing despotism and giving Russia the political forms within which a "struggle of ideas" will be possible.[17]

Peaceful propaganda, even if it won popular acceptance, would do no good since the government was adamant in its nonrecognition policy toward public opinion. Only violence, therefore, had any prospect of bringing results. But violence should not be dissipated in general terror. In Tikhomirov's opinion, it must be concentrated at the center, against the tsar himself, for maximum effect. So, confident that they were carrying out their solemn duties as citizens, giving even their lives to improve their country, they knit themselves into an organization as tightly disciplined as Nechaev could have wished. The aim of "terroristic activity," Tikhomirov wrote in the program of the Executive Committee, "is to explode the myth of governmental power, to provide continuous proof of the possibility of a struggle against the government, to raise in that way the people's revolutionary spirit and belief in the success of the cause, and, finally, to develop forces fit and accustomed to battle." [18] The Committee in effect assumed sovereignty, an *imperium in imperio,* and in its judicial capacity passed sentence of death upon Alexander II. For eighteen months it pursued him with resourcefulness and personal sacrifice, finally killing him with a bomb in 1881. It was not simply that the tsar was reactionary and responsible for his agents; it was rather that the first prerequisite of freedom was that the people be freed from the hypnosis of autocracy, from the myth of the all-powerful tsar who defended the weak against the strong. And they must be freed quickly, as Tkachev had said. The French Revolution had gone astray because of the power of the bourgeoisie, Tikhomirov believed, so the Committee must act while the Russian bourgeoisie was still weak.

Close as these conspiratorial tactics were to those of Tkachev, The People's Will tried always to retain confidence in a popular uprising. They hoped that their assault upon the center of power would be the signal for a general revolution. They hoped to destroy the existing government and thus seize power, but they were reluctant, as Tkachev was not, to think in terms of exercising power. They wanted reform from below, not from above.

We are convinced that all social forms must rest upon the sanction of the people's will, that development of the people is lasting only when it proceeds autonomously and freely, when every idea that is to be embodied in life *has first passed through the consciousness and will of the people.*[19]

If they were successful in taking power, Tikhomirov asked, what then should they do? Create a new structure of government and decree the needed reforms? "We say no. Only in the most unfortunate case, only if the body of the people were to show not a single spark of life, would it be possible to accept such activity." If the people should respond as expected, the Executive Committee would have to help the people "with all its forces," and "hold the central power only in order to help the people to organize itself." [20] This reluctance to exercise power was never tested by temptation, but it shows that faith in the people and hatred of centralized power were strong even among extremists.

The Executive Committee hoped to call a zemski sobor, which was conceived as a constituent assembly. To it they would surrender power and advocate a program:

(1) Continuous representation of the people . . . having full power on all problems concerning the whole State;
(2) broad regional self-government secured by the election of all officials, the autonomy of the *mir*, and the economic independence of the people;
(3) autonomy of the *mir* as an economic and administrative unit;
(4) the belonging of the land to the people;
(5) a system of measures to hand over to the workers all workshops and factories;
(6) complete freedom of conscience, speech, press, assembly, association, and electoral agitation;
(7) universal suffrage, with no limitations of class or property;
(8) replacement of the standing army by a territorial [one].*[21]

The People's Will thus stood between Tkachev and Bakunin. Like the former, it urgently desired to overthrow the government by conspiracy before the bourgeoisie was strong enough to prevent the establishment of socialism. Like the latter, it hoped to stimulate a spontaneous uprising that would bring about cooperation among autonomous communes. The leaders were neither pure Jacobins nor anarchists, and the combination they made of these conflicting ingredients proved very unstable.

The death of the tsar produced no general uprising; the people responded no better to political action than they had to propaganda in 1874. The problem of how to reach the people was still unsolved. The terrorists were forced to reconsider the utility of terrorism, and although not officially disavowed it was for a decade discontinued and it never regained the position it had held in the underground movement.

During this time, when the best efforts of the extreme wing of the *narodniki* appeared to have failed so abysmally, more moderate elements gained in strength. These included the Marxists and the legal populists led by Mikhailovski, Vorontsov, and Danielson.

Mikhailovski had early praised Marx for the subjective idealism and righteous indignation that lay behind the façade of objective science

* It may seem incredible that means could diverge so far from ends as the methods of terrorism diverged from the seemingly reasonable goals of The People's Will. This incredulity is itself a measure of the difference between politics in tsarist Russia and in the West.

and materialism in his system. He admired Marx as an anticapitalist, not as a determinist, and he therefore opposed the Russian Marxists who began to argue that capitalism was inevitable. The Russian path to socialism, in his opinion, could avoid the upheavals and injustices of capitalism in Europe because most of the workers already held the means of production, the land. In western Europe the means of production would have to be taken from their present owners by revolution, but in Russia only a peaceful, conservative development of "those relations of labor to property which at present exist" would be needed, through "the legislative strengthening of the agrarian commune." [22]

But after the failure of The People's Will he grew increasingly pessimistic from an awareness of "the massive, sluggish force of historical atavism imposing its bloody-dirty imprint on the whole epoch." In 1893 he denied that he was a populist and attacked their naïve faith in the virtues and opinions of the people. In the same article he attacked also, as Bakunin had done, the oppressive indignities suffered by individuals within the commune, which he described as rapidly disintegrating.[23] He thus contributed, in spite of his opposition to the Russian Marxists, more strings for their bow: he helped to turn the *narodniki* away from their idealization of the commune, and he helped to spread the atmosphere of pessimism among them.

Vasili Vorontsov (1847–1918), who wrote prolifically as V. V., persistently denied the possibility of capitalism in Russia. The short growing season, he argued, made the farmers dependent for half the year on other employment, and required that industry be geared to this agricultural labor supply cycle. The factories had many workers during the cold season, but "a form of industrial organization under which the factory runs half the year, and stands idle the other half, does not permit production at the lowest possible technical cost. Therefore the product of such an industry, under the capitalistic organization of production, cannot compete in distant . . . markets." [24] And the domestic market was inadequate and was shrinking because of a vicious cycle of falling grain prices, increasing costs, and heavy taxation. Industry could not be run for profit, and must, therefore, be publicly owned or cooperative. In spite of the populists' general antagonism to centralization, Vorontsov came increasingly to advocate the nationalization of various industries. He also changed his mind about the parceling out of the landlords' estates. In the interest of higher productivity they should be nationalized instead, and operated as model farms.

It was as a critic of Marxism that Vorontsov was strongest. He saw clearly that even in western Europe the workingmen were more interested in improving their lot under capitalism than in attaining socialism. Marxism was a rationalization for intellectuals who from idealistic, subjective motives wanted greater social justice. Marx was incorrect, however, in expecting increasing misery for the proletariat. On the contrary, through unions, strikes, and political power the European workers were increasing their share of the output and this process was tending to stabilize capitalism. "The stability of the capitalist structure depends on the extent to which conditions compel the entrepreneurial class to redistribute part of its profits to the workers. . . . If all the products that are produced promptly find consumers, crises—as a general phenomenon—will disappear." [25] The concept of socialism through proletarian revolution had arisen when labor was too weak to attain its economic ends within the system of capitalism, a condition that was no longer present in western Europe. Yet the European Marxists were better than their theory; they did not think only of revolution but helped the workers obtain their reforms. The Russian ones, however, were worse; frozen in the dogma of proletarian revolution, they ignored the interests of the true laboring masses—the peasantry—and argued that nothing could be done to prevent the miseries of capitalism.

All the legal populists agreed that the peasantry need not be, and must not be, sacrificed to capitalism. Vorontsov for many years believed that this could be prevented by a minimal program of reform legislation. Nikolai Danielson (1844–1918), who used the pseudonym Nikolai —on, disagreed and supported centralized economic planning. He stressed the need for increased productivity through industrialization, yet he was sharply critical of the government's policies for promoting industry. Such hothouse capitalism, which tried to finance rapid development by impoverishing the peasants, caused widespread distress and such horrors as the famine of 1891, and at the same time destroyed the only possible market for its own products by reducing peasant purchasing power. Only well planned, balanced development could solve the economic problem, only "the unification of agriculture and manufacturing industry in the hands of the immediate producers, but unification not on the basis of small, separated productive units . . . but on the basis of the construction of large, social production." [26] Vorontsov came to similar views by 1906.

The legal populists studied the Russian economy as carefully as did the Marxists, their sharpest critics. In fact, Vorontsov and Danielson regarded themselves as correct interpreters of Marxism in Russia, as against Plekhanov, Struve, and Lenin, whom they regarded as "apologists for capitalism." The government paid little heed to their policy recommendations, however well founded; but they kept open the question of an exceptional, noncapitalistic path of development, for which the Bolsheviks also came to stand. As a recent student has pointed out, Russia did skip the stage of capitalism as both Marxists and populists then conceived it.*

V

While the debate between legal populists and legal Marxists raged on the surface, a rejuvenation occurred in the underground *narodnik* movement. The tradition of The People's Will never lost its romantic lustre among the more rebellious intellectuals, and groups claiming that lineage continued to appear. In the late 1890's at Minsk a group including Grigori Gershuni was organized; in the Tambov province another was led by Victor Chernov; at Odessa a third with Mikhail Gots appeared; and others arose both in Russia and abroad. By the end of 1901, largely through the efforts of these three men, together with Evno Azef, the police spy, many of these groups had joined together to form the Socialist Revolutionary Party (SR's), the strongest of all the political parties in terms of numbers down to the October revolution. Had it been equally strong in leadership, the outcome of the revolution might well have been different.

In the building and popularizing of the party many persons, of course, participated, but the renovation of *narodnik* doctrine that enabled the organization to compete ideologically with the growing Marxist movement was largely the work of one man, Victor Chernov (1873–1952). Born in the black soil province of Samara, in a petty official's family only one generation removed from serfdom, Chernov was closely attuned to the peasants' psychology. So well did he speak

* Arthur P. Mendell (*Dilemmas of Progress in Tsarist Russia* [Cambridge, Mass., 1961], pp. 232–233) finds that, instead of the Marxist pattern of feudalism—capitalism—socialism, derived from Europe, the "law" of history more frequently seems to be "from a backward rural economy to some variety of noncapitalist, collectivist-bureaucratic economy."

and write for them for twenty years that his own and his party's popularity became unprecedented. Aside from the newcomer Kerenski, who was an SR only in name, he had in 1917, as Minister of Agriculture in the coalitions of May and July, the broadest support of any member of the government. Yet as a minister he was unable to carry out his land program, and as a political leader he was unwilling, after his break with Kerenski, to join his centrist forces with the Left SR's of Natanson in a realignment that could have saved the party. His one-day tenure as president of the long awaited Constituent Assembly, which was dispersed by the Bolsheviks, was the theatrical anticlimax to these failures.

Like the legal populists, Chernov had great respect for Marx, and his theoretical structure was a combination of earlier populist ideas with ideas drawn from Marx and his German followers. For Marx's Russian adherents, however, he had less regard; they were too blindly determined to fit Russia into a European pattern of history. Rejecting economic determinism, he held to the *narodnik* tradition, running back to the Slavophils, that Russia's course of development would be different.

Nevertheless, he began his revision of populism by conceding that capitalism could not be skipped, as Chernyshevski and his previous followers had hoped, and that the mir would not enable Russia to move directly into socialism. From Marx, Chernov also accepted the idea of class struggle. At first he went so far as to concentrate the attention of the new party on the proletariat, expecting it to lead the peasantry into revolution. The peasant uprisings of 1902, however, soon restored the peasantry to the center of attention and facilitated a revision, in line with *narodnik* predilections, of Marxian class analysis. Industrial backwardness and the small size of the proletariat made proletarian revolution a disturbingly remote prospect for Russia, requiring a long period of capitalism to produce enough proletarians. There were plenty of peasants, but Marx had classed them as petty bourgeois counterrevolutionaries. But, said Chernov, Russian peasants are different. Life in the communes had prevented them from acquiring the taste for private ownership characteristic of European peasants and at the same time had imbued them with two convictions that inclined them toward socialism: a conviction that all men have equal right to use the land, and a corollary conviction that the soil should not be subject to exclusive ownership. The prevailing inequalities of the great estates so outraged these convictions that the peasants were ready to revolt—not, as the Russian Marxists thought, because they were bourgeois and antifeudal, but because they were socialistic and anticapitalist. The revolutionary class, therefore, already existed—no need to wait for more proletarians. Chernov's class alignment set the "toilers" (proletarians, peasants, and "toiling" intellectuals) against the "exploiters" (landlords, bureaucrats, and capitalists).

Chernov did not deny class conflicts among the peasants themselves, but he objected to the Marxists' methods of classifying peasants. Whereas Lenin thought the self-sufficient middle peasant was as much a bourgeois as the kulak, and only the landless laborer was dependable, Chernov used labor rather than ownership as his criterion.

We regard the peasantry as being sharply divided into two fundamentally different categories: (1) the toiling peasantry living by the exploitation of its own labor power, and (2) the rural bourgeoisie—middle and small—living to a greater or lesser extent by the exploitation of the labor power of others.[27]

The self-sufficient tiller of his own land and the landless proletarian were both in category one. "The basis of the existence of both groups is *labor*, as a definite category of political economy. . . . Both are *mercilessly exploited*." The fact that one group owned land while the other did not was secondary to the important "distinction of principle" between the economy of toilers and the bourgeois-capitalistic economy. Moreover, Chernov wanted to eliminate these class conflicts, not aggravate them as Lenin wished to do. This he proposed to accomplish by restraining the kulaks through taxation and by providing land for the landless through the confiscation without compensation of all state, church, and landlord lands. The development of capitalism, in his opinion, did not require that capitalism further invade the countryside, polarizing the peasants into wealthy kulaks and landless farm laborers. Far from increasing the forces of the revolution by adding an army of rural proletarians, such an invasion would disastrously reduce such forces by dividing the peasantry against itself and, worse, would destroy the peasants' traditional socialistic attitudes and create a permanent army of tenacious small-holding capitalists.* Chernov thus foresaw

---

* Chernov and the SR's generally accepted the analysis made by Georg von Vollmar and others that, contrary to Marx, small farms were viable and did not tend to be swallowed up into great capitalistic latifundia.

lines of rural development quite different from the urban pattern in industry, which justified quite different party policies.

Chernov conceded that the Marxists were right, however, in expecting the disappearance of the peasant commune, but unlike the earlier *narodniki* he was undisturbed by this prospect. Socialism, in his view, did not depend upon the preservation of the commune. The mir was a restrictive and backward institution that would be outgrown, but it had given the peasantry mental characteristics that would carry over and shape the future. Even without the commune to guide them the peasants would still reject private ownership of the land when its use was redistributed to them by the revolution because they knew that ownership would soon prevent equality of access to the land.

The concept of ownership, Chernov believed, came from the Roman law and had never been accepted by the Russian peasants as being applicable to the land. To them, land could be a "belonging" (*dostoianie*) but not property (*sobstvennost*). Like the air and the sea, the land should be "no one's" (*nich'ia*), not the state's nor the commune's nor the landlord's. "We shall make it *no one's*. Precisely as no one's does it become *the belonging of all people*." [28] Chernov believed that the coming revolution would write these peasant concepts into law. He called this the socialization of land, distinguishing it from the nationalization advocated by Lenin (page 318), which was still contaminated with centralization and the Roman notion of ownership.*

Socialization was not yet socialism, however, for two reasons. First, Chernov expected individual farming to continue until the peasants learned the advantages of cooperative agriculture and until the machinery became available that would permit collective farming. They would then band together voluntarily, and he had no fear that in the meantime they would acquire the proprietary psychology of European peasants. And second, industrial property would not be socialized by the revolution. The SR's realized that the "toiling masses lacked the maturity, and the training in economic self-government, in cooperative association, and in management of autonomous labor organizations requisite to the establishment of a socialist society." [29] They expected instead "a long transition period of 'laborism.' " Capitalism would con-

---

* N. N. Sukhanov (*Zapiski o revoliutsii*, VII [Moscow, 1923], 255) attributes the socialization program to Panteleimon A. Vikhliaev, an agricultural economist. It is likely that he and Chernov thought it out together.

tinue to grow; but with democracy, universal suffrage, and a preponderance of toilers, it could be controlled.

The revolution would, therefore, have two stages, but stages quite different from those of the Marxian system. The Russian Marxists, charmed by the French experience, called the first stage the bourgeois revolution against the feudal autocracy, and appeared to expect events to halt there until the proletariat, increasing in numbers and in misery, attained the strength for a new revolution. Chernov considered such a tactic, leaving power in the hands of the bourgeoisie, a fundamental mistake possible only for a doctrinaire Marxist. For him, the reforms of the 1860's had already brought capitalism to Russia, not by revolution as in France, but by the active help of the autocracy. The tsar was not feudal but the head of an "alliance of reactionary forces" of which "the bourgeoisie was, by all its antecedents, certain to be an integral part." The coming overthrow of tsarism would not be a bourgeois revolution, to be followed perhaps much later by a similarly violent socialist revolution. On the contrary, it would be a toilers' revolution that would go beyond capitalism by ending private land-ownership, and at the same time a political revolution bringing the people to power and enabling them gradually to achieve socialism, largely by legal methods "free of all further catastrophes and revolutions." [30]

Chernov was never so schematic as were the Marxists, the traditions of populism being less deterministic, and he did not dogmatically assume that victory in this revolution would put the SR's in control of everything. He was clear, however, that the revolution would not halt, even temporarily, at a capitalistic stage but would push on toward socialism in Russia and toward proletarian revolution abroad. In this he anticipated both the internal and the external aspects of Trotsky's theory of permanent revolution. He expected the capitalists to oppose these developments, and he thought that in the final stage of the transition to socialism a dictatorship of the toilers might be necessary. As in Marx, this would be dictatorship by the majority, not the protracted minority rule that it came to mean to Trotsky and Lenin.

Chernov's conception of the stages of the revolution, like that of the Mensheviks, thus called for an extended but not permanent period of capitalism in industry and of wary collaboration with the bourgeoisie in politics. Thus the SR's were reformist for the proletariat while revolutionary for the peasantry, a dichotomy which led to criticism and the separation in 1906 of a left splinter group of SR Maximalists who demanded socialization of both industry and land. Against them Chernov argued that the ending of ownership in industry would mean socialism because industrial production, unlike agricultural production, required collective work, which the workers were not yet strong enough to manage. The Maximalists had more faith and perhaps more foresight, for they rejected class collaboration as Lenin was later to do, and expected the revolution to produce a pure toilers' government. No second revolution would then be needed. As a separate group they soon collapsed, but it is strange that, with the absolute majority support that the SR's attained in 1917, there was not a stronger revival of these views. Taken up among Left SR's, they were still rejected by Chernov in favor of the stultifying coalitions with the liberals that prevented the enactment of the party's program.

Russian populism thus presented, during some sixty years, a welter of conflicting and complementary ideas. Personalities ranged from the scholar to the conspirator and the orator, from the terrorist and the spy to most respectable editors and economists. They clashed vigorously with each other over quite basic issues. What did they have in common? For one thing, they all rejected determinism in favor of the freedom and value of the individual and his action. According to this conception, Russia was free to shape her own future and need not follow western Europe. Second, they hated the autocracy and centralized power in general, and they loathed capitalism, which they saw usually through the eyes of Marx. Third, they believed that the people, shaped by the peasant commune, were different from Europeans in being already socialistic. If that trait could be preserved, the country could move directly into socialism, once the enemies were cleared from the people's path. Fourth, they viewed political forms and freedoms as distinctly subordinate to social and economic ends—liberty as subordinate to justice. And fifth, their goal was a classless, socialist society, to them the highest form of organization yet conceived by science and, fortunately, the form for which the people were attuned.

Over the years populism became increasingly sophisticated, refining its knowledge of the economy and its judgment of the people and shedding its more apocalyptic illusions about mass response to minority action. It never lost its character as a movement of the intelligentsia, but it came to enjoy quite unusual support among the ordinary people. Nor did it lose its quality as a spectrum of opinions ranging from the most violent revolutionaries to gradualists who neither desired nor trusted revolution. Its failure to resolve more of the internal conflicts, its preference for the unity of ambiguity and compromise, made populism as embodied in the Socialist Revolutionary Party in 1917 especially indecisive when faced with the dilemmas generated by the war and by power. It achieved majority support through the appeal of its ideals and its program; that support melted away in the disappointments of its performance.

CHAPTER XX

The Liberals

THE liberals of western Europe were once quite radical, and even violent, while they led the struggle for individual rights and political liberty. From the beginning, however, their leading theorists, such as Harrington and Locke, were defenders of private property and minority privileges, so that it was easy later on to convert liberalism into an ideology of individual economic freedom and private capitalism. As its main ends were achieved, it became a doctrine of middle-class moderation and gradual change—the stage of development it was in when Marx linked it with the bourgeoisie. The torch of utopian radicalism had passed to socialist hands and the liberals were on the other side of the barricades.

Yet liberalism is not always bourgeois. The early liberals—for example, the Whigs in England, the Jeffersonians in the United States, the Decembrists in Russia—were primarily rural landowning gentry, not urban capitalists. Liberalism in Russia, all through the nineteenth century, was of this early precapitalist type, and it never did become so clearly an ideology of capitalism as it did in the West. The Russian capitalists, unable to compete with Western industry, were too dependent upon the government to show much interest in an opposition movement. Even in 1895 the leading liberal journal could say:

Our liberals are least of all inclined to adhere to the principle "laissez faire, laissez passer" in any of the areas of state or popular life. . . . Since we do not have a bourgeoisie in the western European sense of the word, we also do not have a bourgeois liberalism, whose interests would be found in conflict with the needs of the laboring masses.[1]

273

I

The liberals were an articulate and potentially influential stratum of society that included many of the provincial gentry and most members of the civilian professions. They were united by a desire for a reign of law and some form of public representation in the government, yet they included a whole spectrum of opinions from Slavophils who wanted to preserve the autocracy to republicans who tried to collaborate with the revolutionaries. They were treated as subversives by the government and scorned as self-seeking compromisers by the revolutionaries, but they had the advantages of education and leisure.

If the Russian liberals continued to resemble the early liberals of the West in their class basis, they were like the later ones in their commitment to peaceful, gradual change. The great achievements of the Western liberals, such as popular sovereignty, limited government, and civil rights, were not gained without revolutions and bloodshed; but when liberalism reemerged in Russia after the reign of Nicholas I, it did not revive the revolutionary methods of the Decembrists. Temperaments that were attuned to violence had been captivated by newer visions of socialism and anarchism, and liberalism never again enjoyed the support of the more daring of the intellectuals. It always tried to occupy a moderate position, opposed to the bureaucracy on the right and to the revolution on the left.

Already weakened by the wide differences of opinion within the movement, the liberals were fundamentally debilitated by their choice of strategy. They not only rejected revolution as a method; they also neglected to build support for their cause among the people. They turned toward the tsar instead, and tried to persuade a government that was not open to persuasion—a choice that the revolutionaries attributed to their fear of the people, fear for their properties and their privileges. This policy was rarely stated so clearly as by Boris Chicherin in 1882:

Only by the harmonious action of the government and the public can we overcome the sickness [terrorism] oppressing us. . . . And the time is coming when the government itself, seeing in us not elements of ferment but a defense of order, will feel the need to enlarge the narrow range of local self-government and to introduce a public basis into the general system of Russian governmental life. . . . To wait with confidence the decision of the supreme power and to show ourselves worthy of our high calling by friendly activity for the public welfare—this, in my opinion, should be our policy.[2]

The liberals were perpetually in the position of petitioners asking the enemy to give in, fearing to reduce their prospects of obtaining "concessions" by offending the tsar or the bureaucrats by asking for too much or appearing "disloyal." On many occasions they were unwilling to say honestly what they thought because they judged that less radical opinions would be more influential. There was a continual process of trimming, of estimating the attitudes of the tsar and his ministers. This process frequently resulted in the watering down of their public statements, and contributed to the impression of weakness and lack of conviction that the liberals were making among the public.

II

The first important centers of liberalism were the zemstvos, the organs of regional self-government created in 1864. These were supposed to represent all classes, but the elections were so arranged that the landowning nobility and gentry entirely dominated the assemblies. Liberalism thus made its début through institutions that were obviously undemocratic. Moreover, the reforms for which they petitioned, being political rather than economic or social, did not appear to deal with the most immediate problems of the people. The socialists were quick to link political reforms with the propertied classes that advocated them, to see proposals for constitutional government as subterfuges to defend privilege, and to brand the liberals as enemies of the people. But how accurate was that assessment? What did the zemstvo liberals really want?

It must be remembered that the reforming impulse that created the zemstvos was quickly exhausted and that from the beginning they were confronted not only with the usual frictions of local and central governments but also with the hostility of a bureaucracy that could not tolerate any independent authority and that repeatedly impeded and curtailed zemstvo activity. In such circumstances very conservative men easily found themselves in opposition to St. Petersburg and ready to support appeals for change. The change most widely demanded was the creation of a central representative body, a "roof" to the zemstvo structure, but on the nature, power, or manner of erection of such a body there was little agreement.

The differences of opinion within liberal ranks are well illustrated by the contrast between Shipov and Petrunkevich, the two most outstanding leaders among the gentry liberals.

From his base in the important Moscow zemstvo, Dmitri Shipov (1851–1920) gradually became the most respected exponent of zemstvo activity, organizer and automatically chairman of the zemstvo congresses. He stood for the Slavophil current of Koshelev and the period of Alexander's reforms, more cooperative and conciliatory toward the government than the early Slavophils had been but still opposed to the existing bureaucratic system. Shipov wanted a revival of the zemski sobor, a consultative assembly that would express public opinion but would have no legislative power and would in no way limit the autocratic power of the tsar. The great evil, in his opinion, lay not in autocracy but in the bureaucracy and its choking of the channels by which the voice of the people should reach the tsar. He therefore called, as the Slavophils had always done, for the liberal freedoms of opinion, speech, press, and assembly. He was strongly opposed, however, to the establishment of a constitution.

The constitutional theory strives for the limitation of the rights of state authority and the enlargement of the rights of popular representation, and this as if to raise to a principle the system of inevitable antagonism and struggle between them. This principle contradicts my whole understanding of life. I adhere to the conviction that a fruitful interaction between authority and popular representation is possible only with their moral solidarity, with the acknowledgement and fulfilment by both sides of the moral duty incumbent upon them.[3]

The people would thus have an advisory voice, along with the bureaucrats, but decision would depend only on the will of the tsar.

In the early years of the twentieth century, as constitutional liberalism became less and less tolerant toward Slavophilism, Shipov drew closer to the government. Faced with revolution in October 1905, he refused to join Miliukov's new liberal party and split the liberals to found the Octobrist Party that cooperated with the government in the Duma.

Ivan Petrunkevich (1844–1928), on the other hand, was the driving force of zemstvo constitutionalism. In the late 1870's, when the government appealed for public assistance against the terrorists of The People's Will, Petrunkevich started a whirlwind of activity that ended in his banishment from Chernigov. He tried to coordinate zemstvo replies to the government's appeal that would attribute the rise of terrorism to the lack of freedom and to "the absence of legality in Russian life," and that would express the zemstvos' complete inability to take any measures against the terrorists due to their lack of power and authority. In this he stayed within the limits of the Slavophils' aims, making no mention of a constitution. At the same time he met with a group of terrorists in Kiev in a fruitless effort to persuade them to give up terrorism, at least temporarily, while all opposition groups worked through legal channels and through illegal publications for a constitution. In 1879 he published such a pamphlet anonymously, raising the demand for a constituent assembly. He argued that limitations of the tsar's power could never be established by a constitution granted by the tsar; therefore "we reject any constitution granted from above and insist on the convening of a Constituent Assembly." Nor, in his opinion, could the zemstvos achieve an effective constitution without popular support. They must first win the confidence of the people by militant advocacy of economic reforms and personal rights.[4]

This sage advice was not followed, and Petrunkevich himself continued to participate in liberal efforts at peaceful persuasion of the tsar. He was dissatisfied with the results of these efforts, but in 1905 he was still telling the liberals to "go boldly to the people, no longer to the tsar."

We must break the narrow bounds of our activity and must go forth to the peasants. Hitherto we have hoped for reforms from above, but, while we were waiting, time has stealthily done its work. Revolution, helped on by the Government, has now overtaken us. . . . We cannot hope to still the tempest, but at all events we must try to avert too great havoc. We must tell the people of the uselessness of destroying mills and homesteads. . . . It is none the less our bounden duty to go to the people. We should have done so before. The *Zemstvos* have existed for 40 years without coming into close and intimate touch with the peasants, and we must lose no time in rectifying our blunder. We must tell the peasant that we are with him.[5]

Between the extremes represented by Shipov and Petrunkevich, many other views were held regarding a reformed government. Some conservatives wanted only the addition of elected representatives of the zemstvos to the existing Imperial Soviet created by Speranski. With the exception of these and other Slavophils, the zemstvo liberals wanted the autocracy to be limited by a written constitution, and much thought was expended on constitutional projects. In 1881 the conservative Chicherin, still looking to the tsar, had believed that "the monarchical system is compatible with free institutions only when the latter come as the fruit of peaceful development and the calm initiative of the Supreme Power itself." [6] But by 1900 even he preferred limited monarchy to autocracy:

It is impossible to limit the bureaucracy without touching that power which it serves, and which more often serves it as a tool—that is, the unlimited power of the monarch. . . . If a reign of law constitutes the most urgent need of Russian society, this need can be satisfied only by a change from the unlimited monarchy to a limited. [7]

Other conservative liberals wanted an assembly, with a share in legislative power, built up by indirect election through the zemstvos at three levels. A type of federal representation of regions would result, and the dangers of direct democracy would be avoided. Others, who felt a need to give the people direct representation at the center, wished to combine an upper house derived from the zemstvos with a directly elected house in a bicameral system on the American model. Still others, more democratically inclined, called for a single house elected by "four-tailed" (*chetyrekh khvostka*) suffrage—direct, equal, universal, and secret. They were able to point to the example of Bulgaria, where the tsar had granted such a constitution in 1878. All these proposals presumed the prescription of the new system by order of the tsar, a new constitution given to the people from above. There were a few real democrats, however, who imagined that the people's representatives, elected by the four-tailed suffrage, could create their own constitution through a constituent assembly, could themselves decide the position of the tsar instead of his deciding their position. There were even a few zemstvo liberals who wanted to use revolutionary means for liberal ends. In the days of The People's Will they set up an underground Zemstvo Union and immediately became involved in the network of police spies. Mikhail Dragomanov, who edited a journal for the Union in Geneva, later explained their view:

Liberalism in Russia cannot employ absolutely "peaceful means," because every declaration concerning a change of the higher administration is prohibited by law. The Zemstvo liberals should have resolutely stepped over the bounds of this prohibition, and at least in this way have demonstrated their power to the government and to the terrorists.[8]

The Zemstvo Union collapsed in 1883, but it appears to have advocated a single-chamber legislature elected by universal suffrage.

Most of these schemes remained vague, containing conflicting elements. Like the *narodniki*, the liberals overvalued unity and did not resolve their differences. They never agreed on any one constitution, nor on a set of principles on which one should be based. They displayed almost no comprehension of popular sovereignty, and there was little sentiment among them for a republic.

III

After their vigorous national activity at the end of the reign of Alexander II, the liberals, like the revolutionaries, went through a decade of local "small deeds" and national quiescence for the remainder of the 1880's. From this they were aroused by the great famine of 1891. The ineptness and callousness of the central government toward this famine sparked renewed conviction that something must be done. Petrunkevich began organizing cladestine constitutionalist conferences. The death of Alexander III provided additional stimulus, and the youth of the new tsar, Nicholas II, caused optimism among the liberal gentry. But they reckoned without Pobedonostsev. Guided by Witte and Pobedonostsev, in January 1895 Nicholas set the tone of his reign:

I am aware that of late, in some zemstvo assemblies, have been heard voices of persons who have been carried away by senseless dreams of the participation of zemstvo representatives in the affairs of internal administration. Let it be known to all that I, while devoting all my energies to the good of the people, shall maintain the principle of autocracy just as firmly and unflinchingly as did my unforgettable father.[9]

This tone, at the beginning of what promised to be a long reign, was very discouraging to the liberal landowners. It discounted in advance the prestige of the nobility, to whose more conservative views other liberals had frequently deferred, thinking them to be more respected by the tsar. There now seemed to be no point to such deference, and within the next five years the center of gravity of liberal opinion moved toward the left.

This was the result of an accelerating change in the composition of the liberal stratum of society. With the gradual decline in the economic position of the landlords after 1861, and with the loss of prestige and power by the zemstvos through the encroachments of the bureaucracy, the landlord element within the zemstvos, and the zemstvos themselves, declined in vigor and importance. At the same time the professional, intelligentsia element grew in numbers and in strength. The zemstvos had long employed a growing number of doctors, teachers, agronomists, statisticians, and other trained persons to work in the countryside, and this "third element," as they were called, expressed its views through the zemstvos and increasingly through its own organizations. As these trends progressed, the late 1890's saw the liberal landlords overshadowed by the better-educated professional men. Professional associations of lawyers, of doctors, of statisticians, superseded the zemstvos as the leading centers of liberal thought.

In 1903 an underground Union of Liberation, a federation of professional and local groups, was organized. On its central committee the Union maintained parity between zemstvo gentry and members of the intelligentsia. It excluded the Slavophils, adopted the slogan "no enemies on the left," and opened its ranks to socialists and revolutionaries. It included, in fact, a number of legal populists and all the former leading legal Marxists. Its first congress (January 1904) considered "political liberty in even its most minimal form completely incompatible with the absolute character of the Russian monarchy" and resolved to seek "before all else the abolition of autocracy and the establishment in Russia of a constitutional regime." It recognized the four-tailed suffrage as essential, and stated as its direct goal "the defense of the interests of the laboring masses." [10] Reacting to the war with Japan in an illegal circular, the Union said that the people, having made the sacrifices of war, "have the right to demand the replacement of the present government of officials and make new rules. The people should abolish the single-handed autocratic rule of the tsar and his subordinate officials and themselves establish a constitution. Down with autocracy! Long live a constitution!" [11] The exclusion of the Slavophils did not bring ideological unity within the Union, for they were replaced on the left by the reform socialists, and during the war the Union included both "defensists" and "defeatists." The conflicts of opinion were clearly evident in a draft constitution prepared by a special committee of the Union. On one hand, this draft spelled out a system patterned on the government of Germany, with a ministry responsible to the tsar, indicating the committee's conciliatory desire to use as much as possible of the existing government. On the other hand, the draft ended with a statement that the "only correct method" for establishing the proposed system was by a constituent assembly—which the government would never accept, and which might draft an entirely different constitution. Even this equivocal document, however, was not officially adopted by the Union.[12]

Many liberals refused to join the Union of Liberation because of its illegal position, and for them a separate Group of Zemstvo Constitutionalists was also formed in 1903. More conservative than the Union, it adopted a defensist attitude toward the war with Japan and made no demands for a constituent assembly. It called for "popular representation in an organic unity of the monarch with the people," which was really a Slavophil position.[13]

The zemstvos themselves remained active, holding "private" nationwide congresses (since public ones were forbidden) in 1904 and 1905. At the largest and most elaborately prepared of these, held in St. Petersburg in November 1904, general support was given to resolutions on civil rights, including a statement that "the individual, civil, and political rights of all citizens of the Russian empire must be equal." A resolution on the peasants considered it essential "(a) to make the peasants equal in individual rights with persons of other estates; (b) to free the village population from administrative tutelage in all aspects of its personal and public life; (c) to protect it through a proper system of courts," but it was silent on the peasants' need for land. No resolutions were passed on social or economic issues, nor were a constituent assembly, a constitution, or even the four-tailed suffrage clearly demanded. Even more revealing of the weaknesses of zemstvo liberalism was the resolution on the future form of government. In deference to Shipov and the Slavophils the preparatory committee had proposed an ingeniously worded resolution for "an always lively and close communion and unity of sovereign power with society" through "the regular participation in legislation of popular representatives, as a separate elected institution," which the Slavophils could approve as a consultative assembly. The committee also proposed some additional phrases to be approved only by the constitutionalist majority, so that the resolution would appear in parallel majority and minority forms. Petrunkevich spoke against this compromise and in favor of a clear limitation of the autocracy, and another delegate boldly said, "There is no reason at this time to take the Slavophil current into consideration." The strength of the Slavophils, however, was indicated by the basic vote on the additional phrase for participation of the people's representatives "in the exercise of legislative power." Of 98 delegates, 38 voted against such participation in power. In other words, after the tide had already set toward the revolution of 1905, nearly 40 per cent of the zemstvo liberals were still opposed to any limitation of the autocracy, even by popular sharing of power in the legislative process.[*14]

IV

Among the professional men who wrested the intellectual leadership of the liberal movement from the hands of the landlords at the turn of the century the outstanding theorists were Struve and Miliukov. The former passed through a liberal phase on his journey from Marx to Wrangel, while the latter led the liberal party from its formation to its victory and collapse in 1917.

Liberalism had been considered hardly respectable by many of the intelligentsia because of its connection with the landlords and because its objectives were political and offered no solution to pressing economic and social problems. It had been antagonistic to socialism and yet unable to defend capitalism or to meet the theoretical arguments of the socialists. These deficiencies were in part remedied by Peter Struve (1870–1944), who brought to liberalism the prestige he had earned as a Marxian socialist.

Struve was a man with an independent mind, son of a nonconformist father who was forced out of a government job for insubordination. Starting his political career as a Marxist agitator, being briefly arrested while still a student at the University of St. Petersburg, Struve quickly

---

* Full texts of the eleven resolutions of this congress are translated in George Fischer, *Russian Liberalism from Gentry to Intelligentsia* (Cambridge, Mass., 1958), pp. 182–188. His treatment of this tenth resolution, however, obscures the essential difference between advisory participation and the sharing of power in legislation, the difference that divided the Slavophil minority from the constitutionalist majority.

abandoned illegal activity in favor of a prolific stream of legal publications that earned him a high reputation. At twenty-five he was regarded as the leading Marxist in Russia, when Marxism itself was at the height of its prestige. He led the attack on legal populism in 1894, then almost immediately began calling in question the basic tenets of Marxism. He remained sufficiently respected in Marxist circles, nevertheless, to be asked by the First Congress of Russian Marxists in 1898 to draft the party program. By 1901, however, he was unable to agree sufficiently with Plekhanov and Lenin to collaborate with them on *Iskra* (see below); and in 1902, with money from a wealthy landowner, he founded in Stuttgart a liberal journal, *Osvobozhdenie* (*Liberation*), which was the leading organ of the liberals until October 1905.

Returning to Russia, Struve sat in the Second Duma as a Constitutional Democrat, held various editorial and academic posts, and continued to gravitate toward the right. In 1909 in a symposium called *Signposts* he attacked the intelligentsia for its nihilism and opposition to the state. Repudiated by the liberals as well as by the revolutionaries, Struve found his way into the White counterrevolution after October 1917 and thence to the emigration.

Struve aimed his attack on legal populism against its doctrines of free will and subjectivism, which, he said, led to unreasonable expectations, disappointments, and pessimism. Reinforcing the Marxian economic determinism with quotations from recent German philosophical determinists such as Simmel and Wundt, he tried to show his readers that the future was bright, that irreversible processes were carrying Russia toward an inevitable socialist triumph. Moreover, against the prevailing antipathy toward capitalism, he argued that the objective, scientific understanding of history that Marx had attained had revealed the necessary and progressive nature of that economic system. Viewed from the standpoint of moral principles, capitalism, with its "extreme economic egotism and individualism, is evil and detestable"; but viewed objectively, "under given conditions, it is the only possible system for raising the productive forces of the country. . . . In this way capitalism is not only an evil but also a powerful factor of cultural progress—a factor not merely destructive but also constructive." [15] The failure of all populist efforts to prevent or to skip over capitalism only demonstrated the errors of their subjective, teleological approach.

As a critic of Marxism, however, Struve very shortly abandoned determinism in favor of free will, a liberal as well as a populist doctrine.

A transition to liberalism was clearly possible for Russian Marxists on the ground that, Russia being still in the feudal stage of history, the next tasks were the achievement of political reforms and the building of capitalism, leaving the struggle for socialism to future generations. This was not the ground that Struve took, although he continued to be complacent about the growth of capitalism.

Touring Europe, he noted the legislative achievements of Marxist labor organizations. Their power enabled them to wrest concessions from capitalist governments, and Struve, like Bernstein, saw in this the refutation of Marx's theory of increasing misery. He went on to revise the doctrine of the intensifying class struggle that could be resolved only by violent revolution. This struggle does intensify for a time, he argued, but at a certain point in the growth of the proletariat the capitalists realize that they must avoid head-on conflict, must fight a retreating action by making concessions to the workers. They then, grudgingly and gradually, legislate the bits and pieces of socialism into existence under capitalism. Revolution is replaced by evolution, and fortunately so, because if socialism were achieved suddenly by a pauperized, brutalized proletariat it would hardly be the utopia Marx and Engels envisioned. Unprepared for the exercise of power, the people would then fall victims of dictatorship.[16]

The idea of proletarian revolution, he now held, was inconsistent with the basic idea of economic determinism. If the political, legal, and cultural superstructure was conditioned by the modes of economic production as Marx had said, then the superstructure must change gradually as the economic base changed. To deny this, to argue that the capitalist governments could resist such changes until overthrown by revolution, was to deny economic determinism and give priority to politics. Marxism had thus always contained an inconsistency, caused by Marx's misapplication of Hegel's dialectic to the class struggle, which in his time was actually intensifying.[17]

If, as the facts seemed to prove, the workers could increase their share of the output under capitalism, then Marx's theory of distribution must be erroneous. This, like most of his system, Marx had based on the labor theory of value. Struve cast aside this cornerstone of Marxism and held that neither economic laws nor the legal position of the capitalists required exploitative distribution under capitalism. The shares of labor and capital were determined by their respective bargaining powers.[18]

Struve now saw in Marxism only a useful myth, lending strength to the labor movement. The Marxists had elevated the antithesis between capitalism and socialism to the level of an abstraction divorced from reality; they had thus come to "a formal mythology and to a generalization of the 'formula of contradiction' that contradicts all human experience." However, this abstract antithesis provided "the psychological and ethical motivation" behind the utopian social democratic movement.[19]

He was able to collaborate with the liberals while he was still a socialist. Even in his most orthodox Marxist publication of these years, the party manifesto of 1898, he set "the aim of winning political liberty," a liberal demand, as "the most important of the immediate tasks of the party." [20] He soon began to discount the longer range goals of socialism itself. "How can one reconcile the aspiration for absolute truth and beauty," he asked, "with the absolute postulate of equality," so dear to the Russian socialists? [21] Gradually the values of liberty and individualism took precedence with him over the egalitarian and materialistic values of socialism.

In 1901 he was invited by the constitutionalist wing of the liberals to edit the journal *Liberation* which they proposed to publish abroad. Through it Struve undertook "to create Russian democracy by relying on class collaboration and not on class struggle." His first editorial called for cooperation between liberals and revolutionaries.

The struggle for freedom can triumph only as a broad national movement, whose paths, forms, and methods should be and cannot but be diverse. . . . The nonrevolutionary elements of society can win the right to call upon the revolutionaries for moderation and to divert them from violence and excesses only when they themselves, having understood that *moderation obligates*, throw into the scales of history their political action and their civic courage.*[22]

Struve also tried to appeal to the Slavophils, but this drew a protest from Miliukov and he desisted.

Early in 1903 Struve advocated that the liberals combine illegal with legal methods of work. By the end of the year this advice was followed

---

* Lenin responded to this call: "We shall welcome the growth of political consciousness among the propertied classes; we will support their demands. . . . Such an exchange of services between liberals and Social-Democrats is already proceeding; it must be extended and made permanent" ("The Persecutors of the Zemstvo and the Hannibals of Liberalism," *Collected Works*, V [Moscow, 1961], 79).

in the creation of the two organizations described above, the underground Union of Liberation and the legal Group of Zemstvo Constitutionalists. Having thus united some of the socialists with the liberals and illegal with legal methods, Struve began to retreat before the revolution of 1905. He argued against the growing sentiment for a republic, saying that republicanism was "incomprehensible and strange" to the Russian masses. He denied the necessity for an insurrection, and held that "in a civil war the attacker is always in the wrong." [23] Expressed when the conflicts were growing sharpest, this desire for peaceful progress was an early hint of his later rejection of the revolution.

In August 1905 the Union of Liberation decided to reorganize as the Constitutional Democratic Party (CD's or Cadets); in October *Liberation* ceased publication, and Struve returned to Russia. He became editor of the journal *Russian Thought* and a professor at the Polytechnic Institute, but his reaction to the revolution was so negative that his intellectual leadership of the liberals was ended. He sat as a Cadet in the Second Duma where he spoke for the right wing of the party, but his evolution toward the right soon carried him outside liberal ranks.

Evincing this change, Struve defended Great Russian nationalism against the separatist nationalisms of the peripheral peoples in the empire. He identified the nation with the state almost as Uvarov had done, and rejected the idea of a federation. The unity of the state must be preserved, he thought, and the Russian language must serve as a bond to hold the various nationalities together. The intelligentsia should not identify the state with the bureaucracy but should "become permeated with the idea of statehood." The revolution had been defeated because of its anarchism, he said, but it had served to impress upon him "the real significance of the state." [24]

By 1909 Struve had become steeped in metaphysical and religious questions. With others such as Nikolai Berdiaev who had followed a similar philosophical path to the right, he published a critique of the intelligentsia called *Signposts* (*Vekhi*). Struve's erstwhile friends were accused of nihilism, materialism, anarchism, and atheism, and called upon to give priority to the internal, spiritual life of the personality rather than to the external life of politics and society. Khomiakov, Dostoevski, and others were set up as guides to a revival of mysticism.

It is small wonder that he was disowned by the liberals and rebutted by Miliukov and others, or that he became a counterrevolutionary.

V

Struve's independence and originality enabled him to make his mark as a critic of other systems, to defend capitalism, and to broaden the appeal and raise the respectability of liberalism. The other leading ideologist of liberalism, Paul Miliukov (1859–1943), was less original but much more tenacious of his opinions. He was an uncompromising Westerner, but the critical and creative thought of the early Westerners, based on their acute awareness of Russia's differences from the West, gave place in him to a naïve faith in Western mechanisms of government and to confidence that their importation into Russia was both natural and inevitable. He was not, however, equally impressed with Western economic arrangements and was strongly opposed to Manchester liberalism.

Born in Moscow, the son of a minor official, Miliukov graduated from the university there in 1886 and proceeded to establish his reputation by his publications in Russian cultural and intellectual history. He also tried to promote the wider dissemination of education and thus ran afoul of the authorities. He was dismissed from the university in 1895, exiled, forbidden to teach, and thereby pushed into politics. His study of history had armed him against Slavophilism and pointed him toward the liberalism of Petrunkevich. From 1902 to 1905 he studied in the British Museum, addressed many audiences in England and the United States, and became widely known as the spokesman for liberalism in Russia. During the spring of 1905 he worked to organize a union of professional groups embracing teachers, engineers, doctors, and others, and his was the main impetus in the formation of the legal liberal party, the Cadets.

Declared ineligible for the first Duma in 1905, he nonetheless guided the Cadets of the Duma, retreating with them to Finland when the Duma was dissolved and helping to draft the Viborg manifesto in which they declared their readiness to follow (not to lead) the people in resistance to autocracy. Again excluded, he directed the CD's from outside the Second Duma, but he was finally seated in both the Third and the Fourth (1907–1917).

As Foreign Minister in the first provisional government, Miliukov reached for a few brief weeks the pinnacle of his influence. To him the honor and obligations of Russia required that the war be continued, and control of the Dardanelles, for him the war's prime objective, remained its objective still. Thus he earned for himself the nickname "Paul Dardanelovich," and was driven from office in May after his statement of war aims.* He undertook to reconcile Kerenski with General Kornilov; this failing, and the attack of Kornilov upon Petrograd having pushed the city soviet into the hands of the Bolsheviks, he fled to Kiev. Thinking the Allied cause was lost, he tried to enlist the Germans in the crusade against Bolshevism that the Allies later launched. This dealing with the enemy cost him his little remaining prestige among the Russians.

Because of his foreign lecture commitments Miliukov declined the proffered editorship of *Liberation* in 1902, but he contributed to the shaping of its policies. In the first issue he emphasized the necessity for the liberals to work through the zemstvos. He suggested that, with the tsar's approval, an assembly of zemstvo and municipal duma representatives should draft an election law by which a national parliament should be elected.[25] Soon, however, he gave the publication a shove to the left by objecting to the inclusion of the Slavophils in Struve's efforts at unity, and by demanding agreement on clear-cut constitutionalist principles.[26]

Miliukov's reaction to the war with Japan was not outspoken defeatism although he refused to be drawn as Struve was at first into support for the autocracy. He called for the continuation of normal oppositional activity, including the slogan "Down with autocracy!" [27]

Aware that the conflict between the government and the revolutionaries was growing sharper, he saw the role of the liberals as that of mediators between these extremes, a role for which they were qualified by being "oppositionary without being revolutionary." Their chances of success as mediators depended on the possibility of liberalism influencing the government "without becoming untrue to the public opinion which is the only source of its power." Miliukov's liberalism, therefore, was pragmatic, a reflection of what he took to be public opinion, not of philosophical principles.

---

* One of the most fateful things he did as Foreign Minister was to insist upon the release of Leon Trotsky, held by the British in Halifax in spite of the transit visa they had given him.

The program of the group [the liberals] also depends largely upon the general state of public opinion at a given moment, being more or less advanced according to the more or less pronounced radicalism of this opinion. It thus reflects public opinion; with public opinion it stands or falls.[28]

Like Struve, Miliukov believed that government in Russia, as in the West, must eventually rest not upon the intelligentsia and landowners but upon the suffrage of the masses. The CD's, therefore, should cooperate with the parties to their left that claimed mass support, the Social Democrats and Socialist Revolutionaries. Finding that these groups expected a political revolution to precede the social one, he accepted their first phase as the final phase, and thought that hard political realities would prove the impracticability of the social and economic objectives of the leftists.

His solution for the peasants' problems was state aid in their purchases of additional state lands and parts of the larger estates that the landlords would be required to sell—a solution that would modify prevailing property arrangements slightly but that seemed to the SD's and SR's to be a scheme for continuing the hated redemption payments. During and after the revolution of 1905 these differences of ultimate aim separated Miliukov more and more from Chernov, Trotsky, and Lenin in proportion as these leaders expected the revolution to develop into a second, socialist, phase. From Martov, the Menshevik leader, on the other hand, his position was not so far removed, since Martov continued to expect a lengthy phase of capitalistic development. There is little evidence in Miliukov's writings, however, that he understood the differences of theory that divided the groups to the left of him.

The triumph of the CD's, who were by far the largest party in the First Duma, did not budge Miliukov from his attitude of opposition to the government. It is sometimes argued that the Cadets, by their intransigence in the Duma and by their stiff-necked rejection of positions in the ministry offered by both Witte and Stolypin, lost a great opportunity to achieve parliamentary government gradually. Their all-or-nothing attitude left the government no chance to compromise, whereas if they had entered the ministry they could have influenced the tsar, earned his confidence, and gained their ends step by step. Miliukov, however, felt no sincerity behind the offers of portfolios. By entering the government, he judged, his party would become entangled in policies it would be unable to change and would thus be discredited among the people. Having served the government's purpose, the liberal ministers would be cast aside. It is probable that in this estimate of the government's motives Miliukov was correct; at least it was a realistic judgment of the prospects.

By 1909, however, there was a notable absence of antagonism in his attitude of opposition. Safely seated in the Duma, he persuaded himself that Russia was enjoying a constitutional regime. In spite of Stolypin's antidemocratic evisceration of the Duma, Miliukov made in London the often-quoted remark that, as long as the Duma controlled the budget, "the Russian Opposition will remain His Majesty's Opposition, and not an opposition to His Majesty." [29] He reacted less negatively to the outbreak of war in 1914 than he had done ten years earlier; he even supported the government for a time and suspended his efforts for reform.

Within a year, however, he became convinced that only reform could save the country from defeat, and he resumed his opposition. By August 1916 he had won over a majority of the conservative Duma to his position. He made vehement attacks upon the German influence centering around the tsarina, using the phrase "treason or folly," and generated enough oppositional momentum to take advantage of the bread riots of February to secure the tsar's abdication and a Duma ministry—a "legal" revolution.

It was at this point rather than in 1906 that Miliukov showed so plainly the unreality of his basic opinions. He conceived liberalism as a reflection of public opinion, but he was unable to comprehend the un-gentlemanly public to the left of him, especially its elemental impatience with legal formality. As Miliukov saw the situation, the tsar and his ministers had resigned, the Cadets were legally in power, and his policy of patience was reaping its reward. The constituent assembly would establish parliamentary responsibility under a constitution, and all the forms of legality would be preserved. But in their addiction to legality the Cadets displayed a lack of understanding of the forces that had brought them to power. The war-weariness and hunger that had produced the riots and the revolution seemed to make little impression on Miliukov. His was an almost purely political conception of reform. Still a monarchist, he promised the Duma a new tsar, a brother of the old one, amid shouts of protest from the republicans, and only late in the summer did he abandon monarchy. Basic reforms were put off to the constituent assembly and the date of the assembly was pushed back further and further. Whether Miliukov feared the people, as the socialists said, or not, he was clearly out of touch with the masses and with the revolution.

Yet this unreality of Miliukov's opinions was not appreciated by the liberals of the West. Here he continued to be regarded as a foremost authority on Russia, and he contributed substantially to the general misapprehension of developments there—the first of a long series of "experts" to interpret each turn of events as evidence of the weakness and impending collapse of the Soviet power. But even he came to realize something of the people's attitude toward the Cadets. In 1921 he made the bitter admission that the masses did not know them but that "the very fact of their participation in the revolutionary Cabinets was sufficient to discredit the Government in the eyes of the masses." [30]

Liberalism in Russia started among landowners, and their perspectives conditioned its meaning and its public image. It never entirely overcame that stigma. No radical change of methods or of aims resulted from the ascendancy after 1900 of the intellectuals. Individual liberals understood the need for popular support as early as the 1870's, but liberalism never reached the masses. Within landowning and professional circles the liberals represented and kept alive a reasonable alternative between autocracy and revolution, the alternative of limited government attained by peaceful means. Liberalism thus provided a path by which wealthy and conservative but dissatisfied men could oppose the government, and thereby it reduced drastically the government's already very narrow basis of support. The spectrum of opinion in liberal ranks was so broad and their unity so precarious that Witte was able to split the movement by promising a Duma. The more conservative liberals ceased their opposition and gave the government a new lease on life, but the Cadets retained a large following in the zemstvos and in the Duma.

Even so, measured by any criterion, Russian liberalism was a failure. It failed, not because of the power or ruthlessness of the Bolsheviks, but because of its own weaknesses and errors. Among these were the following: (1) It chose to gain its ends from the tsar, not from the people, and to persuade him by supplication, not by strength. (2) It therefore bargained for the support of the nobility instead of building a mass following among the people by means of an adequate program of economic and social as well as political reform. (3) It did not build for itself, after the emancipation of 1861, a broad economic base of individual peasant proprietors by the active promotion of small peasant farms and the erosion of communal land tenure. The psychology of the peasants was thus left communal and not conditioned to individualism. (4) The liberals did not combine with conviction the two insights of Chicherin and Petrunkevich—the one, that the bureaucracy could not be brought under the law while the tsar stood above the law, and the other, that the tsar could be brought under a constitution only by a mass movement. (5) They remained almost entirely nonrevolutionary, whereas the liberals of other countries, when faced with unyielding governments, had found popular support and had resorted to revolution. All these weaknesses can be summarized in the statement that the liberals faced the tsar rather than the people. He, seeing them weak, could reject their "senseless dreams."

Yet after half a century of failures they finally did persuade the tsar. In 1917 he voluntarily stepped down; he and his brother Mikhail gave the liberals not concessions but in effect carte blanche. Then, in their hour of victory, the psychological consequences of their early choice of the tsar over the people emerged, like Nemesis, to destroy them. The people did not understand them nor they the people, and they continued to make unpopular choices. They had won the tsar, but they still could not rule without the people.

CHAPTER XXI

The Marxists

BETWEEN the promulgation of the *Communist Manifesto* and the organization of the first group of Russian Marxists a period of thirty-five years elapsed. This lag had several important consequences.

During this time Marxism had undergone extensive theoretical development in response to Western experience and had been subjected to a variety of interpretations. Marx himself had said in 1872 that the revolution might come in England and the United States by majority vote, rather than by violence, and had thus led the way to revisionism. The economic emphasis in his later writings contrasted with the stress on political organization and action in the *Manifesto*, and had a more deterministic quality. This presented to his Russian followers the dilemma of reconciling themselves to a lengthy period of capitalism or else revising the doctrine to provide a short cut to socialism.

Another result of the late arrival of Marxism was that other doctrines, including the anarchism of Bakunin and the Blanquism of Tkachev, enjoyed a head start. The Russian socialists and revolutionaries accumulated experiences different from those of the West and progressively refined their own indigenous theories, which had the additional advantage of closer affinity with Russian traditions and circumstances. Marxist claims to universal laws of history were always faced with the widespread and deeply rooted belief that Russia was fundamentally unique and would find a separate path to socialism.

I

The conditions in Russia were surely different from those in which Marxism had arisen. Industrial development was retarded and capitalism was even more so. From the time of Peter's military factories the entrepreneurs had been more dependent upon governmental favors and contracts than their counterparts in the West. They therefore lacked attitudes of independence and were unenthusiastic about the "bourgeois" revolution required by the Marxist pattern of history. The lower classes also failed to fit the pattern. Since the population was about 90 per cent peasant, illiteracy and the difficulties of propaganda and organization were correspondingly greater than in the West. Some of the factories were quite large, but the workers in them tended to preserve their old connections with the farms and villages whence they came and thus frequently failed to develop the attitudes of an urban proletariat. Marxism was therefore handicapped by the weakness of the two classes that were to play the major roles in the drama of revolution. It was further handicapped by its tendency to discount the peasantry—that vast reservoir of misery and of strength—and the peasant commune, the peculiar institution on which so many socialists based their hopes of avoiding capitalism.

There were, nevertheless, certain features of Russian life that gave Marxism some advantages over other theories. Marxism was based on class warfare, not on mutual understanding, and Russian classes were very far apart. Marxism demanded revolution, not reform, and the contempt of the bureaucracy for public opinion had convinced many that reform was impossible. The centralization of the government stimulated centralization among its enemies, which favored an organized urban movement rather than the decentralization of the anarchists and the peasants. And in the realm of philosophy, many of the Westerners, anarchists, populists, and liberals based their views, as did Marx and Engels, on the French socialists and on Hegel and the Left Hegelians.

Marx and Engels themselves had given considerable attention to the problems raised by Russia. They had been sufficiently impressed to undergo the tortures of learning Russian, and they studied the economic statistics in detail. Marx viewed the village commune as a primitive Indo-European institution, and he thought that, although already severely damaged by capitalistic influences, it still, in 1877, provided the Russians with "the finest chance ever offered by history to a people" to avoid "all the fatal vicissitudes" of capitalism. In 1881 he denied that the analysis in *Capital* applied to the mir, and insisted that "this community is the mainspring of Russia's social regeneration"; but he also warned that it must be allowed to develop spontaneously and that the "deleterious influences" undermining it must be eliminated.[1] These requirements could be met only with help from the West: "If the Russian revolution becomes the signal for a proletarian revolution in the West, so that both complement each other, the present Russian common ownership of land may serve as the starting point for a communist development."[2] Marx and Engels were then optimistic that the nonproletarian but restless Russians, who had recently assassinated a tsar, would provide the spark to ignite a proletarian revolution in Europe, but by 1893 Engels thought that it was too late. Scientific socialism could arise only dialectically from the antagonisms of capitalism. It was impossible "to develop a higher social form out of primitive agrarian communism unless—that higher form was *already in existence* in another country, so as to serve as a model."[3] The model was not in existence, so capitalism was unavoidable—in Russia as elsewhere.

II

Marx and Engels had been hopeful, however, at the time when the first Russian Marxist group, The Emancipation of Labor, was formed in 1883 in Geneva. This was the group organized by George V. Plekhanov (1856–1918), who led the moderate wing of Land and Liberty when it broke away from The People's Will in 1879, with the help of Vera Zasulich, Paul Axelrod, and Leo Deutsch. Coming from the rural gentry, Plekhanov, though well educated, was irascible and conceited and thus handicapped as a political leader; yet his mind and pen were sharp.

The apparent failure of both Lavrov's propaganda and Zheliabov's terrorism had opened the way for Marxism, which was already the dominant trend in Western socialism. Difficult problems of theory had to be solved, however, before Marxism could be made appealing to Russian socialists. Plekhanov attacked these problems with vigor and imagination.

Against Tikhomirov, who had survived the destruction of The People's Will, Plekhanov wrote his basic book *Our Differences* (1884), arguing the futility of conspiracy when it lacked the support of the class-conscious masses. He branded this as utopian Blanquism derived from Tkachev. In rejecting Blanqui, Plekhanov was undoubtedly following Marx and Engels, but in reply to the book Engels wrote that Russia was "one of the exceptional cases where it is possible for a handful of people to *make* a revolution." [4] He thus encouraged immediate political action, but Plekhanov was impelled by factional differences to embrace a more cautious and deterministic interpretation of Marxism. He chose the stance of "scientific" historical materialism, which may have had a broad appeal, but which also made more difficult the later adoption of conspiratorial tactics.

Yet Plekhanov was far from surrendering to determinism. "Dialectical materialism not only does not strive, as its opponents attribute to it, to convince man that it is absurd to revolt against economic necessity, but it is the first to point out how to *overcome* the latter. . . . It depends on us to make *necessity* the obedient slave of *reason*." [5] The revolution must have mass support and this could not be generated by propaganda among the peasants. It must come from an urban proletariat conditioned by factory life through the industrialization of Russia. But this did not, as the *narodniki* claimed, mean an indefinite period of capitalism: "Our capitalism will fade before it has time to blossom *completely*." Profiting from Western experience and advanced technology, Russia would press quickly through the capitalist stage of history and be ripe for socialism.[6] Thus, while abandoning the mir and with it the hope of skipping capitalism entirely, he retained a modicum of Russian "exceptionalism."

In this analysis Plekhanov retained also the traditional distinction between a political and a social revolution. Combined with Marxism this meant that Russia, being in the feudalistic stage of history, would first undergo a bourgeois-democratic revolution, then, after the growth of the proletariat, a proletarian-socialist revolution. Like the *narodniki*, he believed that the socialists would have to lead both of these revolutions. Because of the "underdevelopment of the middle class," which "is incapable of taking the *initiative* in the struggle against absolutism, . . . our socialist intelligentsia has been obliged to head the present-day emancipation movement, whose direct task must be to set up free political institutions in our country." [7] While adhering to the Marxist pattern of history, and emphasizing the importance of economic development, he thus provided ample opportunity for revolutionary initiative.

Plekhanov charted the course of Russian Marxism by the earlier, more voluntaristic writings of Marx, trying to steer the movement between the optimistic, impatient, and to him visionary ideas of the *narodniki* and anarchists on the one hand, and the economic determinism that shaded into liberalism on the other. As in 1879, however, he failed to convince most of the socialists, and the revolutionary movement was permanently divided into mutually antagonistic Marxist and non-Marxist currents.

The Marxist current itself seemed to have a perennial tendency to flow toward liberalism. From 1895 the revisionism of Bernstein diverted many of the Marxists of the West into peaceable reformist activities, and similar ideas in Russia pushed three separate sections of the movement toward economic determinism—the legal Marxists, the Economists, and the Mensheviks.

Of these, only the first group made the full transition to liberalism. The legal Marxists were writers, publishing somewhat abstract and scholarly economic analyses openly under the censorship. These men, especially Struve, Berdiaev, and Bulgakov, did yeoman service for Marxism through their criticisms of the legal populists (page 283). Their primary objective was to demonstrate that Russia was already far along in the development of capitalism, and that all theories aiming at the avoidance of capitalism must therefore be abandoned. With the help of Plekhanov and Lenin (Vladimir I. Ul'ianov, 1870–1924), both writing openly under pseudonyms in the 1890's, they made this demonstration so convincingly that even Chernov accepted it. Yet they were never very radical and never entirely satisfied with the economic analysis of Marx. Bernstein's criticisms, added to their awareness that the facts of Russia did not always fit the theories of Marx, gradually disenchanted them. Between 1895 and 1900 they completed their migration from Marxism into the ranks of the liberals.

While these literary debates were going on in the open, efforts were also made to spread Marxism underground, among the workers of the cities. In St. Petersburg both Lenin and Martov (Iuri O. Tsederbaum, 1873–1923) participated in these efforts, and, like the *narodniki* before them, they immediately encountered the difficulties of bridging the chasm between the intelligentsia and the masses. From the beginning Plekhanov had been aware of this problem. In his pamphlet *Socialism and the Political Struggle* (1883) he had written:

The strength of the working class—as of any other class—depends, among other things, on the clarity of its political consciousness, its cohesion and its degree of organization. It is these elements of its strength that must be influenced by our socialist intelligentsia. The latter must become the leader of the working class in the impending emancipation movement, explain to it its political and economic interests and also the interdependence of those interests and must prepare them to play an independent role in the social life of Russia.*[8]

Martov too, in his first pamphlet ten years later, had contrasted "consciousness" of the workings of economics and history possessed by the intellectuals with the "spontaneity" of the illiterate workmen who were organizing a union movement without understanding the interconnections of politics and economics or the ramifications of the class struggle. He concluded that neither spontaneity nor consciousness was adequate alone and that they must be combined.

From his exile in Vilna, Martov brought back an important method for combining them. By sad experience the Polish SD's had learned that the education of factory workers in study circles only served to enable the most capable workers to rise into the middle class, deserting the class they were being trained to lead. The Poles, therefore, had worked out a different technique. As drawn up by Arkadie Kremer and edited by Martov in a pamphlet *On Agitation* (1894), this technique called for the gradual development of consciousness among the workers, not by teaching, but by active participation of the socialist intellectuals in the spontaneous workers' movement, in mass meetings, and in strikes. Their propaganda should be written around actual factory situations, so that their arguments would be clear and significant to the worker from his own experience. The intellectuals, by stimulating and helping in the pursuit of immediate economic goals and by interpreting the experiences of the resulting struggles, would win the confidence of the workers, would enable them to understand the necessity for longer range political goals, and would earn positions of leadership in the coming political struggle.[9]

Martov regarded these tactics as means toward a revolutionary political end, and as such they were the basis on which he and Lenin attempted to consolidate the Marxists of St. Petersburg in a Union of Struggle for the Liberation of Labor—activities that led to their arrest and exile late in 1895. But *On Agitation* stressed so much the need to

---

* The Austrian Social Democrats, in their Hainfeld Program of 1888, accepted this view, and the German party incorporated it into the Erfurt Program in 1891.

adjust propaganda and agitation to the understanding and to the immediate interests of the workers that political objectives were pushed into the background. Such political objectives as civil liberties and a parliamentary republic had never been popular among Russian socialists, and soon a group of Marxists began to reject them explicitly. These were the Economists, the faction resulting from the second major split in Russian Marxism.

III

Economism was an attempt to revise Marxist doctrine in the light of empirical facts, somewhat like the revisionism of Bernstein in Germany. The fundamental law of the labor movement was that it followed the line of least resistance, the Economists said in their *Credo* drawn up by Ekatarina Kuskova in 1899.* In the West, with its free institutions, this line included political activity; but in Russia, without such institutions, "the line of least resistance will never tend in the direction of political activity." The economic struggle, on the other hand, was possible and was actually being waged by the masses themselves. Through his conflicts with the government in the course of this struggle, "the Russian worker will at last create what may be called the form of the labour movement" best suited to Russia.†

This optimistic confidence in the growth of class consciousness from the spontaneous labor movement was consonant with the materialist psychology of Marx's *Capital* although not with recent Western experience. It also had deep historical roots in the apolitical attitudes of Slavophils, *narodniki*, and anarchists, and it encouraged the hope for a special Russian path to socialism. It therefore proved popular for some six years beginning in 1896, the Economists gaining control of the St. Petersburg Union of Struggle and of the émigré Union of Russian Social Democrats Abroad.

Economism labored, however, under two severe handicaps. Its special path to socialism lay through an extensive period of capitalism, and

---

* In addition to Kuskova (1869–?), the Economists included her husband, Sergei N. Prokopovich (1871–1955), later Minister of Food under Kerenski, and Martynov (A. S. Piker, 1865–1935) and Akimov (V. L. Makhnovets, 1873–1921), their leading theorists.

† The text of the *Credo* is in V. I. Lenin, *Selected Works*, ed. J. Fineberg, I (London, n.d.), 516–519, quotations from p. 518.

the Economists denied the possibility of shortening this period by the infusion of class consciousness into the workers through a political party. They thus largely deprived the intellectuals of their *raison d'être* in the labor movement. Moreover, they were willing to wait for the bourgeoisie to lead its own revolution, and called for collaboration in "liberal opposition activity" against the autocracy. In this manner the proletariat, instead of leading the revolution, seemed to be reduced to the role of auxiliary troops for the bourgeoisie. Economism, in fact, challenged the whole pattern of Russian Marxism as Plekhanov had been presenting it since 1883.

Against this extreme form of deterministic Marxism, Plekhanov and his voluntaristic followers, from their various places of exile, volleyed and thundered. To coordinate their efforts and combat the ideas of Economism they started, early in 1901, the famous newspaper *Iskra* ("The Spark") and the less successful theoretical journal *Zaria* ("The Dawn"), with Plekhanov, Axelrod, Zasulich, Lenin, Martov, and Potresov as editors. Printed abroad and smuggled all over Russia, these journals spread both news and polemical argument, and the distribution of them gave much practical experience in underground organization.

Against the Economists also Lenin wrote his important book *What Is To Be Done?* (1902). "The history of all countries," he declared, "shows that the working class, exclusively by its own effort, is able to develop only trade union consciousness," not class consciousness, and "trade unionism means the ideological enslavement of the workers to the bourgeoisie." [10] In this Lenin went beyond the views of Plekhanov and the Western Marxists that the factory worker, in his increasing misery, needed the help of the socialist intellectual to understand the necessity for the destruction of capitalism (page 298). Factory experience, he believed, far from shaping men into socialists, would in itself serve only to freeze them in the stance of a tug of war with the bourgeoisie, unable to let go of the rope and march forward to an entirely different, cooperative economic system. The role of the intellectuals, therefore, was not simply auxiliary or catalytic; it was fundamental and indispensable.

In this book Lenin also went beyond the earlier Marxists in his conception of the role of the party. The party was not only needed to educate the workers and to organize the mass struggle that they would inevitably initiate; it was needed as the fighting vanguard of the proletarian army. It must, therefore, be based on a hard core of professionals.

"We can never give a mass organisation that degree of secrecy which is essential for the persistent and continuous struggle against the government." Centralization and discipline were not only desirable, they were essential. Yet "the centralisation of the more secret functions in an organisation of revolutionaries will not diminish, but rather increase the extent and quality of the activity of a large number of other organisations intended for wide membership." [11]

Lenin's conviction, made explicit in *What Is To Be Done?*, that without the Marxist party the workers would never achieve socialism, underlay all of his later adaptations of Marxism. It caused the long and rancorous controversy with the Mensheviks over the nature of the party. It distinguished the "vanguard" from the main body of "troops" in a way that made possible the seizure and retention of power by a minority. It shaped his attitude toward the Workers' Opposition in 1920, which irreversibly replaced revolutionary enthusiasm with party discipline. And it led ultimately to a bureaucratic regime of tutelage instead of the freedom and equality that had been the goal.

IV

The struggle of the *Iskra* leaders against the Economists culminated in the Second Congress of the Russian Social Democratic Labor Party. A First Congress had been held at Minsk in 1898 for which Struve drew up the party program, but the central committee there elected was soon arrested and the organization collapsed. Several efforts to convoke a new congress were made under Economist auspices but were successfully blocked by the Iskraists until they felt themselves strong enough to control the gathering. In 1903, by excluding certain groups under various pretexts, by controlling the credentials committee, and by so planning the agenda that other unwanted groups would be provoked into withdrawal before crucial votes were taken, Plekhanov and his friends assembled a congress broad enough to be accepted as representative of Russian Marxism, and yet dependable. He and Lenin were the guiding spirits in these manipulations, but Martov and the other *Iskra* editors were undoubtedly participants in them.

This Congress resulted, however, in two parties instead of one—the Bolsheviks and the Mensheviks. The first fissure in the *Iskra* ranks, although not the split, came on Point 1 of the Rules, the definition of a party member. Lenin's formulation required that party members be members of party organizations. This seemingly innocent requirement was, in Lenin's mind, the basis for party discipline. A loose aggregation of proletarians and intellectuals was not enough to lead and guide the revolutionary movement, in his opinion; all members and all activities must be subject to centralized control. When he explained his formulation, however, it was seen to call for more discipline than the Congress wanted. His draft was rejected in favor of Martov's, which required only that members work "under the direction" of party organizations.

The differences between the two men on the nature of the party were subsequently greatly sharpened and are sometimes read back into the Congress. Lenin is pictured as an élitist conspirator, interested only in a party of professional revolutionaries, while Martov is thought to stand for a mass party and socialism by majority vote. At the time, however, they were much closer together. Like Lenin, Martov came from an urban, intellectual, middle-class family. He was Jewish but not religious, and he had worked with Lenin longer and more closely than any of the other editors. Martov denied that he was opposed to a conspiratorial organization, but insisted that "for me a conspiratorial organization has meaning only in so far as it is enveloped by a broad Social Democratic Labor Party." Lenin, in similar vein, told the Congress that "it should not be thought that Party organizations must consist solely of professional revolutionaries. We need the most diversified organizations of every type, rank and shade, starting from extremely narrow and secret ones and ending with very broad, free, *lose Organisationen*." [12]

Nor were Lenin and Martov then so far apart in their attitudes toward majority rule within the party. Martov had not objected to the tactics by which the constituent base of the party had been deliberately narrowed in order to secure an *Iskra* majority at the Congress, and he had helped to drive the Jewish Bund out of the party by his attack upon its federal plan of organization. Lenin, on the other hand, bowed to Martov's majority on Point 1 of the Rules and did not reopen the matter later when he had a majority. He insisted tenaciously upon the name "Majority" (Bolshevik), for his faction, even when it became miniscule. Both men tended to see a majority as a means of control; yet it was against the way in which Lenin proposed to use his Congress majority that Martov finally stood up in anger.

The split in the party came when Lenin proposed a new editorial board of three, excluding Axelrod, Potresov, and Zasulich. Lenin's motives remain unclear, but they probably arose from his changed conception of the role of *Iskra*. Before the Congress the paper had worked for a unified party and for the destruction of Economism, which all six editors wanted. The party now being unified, a new task was posed—the centralized direction of a disciplined party, a task for which Plekhanov had a bent and with which Lenin may have expected Martov to cooperate.

Formerly our Party was not a formally organized whole, but only the sum of separate groups, and therefore, no other relations except those of ideological influence were possible between these groups. *Now* we have become an organized Party, and this implies the establishment of authority, the subordination of lower Party bodies to higher Party bodies. . . . Refusal to accept the direction of the central bodies is tantamount to a refusal to remain in the Party, it is tantamount to disrupting the Party; it is a method of *destroying*, not of convincing.[13]

Lenin carried the Congress for his proposal—Plekhanov, Martov, and himself as editors—but he badly misjudged Martov and the mood of the minority who followed him. Plekhanov voted with Lenin and was thus among the original Bolsheviks, but Martov refused to serve on the new board. As the resulting polemics clarified and widened the differences separating the two factions, Plekhanov saw the impossibility of imposing party discipline on the Mensheviks and went over to Martov, taking *Iskra* with him. Lenin soon lost control of the Central Committee as well and was almost isolated, with all the influential leaders against him.

It appears that Martov's initial revulsion against Lenin's seemingly needless expulsion of his old colleagues from the editorial board was sharpened by a sudden realization of the ways in which Lenin was determined to use the contrived Congress majority. *What Is To Be Done?* had stressed centralization and secrecy against "the implausible 'principle' of democracy in revolutionary affairs," and Martov presumably knew from conversation how far Lenin's ideas had progressed. Yet he seems not to have realized that, in Lenin's mind, the Congress was intended to establish centralized discipline over all Russian Marxism. Knowing that most of the Marxists, including the groups that had not been invited to the Congress and those that had walked out, would not accept such control, he rejected the Congress majority in favor of what he thought was the attitude of a majority of the Marxists. Lenin, on the contrary, could not "imagine any other way of avoiding a split in a party that is at all organised except by the submission of the minority to the majority." [14]

In addition to this practical difficulty of Lenin's party discipline, Martov recognized more basic disagreements of theory. A tightly disciplined party was necessarily a narrow party, whereas the proletarian revolution was supposed to be a revolution by a majority of the people. Moreover, this political change was dependent upon the underlying economic development of Russia, which could not be advanced by the hothouse stimulation of class consciousness by professional revolutionaries. And ahead of the proletarian revolution must come the bourgeois revolution and a period of republican government for which a mass party was needed.

As the polemics pushed them farther apart each side exaggerated and distorted the position of the other. In Lenin's tight underground party Martov saw a profound distrust of historical materialism, of democracy, and of the proletariat, and a dangerous and quite un-Marxian desire to skip the stage of capitalism by a Blanquist conspiracy. Lenin, in his turn, saw that the Economists were joining the ranks of the Mensheviks, that Martov was giving aid and comfort to the liberals, and that Axelrod was calling for a broad labor party embracing non-Marxists—thus misleading the workers into the service of the hated bourgeoisie. Each man, of course, denied the accusations, but it is possible that each saw the other more clearly than he saw himself.

In any event, in reaching for tighter party discipline Lenin had broken the already precarious unity achieved by the Second Congress. He then persisted in his separate views just at a time when the internal situation in Russia was building up, through strikes, demonstrations, and bloodshed, to the revolution of 1905. The two factions proceeded to dissipate their energies in polemics, each attempting to refute the ideas and block the actions of the other, thus confusing the minds and weakening the wills of the workers, when a coordinated effort might have ended the autocracy.

That revolution could have succeeded at that time is doubtful, however, because both factions still believed that a period of liberal bourgeois rule would follow the overthrow of the old regime, and the liberals themselves were not united in opposition to autocracy (page 282). Before 1905 no one had suggested that the workers themselves could govern without the liberals, and when this notion was advanced it was rejected as heresy by both Mensheviks and Bolsheviks. These revolutionaries, it seems, were too entangled in Marxian dogma to make a revolution.

V

The idea of a workers' government—the first suggestion from a Marxist that power might be seized and held by a minority—came from Parvus in introducing a pamphlet by Trotsky early in 1905.* "If the Social Democratic party is at the head of the revolutionary movement," he wrote, ". . . then this government will be social democratic. . . . It will be a complete government with a social democratic majority." [15] For a generation and more the accepted doctrine among all types of Russian socialists had been that the liberals were incapable of leading a revolution and that the autocracy must be overthrown by the socialists. It seems an easy step from there to the idea that the socialists would then rule, but for the Marxists an insuperable difficulty blocked that step. Politics must rest firmly on economics, and until economic development was sufficient for socialism, the government could not be socialist. As Lenin summed it up, on reading Trotsky's pamphlet, "This cannot be, because only a revolutionary dictatorship relying on the overwhelming majority of the people can be at all durable. . . . The Russian proletariat, however, at present constitutes a minority." [16] The expectation of majority rule was then universal among Marxists, and it entailed a period of capitalism for the production of the proletarians. The new government, therefore, must be bourgeois.

By the end of 1905, however, Trotsky had developed this basic idea into the theory of "permanent revolution," the first Marxist attempt to escape from the expectation of two revolutions and the intervening period of capitalism—the theory that the irresistible momentum of events would sweep the revolution, without a pause, from its bourgeois phase into its proletarian phase and on into socialism.

* Leon Trotsky, *Do Deviatago Ianvaria* (Geneva, 1905). Parvus (Alexander L. Helfand, 1869–1924), a Russian Jew resident in Germany, had supported Kautsky against Bernstein in the German SD party and tried to reconcile the factions in the Russian party. He was then greatly respected as an economist and political theorist. Trotsky (Lev D. Bronshtein, 1879–1940), son of a Ukrainian Jewish kulak, was already well known as a contributor to *Iskra* and as a pamphleteer.

The proletariat, once having taken power, will fight for it to the very end. While one of the weapons in this struggle for the maintenance and the consolidation of power will be agitation and organization, especially in the countryside, another will be a policy of collectivism. Collectivism will become not only the inevitable way forward from the position in which the party in power will find itself, but will also be a means of preserving this position with the support of the proletariat.[17]

After overthrowing the tsar the revolutionaries would not, indeed could not, calmly hand over power to the liberals. "Every passing day will deepen the policy of the proletariat in power, and more and more define its *class character*." [18] Seizures of the factories and the land by workers and peasants would drive the liberals back to reaction, but by protecting the peasants in their redistributions of land the revolution would gain mass support. The deficiency of proletarians would thus be remedied. The revolution would have majority support and there would be no need to wait for the growth of the proletariat. Like the other Marxists, however, Trotsky expected the peasants, who were petty bourgeois and not socialists, to desert the revolution when it entered its socialist phase. Both Lenin and Martov thought that this would destroy a workers' government and discredit socialism, and that power must not be taken until the dependable class base was prepared. Trotsky, on the contrary, believed that Western Europe was ripe for revolution and would come to the rescue before the peasants deserted.

Left to its own resources, the working class of Russia will inevitably be crushed by the counter-revolution the moment the peasantry turns its back on it. It will have no alternative but to link the fate of its political rule, and, hence, the fate of the whole Russian revolution, with the fate of the socialist revolution in Europe.[19]

The Russians could provide the spark for the socialist revolution in Europe, as Engels had hoped, and thus they could link hands with the international proletarian forces that would destroy capitalism everywhere.

This theory of permanent revolution, and Lenin's criticism of it, were later used to discredit Trotsky, although it clearly contains the key to the success (and the failures) of October 1917.

Lenin, in his polemical zeal, missed the significance of this new approach, but he was not so far from Trotsky's position as Stalin later professed to think. He wrote of "making the Russian revolution . . . a

movement of many years" which would touch off the socialist revolution in the West. "The revolutionary wave in Europe will sweep back
again into Russia and will convert an epoch of a few revolutionary
years into an era of several revolutionary decades." While insisting that
"we all draw the distinction between bourgeois revolution and socialist
revolution," he blurred that distinction by saying that "in history
certain particular elements of both revolutions become interwoven."
And he brought the period of bourgeois rule into question in July 1905
when he wrote that the workers and peasants "will not surrender" the
democratic revolution "to the contemptibly cowardly and greedy
bourgeois and landlords." In September, moreover, he realized that the
Marxists, by insisting on the bourgeois-democratic character of the
revolution, were losing ground to the Socialist-Revolutionaries who
promised socialism in the countryside (page 269). Trying to counter-
act this loss, he proclaimed that "from the democratic revolution we
shall at once, according to the degree of our strength, the strength of
the class conscious and organised proletariat, begin to pass over to the
socialist revolution. We stand for continuous revolution. We shall not
stop half way." [20]

His differences with Trotsky were, nevertheless, substantial. Lenin is
usually credited with fitting the peasantry into the Marxist system, but
at this time he was clearly not ready to regard them as an adequate base
for a government. Trotsky, on the other hand, who was to be accused
of lacking faith in them, thought the peasants a sufficient substitute, at
least temporarily, for the masses of proletarians required by the schema
of Marx. Conspirator though he was, Lenin did not believe that a
minority, even of dedicated revolutionaries, could achieve socialism.
He still believed in the necessity for a broad basis of class consciousness
and a proletarian majority. And he was less confident than Trotsky in
revolution in the West.

The year 1905 was a year of great activity and hope in all sectors of
the politically conscious public, from the Slavophil liberals to the most
radical revolutionaries. From Bloody Sunday on January 9 (old style),
when the government began the revolution by firing into an unarmed
crowd of petitioners led by a priest who was also a police agent, public
agitation and unrest mounted to a crescendo in the mass strikes of
October. For a brief period the Petersburg soviet—the committee set
up by groups of workers, on the tsar's invitation, to express their
wishes—enjoyed wide popular support as the only representative body

in Russia. Trotsky, who was its president, added much thereby to his experience and to his prestige. He adhered to the opinion that "the Soviet was indeed the embryo of a revolutionary government." [21] At times Lenin agreed, but the soviet was controlled by the Mensheviks and he was generally uncomfortable with such broadly based bodies, so he remained sceptical toward it and changed his estimate of it several times.* Lenin, in fact, did not return to Russia until November, after Count Witte had cleverly divided the tsar's enemies by his proposal for a representative Duma. The government thus regained the initiative, arrested the soviet, and diverted the energies of the revolutionary movement into the charade of elections and a powerless parliament. Had the Mensheviks rejected the Witte Duma as decisively as did the Bolsheviks the story might have been different.

During the years of disappointment that followed the defeat of the revolution of 1905 the Bolsheviks and Mensheviks drifted farther apart, in spite of the efforts of Trotsky and at times of Plekhanov to stand outside the factions and draw them together. Their differences are evident in their readings of the political situation and in their attitudes toward other classes, the liberals, and the peasants.

When the lack of power in the First (Witte) Duma had been demonstrated, it was clear to Martov that the "feudal" regime had not been ended, that two revolutions still lay ahead, and that the liberals remained revolutionary. Even in 1906 he opposed renewed strife between the bourgeoisie and the proletariat since it would "strengthen the position of the autocracy and thus would retard the progress of the emancipation of the people." [22] The Stolypin regime he saw as a backward step in feudalism, making the bourgeoisie still more revolutionary. Neither the liberals nor the peasants, who had not yet gone to "the school of the capitalist bourgeoisie," could be integrated into a Marxist party, but the SD's should support both the Cadets and the SR's in their "manifestations of their struggle against the present regime." The Mensheviks therefore proposed, at the Fifth Party Congress in 1907:

To enter into agreements with these parties in separate, definite cases, guided by the demands that the task of strengthening the attack on the autocracy places upon Social Democracy, in order to use them in the

* On his changing attitude see Bertram D. Wolfe, *Three Who Made a Revolution* (Boston, 1955), pp. 312–318, 368–370. These shifts of opinion left an ambiguous legacy for his followers when the soviet reappeared in 1917.

interests of broadening the current of the revolution and of the attainment by the proletariat of its own great goal.[23]

Lenin, on the contrary, was not so sure that the government was entirely "feudal." The Cadets' acceptance of the Duma marked their desertion of the revolution, he thought, and even after Stolypin's revision of the election laws in 1907 he continued to refer to the government as a "bourgeois monarchy." He made a distinction, however, which Martov did not make, between the stages of economic development in the cities and in the countryside. Landlord-peasant relationships were still feudal; the petty-bourgeois peasants were still revolutionary, therefore, while the urban bourgeoisie was not. The Cadets and SR's were not at all alike: the former were class enemies, the latter, allies. The peasants, in Lenin's view, had more "direct revolutionariness" than had the proletarians, and he thought continually on the problems of their position in the revolution. He revised Marx's "dictatorship of the proletariat" into the new formula, "the revolutionary-democratic dictatorship of the proletariat and the peasantry," an ambiguous formula that encapsulated several features of his thought. It indicated, for one thing, that Lenin saw an important part of the bourgeois revolution ahead of him, not behind. For another, it showed, in spite of its radical tone, that he expected a nonsocialist regime based on the peasantry. And for a third, it emphasized his expectation of majority support and his rejection of minority government. This formula, however, failed to win the peasants. While he struggled against the Economists and then the Mensheviks, within the confines of Marxism, the peasants were organized into the SR Party by Chernov and others who were less restricted by the system of Marx.

VI

The First World War, which shattered the international socialist movement, also further fragmented Russian Marxism. Plekhanov immediately supported the war and the tsar's government, although, like Miliukov, he soon abandoned the latter. He justified this "social chauvinist" position by arguing that Germany, if victorious, would convert Russia into an agrarian province, would prevent the growth of industry, and would thus delay for many years, if not indefinitely, the possibility of proletarian revolution. He broke with Martov and withdrew from the Mensheviks, yet after the February revolution he refused an invitation to join Kerenski's government. Most of the Mensheviks tried to oppose the tsar's government at the same time that they supported the war effort, an ambivalent position from which the February revolution released them. They were led by Tseretelli and Dan, who entered the ministry and showed themselves quite reactionary in the "July Days." Martov, on the contrary, opposed the war as well as the government and stood apart from the Menshevik ministers on the ground that the bourgeois elements in Kerenski's government would never agree to the radical parts of the SD program. He worked for a new coalition of all socialist parties, for, as always, he did not believe that the proletariat alone could rule. On the extreme left of the Mensheviks, he still could not join the Bolsheviks. They, too, had opposed the war from the beginning, with Lenin's idea of converting the "imperialist" war into a civil war, but they had come to stand for minority government by the SD's alone, in the absence of an adequate economic base. This, Martov could not accept.

The Bolsheviks justified this position in Marxist theory by means of two of Lenin's ideas of 1915, ideas that made possible the silent absorption of the theory of permanent revolution, and that have exerted tremendous long-range influence on world Communism. These were his "law of the uneven development of capitalism" and his theory of imperialism.

With international socialism in ruins, and with the separate national Marxist parties themselves divided, it was difficult for a man as impatient as Lenin to retain the idea that socialism in Russia must await revolution in the "advanced" countries. The idea that Russia could lead the way to socialism, which had been heresy when enunciated by Parvus and Trotsky in 1905, had become, in ten years time, the only alternative to pessimism. Yet Marx had said that the political superstructure was dependent upon the economic base, so Lenin proceeded cautiously in his efforts to free politics, which was his forte, from economics, in which Russia was so backward.

In his first response to the outbreak of war, and in the manifesto of the party central committee, Lenin had advanced as a slogan the "United States of Europe."[24] This slogan was widely accepted and defended by Trotsky, Bukharin, and others, but by March 1915 Lenin had turned against it. A United States of Europe was "either impossible or reactionary under capitalism," he now argued, because the European capitalists could unite "only for the purpose of jointly suppressing socialism." Socialist revolutions must precede the union of nations, and these will not come simultaneously because "uneven economic and political development is an absolute law of capitalism. Hence the victory of socialism is possible, first in a few or even in one single capitalist country." [25] Lenin made no claim that Russia might lead the way, but neither did he say that the economically advanced countries must lead. For the time he was content to justify the freedom of action of each national party. This almost casual argument, however, was later to become one of the pillars of Stalin's doctrine of socialism in one country.

Lenin himself used it in constructing his theory of imperialism. The willingness of the workers to support bourgeois governments in the prosecution of the war had seriously undermined the Marxist dogmas of international proletarian solidarity and class warfare. It had been suggested by Kautsky and others that the exploitation of colonial empires placed the proletarians of the advanced countries in a symbiotic relationship with the capitalists and thus destroyed their will to revolution. Moreover, international cartels seemed to reduce the competitive contradictions of capitalism, to stabilize and strengthen it. Lenin denied these conclusions. Capitalism, he argued, culminated in a final and economically necessary stage of imperialism, a stage of acute crises and military conflicts. Since capitalism developed unevenly, both within and between countries, no cartel agreement could be stable. And no agreement between imperialist governments, acting as agents of their capitalists for the political or economic division of the world, could be more than a temporary truce between wars. True enough, the profits squeezed from the colonial peoples were used to "bribe" the workers of the imperial nations. But this not only served to separate the opportunists from the real revolutionaries, it also brought all the colonial victims of capitalism into the ranks of the world revolution. In this stage of development all countries were bound together economically, and capitalism must be analyzed not nationally but internationally. The relative advancement of a given nation was less crucial for revolution in that nation than was the condition of international capitalism as a whole.

This line of thought brought Lenin, belatedly and by a different route, to two opinions that Trotsky had reached in 1905. The first was that the socialist revolution might start, not in the West where the workers were being bribed, but in a backward, semicolonial or colonial country—in Russia, for example. The other opinion was that, since capitalism had reached its ultimate imperialist phase, the capitalist development of separate countries might not be necessary. The expectation of two revolutions in Russia, the first bourgeois and the second proletarian, had always rested on the idea that the economic base for socialism must exist in Russia itself. If this were not necessary, if an international base were sufficient, then the two revolutions might somehow be telescoped into one. Unfortunately, in his *Imperialism* (1916) Lenin did not make these implications of his theory entirely clear. Perhaps he was not himself quite reconciled to the idea of an international revolution without an adequate international organization to control it. In any event, Lenin's followers failed to grasp the significance of his new views and were shocked by his "April Theses" when he returned to Russia.

Russian Marxism had thus come almost full circle. In 1883 it had been accepted as a system of revolutionary legitimacy by Plekhanov and his friends, who had denounced the political aims and methods of The People's Will, a system that accounted for the status quo and the failure of revolution in Russia and at the same time promised inevitable success through economic development. In the 1890's its class analysis and its schematic requirement of two revolutions, with an intervening period of the universally hated capitalism, served to separate its adherents from the tradition of a special path to socialism, circumventing capitalism, and thus from the reviving stream of *narodnik* thought and from the peasants. Yet by 1916 in Lenin's hands, and earlier in Trotsky's, Marxism had been so much revised that political revolution might be tried, as Tikhomirov had said in the 1880's, without waiting for the economic development of Russia, and the revolution, led by professionals, might drive on into socialism without a majority of proletarians.

PART SIX

The Soviets

CHAPTER XXII

The First Decade: Left, Then Right

AFTER the February revolution the leaders of Russian Marxism began to return to Petrograd. Unable to secure permission to travel through Allied territory, the exiles in Switzerland, at the suggestion of Martov and with the help of Parvus, finally crossed Germany in a sealed train. Their arrival was thus delayed until April, and in the meantime Stalin (Joseph V. Dzhugashvili, 1879–1953), arriving in March from Siberia, had an opportunity to display his leadership qualities.

The Petrograd Bolsheviks included a radical group led by Molotov and some conservatives around Kamenev. The city soviet was again in the hands of the Mensheviks, but Molotov, as editor of *Pravda*, had already advanced the famous slogan, "All power to the soviets!" Stalin, on his arrival the only member of the Central Committee present, took over the editorship, but he managed to avoid either supporting or rejecting this slogan. He was elected to the executive committee of the soviet, but he clearly did not see in it the focus of power that Lenin and Trotsky were to see. Still expecting two distinct stages of revolution, he thought in terms of an extended period of bourgeois democracy and advocated the spread of Bolshevik influence among the peasants. He wanted additional soviets in the provinces and their affiliation in an All-Russian soviet; even further, he wanted a national constituent assembly that would "enjoy authority in the eyes of all sections of society." In this conciliatory manner he moved toward the broad people's party of Axelrod and Martov as the appropriate instrument for open politics under the Provisional Government. He even began negotiations with the Mensheviks.

Lenin's "April Theses" fell with the suddenness of a spring shower on this conservative leadership, which was still following his prewar ideas. "The present situation," he said, "represents a *transition* from the first stage of the revolution . . . *to the second stage,* which must place power in the hands of the proletariat and the poor strata of the peasantry." No support should be given to the Provisional Government; "not a parliamentary republic . . . but a republic of Soviets" must be the aim. It was an "immediate task" to "bring social production and distribution of products at once under the *control* of the Soviets of Workers' Deputies." [1]

These bold new conclusions Lenin hinged on the concept of "dual power." "*Nobody* hitherto thought, or could have thought, of a dual power"; but now, "side by side with the Provisional Government, the government of the *bourgeoisie,* there has developed *another government,* weak and embryonic as yet, but undoubtedly an actually existing and growing government—the Soviets of Workers' and Soldiers' Deputies." According to the old ideas the rule of the proletariat "must come after the rule of the bourgeoisie," but in actual fact both already held power. "He who continues to regard the 'completion' of the bourgeois revolution *in the old way* sacrifices living Marxism to the dead letter." [2]

Lenin thus made it clear that he had no desire to halt the revolution, even temporarily, at its bourgeois-democratic stage. On the contrary, the international crisis of capitalist imperialism seemed to him a now-or-never opportunity to push on to socialism. He did not explicitly accept the theory of permanent revolution, but his implicit acceptance was enough for Trotsky, who joined the Bolsheviks in July.

All through the summer they worked for control of the soviets, in which they saw the Russian equivalent of Marx's favorite revolutionary instrument, the Paris Commune of 1871. In this campaign Lenin wrote his most famous pamphlet, *The State and Revolution,* which reflected strongly the writings of Marx in defense of the Commune. The Commune had included important anarchistic elements in the followers of Proudhon and Bakunin, and Marx, defending them in his *Civil War In France* (1871), had leaned closer to anarchism than usual, stressing such ideas as political freedom and economic equality under socialism, the simplicity of administration, and the withering of the state. Lenin, too, stressed these ideas, painting an optimistic picture of the future and making many statements that continued to haunt him and his successors.

Among these statements, pregnant with future trouble for the world and for world Communism, was this: "The substitution of the proletarian state for the bourgeois state is impossible without a violent revolution."[3] In 1916 young Nikolai Bukharin (1888–1938), one of the few Bolsheviks with a university education, had advanced the theses that the objective of the revolution was not to capture the bourgeois state machinery but to smash it, and that the "withering away" applied to the proletarian state that replaced it.[4] Lenin had promptly contradicted him, arguing that the revolution would use the "existing machinery of government."[5] But subsequent more careful study of Marx and Engels on this point had led him to the conclusion that Bukharin was substantially correct. Hence the practical conclusion: the Provisional Government should not be entered or captured; it should be smashed and a new government built on the soviets. Marx's idea of capturing power by parliamentary methods was thus abandoned and Bolshevism was linked to force and violence even before the seizure of power.

During the assault on Petrograd by General Kornilov, the Provisional Government lost prestige and the Bolsheviks proved themselves to be the most resolute defenders of the city. This earned them a majority in the soviet, and Lenin, in hiding since the riots of July, concluded that the country would support an armed seizure of power. Kamenev and Zinov'ev strongly opposed this, and Lenin had to appear personally (in disguise to avoid Kerenski's police) to convince the Bolshevik Central Committee. The city soviet appointed a Military Revolutionary Committee with Trotsky as chairman; it arranged the details of the seizure, which was accomplished almost without bloodshed. It was proclaimed in the name of the soviet, which gave the October revolution a broader basis than Lenin's plan for action in the name of the Bolshevik Party would have done. The following day (October 25, old style) a nationwide Congress of Soviets assembled in Petrograd, representing some twenty million voters. It contained a Bolshevik and Left SR majority of over two-thirds, and sanctioned the transfer of "all power to the soviets." *

Other important slogans of the uprising were "Peace, Land, and Bread" and "Workers' Control of Industry." They well expressed the basic nature of the failures of the Provisional Government and of the tasks of the new one.

---

* The most brilliant eye-witness account of these events is John Reed, *Ten Days That Shook the World* (New York, 1919).

The decrees on peace and land were issued on October 26. The former appealed to all belligerent governments and to their peoples for an immediate armistice and peace negotiations. It clearly accepted the possibility of a separate peace without the Allies, which had been a hurdle too high for Kerenski to attempt.

The land decree, presented to the Congress by Lenin, was not Lenin's program but that of the Socialist-Revolutionaries. In the debates of the preceding decade Lenin had called for the nationalization of the land, central control, and distribution on a rental basis. He had been opposed, however, on the ground that the central government was expected to be bourgeois. The Mensheviks proposed "municipalization"—ownership of the land by local (*volost* or *uezd*) governments and redistribution of its use, but not ownership, to the tillers. The SR's had gone further. Having faith in the village commune, which the Marxists lacked, they wanted "socialization"—abolition of all ownership, collective possession of the land by the communes, and allocation by the peasants' committees.* Chernov, who had formulated this program, had been Minister of Agriculture for months but had not carried it into force. Now, the Bolsheviks lost no time. At the Congress of Soviets, even after Chernov and the Right SR's walked out, the Left SR leader, Kamkov, secured a majority for the peasants' committees, and Lenin bowed to this decision in drafting the decree. It was not until 1919 that the land was nationalized.

The peasant support that this decree secured for the revolution was not expected to be permanent. The great hope was still for revolution in the West. This was the key to Trotsky's delaying tactics in the peace negotiations with Germany at Brest-Litovsk and to the propaganda effort that accompanied them. He tried to save the territory of Russia, and failing, he broke off the negotiations with the formula, "no war, no peace." The Germans renewed their invasion and issued an ultimatum containing territorial demands that brought a crisis in the Bolshevik Central Committee. Lenin had wanted concessions to gain peace in the first negotiations, and he now insisted that, in spite of the cost, the ultimatum must be accepted. Against him stood the Left Communists

---

* Against all these programs Stalin had argued in 1906 that the peasants' own seizures of the land as private property should be supported, since this would promote capitalism in the countryside, would intensify the class struggle between landless peasants and the kulaks, and thus would promote the revolution. At the Fifth Party Congress (1907) the Bolshevik majority adopted both Lenin's and Stalin's proposals as alternatives.

led by Bukharin, arguing for Lenin's old program of converting the imperialist war into an international civil war. The workers of the world, Bukharin believed, would not let the revolution be crushed by the Kaiser's armies. Fighting a retreating war against the German invaders, across the whole expanse of Russia if necessary, the revolution would rally the support of the Russian people and exert irresistible influence upon the proletariat abroad. If, on the other hand, the ultimatum were accepted, the revolution would be tainted by compromise with imperialism, and a new ultimatum might be presented immediately. Bukharin's argument was consistent with Marxist traditions of proletarian solidarity, and also with ideas of Russian dependence on the West that Trotsky had advanced in 1906 (page 306) and that had become accepted in the Party. So Trotsky was inclined to agree with him. Yet they all knew how determined Lenin was for peace: continuation of the war would mean war also against Lenin. "We cannot wage revolutionary war with a split in the party," Trotsky concluded. He and three followers abstained from voting in order to preserve unity and allowed the vote to stand at seven for peace and four for war.* To Bukharin this decision meant abandonment of the international revolution and the decay of the moral authority and idealism of the Party. To Lenin, on the contrary, this was a Tilsit peace, a respite in which to prepare for the world revolution. "It is the absolute truth," he still thought, "that without a German revolution we will perish"; [6] yet it would be irresponsible to gamble on inducing one by war.

After "Land" and "Peace," the slogan "Workers' Control of Industry" expressed the most popular objective of the revolution—and the most elusive. All through 1917 spontaneous factory committees had seized control during disputes with management, much in the manner that Trotsky had predicted. They were strongly influenced by anarchosyndicalism, but Lenin supported and defended them. "Workers' control," he had said in June, ". . . should be immediately developed . . . into complete regulation of the production and distribution of goods by the workers." [7] In *The State and Revolution* and other writings he seemed to regard control as a simple matter of accounting, auditing, and the like: "It is quite possible, immediately, overnight, after the overthrow of the capitalists and bureaucrats, to supersede them in the *control* of production and distribution, in the

---

* The situation and Trotsky's motives are well analyzed in Isaac Deutscher, *The Prophet Armed* (New York, 1954), pp. 382–392.

work of *keeping account* of labour and its products by the armed workers." Moreover, such control would be exercised over the whole economy: "The whole of society will have become a single office and a single factory with equality of work and equality of pay." [8] Such accounting and control, however, Lenin distinguished more and more clearly from the management of the factories. The factory committees, on the other hand, frequently assumed the management role—often because the old managers refused to obey them. In theory the committees stood for the nationalization and planning of industry, but in practice they tended, especially after October, to regard the factories as their own, in short-range local terms. Beset by the dilapidation and shortages of materials and transport after three years of war, they were unable to reverse the decline in production. In fact, they contributed to the chaos in industry, and lost Lenin's support.

The Marxists had given surprisingly little attention to the problems of administering the economy before their victory confronted them with the necessity to administer it. They were ill-prepared and hardly aware of the magnitude and complexity of their task. The government's first solution was to centralize workers' control by subordinating the factory committees to the trade unions and by integrating the unions themselves into the machinery of government. In the resulting struggles the tone of the revolution was changed.

At the First Congress of Trade Unions (January 1918) the Mensheviks raised the issue of the independence of the unions. Martov and Maiski argued that the working class must be able, through the trade unions, to defend itself against the government, since the revolution and the resulting government could only be bourgeois and not socialist. Resting on both proletarian and nonproletarian (peasant) elements, the government, Martov went on, "cannot direct its economic policy along lines of the consistently and clearly expressed interests of the working class." [9] Even among the Bolsheviks the government's policy caused misgivings. Lozovski, a recent recruit from Menshevism, pointed out that if the unions became organs of government their decisions would be carried out by compulsion. The spontaneous solidarity of the working class would thus be replaced by coercion. Zinov'ev, on the other hand, insisted that the workers could have no interests different from those of the workers' state, and the unions therefore had no need for independence.

The Congress resolved that the unions ought to be "organs of state power," and that they "ought to take on themselves the main burden of organizing production and of rehabilitating the country's shattered productive forces." [10] They were, in fact, entrusted with the discipline and distribution of labor, the administration of the social insurance system, and other duties. A year later, at the Second Congress, the "statization" of the unions was carried further. The unions were given control over wages and conditions of labor, but strikes in nationalized industries were ruled out.

In the meantime the government, on Lenin's insistence, had adopted some very nonproletarian measures to increase production, including incentive wage schemes such as piece rates, labor discipline, and the use of "bourgeois specialists" at high salaries. Lenin also advocated one-man management instead of committees, and even negotiated with some wealthy entrepreneurs in attempting to organize joint monopolies with state and private capital. Lenin admitted that wage differentials were "a departure from the principles of the Paris Commune and of every proletarian state, which call for the reduction of all salaries to the level of the wages of the average worker"; but some high salaries were necessary, he argued, "owing to the considerable 'delay' in introducing accounting and control." He also defended the use of managers with "individual dictatorial powers" on the ground that "large-scale machine industry . . . calls for absolute and strict unity of will," which could be secured only "by thousands subordinating their will to the will of one." [11]

The same Left Communists who opposed Lenin's peace policy also attacked his economic policy with vigor. They established their own theoretical journal *Kommunist*, and in its first number Bukharin denounced the new policies:

The introduction of labour discipline in connection with the restoration of capitalist management of industry cannot really increase the productivity of labour, but it will diminish the class initiative, activity and organisation of the proletariat. It threatens to enslave the working class. . . . The Communist Party would have to rely on the petty bourgeoisie, as against the workers, and in this way would ruin itself as the party of the proletariat.[12]

Still more severe was Osinski in the second number:

We stand for the point of view of the construction of the proletarian society by the class creativity of the workers themselves, not by ukase of "captains of industry.". . . We proceed from trust for the class instinct, to the active class initiative of the proletariat. . . . If the proletariat itself does not know how to create the necessary prerequisites for the socialist organization of labor—no one can do this for it and no one can compel it to do this.[13]

Even the Menshevik Isuv attacked Lenin from the Left: "Lacking a genuinely proletarian character from the very outset, the policy of the Soviet government has lately pursued a still more undisguised course of compromise with the bourgeoisie and has assumed an obviously anti-working-class character." [14]

With the outbreak of the civil war in May 1918, these disputes, still unresolved, died down as the revolutionaries mustered all their resources against the White generals, the Czech Legion, and the invading forces of Britain, France, Japan, Poland, and the United States.* An emergency policy of "War Communism" was adopted—from each according to his ability for the defense of the revolution, with strong incentive and disciplinary measures. The unions, working closely with the government, assumed additional administrative duties in military recruitment and the supply services. The Eighth Party Congress (March 1919) drew up a new program that reflected this gradual "statization" of the unions:

The trade unions ought to come actually to concentrate in their hands all the administration of the entire national economy as an economic unit. . . . The participation of the trade unions in economic management . . . is, moreover, the principal means of the struggle against bureaucracy in the economic apparatus.[15]

Yet the supplies of goods continued to dwindle, and in their absence only paper promises could be given to the peasants for their grain. Contribution according to ability meant, in practice, confiscation of surpluses, with the help of "committees of the rural poor"; and the wealthier peasants—as could have been foreseen by Marxist theory and by common sense—responded in many cases by restricting acreage to their own needs. Food shortages in the cities, added to the drain of manpower to the front, further sapped industrial production. The Red Army, under Trotsky's leadership, defeated all its enemies, but before

---

* These invasions, and the assistance given to the tsarist generals, confirmed the Marxist class analysis and instilled in the Russians an abiding conviction of the military danger from world capitalism.

the civil war was over in November 1920 the economy was in chaos, black-marketing and brigandage were rife, and the proletariat itself, the backbone of the revolution, was melting back to the land.

Drastic new methods were urgently needed. As War Commissar, Trotsky was acutely aware of the extent and the depth of the difficulties. Early in 1920 he proposed two new approaches of opposite tendency: more freedom in agriculture and more discipline in industry.

In agriculture he proposed to replace the requisitioning of surpluses with an incentive system. A tax on agricultural income should be "set up in such a way that it is nevertheless more profitable to increase the acreage sown or to cultivate it better." [16] This idea was rejected by the Party, but a year later such a tax was established to start the New Economic Policy (N.E.P.).

Trotsky found more support for his second approach, the "militarization of labor." At the Third Congress of Economic Soviets in January, with the help of Tomski, the trade union leader, he pushed through a resolution calling for the use of army-recruiting machinery for the mobilization and allocation of labor. In the same month, when the White menace in Siberia collapsed, the Third Red Army was converted into the First Red Army of Labor and put to work. These measures were endorsed by the Ninth Party Congress in March.

Even so, this policy provoked strong objections both within the Party and without. The Mensheviks argued that compulsion would reduce production, not increase it. Just as wage labor under capitalism, being more free than slave or serf labor, had been more productive, so under socialism, labor should be still more free and more productive. Taunting the Mensheviks for admitting that the regime was socialist, Trotsky vigorously defended compulsion. Labor in the capitalist market had never been free; it was subject to economic compulsion. In Russia at present, however, that system could not be used.

Industry can at present give practically nothing to the village; and the market no longer has an attractive influence on labor-power. Yet labor-power is required. . . . The only way to attract the labor-power necessary for our economic problems is to introduce *compulsory labor service.* . . . It is necessary once for all to make clear to ourselves that the principle itself of compulsory labor service has just so radically and permanently replaced the principle of free hiring as the socialization of the means of production has replaced capitalist property.[17]

The mobilization and distribution of labor required a single coordinated economic plan, and Trotsky became the foremost exponent of planning.

The transition to Socialism, verbally acknowledged by the Mensheviks, means the transition from anarchical distribution of labor-power—by means of the game of buying and selling, the movement of market prices and wages—to systematic distribution of the workers by the economic organizations of the county, the province, and the whole country. Such a form of planned distribution pre-supposes the subordination of those distributed to the economic plan of the State.[18]

He proposed such a comprehensive plan to the Ninth Party Congress, but, although the idea was endorsed, it was given no implementation.

Trotsky also told the Congress that "militarization [of labor] is unthinkable without the militarization of the trade unions as such." [19] This meant more extreme statization of the unions. Tomski did not oppose statization, but trade union opposition was indicated by some theses drawn up by Shliapnikov. Attempting to defend the independence of the unions, Shliapnikov insisted on the old distinction between economic and political power and also emphasized the difference between policy making and administration. He thus arrived at three structures that should be kept separate: the Party for policy making, the soviets for political administration, and the unions for economic administration.[20] The Congress, however, rejected his views.

Militarization of labor also involved the issue of management by committees versus the one-man management long advocated by Lenin and Trotsky. This issue touched a sensitive nerve in the Party. When individual management had been adopted for the railroads early in 1918 the significance of its implications was immediately grasped by Eugene Preobrazhenski (1886–1937), a far-sighted young economist. In the last issue of *Kommunist* he voiced a widespread fear: "The party apparently will soon have to decide the question, to what degree the dictatorship of individuals will be extended from the railroads and other branches of the economy to the Russian Communist Party." [21] Now at the Ninth Party Congress this issue aroused still more vigorous debate. Tomski had gone along with the militarization of labor, but he introduced theses at the Congress defending "the presently existing principle of collegial management of industry" as being "the only one able to insure the participation of the broad non-party working masses through the trade unions." [22]

Lenin termed this "utter nonsense." * He lectured the Congress on "a little bit of theory" as to "how a class governs and in what the rule of a class consists." "The domination of the proletariat consists in the fact that the ownership of property by landlords and capitalists has been abolished. . . . The prime thing is the question of property." Individual management did not violate proletarian ownership. The bourgeoisie at first used the feudal lords as expert administrators, and the proletariat must similarly use bourgeois managers until its own people were trained.[23]

Undaunted by this reasoning, conservatives like Rykov as well as radicals like Osinski and Sapronov of the Democratic Centralist group defended collegial management. The latter group argued the practical value of the old committees as schools of administration for the workers and as "the strongest weapon against the renascence of departmentalism and bureaucratic deadening of the soviet apparatus." The Congress, approving one-man management as the "oft-proclaimed principle" of individual responsibility, left the "collegial principle" for policy making but insisted that it must give way to the "individual principle" in the process of execution.[24] This distinction was too ambiguous to protect collegial control in the factories; the workers' committees, already abandoned in the military sphere, were rapidly replaced in industry. The Party had taken another stride toward the one-man rule that Preobrazhenski had foreseen.

The Party having decided to continue War Communism and to adopt the militarization program, Trotsky proceeded to show what this meant in practice. Placed in charge of the almost paralyzed railways, he mobilized the rail workers, established a five-year plan for the locomotive industry, and rehabilitated the nation's transport system. He also showed what he had meant by the "militarization of the trade unions": he secured the dismissal of the rail union leaders and integrated the union into the administration. When, in November, he called for a similar "shake-up" of union leadership in general, however, he triggered the most serious controversy among the Bolsheviks that had occurred since the treaty of Brest-Litovsk. It revolved around the role of the trade unions, but it brought to the surface all the hidden dissatisfactions with the course of the revolution since October 1917. It

* He and Bukharin had struggled in vain to block Tomski's theses two weeks earlier in the Party fraction of the Central Council of Trade Unions. Now he was sure of his majority.

was bitter because on all sides it was believed that the fate of the revolution was at stake.

The Party program of 1919 (quoted above) had reflected the use of the unions in bringing the factory committees under control, but it had not solved the problem of the relations of the unions to the government. If, as Marxist doctrine had always professed, and as Lenin's *State and Revolution* had emphasized, the state would wither away, this problem too would wither; but in the meantime a complete structure of economic soviets had been set up within the government, vying with the trade union structure for control of the economy. Did statization of the unions mean the absorption of the one structure by the other? If so, by which? And if not, which should prevail? More fundamentally, was the proletarian revolution ultimately to be guided by the workers organized in unions or by the professional revolutionaries, intellectuals, and others operating through the Party and Party-controlled state?

The answer to this basic question could hardly be doubtful to those who had absorbed Lenin's attitude. Since, in his opinion, factory experience led only to "trade-union consciousness," not to class consciousness (page 300) and did not make the workers socialists, it followed that socialism itself required that the Party be dominant. Economic influences were important but not in themselves sufficient. The primacy of economics, which Marxism had always asserted, Lenin still accepted on broad international terms as described in *Imperialism;* but in immediate, concrete affairs, politics was not determined by economics. He had long acted on the assumption that politics was independent if not primary, at least in the short run, although this had been implicit rather than explicit in his thought. Then, at the Ninth Party Congress, he and Bukharin found for the trade union resolution the happy yet ambiguous formula, "Politics is the most concentrated expression of economics." As the trade union controversy grew sharper, however, Lenin repeated this formula and went on to make his view explicit: "Politics cannot but have precedence over economics. To argue differently means forgetting the A B C of Marxism." [25] This meant that politics could determine economics, and was, actually, a major revision of Marxism, a basic element in the conversion of it into Marxism-Leninism. This extreme, dogmatic voluntarism colored the outcome of the trade union debate and, in fact, the whole history of the revolution.

Trotsky, whose views were even more extreme, was an outspoken advocate of the absorption and subordination of the unions by the government. Since the revolution in the West had not materialized, and since the regime needed to retain the support of the peasants, it was necessary to provide them with goods by increasing industrial production. The unions must become "production unions," cooperating with the government in a desperate effort to revive the economy. He was supported by Bukharin, who called for joint sessions of the union and soviet organs, and members in common. This innovation would accomplish both the statization of the unions and the unionization of the state, and the final result would be "not the absorption of the unions by the proletarian state, but the disappearance of both categories—of the state as well as of the unions, and the creation of a third—communistically organized society." [26]

The Workers' Opposition group, on the other hand, while agreeing on the urgency of increasing production, believed that the subordination should go the opposite way. It was led, after the defection of Tomski, by Shliapnikov, a proletarian who had been the first Commissar of Labor. He interpreted the Party program to mean that, since the management of production would still be necessary after the state withered away, it should be entrusted to the unions and not to the state. The unions must, therefore, administer the economy independently, and all administrative organs must be elected by the workers and culminate in an All-Russian Producers' Congress. This would achieve the "unity of will" that Lenin and Trotsky emphasized, "and also a real possibility for the influence of the initiative of the broad working masses on the organization and development of our economy." [27]

Lenin supported Trotsky's line until November, but then, seeing the deepening rancor and extremism of the opposing sides, he struck out on a new third line. He was then planning the "retreat" into the N.E.P., which required drastic revision of many positions previously taken. Blandly going back to Martov's idea at the First Congress of Trade Unions three years before (page 320), Lenin now held that the unions still must defend the workers against the state because it was in fact a "workers' and peasants' state" with "bureaucratic distortions." Statization, therefore, was wrong; the unions should remain independent.

The trade unions are not state organisations, not organisations for coercion, they are educational organisations, organisations that enlist, that train; they are schools, schools of administration, schools of management, schools of Communism.[28]

Contrary to both Trotsky's and Shliapnikov's interpretations, the Party program of 1919 did not aim at organization of production through the unions. The dictatorship of the proletariat must be exercised by the class-conscious Party of the proletariat, not by the whole class organized through the unions, since the class was "still so split up."

Out of this controversy came a last eloquent restatement of the idealism that had inspired the revolution in 1917. This was *The Workers' Opposition* (1921) by Alexandra Kollontai (1872–1952), the first Commissar of Public Welfare and an ardent advocate of the emancipation of women. Although far from a proletarian in origin, she saw the situation in sharp working-class focus.* The revolution, she believed, had opened the flood gates of proletarian energy and creativity, but the Party leadership, thinking in terms of coercion and control, was moving ever farther away from the class it professed to lead, and was stifling the creative energies of the workers. Through the admission of careerist intellectuals and bourgeois experts, the Party had become permeated with nonproletarian ideas and had begun to display "bourgeois class hatred of the proletariat" as organized in the trade unions. To interpret the Party program so as to deny union control of the economy, or to relegate it to an indefinite future, was sophistry, bad faith, and bad Marxism. "Experts" trained in bourgeois methods were not likely to create the "new forms of production in industry" that proletarian control required. "New incentives for intensification of labor" were not to be found by the bureaucratic, dictatorial methods so dear to the bourgeois mind. They would arise from the creativity of the workers themselves that would come with a resurgence of the spontaneous enthusiasm they had displayed in 1917. Such enthusiasm and the confidence of the proletariat could be recaptured, however, only if the Party showed confidence in the proletariat by a return to democracy and equality. It must purge itself of bourgeois elements and return to the class principles of democratic elections, committee management, and "freedom of opinion and criticism inside the party." [29]

This trade union controversy was carried to the floor of the Tenth Party Congress in March 1921, where Kollontai demanded "a system of widely extended democracy and trust toward the masses," and insisted that "we must recognize, owing to Party currents, the right to organize

---

* "Her thinking could well represent man's highest ascent toward faith in the proletariat" (Robert V. Daniels, *The Conscience of the Revolution* [Cambridge, Mass., 1960], p. 128).

discussions, and must give an opportunity to the representatives of various currents to defend their views." [30] Similar demands were made by the Democratic Centralists also. Trotsky, in reply, displayed most blatantly the attitude she had condemned. "The Workers' Opposition has come out with dangerous slogans," he said. "They have made a fetish of democratic principles. They have placed the workers' right to elect representatives above the party, as it were, as if the party were not entitled to assert its dictatorship even if that dictatorship temporarily clashed with the passing moods of the workers' democracy." [31] Far from making concessions to the demands for democracy, he and Bukharin joined with Lenin to push through the Congress a rule outlawing the organization of factions within the Party. This rule reflected the Party's panic at the Kronstadt uprising and was aimed especially at the Workers' Opposition, but it marked the end of free opposition to the central leadership.

The Tenth Congress overwhelmingly supported Lenin's views on the trade unions, and also instituted his New Economic Policy (N.E.P.). Lenin admitted frankly to the Congress that "we made many mistakes; we went too far," and then proceeded to justify the change in policy:

In the main, the position is as follows: we must satisfy the economic needs of the middle peasantry and agree to free turnover, otherwise, owing to the delay in the international revolution, it will be impossible, economically impossible, to retain the power of the proletariat in Russia.[32]

This reintroduction of capitalism was to be a "transitional measure," a temporary retreat. It aroused surprisingly little opposition at the time,* since the old policy toward the peasants was so clearly bankrupt. The N.E.P. was, moreover, a success: slowly and unevenly the economy began to revive.

The task of fitting the new capitalist policy into socialist theory fell to Bukharin. The result was a theoretical structure with remarkably broad implications. The crux of it was the necessity to preserve peasant support for the revolution.

Bukharin reached back to his 1915 theory of the "stabilization of

---

* Kollontai, though, had written against those who raised the question "Have we not gone too far?" She asserted, "The workers demand a clear-cut, uncompromising policy, a rapid, forced advance toward communism" (*The Workers' Opposition in Russia* [Chicago, 1921?], pp. 9, 13).

capitalism" * on which Lenin had drawn in formulating his theory of imperialism. Under capitalism, Bukharin held, competition leads to the elimination of competitors, to the formation of great national combines of cooperating capitalists, and to the displacement of economic competition within nations by a much fiercer political and military competition among nations, in which the governments execute the wills of these great combines. The upper strata of the proletariat in each country shares in the fruits of victory in this competition and in the exploitation of colonial peoples and is thus bribed away from revolution. Capitalism becomes stabilized within the advanced countries except in the periods of war. The Marxist expectation of ever more severe economic crises is thus transferred to the international arena, and the prospects of revolution are connected with war. During and immediately after the wars the "tide of revolution" would rise, but between wars it would ebb. And—the basic conclusion—since Europe was between wars, revolution was not to be expected there, and the Russian revolution could be preserved only with the help of the peasantry.

The peasants, therefore, must be appeased; there was no alternative. But this did not, to Bukharin, involve an abandonment of socialism. On the contrary, the N.E.P. was the shortest path to socialism. By pursuing their own economic interests the kulaks and nepmen would expand production in the private sector of the economy and thus would provide the surplus needed for industrialization in the socialist sector. At the same time they would become increasingly entangled in the networks of credit, markets, transport, and supplies controlled by the state. The socialists, holding the "commanding heights" of government, cities, banks, industry, foreign trade, and the like, could later gradually squeeze the kulaks and nepmen out through the market, and "the market itself will sooner or later die out." Under the dictatorship of the proletariat the forms of the class struggle were different, and the struggle itself would eventually wither away as the other classes "grow into socialism." †[33]

* See his *Imperialism and World Economy* (1915; New York, 1929).

† Bukharin was the architect of the popular front policy in the Comintern, but this was based on his stabilization theory and not on the withering away of the class struggle, which was confined to the proletarian dictatorship. This policy, therefore, was always regarded as temporary, applicable only between wars.

Bukharin found in the necessity to preserve the support of the peasants a determinant of economic policy not only in the private sector but in the public sector as well. He believed that the demand for consumer goods was the "direct driving force" behind industrial production. Most of the consumers were peasants, so it followed that "the development of industry is dependent on the development of agriculture." All elements of the national economy must be kept in equilibrium, and since agriculture could not be expanded rapidly, Trotsky and his followers were wrong in advocating too rapid industrialization. "The reverse side of the upsetting of the necessary economic proportions is the shaking of the *political* balance of the country." [34] Too great a squeeze, in other words, applied too soon through price differentials, taxes, and the like, to get resources for industrialization, would turn the peasant masses against the government and destroy the revolution. Such a breakdown of the worker-peasant alliance in Russia would, moreover, have serious repercussions for the world revolution as well. The peasants of colonial countries, as Lenin had said in *Imperialism*, were natural allies of the proletariat; to alienate the Russian peasants would undermine this alliance all over the world and greatly hamper the spread of revolution.

This reasoning, however, did not go unchallenged. Before the N.E.P. was a year old, uneasy impatience was expressed by Preobrazhenski. He criticized the working of the N.E.P. and urged the development of state farms and collective farms as "the basic form of the transformation of the peasant economy into a socialist economy." He rejected as impossible Bukharin's idea that the peasants could be induced to give long-term support to the proletarian revolution. He was haunted by the fear that the kulaks and nepmen, strengthened by the new policies, would join forces with world capitalism in a new economic, political, and military effort to crush the Bolshevik regime. In the absence of revolution in the West, the only hope lay in rapidly building up Russia's own proletariat. The country was in great danger from both internal and external enemies in the period after the revolution, when the incentives and controls of capitalism were lost, and before the achievement of socialism, when the advantages of a rationalized economy would be attained. "To run quickly through this period, swiftly to reach the moment when the socialist system will unfold all its natural advantages over capitalism—this is a question of life and death for the

331

socialist state." It should, he thought, be rushed through by central planning, collectivization in agriculture, and rapid industrialization with emphasis on heavy industry.[35]

For such a program great resources would be needed in the socialist sector. The accumulation of capital by the nepmen and kulaks did not provide such resources, as Bukharin thought; on the contrary, it only strengthened the class enemy. The socialist sector must, therefore, resort to what Preobrazhenski called "primitive socialist accumulation." * This required the systematic transfer of resources from the private sector by taxes and monopoly prices; it required, in a word, the exploitation of the peasants. He expected them to resist and was acutely aware of the bitterness that real industrialization would engender. Yet primitive socialist accumulation was an objective law of the economy, he was convinced, and it would prevail in spite of the subjective desire of the leadership to continue the N.E.P.

While these differences of opinion regarding economic policy were growing sharper, and before any signal had been given to terminate the N.E.P., Lenin lost his grip on affairs through apoplexy. Immediately a troika of Zinov'ev, Kamenev, and Stalin took effective command and sounded the watchword of "collective leadership"—less from a belief in that principle than from a desire to exclude Trotsky, the man most clearly eligible, from a succession to Lenin's mantle. Trotsky seemed reluctant to assert himself and was repeatedly outmaneuvered. The details of the power struggle would not be appropriate here, so only a few issues of substance will be mentioned.

Trotsky had never considered the N.E.P. to be inconsistent with central planning and rapid industrialization. He continued to stand for these policies, and it is probable that his connection with them actually delayed their adoption. In any event, he was increasingly critical of the trend toward capitalism that seemed to him to be involved in Bukharin's equilibrium theories and the continuance of the N.E.P.

Open advocacy of such views, however, exposed Trotsky and his adherents to charges of violating the Party rule against factions, a rule he had helped to establish. By temperament he was one of the least tolerant of the leaders, yet when the "New Course" toward intra-Party

---

* This phrase was parallel to Marx's capitalist "primitive accumulation" discussed in volume I of *Capital*. Preobrazhenski gave credit for the phrase itself to V. M. Smirnov (Preobrazhenski, *Bumazhnye den'gi v epokhu proletarskoi diktatury* [Tiflis, 1921], p. 71).

democracy was proclaimed at the end of 1923 he appealed to the Party for the "renovation of the party apparatus," to clear out of the leading posts "those who, at the first word of criticism, of objection, or of protest, brandish the thunderbolts of penalties before the critic." [36] He failed to reach the proletarians of the Party, however, and drew from Shliapnikov the judgment that "in the present controversy the only goal of Comrade Trotsky and the Opposition is simply to seize the apparatus." [37] Trotsky still believed that the rule against factions was correct; he still believed in the overriding importance of Party unity; so he was still committed to the system that was destroying him.

Beginning in 1923 Trotsky was accused of "underestimating the peasantry." The N.E.P., and the stress that Bukharin laid on the peasants in his justification of the N.E.P., had resulted in a reversal of official expectations regarding the peasants. For forty years the Russian Marxists had expected only temporary peasant support for the proletarian revolution and had looked to the proletariat of western Europe as the main army of the class war. The decision to take power in 1917 had rested on those same expectations, and as late as 1921 Lenin had named "timely support from the Socialist revolution in one or several advanced countries" as the first condition for the success of the revolution in Russia.[38] "Agreement with the peasantry" was his second condition, but it had come to be much the more important. True, Bukharin's stabilization theory led to dependence on the peasants only until the next "rising tide" of revolution at the time of the next war, but that might be many years. When he added to this theory his withering away of the class struggle, with the kulaks and nepmen growing into socialism, moreover, the old expectation that the peasants would "desert the revolution" was effectively abandoned. Trotsky did not accept this. By pushing for industrialization instead, he showed himself unrepentantly guilty of the new sin, underestimation of the peasantry.

Trotsky attempted an appeal to history. In *The Lessons of October* (1924) he traced the influence within Lenin's Party of "two tendencies of utmost principled significance," the one proletarian, the other democratic, i.e., petty bourgeois. He portrayed Lenin's "anger, protest and indignation against a fatalistic, temporizing, social-democratic, Menshevik attitude" as he struggled against the latter tendency even in the Bolshevik Central Committee. He recalled, as a prime example, the defection of Zinov'ev and Kamenev on the eve of the revolution, and hinted that similar right-wing cowardice was now holding back the

Party.[39] He also suggested that the course of events had largely confirmed his theory of permanent revolution. This claim, however accurate it may have been, gave his enemies a club with which to beat him, for it implied a criticism of Lenin, who had rejected that theory.

The troika lost no time in turning history to its own uses in extended polemics on the theme, Leninism or Trotskyism. The numerous differences between the two men over a twenty-year period were exploited. The pattern of exaggerations and distortions was set and the writings of Lenin were elevated as an authoritative canon. Truth was to be found, not by objective analysis, but by canonical quotation and interpretation. Trotsky also tried to join the new priesthood, presenting himself as a better Leninist than his detractors.

In this process the theory of permanent revolution was twisted into a new major heresy. It was elaborately distinguished from Lenin's idea of "uninterrupted revolution" and set in contrast to Stalin's new orthodoxy, socialism in one country.

The troika was intent on explaining the regime in Marxist terms as a workers' government in a peasant country, and on exorcising the widely held if rarely voiced suspicion that it was not really socialist. The success of proletarian revolution where the proletariat was weak had been explained in internationalist terms: the chain of capitalism had been broken at its weakest link. But is was necessary also to show that socialism was possible in an isolated country. For this Stalin relied chiefly on Lenin's "law of the uneven development of capitalism" (above, page 311). In doing so, he found it convenient to play down the international aspect of Marxism, which could not be attacked directly, by attacking Trotsky's application of it in the theory of permanent revolution. His recognition of the need for Western support for a minority proletarian government in Russia was treated as a disparagement of the Russian peasantry—indeed of the whole Russian people. This aspect of the theory, Stalin averred, was the basis for Lenin's criticisms.

Lenin's statement that "the victory of Socialism is possible first in a few or even in one single capitalist country," [40] was interpreted as applying not only to the victory of revolution (which Lenin seems to have had in mind) but also to the postrevolutionary "building of socialism." Yet Stalin proceeded gradually in his revision of Marxist internationalism. At first, in April 1924, he admitted that "formerly, the victory of the revolution in one country was considered impossible";

but he argued that the facts led "not only to the possibility, but also to the necessity of the victory of the proletariat in individual countries." Even so, victory in one country "does not yet mean that the complete victory of socialism has been ensured."

For the final victory of socialism, for the organisation of socialist production, the efforts of one country, particularly of a peasant country like Russia, are insufficient; for that, the efforts of the proletarians of several advanced countries are required.[41]

By December, however, his stance was much firmer. He had found in Lenin's pamphlet *On Co-operation* (1923) the statement that Russia contained "all that is necessary and sufficient" for building a "complete socialist society." [42] He therefore shifted his ground and redefined the "complete victory" of socialism as "a complete guarantee against the restoration of the old order," for which "the united efforts of the proletarians of several countries are necessary." * He also added the word "probable" to Lenin's "possible." [43] Then in 1926, writing against Zinov'ev after their split, Stalin insisted that the building of a socialist society in one country could be completed. The internal contradictions of Russia and the N.E.P. could be completely resolved. But the resolution of the external contradictions—the ending of the "capitalist encirclement," with its threat of a restoration of capitalism—still required revolution abroad.[44]

Stalin disclaimed originality and diligently attributed this theory to Lenin although he was unable to find quotations that gave it much support. All of the Left Opposition regarded it as rank heresy, and Zinov'ev, in his *Leninism* (1925), mustered many passages from Lenin against it. The "Declaration of the Eighty-four" (May 1927) went so far as to term it "the untrue, petty-bourgeois 'theory of socialism in one country,' which has nothing in common with Marxism, with Leninism." [45] The argument was lengthy and increasingly virulent, but Stalin, supported by Bukharin and by the Party apparatus, gradually drove his opponents from their positions of power.

---

* It was necessary to preserve a distinction between the "victory of socialism" and the "final" or "complete" victory, because Lenin had said very explicitly that "the complete triumph of the socialist revolution is inconceivable in one country alone and demands the most active collaboration at least of several advanced countries, among whose number Russia cannot be counted" ("The International Situation" [1918], *Collected Works*, ed. Alexander Trachtenberg, XXIII [New York, 1945], 275). Trotsky had quoted this at the Fifteenth Party Conference (*Pravda*, Nov. 6, 1926, p. 5).

The Opposition was handicapped, if not emasculated, by its acceptance of two dogmas, the necessity of Party unity and the authority of Lenin's writings. Together these dogmas required a monolithic, organized orthodoxy; they were the ideological bases of Stalin's dictatorship. By the end of 1927 Trotsky, Zinov'ev, Kamenev, Preobrazhenski, Radek, and many other leaders had been expelled from the Party.

This marked the furthest swing of the Party to the Right. Lenin had pushed the Party pendulum, through the war years and down to the seizure of power, vigorously toward the Left. Immediately thereafter, with the abandonment of his own land program in favor of the SR program, he had begun the retreat from the old revolutionary ideals under pressure of practical considerations. Workers' control was abandoned; incentive wages, bourgeois experts, individual management, and other capitalistic methods were reintroduced. With the N.E.P., capitalism itself was restored in internal trade and agriculture. Lenin's successors carried further the policy of wooing the peasants. They justified their retreat from world revolution, and they effectively eliminated all criticism from the Left. At the end of its first decade the Russian revolution, like its predecessors in England, America, and France, seemed set on a Thermidorian course.

There were, nevertheless, indications that the trend toward the Right was not permanent. War Communism had been a temporary reversion to the Left, but revolutionary attitudes remained current. Faith in Marxism and the commitment to proletarian socialism, however flexibly they might be interpreted, were not repudiated. The nationalized sector of the economy was favored, and the great electrification plan moved forward. Moreover, the theory that underlay the later stages of the trend toward the Right, Bukharin's idea of the stabilization of capitalism (page 330), was a cyclical theory that presumed a resurgence of revolution.

Even so, the long-range impact of this ten-year trend, both on the theory and on the practice of Marxism, were tremendous. A few of these effects on Marxist theory will be examined in Chapter XXIV.

Russian Marxism in 1927 was far from the majoritarian ideas of Marx and even from the ideals of Lenin's *State and Revolution*. Many of the valiant adaptations that Plekhanov had made to fit the conditions and traditions of Russia had been superseded by new adaptations stimulated by the drive to gain and hold power. Some very difficult revisions of theory had been made, to the satisfaction of the leadership at least. The bourgeois-democratic and proletarian-socialist revolutions had been telescoped. The failure of proletarian revolution in the advanced countries and its success in a backward country had been explained. A minority government and severe restrictions on democracy had been justified. Capitalist methods and even capitalism itself were in use—for socialist ends. The regime had reoriented itself to depend upon the peasants instead of the Western proletariat. For the workers "militarization" had been justified, and for the peasants, increasing freedom. And for the time being, at least, an isolated national struggle for socialism had been substituted in place of the struggle for world revolution.

Pragmatic as the motives may have been for many of these adaptations, there was no relaxation of the requirement that all lines of policy must be justified by Marxist theory. The deterministic economic element in such justifications was diminished by the addition of Lenin's writings to the texts of Marx and Engels to form a vast canon of Marxism-Leninism, and the independence of politics was increased. Bukharin's theories still retained some respect for economic determinism, but Russian Marxism, once started on a voluntaristic path, had gone ever further and had become remarkably flexible.

CHAPTER XXIII

The Autocrat and After

THE expulsion from the Party of Trotsky, Zinov'ev, and the other Opposition leaders was not followed by the Thermidorian degeneration they expected. On the contrary, Stalin almost immediately halted the drift to the Right and pushed the Party pendulum strongly to the Left. It seemed that he had cynically waited until he had eliminated the leftist leaders and then had stolen their policies. Or perhaps he now felt strong enough to stand alone and cynically chose a Left turn as a means to eliminate Bukharin and Rykov.

There remained, of course, important elements of continuity in official policy. The doctrine of socialism in one country, with its concomitant isolationism and subordination of the Comintern to the defense of the Soviet Union, was still the pivotal element. The stress on Party unity, the ban on factions, the insistence on Marxist-Leninist orthodoxy, and the bureaucratic centralization of power developed steadily toward dictatorship.

I

It was in the field of economic policy, an area of perennial controversy, that the change came. The harvest of 1927 did not find its normal path to the market, and by the end of the year an acute shortage of grain developed in the cities. The wealthier farmers, strengthened by three years of good harvests, were withholding their crops in hopes of forcing the government to raise its fixed price. Traveling through the country on a foraging mission, Stalin concluded that Bukharin's policy of winning the kulaks over through concessions had broken down, and that "so long as there are kulaks, so long will there be sabotage of the grain procurements."[1] The class struggle, instead of withering away, was becoming more intense, and the kulaks, far from growing into socialism, were striking at the socialist regime itself. Stalin struck back with an "offensive against the kulaks."

To Bukharin this change of policy was both unnecessary and disastrous. Under pressure from Preobrazhenski and the industrializers he had agreed to a differential between the prices paid by the farmers for industrial goods and those they received for their crops—a differential designed to siphon resources into industry although at a slower rate than that advocated by Preobrazhenski. He now saw this price structure as the source of the difficulty in grain supplies. He therefore proposed to revise the differential and even to buy grain abroad if necessary. In his opinion there was no occasion to abandon the reasoning by which he had justified the N.E.P. There was still no rising tide of revolution abroad, so it was still essential to conciliate the peasantry. The Communists still held the "commanding heights," so such concessions were not dangerous. The danger, and a real one as he saw it, was that Stalin's offensive would goad the kulaks into leading a great uprising against the government.*

Stalin, as usual, was careful to disguise his Left turn as the carrying out of earlier Party decisions. Yet he did not reach back to the long-orthodox expectation that the peasants would desert the revolution. He denied that the offensive against the kulaks was a repudiation of the "*smychka*," the union of the peasantry and the proletariat in the building of socialism. It was not a repudiation of the N.E.P. or a return to War Communism.

The alliance of the working class with the peasantry means reliance on the poor peasants, alliance with the middle peasants, and a fight against the kulaks. Whoever thinks that under our conditions alliance with the peasantry means alliance with the kulaks has nothing in common with Leninism. . . . Our policy is a class policy.[2]

The Fifteenth Party Congress, meeting in December 1927 before the conflict arose, had adopted routine resolutions in favor of planning, industrialization, and voluntary collectivization of agriculture. These resolutions Stalin now proposed to implement in earnest.

---

* Bukharin's views are well stated in his "Notes of an Economist" (1928) in Bertram D. Wolfe, *Khrushchev and Stalin's Ghost* (New York, 1957), pp. 295–315.

The redistributions of land after the revolution had greatly reduced the proportion of large farms, Stalin pointed out, and the small farms did not market much grain; yet the large kulak farms could not be depended on. "It follows then that we must do our utmost to develop in the countryside large farms of the type of the collective farms and state farms and try to convert them into grain factories for the country organised on a modern scientific basis." [3] Large collective and state farms had generally, from the beginning, been regarded as desirable, but it had been thought that extensive collectivization must wait until the factories were able to supply such farms with machinery. On the other hand, the rate of growth in industry, according to Bukharin's equilibrium theory, was limited by the rate of growth in agriculture. The economy was thus caught in a vicious circle from which Stalin, disenchanted with such economic arguments, proposed to break out. He had learned from Lenin the power of politics over economics, and he proposed to exert it.

All through 1928 the argument continued in the Politbureau, but without any admission, even to the Central Committee, of differences among the leaders. Only an anonymous "Right deviation" was castigated in public, which seems a strange tactic if Stalin's motive from the start was to destroy his opponents. Bukharin, Rykov, and Tomski helped to preserve the façade of unity, having seen the futility of open opposition. By doing so, however, they gave the new policies the appearance of unanimous decisions and themselves the appearance of covert antagonists of established policies when their opposition became public in August 1929.

In the meantime the strength of the Party was thrown behind the collectivization of agriculture, and industrialization proceeded at an ever more hectic pace. Market demand as a guide to production was brushed aside by political decisions to allocate men and resources, much in the manner that Trotsky had long advocated. In April 1929 the first five-year plan, coordinating these political allocations, was approved over the opposition of most of the economists. Preobrazhenski, who returned to the Party after Stalin's Left turn, was soon a conservative arguing on grounds of objective economic conditions against the more extreme planners. The dominance of politics in Stalin's economic thought was clearly displayed when, in 1934, he told the Seventeenth Party Congress:

The part played by so-called objective conditions has been reduced to a minimum. . . . What does this mean? It means that from now on nine-tenths of the responsibility for the failures and defects in our work rest, not on "objective" conditions, but on ourselves, and on ourselves alone.[4]

At this same Congress Stalin also attacked as "a reactionary petty-bourgeois absurdity" all surviving ideas of egalitarianism.

By equality Marxism means, not equalisation of personal requirements and everyday life, but the abolition of classes. . . . Marxism has never recog-nised, and does not recognise, any other equality. . . . It is time it was understood that Marxism is an enemy of equalisation.[5]

II

During this time winds from abroad were fanning the fires of Stalin's forge. In China in 1927 the united front policy suffered such a severe humiliation that it never recovered. The expulsion of the Communists from the Kuomintang was explained away in Russia, but at the same time Stalin noted that world capitalism was becoming less stable. "We are living on the eve of a new revolutionary upsurge both in the colonies and in the metropolises," he told the Fifteenth Party Congress. "Stabilisation is giving rise to a new revolutionary upsurge." The period of "peaceful co-existence" was "receding into the past." War was inevitable but it could be postponed. "Therefore, the maintenance of peaceful relations with the capitalist countries is an obligatory task for us. Our relations with the capitalist countries are based on the assump-tion that the co-existence of two opposite systems is possible. Practice has fully confirmed this." [6] Yet the Comintern abandoned the united front tactic in 1928, and the resulting conflicts with the Social Demo-crats in Germany may have eased Hitler's road to power.

The deepening world economic crisis of the following years con-firmed Stalin's prognosis, and he had the prescience to foresee that the Soviet Union would shortly have to meet a military challenge. "We are fifty or a hundred years behind the advanced countries," he said in 1931. "We must make good this distance in ten years. Either we do it, or we shall go under." [7] Industrialization thus became a struggle for national survival.

From 1933, when Hitler gained power, a new atmosphere pervaded

Russia. The chronic fear of the capitalist encirclement gave place to a paranoid obsession that played a part in the great trials and purges in which all the opposition leaders perished—much as the counterrevolutionary invasions of France had led to the reign of terror in 1793.

By 1936, ten years after Stalin had argued against Zinov'ev that the building of socialism in one country could be completed (page 335), he held that it was already achieved. Describing the new constitution, which Bukharin had helped to draft, he stated that it was based on the fact of socialism. "Our Soviet society has already, in the main, succeeded in achieving socialism; it has created a socialist system, i.e., it has brought about what Marxists in other words call the first, or lower, phase of communism." It followed that "there are no longer any antagonistic classes in society; that society consists of two friendly classes, of workers and peasants." [8] The transition to the higher phase of communism ("to each according to his needs") required an abundance of goods and services not yet available, but by 1939 Stalin thought the country was "moving ahead, toward communism."

"The complete victory of the socialist economic system" had been achieved, but Stalin had not forgotten the capitalist encirclement. At the Eighteenth Party Congress in 1939 he undertook to justify the continued existence of the state under socialism. A tool of class oppression, the state, it had been thought, would wither away when class antagonisms were ended, but Stalin pointed out that the state still had two functions, one internal, the other external. Within the Soviet Union the state was still needed to administer the economy, and abroad there was still capitalism, still class antagonism against Russia, so the defense of the country required it. Even under communism, he went on, because of the capitalist encirclement the state would remain. But if this were replaced by a socialist encirclement the state would wither away.[9]

In his *Dialectical and Historical Materialism* (1938) Stalin grappled with the typically Marxist problems of the relations of the ideological and political superstructure to the economic base. For Marx the latter was primary and the former was derivative. Yet the voluntaristic drive of Russian Marxism had always been impatient with the restraints that an underdeveloped economy, if primary, would impose on the revolutionaries' desire for socialism. Lenin, after carrying off the October revolution with little regard for the economic base, had asserted the primacy of politics over economics (page 326), and Stalin now tried to integrate this assertion into the theoretical system. He made use of a concept of "tasks" different from that of Marx.* "The concrete conditions of the material life of society" were indeed "the determining force of social development."

New social ideas and theories arise only after the development of the material life of society has set new tasks before society. But once they have arisen they become a most potent force which facilitates the carrying out of the new tasks set by the development of the material life of society, a force which facilitates the progress of society. . . . Thus social ideas, theories and political institutions, having arisen on the basis of the urgent tasks of the development of the material life of society, the development of social being, themselves then react upon social being, upon the material life of society, creating the conditions necessary for completely carrying out the urgent tasks of the material life of society, and for rendering its further development possible.[10]

"Tasks set by the development of material life" (a deterministic concept) were thus equated with "tasks of the development of material life" (a voluntaristic concept). The superstructure of ideas and institutions, by recognizing social needs and meeting them, within the limits of resources, could direct the development of society.

This meaning became even clearer when Stalin returned to the subject after the second World War. In *Marxism and Problems of Linguistics* (1950) he stated:

The superstructure is a product of the basis, but this by no means implies that it merely reflects the basis, that it is passive, neutral, indifferent to the fate of its basis, to the fate of the classes, to the character of the system. On the contrary, having come into being, it becomes an exceedingly active force, actively assisting its basis to take shape and consolidate itself, and doing its utmost to help the new system to finish off and eliminate the old basis and the old classes.[11]

* Marx wrote, in the preface to *The Critique of Political Economy* (1859), "New, higher relations of production never appear before the material conditions of their existence have matured in the womb of the old society itself. Therefore mankind always sets itself only such tasks as it can solve; since, looking at the matter more closely, it will always be found that the task itself arises only when the material conditions for its solution already exist or are at least in the process of formation" (Karl Marx and Friedrich Engels, *Selected Works*, I [Moscow, 1951], 329). Marx's concept was deterministic; Stalin's only appeared to be so.

343

He then gave a prime example:

In a period of eight to ten years we effected a transition in the agriculture of our country from the bourgeois, individual-peasant system to the socialist, collective-farm system. This was a revolution which eliminated the old bourgeois economic system in the countryside and created a new, socialist system. . . . And it was possible to do that because it was a revolution from above, because the revolution was accomplished on the initiative of the existing power.[12]

The year before he died, however, Stalin had to try again to clarify this murky problem. "Some comrades," encouraged by his *Linguistics*, it seems, had come to believe that the Soviet state was not bound by objective laws of economics but could "abolish" existing laws and "create" new ones. In his last major theoretical work, *Economic Problems of Socialism in the U.S.S.R.* (1952), he tried to set them straight. Economic laws, like other laws of science, are objective and independent of the will of man, he said; but they are different, also, since they are "impermanent," operating "for a definite historical period, after which they give place to new laws." These new laws are not created; they arise from the changes in "economic conditions." But they encounter resistance from "the obsolescent forces of society." A force, such as the worker-peasant alliance in Russia, is necessary to overcome this resistance. Thus, by recognizing the new laws of the economic relations required by changes in the economic base, and by using the necessary force, the Soviet state had enabled these new laws to prevail. The active superstructure had helped its base to consolidate itself, but only by understanding and using objective law. Only in conformity with law could the economy be directed.[13]

In this same pamphlet Stalin examined some of the problems of the transition from socialism to communism. It was not enough, he said, that consumer goods be adequate to satisfy the people's needs. The relations of production must be changed. And this involved the relations of town to country and of mental to physical labor.

Specifically, the "group property" found on the collective farms must become "public property." The farmers owned their products, while the land and machinery were already publicly owned; but farm products could not simply be nationalized, as capitalist industry had been, because they were socialist property. This property came on the market in the form of commodities, but "commodity circulation is incompatible with the prospective transition from socialism to communism." Furthermore, group property and commodity circulation were obstacles to the extension of effective central planning to agriculture. Therefore a way must be found to exclude the collective farm output from the commodity market and to include it in "the system of products-exchange between state industry and the collective farms." [14]

At present, Stalin believed, the collective farmers saw the market as the basic form of the relationship between town and country, between industry and agriculture. This attitude could be changed only gradually. The old antagonistic exploitation of the countryside by the town had disappeared under socialism, as had the antagonism between mental and physical labor, but distinctions remained between the two forms of labor and between industry and agriculture. The latter distinction consisted mainly in the difference between public ownership and collective-farm ownership. The ending of commodity production and the transition to communism required the elimination of these distinctions, for which Stalin had no ready formula. He seemed inclined to rely, not on another revolution from above, but on education. The well-rounded man so dear to Chernyshevski, William Morris, and others, equipped with multiple skills by greater leisure and "compulsory polytechnical education," would feel at home in both town and country. Aided by the mechanization of agriculture, he would so blend the productive forces of the cities with those of the countryside that no difference in economic base could remain to justify a separate form of ownership for agricultural products. [15]

III

With the end of Stalin's dictatorship in 1953, as with the relaxation of Lenin's grip in 1922, his successors proclaimed the principle of "collective leadership" which would "reestablish the Party standards worked out by Lenin." The new rulers were described as "a working collective of leaders whose relations are based on ideas and principles permitting neither of mutual forgiveness nor personal antagonism." [16]

The old ideas of Party unity and orthodoxy, however, still gripped the leaders. There is a fundamental conflict between the belief that there is, for Russia, only one correct interpretation of Marxism, and the belief that several coordinate leaders can interpret it. As before, this conflict was resolved by the emergence of a single preeminent inter-preter, Nikita Khrushchev (1894–   ).

Khrushchev was the first of the top leaders who had learned at first hand the life of the proletariat. Joining the Bolsheviks in 1918, he had worked his way up through the Party and had mastered Stalin's meth-ods well. Yet his own involvement did not deter him from his famous attack upon Stalin in a secret speech at the Twentieth Party Congress in 1956. It should be remembered, however, that the attack was upon Stalin's mistakes and his personal qualities of suspicion, vindictiveness, and unwillingness to take advice, more than upon his theories or methods.* Khrushchev did condemn Stalin's conduct of the war and some of his purge activities, but he by no means denounced his career as a whole nor did he rehabilitate Stalin's victims. Khrushchev's sup-pression of the Hungarian uprising later in the year dispelled any illusions as to the extent of the "thaw." "We did not criticize Stalin for being a bad Communist," he told the enemies of Communism. "We criticized him for certain deviations, negative qualities, for committing grave mistakes. . . . [But] for all of us . . . Stalin's name is insepara-ble from Marxism-Leninism." [17]

Under Khrushchev the "cult of the personality" did not return to the Kremlin. Khrushchev's regime was different, not only because he had a robust sense of humor, but because many of his attitudes and values were different. These resulted in some substantial revisions of theory.

The basic element behind Khrushchev's departures from earlier doctrine was his optimistic estimate of the class struggle. Stalin, in repudiating Bukharin's views, had argued that the class struggle was becoming more and more acute, and his subsequent experiences with Chamberlain, Hitler, and Truman hardly required him to change that opinion. Khrushchev, on the other hand, held that the most acute stage of the struggle between capitalism and socialism, both within the Soviet Union and in the international arena, had passed. "Great harm to the cause of socialist construction and the development of democracy inside the party and the state" had been done, he said, by Stalin's retention of his formula, "which is only correct for certain stages of the transition period," after socialism had triumphed.[18] Khrushchev did not revive the idea of the withering away of the class struggle, nor did

---

* An interesting parallel might be drawn with Kurbski's criticism of Ivan IV.

he rehabilitate Bukharin, but he believed that some of the tensions of the Stalin era could be relaxed.

We have entered a stage in the contest between labour and capital, between socialism and capitalism, when the relation of forces is decided by peaceful co-existence and peaceful competition. And this competition shows which of the two systems can best develop the productive forces and raise labour productivity; which of the two systems can best satisfy the material and spiritual requirements of the people.[19]

His certainty of victory was "based on the fact that the socialist mode of production possesses decisive advantages over the capitalist mode." [20] This note of optimistic pragmatism, inviting comparison in the areas of material and spiritual satisfactions where capitalism has thought itself strongest, is the keynote of modern Soviet policy.

This change of attitude was not simply a reflection of the different personalities of Stalin and Khrushchev. It had a strong foundation in both fact and theory. The defeat of the preponderant part of Hitler's armies by Russia, followed by the spread of Communism in eastern Europe and in China, served to lift Russian self-confidence to new heights. The desperate feeling of dependence on revolution in western Europe or on the peasantry was gone, and with it the need to protect the Soviet Union by promoting subversion abroad. Moreover, so great a part of the world's resources had been removed from the control of the leading capitalist countries into either socialist or "neutralist" control, and the industrialization of Russia had been so successful, that the world's balance of material strength was much less adverse than formerly. This, plus the "balance of terror" of modern weapons, made the expectation of predatory capitalist attack less tenable.

The postwar factual situation was soon reflected in the realm of theory. Khrushchev noted early in 1958 that the concept of capitalist encirclement needed clarification because, with the formation of a world socialist system, "you cannot tell who is encircling whom— whether the capitalist countries encircle the socialist countries, or vice versa." [21] Moreover, in contradiction to earlier Marxist thought (still persisting in China), he argued that "war is not fatalistically inevitable." "Developments indicate that it may actually be feasible to banish world war from the life of society even before the complete triumph of socialism on earth, with capitalism surviving in part of the world." [22] This theory amounted to a separation of revolution from world war, contrary to the old idea of a "rising tide" at such times (page 330), but not necessarily from local wars. The development and the aftermath of the Second World War, however, had so exactly conformed to the old ideas that Khrushchev's view proved unacceptable to the Chinese Communists. Yet Khrushchev and his successors adhered to it tenaciously.

IV

Khrushchev gave much emphasis to the doctrine of "peaceful co-existence of countries with different social systems," and termed it "a fundamental principle of Soviet foreign policy." [23] He attributed it to Lenin although Lenin had frequently reiterated the impossibility of a socialist state living side by side with capitalist states.* He knew that Lenin had expected the peace to be broken by the capitalists, and that he had in practice pursued a peace policy, as at Brest-Litovsk. Stalin had used the phrase "peaceful co-existence," usually in quotes, a few times in the 1920's in connection with the idea of the stabilization of capitalism, but for Stalin the phrase referred to a phenomenon or temporary condition. For Khrushchev, on the other hand, an extended period of coexistence was possible, since world capitalism could no longer with impunity attack the Soviet Union. Survival in the nuclear age made this policy imperative, but Khrushchev also believed that it was desirable, from the Soviet point of view, because he believed in the superiority of socialism over capitalism in long-range economic competition.

Marx had expected the destruction of capitalism as a result of the contradictions within it—the aggravating crises, the growing misery and strength of the masses, and the final revolutionary struggle. Khrushchev did not deny Marx's analysis, but he supplemented it. In addition to the acute crises of capitalism, he stressed its chronic inefficiency. Marx, Veblen, and others had described the inefficiencies of capitalism, but Khrushchev saw their long-range significance for the class struggle. Having experienced the phenomenal growth of Soviet industry, he was convinced that the capitalist countries were not able,

---

* See, for example, Lenin's "War and Peace," *Selected Works*, VII (London, 1937), 288, and his report to the Eighth Party Congress, *ibid.*, VIII, 33.

even in periods of prosperity, to match the socialist rate of economic progress. Hence the Soviet Union would surpass the United States in per capita production and would eventually attain the world's highest standard of living. As a materialist he believed in the persuasiveness or propaganda value of material goods. The rest of the world would notice the superiority of socialist methods, and capitalism would be overthrown by the cupidity, if not by the desperation, of the masses.

When the Soviet people will enjoy the blessings of communism, new hundreds of millions of people on earth will say: "We are for communism!" It is not through war with other countries, but by the example of a more perfect organisation of society, by rapid progress in developing the productive forces, the creation of all conditions for the happiness and well-being of man, that the ideas of communism win the minds and hearts of the masses.

Capitalism replaced feudalism because it was more productive than the feudal system. Communism will defeat capitalism by making use of its advantages, by showing the peoples that the communist system is more productive than the capitalist system. This is the crux of the matter.[24]

Khrushchev's best-known *mot*, when he visited America in 1959, reflected this line of thought: "We will bury you."

There were, and are, important qualifications to the doctrine of peaceful coexistence that need to be remembered. In the first place, it does not imply any cessation of the struggle between capitalism and socialism in the realm of ideology. Yet this struggle, Khrushchev insisted, must not be confused with "the question of relations between states." Second, it does not imply the maintenance of the status quo as that term is usually understood. For Khrushchev, the existing situation included a dynamic trend toward socialism, with a series of local revolutions, like that in Cuba, gradually eroding the area of capitalism. There was no need for the "export of revolution," and there must also be no "export of counterrevolution." Each nation must be free to choose its own social system. And third, peaceful coexistence is not expected to be permanent, because capitalism is not thought to be permanent. A severe capitalist crisis may erupt into international war at any time; but, barring that, coexistence will continue until the last capitalist country succumbs in the economic competition between the two systems. As with feudalism, backward enclaves of capitalism may remain for a long time, but probably will not, for the advantages of economic abundance under communism will be so obvious.

Would other nations, in making their transitions to socialism, follow the path that Russia had trod? The establishment of Tito's Communist regime in Yugoslavia without benefit of the Red Army had raised the issue of "separate paths to socialism." Stalin, for a time, appeared to accept this idea, but he later insisted on closer conformity. Khrushchev again widened the limits of acceptable variation. He quoted to the Twentieth Party Congress Lenin's remark of 1917 that "All nations will arrive at socialism—this is inevitable, but not all will do so in exactly the same way." [25] He had words of praise for People's Democracy as an alternative to the Soviet form; then he continued:

It is probable that more forms of transition to socialism will appear. Moreover, the implementation of these forms need not be associated with civil war under all circumstances. Our enemies like to depict us Leninists as advocates of violence always and everywhere. True, we recognize the need for the revolutionary transformation of capitalist society into socialist society. . . . But the forms of social revolution vary. It is not true that we regard violence and civil war as the only way to remake society.[26]

He went on to raise the question "whether it is possible to go over to socialism by using parliamentary means." Undaunted by the ghost of Bernstein, he answered in the affirmative.

The winning of a stable parliamentary majority backed by a mass revolutionary movement of the proletariat and of all the working people could create for the working class of a number of capitalist and former colonial countries the conditions needed to secure fundamental social changes.[27]

That peaceful path had not been open to the Russians in 1917, but the growth of socialism and democracy since that time had brought radical changes. "In the present epoch," he said in 1961, "the tasks of the popular-democratic, the national-liberation and the socialist revolutions are drawing closer and becoming more interwoven," because all three are "directed primarily against one principle foe—imperialism, the monopolist bourgeoisie." Khrushchev thus added, for colonial countries, the revolution of independence to the two revolutions familiar to Russian Marxism, and attempted to telescope all three as Trotsky and Lenin had telescoped the two. Moreover, working from the ideas of Lenin's *Imperialism*, he believed that, in view of the large bloc of socialist states, the transition of a particular country to socialism was not dependent upon its own stage of economic development. "Today practically any country, irrespective of its level of development, can enter on the road leading to socialism." [28]

V

Another transition, however, that from socialism to communism, occupied Khrushchev more. The emergence of new socialist countries at different levels of development stimulated him to formulate a new "law of the even development of socialism." According to Lenin's "law of the uneven development of capitalism," on which the doctrine of socialism in one country had rested, the unplanned methods of production under capitalism caused some countries to pull far ahead of others. The planned methods of socialism, on the contrary, Khrushchev suggested, would enable the socialist nations to coordinate their efforts and, by mutual aid, to narrow progressively the differences in their levels of economic development. All the socialist countries could enter the final stage of communism "more or less simultaneously," at least "within one historical epoch." From this law it followed that the Soviet Union, having the most advanced industrial capacity, should not rush ahead into a plethora of consumers' goods under communism without regard to her poorer neighbors. She should instead cooperate in the organization of a more efficient international division of labor. This would result in greater output for all through more rational use of all resources. Moreover, this policy would avoid among socialist nations the "have" and "have not" jealousies of capitalistic international relations and lead to stronger international solidarity.[29]

Khrushchev was not able, however, to carry his "law" into effect as public policy. His international planners and negotiators did not display adequate generosity and understanding toward the less developed countries of the socialist bloc. They were unable to dispel the suspicion among these countries, which stood to gain so much economically from such a policy, that economic interdependence with the Russian giant would bring political dependence as well. The economic gains did not seem to justify the political risks of the erosion of sovereignty. Thus the heritage of socialism in one country and the long discounting of proletarian internationalism came to be separate socialisms in separate countries and the survival of nationalism.

The transition from socialism to communism within the Soviet Union also has received increasing attention. The old Marxist categories continue to structure the development of thought, but they are undergoing significant evolution.

This transition, according to Khrushchev, is "a law-governed historical process that cannot be violated or bypassed at will." Communism can come "only after socialism is fully consolidated." The transition from capitalism to socialism involves the class struggle and requires radical and sweeping changes in social relations. That from socialism to communism, on the other hand, "develops on its own foundation," gradually, without antagonistic classes and without a radical break-up of social relations. "Communism stems from socialism as its direct continuation." [30]

In the new Party program adopted by the Twenty-second Congress in 1961, a period of twenty years was assigned for this transition, the first time a definite date was set for the achievement of communism "in the main." "The Party solemnly proclaims: the present generation of Soviet people shall live in communism!" This will require, in the economic sphere, "the world's highest living standard" and an abundance of material and cultural values. "The bowl of communism is a bowl of abundance, and it must always be full." * In the social sphere, the "essential distinctions" between classes, between town and country, and between mental and physical labor must be eliminated. "Classes will fuse into a classless society of communist working people." And finally, in the political sphere, "all citizens will participate in the administration of public affairs" through "a most extensive development of socialist democracy" in "communist self-government." [31]

In 1961 Khrushchev announced the end of the dictatorship of the proletariat. This concept had always rested on the idea of the state as a class instrument; so, logically, with the disappearance of distinctions among classes, class rule would have no basis. The class dictatorship must be converted into a "state of the whole people." "The working class," he held, "is the only class in history which does not entertain the purpose of perpetuating its domination. Until now the state has always been an instrument of dictatorship by this or that class. In our country,

---

* Certain items, such as medical services, maintenance of children, education, housing, transportation, utilities, and restaurant meals, will reach adequate supply, according to the plans, before others and will be made free. Other items will be reduced in price and wages increased until eventually "commodity-money relations will become economically out-dated and will wither away."

for the first time in history, a state has taken shape which is not a dictatorship of any one class, but an instrument of society as a whole, of the entire people." Similarly, the Communist Party of the Soviet Union became "the Party of the entire people." [32]

It is interesting that Khrushchev took these steps while distinctions of class were still present, the workers and peasants being regarded as separate but friendly classes. No relaxation of internal control or external defense was involved, but the tenacity of the hope that the state will wither away was evident in his emphasis on "public self-administration"—the piecemeal transfer of governmental functions to "mass organizations" such as trade unions and cooperatives.

The state of the whole people is a new stage in the development of the socialist state, an all-important milestone on the road from socialist statehood to communist public self-government. . . . The process of its withering away will be a very long one; it will cover an entire historical epoch.

In the meantime he expected self-administration and state administration to "intermingle." "In this process the domestic functions of the state will develop and change, and gradually lose their political character." And, after a communist society is built in the Soviet Union, and "provided socialism wins and consolidates in the international arena," he said positively, "there will no longer be any need for the state, and it will wither away." [33]

Khrushchev, like Stalin, attached great importance to the problem of the relations between collective-farm property and public property. In the early 1950's he pushed for the amalgamation of collective farms into larger and more efficient units and for the creation of urbanized "agro-towns" with extensive community facilities. Where Stalin had refused to sell tractors to the collectives because that would extend the sphere of commodity circulation, Khrushchev proceeded to sell the machines, to reorganize the machine and tractor stations, and to entrust the farms with their own building and electrification programs. He thereby converted a large amount of the farms' undistributed funds into nondistributable assets. He argued that "the wealth of every collective farm has been created with the decisive help of the state and that this wealth essentially belongs to the entire people. . . . In present-day conditions the collective farms' indivisible funds essentially approach [the status of] public property." [34] The forms of property, he held, "develop in accordance with economic laws and depend on the nature and level of the productive forces." The solution, therefore, was "to raise the degree of socialization" of collective-farm property through improving the farms' mechanization, their management, and their productivity. When, through technology, the productive forces of agriculture approximated those of industry, it would be possible for the farms, along with the towns, "to go over to communist forms of production and distribution." The essential distinction between town and country would thus be overcome.[35]

In this connection Khrushchev also reinstated the old idea of equality that Stalin had denigrated (page 341). He agreed with his predecessor that "levelling" under socialism would be unjust and would delay the transition to communism. However, as class distinctions are eliminated and full communism is built, he said, "there will emerge communist equality, that is, complete social equality of people implying identical relations to the means of production, complete equality in distribution, and harmony of individual and society on the basis of an organic blending of personal and public interests." [36]

The other Marxist problem of the elimination of the distinction between mental and physical labor, like that of town and country, would be solved under communism, but in Khrushchev's opinion it was more difficult to solve. The key lay in education. Workers and peasants must be educated to the level of technicians and engineers, "to the level of the intelligentsia"; and at the same time secondary education must be combined with work on farms or in industry. Personal experience of both mental and physical labor would break down the psychological barriers between them. Once ideas of exploitation were eradicated, man would realize that he himself must work if he would eat. Thus the "new man" would be created, the man of communism, who would feel labor to be not a burden but life's prime need.[37]

The self-discipline of the new man will, however, be reinforced by the discipline of the machine. "The machine industry," Khrushchev saw, "has a set rhythm that calls for a corresponding arrangement of the work." * To enjoy in abundance the products of the machines, man must tend them on schedule. Hours of labor will be reduced and hard physical labor and "all unskilled labor" will be eliminated; but the planned allocation and social regulation of labor will continue under communism.[38]

* For a more thorough analysis of this idea see Rexford G. Tugwell, *The Industrial Discipline* (New York, 1933).

VI

The most significant development between the Twenty-second and Twenty-third Party Congresses was the deterioration and break in friendly relations with China. Although a power struggle, this dispute has ideological content and is clarifying Communist thought.

When Khrushchev formulated his "law of the even development of socialism" in 1957 (page 351), the enormous population and deep poverty of China seemed to defy such a law. The delays and sacrifices that would be required of the Russian people to raise the Chinese to their own economic level were beyond calculation. The suggestion was soon made by Stepanian that the law of even development might be applied separately to two groups of socialist countries, a European and an Asiatic group.[39] Within each group the differences between countries were much less than those between the groups, and thus the law would not require such great sacrifices. Khrushchev branded this suggestion as revisionism, yet his law was hardly applied seriously to China. Even the existing trade and aid agreements between the two countries were soon being broken.

This failure was in part due to the insistence of the Chinese leaders on their own interpretations of Marxism. Khrushchev was unwilling to recognize Mao Tse-tung as a higher oracle of Marxism-Leninism, but he changed course more than once to meet Mao's ideas. "The Communist Party of China," he said in 1959, "is employing many original forms of socialist construction. But we have no disagreements with it, nor can there be any disagreement." The Party platform of 1961 found a place, though not a prominent one, for "the law of planned, proportionate development" of socialist countries.[40] Yet this formulation was itself a relaxation of Khrushchev's earlier idea of "even development."

Between 1960 and 1963 the differences between Khrushchev and Mao gradually became sharper and emerged into the open. They hinged on the international class struggle and the role of war in the overthrow of capitalism. The Russian and the Chinese revolutions had both occurred in times of war, but the Chinese revolution was much more directly the result of Communist military activity. The Russians carried the responsibilities of a thermonuclear power and were more impressed with the necessity to avoid a third world war. They enjoyed a highly productive and vulnerable economy and felt the attractiveness of peace and plenty. The Chinese, on the contrary, felt a closer affinity to the "have not" nations of the world and were tempted to bid for the leadership of world Communism by adopting a more militant line. These vast differences in the situations of the two countries found expression in divergent interpretations of Marxist theory.

Problems of the balance between voluntaristic and deterministic currents of Marxism lay close to the heart of the controversy. The Chinese Communists tend more toward voluntarism in proportion as the prerevolutionary conditions of China were even farther than those of Russia from the conditions envisioned in Marx's economics.* As the Russians' economy becomes more powerful they tend to emphasize more the economic forces in the world revolution, and their revolutionary ardor becomes suspect.

The Chinese admitted that the economic achievements of the Soviet Union "play an exemplary role and are an inspiration to the oppressed peoples and the oppressed nations." But, they insisted, "this exemplary role and inspiration can never replace the revolutionary struggles of the oppressed peoples and nations." Therefore peaceful coexistence and economic competition between socialism and capitalism were not sufficient for victory in the class struggle. Local wars of national liberation and violent proletarian revolutions were necessary: "As a matter of fact, there is no historical precedent for peaceful transition from capitalism to socialism." [41] Peaceful coexistence, while both possible and desirable, could not be preserved by cooperation with the imperialists but only by active struggle against them.

The Russians, in response, denied that they were depending solely on economic competition to destroy capitalism or that they had extended peaceful coexistence beyond the area of interstate relations in opposition to anticolonial and civil wars. They were impressed, however, with the danger that such local wars might trigger a nuclear holocaust. Khrushchev attacked "the newly-fledged theoreticians" who thought the road to victory for socialism lay through "wars between states," desolation, bloodshed, and the death of millions. "Were the Communists to be guided by a 'theory' such as that, it would repel the masses instead of attracting them." He reminded them of Marx's basic point that capitalism is inevitably destroyed by its own internal contradic-

---

* This is one of the reasons for the continued admiration of the Chinese for Stalin, the supreme voluntarist.

tions. "According to this doctrine, the working class defeats capitalism by its class struggle against the exploiters and not by starting wars between countries." But he still appealed for mutual tolerance and forbearance: "It does not befit us to proceed like churchmen and engage in 'excommunicating' from socialism." [42]

The Chinese, however, intransigently continued to extend the ideological conflict. They traced its roots back to the Twentieth Congress of the Soviet Party and Khrushchev's criticism of Stalin. From that point on, they held, the Russian leaders had abandoned international proletarian solidarity and the world revolution in favor of "great power chauvinism" and a capitulationist peace with the United States, the world leader of capitalism, imperialism, and counterrevolution. The Chinese defended Stalin and argued that imperialism could be defeated, and world war prevented, not by agreements with the United States but only by successful revolutions. They went on to attack Khrushchev for deviating from Marxism-Leninism toward social democracy and capitalism, and for naïvely trusting in class collaboration. They criticized him for ending the dictatorship of the proletariat before full communism was attained and before the world struggle between classes was finished. They ridiculed his state and party "of the entire people" as completely non-Marxian concepts. They accused him of trying to stop the debate and to impose his revisionist line upon world Communism by applying discipline and majority rule among fraternal Communist parties, whereas such differences regarding fundamental principles could be resolved only by "unanimous agreement in accordance with the principle of consultation." [43]

Both the Russians and the Chinese exaggerated and distorted their opponents' positions. Neither side has been willing to retreat and the polemics have increased in virulence. The result has been a deepening split in international Communism—the most serious since that between Stalin and Trotsky and even more portentous.

VII

In October 1964 Khrushchev fell from power and the leadership became even more "collective" and bureaucratic. Some of his reorganizations of the Party and government, such as rotation in Party office, were abandoned, but Brezhnev and Kosygin continued to reiterate the principal elements of both theory and policy stressed by Khrushchev. Peaceful coexistence, the building of communism through expanding production, the state and the party of the whole people, and the spread of Communism by demonstrating its economic superiority over capitalism—all under attack from China—remained as key elements. Very little new theory has been advanced, and the Twenty-third Party Congress (March–April 1966) showed great reluctance to explore the frontiers of Marxist thought.

This conservatism was most significantly apparent in the view, frequently expressed by Brezhnev, that the development of Marxist theory is a principal task of the social sciences. Theory is to be derived empirically from deeper, more scientific study of Soviet society.

At the same time, this attitude carried the implication of a greater role for public opinion in the shaping of policy. Soon after taking office Brezhnev said on Red Square, "The great Lenin taught us Communists strictly and undeviatingly to fulfill the will of the people, to rely on their experience in arriving at political decisions, constantly to take the pulse of the people's life." [44] Yet public opinion was to remain outside the government—as in the old Slavophil ideal. It was a phenomenon to be studied, not a force from which government itself is derived.

The new leadership wished to avoid the "subjectivism" of which it accused Khrushchev. Since Marxism is scientific socialism, the methods of modern social science—not insight or intuition, individual or collective—must be applied to the direction of public policy. In particular, the achievements of economics were to be applied. Stalin's idea that commodity production is a reflection of the two forms of socialist property, public and collective-farm, and is therefore destined to disappear when these become one form (page 344), was replaced by a new theory of the "objective necessity of commodity production under socialism." The "law of value" is not simply an accounting concept; even within the public sector of the economy it must guide the rational allocation of resources.

As applied to the planning process this meant complete cost accounting and respectful attention to consumer preferences as expressed in market demand. Planning and a market economy were not opposing concepts: "A plan that is not based on the market is as powerless against disproportions as is a market that is not organized by a plan. It is precisely the dialectical unity of the plan and the market that gives rise to the most effective system of economic management of the socialist economy." [45] Socialist distribution according to contribution required that the latter be measured by products sold rather than by output, and the planning indices were revised accordingly. Thus, "trade becomes a mechanism for controlling and testing the validity and effectiveness of the plans. The consumer expresses the final judgment on the expediency of this or that labor expenditure, and his voice becomes important in determining the rate of growth of this or that line of production." [46] Subjective, political decisions as to what should be produced were to be replaced by decisions based on market research.* The balance between the voluntaristic and the deterministic strains of Marxism was thus shifted a little toward the latter.

The search for economic incentives continued. Factory managers were encouraged to produce at a "profit" by being empowered to retain and use part of such surpluses.† At the same time the factories must pay interest on their capital equipment, and therefore must manage carefully its rational use and calculate sharply the expected return from any investment in additional equipment.

This drive for the rationalization of industry and agriculture was a continuation of Khrushchev's great push toward the world's highest standard of living. The consumers were to benefit from increased national production by four pathways—through higher wages and pensions, lower prices, reduction and elimination of some taxes, and expansion of the free services supported by public funds. As a *Pravda* editorial frankly said, "Communists are not fighting to make future generations happy through the ascetic self-denial of those living now— they call for paving the way to a better future for their descendants by doing everything to make life happier and richer today, for their contemporaries." [47]

Like Khrushchev, Brezhnev and Kosygin saw the pursuit of economic plenty as a substantial contribution to the world revolution, in fact the most important one that the Soviet Union could make. "More than

---

* These were recognized as being partly political: "The Party rebuffs all attempts to divorce politics from economics or to counterpose the two. . . . The divorce of politics from economics inevitably leads to attempts to solve economic tasks through arbitrary fiat, without reckoning with scientific data and objective economic laws" (L. Leont'ev, "The Unity of Economics and Politics," *Current Digest of the Soviet Press,* XVII, no. 10 [March 31, 1965], 7, from *Pravda,* March 7, 1965, p. 2).

† Profit under socialism was said to be an accounting category, not based on exploitation as under capitalism.

ever before," Kosygin told the Twenty-third Congress, "do we appreciate today the depth of perception in Lenin's statement that our socialist state exercises its chief influence on the world revolution by its economic policy." [48] This policy made possible improved support for the national liberation struggle and for the new nations; it demonstrated the advantages of socialism over capitalism; and it built military strength to restrain the predatory imperialist powers. Yet emphasis was placed, not only on "the development of the Soviet economy," but on "those of the other socialist countries" as well.

It is not surprising, however, that this argument sounded like a rationalization of selfishness when heard on an empty stomach. From the Chinese point of view the great stress on incentives, profits, money, and the market meant not the rationalization of the economy but the reintroduction of capitalism. Coupled with efforts to reach agreement with the United States, the leading imperialist power, in the international arena, this amounted to a complete abandonment of the revolution under cover of hypocritical pleas for socialist unity. Chinese criticism became harsher; the Russians were accused of trying to divide the world with the Americans.

The four decades since Stalin took command have witnessed substantial developments of Marxist thought in the Soviet Union. Some perennial problems continue to attract attention, such as the relations between base and superstructure, the role of the state, and the methods of planning. Other matters, once urgent issues, have been laid to rest, among them socialism in one country, divergent paths to socialism, and the dictatorship of the proletariat. As economic power grew, especially after the great test of the Second World War, prestige and confidence have grown. Progress has been made in building a new socialist ecumene with Moscow as its center; paranoia has abated; and the leadership seems more businesslike—perhaps more bourgeois—than ever. Policy seems less volatile, less voluntaristic, more predictable. It must still be justified by Marxist theory. And here lies one of the main effects, perhaps advantages, of the break with China: the justifications of policy are now subject to sharp scrutiny, not only from the capitalist West but also from the Communist East.

CHAPTER XXIV

Some Perspectives

THE Russian political tradition is a quite intricate fabric. Efforts to simplify it into a straight warp and woof of Norman versus Mongolian influences, of Byzantine versus Slav, or of Marxism versus oriental despotism, have led as much to distortion and misunderstanding as to clarity and insight. The variety of such interpretations should, in itself, arouse scepticism toward an overemphasis on any one of them. Even so, after the foregoing survey some generalizations are necessary; with these words of caution, they will be attempted.

I

It should be clear that an understanding of Russian political thought cannot begin with the October revolution, nor with the nineteenth century, nor with Peter. As in most if not all cultures, the continuities outweigh the innovations, and the most radical ideas, when implemented in practice, must make their peace with the inherited environment, including the old ideas.

Among these continuities none seems more firmly established than the chasm that has separated the Russian government from the people. This was not, of course, a uniquely Russian phenomenon, but several features of Russian history deepened it. The Varangians, as conquerors and as mercenary soldiers among an agrarian people, were set apart and held themselves apart from the Slavs by their language, their habits, and their interests. After they became Slavicised, the movements of princes and their retinues from town to town perpetuated this separation. During the Mongol period, the duties of the princes as agents of the khans, and their own use of the danger of destruction by the Tatars to complete their suppression of the *veche*, further divided the interests of the princely government from those of the people. Their exclusion of the people from participation in the government was never remedied, and in the nineteenth century it was even elevated into a virtue by the Slavophils.

Aided by the church and the ideas of autocratic rule that the churchmen brought from Byzantium, the House of Riurik raised itself above both the people and the other aristocrats, and the grand princes exalted themselves over the other Riurikides. A number of historical influences—the Mongol court at Sarai, the fall of the Byzantine empire, Ivan III's marriage to a Byzantine princess, the doctrine of Moscow as the Third Rome, use of the title of tsar, the conquest of the Volga khanates—all served to reinforce this trend toward autocracy. As this trend culminated with the personality of Ivan IV, and time and again thereafter, rivalries among the boyars and conflicts between greater and lesser aristocrats helped to consolidate and protect the autocracy.

The Western medieval doctrine that the king was under the law, and the concepts of limited government that were built up in England from the time of the Magna Carta, had no counterparts in Russia. Moreover, the great rivalry of Empire and Papacy, which contributed so substantially to the sharpening and development of political concepts in the West, was avoided by the use of Byzantine ideas of church-state collaboration, which led to the subordination of the church. In "Holy Russia" there was no need to search for a secular justification of political power, a search that led, in the West, to theories of the social compact and the doctrine of popular sovereignty. The autocracy rested instead on its mission, both temporal and spiritual in Byzantine style, to care for its faithful sheep. The Mongols too, it should be remembered, justified themselves by an ideology of a great, messianic mission; and, much later, so would the Marxists. Power in Russia was thus closely linked with ideology long before and long after Uvarov produced his formula, Orthodoxy, Autocracy, and Nationality.

The people themselves were accorded no voice in the interpretation of the ideology. The government and the church, having the true faith, had also a responsibility to maintain its doctrinal purity against all errors, internal and external, religious and political. A free play of public opinion would be useless, dangerous, and intolerable; orthodoxy required centralized interpretation. Against the West, heretical in social and political as well as in religious thought, an attitude of hostile isolation must be maintained. At the same time, the material achievements of the West were respected, and repeated attempts were made from the fifteenth century to acquire Western technology without becoming infected with too many Western ideas. For this official attitude the Slavophils provided a philosophical foundation, but even so their independence of opinion attracted the hostility of the government.

Into this traditional pattern of attitudes and purposes some features of Marxism fit beautifully. Its messianic, universal program would link Russia with the outside world, ending her isolation through a new secular orthodoxy. It promised the material advantages of industrialization while it not only rejected but even promised to destroy the institutions of the West. Yet others of its features did not fit at all. The underdeveloped conditions of the economy confronted the Marxists with a choice between intolerable delays in achieving power or drastic revisions of theory and practice to speed up the revolution. The Bolsheviks, having chosen the latter, thereby cut themselves off from European social democracy, and thus preserved the tradition of ideological exclusiveness that reached back to the fifteenth century. In Lenin's Party and later in the government, the pursuit of doctrinal purity, in isolation, led again to centralized interpretation and the suppression of divergent opinion.

II

The backwardness of Russia, which made her vulnerable to revolution and which required a special form of Marxism, was the result of centuries of discouragement of local and individual initiative. To the grand princes, ambitious to centralize power, all independent activity was threatening. The uprooting and transplanting of many people in the Mongol period and in the fifteenth and sixteenth centuries, the use of temporary land tenures, and the activities of Ivan IV, effectively eradicated attitudes of independence among the aristocrats. Among the peasants, their dependence upon the landlords and the practice of land reallocation through the mir had much the same effect in stifling initiative. So little was the psychology of individualism developed that even those who left the land for urban employment frequently joined in artels, sharing in common both work and wages. The concepts and practices of the zemski sobors, and their failure to develop into an independent parliament, well illustrate the situation. The bureaucracy too, as it expanded, tried to keep control of local activities and to prohibit those it deemed too independent.

Under an unlimited autocracy, and in the absence of traditions of local autonomy or of individualism, it was not likely that doctrines of individual rights, as they developed in the West, would penetrate effectively. They, of course, did not. Instead, such doctrines—especially after the French Revolution—were regarded, except by the radicals, as a dangerous Western heresy. In spite of several attempts by the government to reform itself, from Alexis to Alexander II, it never succeeded even in establishing a reign of law. Such basic elements as the separation of powers and the independence of the judiciary proved irreconcilable with autocracy.

Economic doctrines of individual enterprise were similarly handicapped by the lack of a supporting tradition. From the beginning, when the Kievan princes had led the trading flotillas down the Dnieper to Byzantium, through the eighteenth century, when government-sponsored factories began the industrialization of Russia, economic initiative came from the central government. While the entrepreneurs of the West, armed with the *laissez faire* doctrine of Adam Smith, were freeing themselves from government controls and increasing the momentum of the industrial revolution, those of Russia remained, on into the twentieth century, largely dependent upon, and subservient to, the government.

The pursuit of pecuniary gain never attained the prominence or the prestige that it was accorded in Europe and America. The rationalizations by which first the Roman church and then the Protestants had reconciled private property with religion were never so successful among the Orthodox. Coming late to Russia, capitalism came under the disadvantages of its Western origin and its well-documented defects of urban poverty, cyclical unemployment, child labor, and the rest. It met with the approval of no substantial segment of the population, the bureaucracy preferring state enterprise, the nobility their manorial economy, the intelligentsia socialism, and the ordinary people their cooperatives, the artel, and the mir. Its base remained narrow and it never built up a powerful middle class dedicated to its preservation. In October 1917, therefore, there was no massive, deep-seated, and confident psychology of private enterprise confronting the Bolsheviks like those that defeated the Chartists in England and the Commune in Paris.

III

There were other deep-seated elements of thought, however, that powerfully influenced the course of the revolutionary movement and the subsequent history of the Soviet Union.

The attitude of the autocracy, of the tsar and his officials—that public opinion had no status, that they would consult only those whom they wished to consult, and that they retained all power of decision—was deeply discouraging to the pursuit of political reform by peaceful and legal means. Those who hoped for reform by the tsar, from Kurbski to Miliukov, were usually disappointed and left with the conviction that peaceful methods were hopeless.

Many of the revolutionaries of the last century firmly grasped the idea that the nature and tactics of the regime under attack determined the nature and tactics of the attackers. The centralized autocracy, deaf to reason and using spies and administrative exile without trial to eradicate its enemies, drove the latter to the use of corresponding methods of centralized conspiracy and terrorism. Among the *narodniki* the peaceful propaganda of Lavrov lost ground to the violence of Zheliabov. The Mensheviks' search for a broadly based labor party lost out to the direct action of the Bolsheviks. In spite of the opprobrium of Nechaev, tight, disciplined organization prevailed over the loose methods of the anarchists. In the end the best disciplined of the revolutionary groups, the Bolsheviks, were also the most successful.

This conditioning left its mark permanently on Russian Marxism. Without it the Marxists might never have won power anywhere, but with it the nature of Marxism itself was changed.

Capitalism was well established in the West before Marx wrote, and he gave no attention to the idea, fantastic on its face, that feudalism might be overthrown and capitalism established under proletarian leadership. Yet such was the quandary of the Russian Marxists. So little strength had the bourgeoisie, and so little will to attack the government, that the revolutionary socialists early reached the conclusion that they must themselves assume the liberals' task, the political revolution, as well as their own social and economic revolution. Plekhanov took this conclusion, in large part, over into the Marxist movement—which he could hardly avoid doing and still pretend to a revolutionary role. But this conclusion entailed momentous consequences. It required that the proletariat push forward a nonsocialist struggle, the primary bene- ficiary of which would be the hated class enemy, the bourgeoisie. It required that this political struggle be undertaken before, and apart from, the struggle for socialism. It required that the Marxists organize and carry out a minority revolution very different from the over- whelming majority revolution that would later destroy capitalism. It thus gave great weight to the wills and actions of the professional revolutionaries and less weight to the conditioning of men's minds by their factory experience. Economic determinism seemed to be sub- merged by a willful determination to end the autocracy. Could this be Marxism? It is small wonder that the legal Marxists and the Econo- mists objected.

Western Marxism, however, embraced two very different attitudes and strains of thought. On the one hand there was the deterministic strain expressed in *Capital* for which the incremental processes of technological change inevitably evolve corresponding patterns of eco- nomic, political, and legal relationships through a dialectical series of class conflicts in which all parties play objectively determined roles. The eventual victory of the proletariat and communism is inescapable, and the moral rights and wrongs of the conflicts are reduced to progressive and conservative forces. On the other hand there was the voluntaristic, eschatological strain found in the *Manifesto* with its clarion call, "Workers of all countries, unite!" In this strain scientific objectivity is forgotten as righteous indignation wells up and demands herculean labors to destroy the exploiters. This last cosmic conflict won, the vision extends to an anarchist's paradise of brotherly coopera- tion in peace and plenty, without avarice or coercion, without classes and without the state.

Determinism was attractive to some of the radicals after eighty years of unsuccessful revolutions under other banners. It promised an inevita- ble victory. Against it, however, were the equally inevitable period of capitalism, which the socialists were determined to avoid, and the resulting delay in achieving socialism. The voluntaristic strain, standing for more active efforts to shorten that period, started with an advantage that increased as its adaptations to Russian conditions improved.

These conditions were so different from those of the West in which Marxism arose as to demand great originality on the part of the Russian Marxists. They met this demand, in general, by integrating elements of Russian thought and experience into the Marxist system.

To lead a minority revolution for political freedom, with the help of the bourgeoisie and without immediate expectation of attaining either power or socialism, was a task for which Marx's writings gave little guidance. For it, the revolutionary tradition was more directly relevant. The lessons of the Decembrist revolt and the conspiratorial experiences of Nechaev and The People's Will, and the arguments of Tkachev, all pointed toward a tightly disciplined, secret organization of professional revolutionaries. To more traditional Marxists, however, this smacked of Blanquism and Bakuninism and seemed illusory in the absence of a mass organization capable of attracting majority support. Hence the tension at the Second Party Congress in 1903 and the unbridgeable gap between Bolsheviks and Mensheviks.

In any event, the conspiratorial tradition, integrated into Marxism by Lenin, made Marxism-Leninism a more effective revolutionary instrument than Marxism had ever been. But this tradition, exerting its influence before a mass movement was feasible, set an elitist tone in Lenin's Party in a way that never changed. Especially after Parvus and Trotsky, via the theory of permanent revolution, and Lenin, via his theory of imperialism, had concluded that the bourgeois-democratic revolution could be carried on into the proletarian-socialist revolution was the idea of a capitalist period abandoned and with it the idea of majority revolution. The professionals, with proletarian support and the expectation of revolution in the West, could take and hold power. They should not surrender power to the bourgeoisie. But neither, they rapidly concluded once power was in their hands, should they surrender it to anyone else—not even the Constituent Assembly or the proletariat itself organized through trade unions.

This independent attitude of Lenin's proletarian Party toward the proletariat was not of purely postrevolutionary vintage. It derived from the class relations of the *narodnik* movement and from Lenin's early conclusion that factory life did not make the workers socialist or enable them spontaneously to see the necessity for political revolution. Class consciousness and political purpose had to be imparted to them, he believed, by the professionals, by the socialist intelligentsia. This belief, however accurate it may have been, ran clearly counter to the materialist psychology of Marx, which Lenin continued to accept. Its effect was to set the vanguard Party above the proletariat. It also loosened the connection between Party decisions and the objective economic situation.

Closely related to these elitist influences of the conspiratorial tradition was its influence in shifting the emphasis of Marxism from economics to politics. There was strong sentiment among the early socialists against political action, but by 1879 the political situation seemed so intolerable to The People's Will that it gave the political revolution top priority. Marxism, on the contrary, taught that the political superstructure reflects the economic base, and if interpreted deterministically, this would call for an extended growth of capitalism before and after the autocracy could be overthrown. To make Marxism palatable, and to meet the challenge of its *narodnik* and SR critics, the Marxists had to escape from this difficulty by telescoping their two revolutions into one. They were thus under pressure from the urgencies of the revolutionary movement to deny strict economic determinism and to act through politics without being unduly restrained by the backwardness of the national economy. The habits acquired and the theories that justified them led ultimately to Lenin's explicit assertion of the priority of politics over economics and to Stalin's idea of revolution from above.

These influences of earlier Russian experience and thought upon the practice and theory of Russian Marxism were exerted from its beginning, gradually and cumulatively. By 1917 Lenin and his followers were no longer inhibited by the retarded condition of the economy or by the absence of a proletarian majority in the population.

IV

Lenin's and Trotsky's decision to try political revolution without waiting for Russian economic development set in train inexhaustible consequences for Russia, for the world, and for Marxist theory. Since Marxism was a well-integrated fabric, the omission or revision of some of its elements, especially such basic elements, led inevitably to the revision or replacement of others. Some of these changes were improvements, from the point of view of the revolutionaries. Others, even from the same viewpoint, entailed undesired consequences. A few of these, as they related to Marxist theory, may be briefly examined.

First, the decision to seize power was based primarily on assessments of the domestic and foreign political situations. Lenin and Trotsky thus gave to politics an independence from the stage of economic development that Marx and Engels had never allowed. The tenuous connection they maintained with Marx's economics, through Lenin's theory of imperialism, linked the Russian revolution to its international context. Yet this link was largely abandoned in Stalin's theory of socialism in one country, and the regime was left with little basis in Marx's "scientific socialism."

Second, the decision to take power without a proletarian majority in the population—followed, step by step, by the replacement of factory committees with individual managers, the substitution of appointments for elections, and the suppression of opposition (from other political parties, from within the Bolshevik Party, and finally from within the Politburo itself)—led, much as the Mensheviks had predicted, to a dictatorship and not to the democracy that had inspired the idealists among the Bolsheviks. The dictatorship of the proletariat became the dictatorship of an individual as Lenin's theories of Party discipline sanctified a replication of the old national pattern of centralized, autocratic government. The old separation between the tsar's government and the people gradually returned, and with it the hatred and contempt of the old rulers toward any independent public opinion.

Third, the egalitarian ideals of Marxism were also buried under the weight of incentive schemes, the N.E.P., and bureaucratic rationalizations. The regime became less and less able to command, at home and abroad, the driving force of moral indignation against economic injustice, which had been one of the most attractive features of Marxism. Stalin later repudiated equality, even as a long-range goal.

Fourth, the special Russian circumstances, and the long tradition of difference from the West, encouraged a drift away from the international proletarian solidarity envisioned by Marx and Engels. It began with the acceptance of the German ultimatum and culminated in the united front policy of the Comintern and the doctrine of socialism in one country. It was a process with far-reaching effects that are still being felt. Hope for proletarian revolution in the West gave place to fear, both real and paranoid, of the capitalist encirclement. A self-righteous, isolationist psychology like that of Muscovy pervaded the

Party and diverted the Third International from its revolutionary mission to the conservative defense of the Soviet Union by any expedient means.

Fifth, the expectation of military attack, with no relief expected from revolution in the West, spurred the industrialization of the nation to a hectic pace. The building of socialism became the building of military strength; and this, in turn, induced in the West an exaggerated fear of the Soviet Union, aggravating its fear of socialism. Tensions were increased, and war came. Soviet strength helped the West, but it also increased the fear. This same industrialization, however, led to Khrushchev's belief that capitalism could be overthrown by international economic competition. This belief might reduce tensions, but in the opinion of the Chinese, it might also draw the teeth of Marxism.

And finally, the suppression of the Left Opposition in the name of discipline led to splits in foreign Communist parties, to the formation of a Fourth International, and to the further fragmentation of the Marxist movement. The subordination of Comintern policy to Soviet needs and Russian Party orthodoxy engendered a parallel growth of nationalistic attitudes abroad, and the stage was set for the drama of separate national Communisms wherever revolution might succeed. The price of socialism in one country included the reconciliation of Marxism with nationalism. Thus was forfeited the last hope for the realization of Marx's great dream of the ending of nation states.

Such drastic departures from western Marxism are easily made to appear as ruthless rejections of theory in the cynical pursuit of power. So it is important to remember that, at each step along the way, the new departures were integrated into the remaining fabric of Marxist theory. This was accomplished through a polemical process of exceptional vigor, which set a pattern that continues to prevail in international Communism. A new orthodoxy was established, again connected with the government but standing above it and not below it as the Orthodox church had stood. But it is a flexible orthodoxy that was not frozen even by the canonization of Lenin and his writings. Theory retains its importance and its relevance to practice. New circumstances elicit not only practical responses but also new theoretical developments.

The connection of ideology and power thus assumed a new form parallel to the old connection between church and state. Secular salvation was linked to the preservation of the new true faith, Marxism-

Leninism. For a long time this was an exclusive faith, cherished in isolation as the Third Rome had cherished its doctrinal purity, but with more effective ecumenical, messianic claims, this time expressed in the Communist International. After the appearance of additional Communist countries, however, and especially after the ideological dispute with China,* it was no longer an exclusively Russian doctrine. Control over interpretation could no longer be maintained. It remains to be seen whether the long-run effect of this will be the establishment of separate national "churches" of Marxism-Leninism or the integration of broader international thought and experience into a single "church."

V

The Soviet attempt to apply the theories of Marxism, having continued for half a century, may be assessed as the most significant experiment in government and politics since the introduction of the large-scale representative republic. Its great importance as an experiment lies in its combination of economic with political power in the hands of the central government. It has the further importance of being dedicated to the achievement of a long-range theoretical goal rather than responding to the current will of one or of many. Both of these, on first sight, look like formulas for tyranny; and the Soviet people have in fact experienced tyranny. But the experiment and its significance do not end there.

In previous theories of government, from ancient times, the problems of the relations of political and economic power have been recognized. In the West, ever since the two aspects of the Latin word *dominium* were distinguished in the late Middle Ages, the tendency has been to set the one against the other. After Adam Smith the cleavage became increasingly sharp as economic interests sought to escape public control. The defense of property, it was said, is the defense of liberty. Independent economic power could be used as a restraint upon the abuse of political power. In general, it might be said that, as a result of Western thought and institutions, political power has been brought under much more effective democratic control than has economic power.

The Russians in 1917, on the other hand, were in a very favorable

---

* Khrushchev saw the similarity to a religious dispute.

position to undertake a new approach to these problems. Their language, reflecting their ideas and attitudes, retained several words combining the concepts of authority and ownership. They habitually expressed the idea of possession, "I have," by the equivalent of "by me is," and in the mir and artel they had long been familiar with communal land and goods. The time, moreover, was ripe for a new experiment. Technological advances had brought industrial units to such size that miscalculations in their management caused very widespread social evils: the business cycle was clearly too costly. At the same time, the increasing size of units brought with it the tempting idea that they might be centrally integrated into a system of planned production. The Russians, however, handicapped by their lack of experience with democracy and by their overwhelming illiteracy and poverty, were not in a favorable position to guard their experiment against the recrudescence of the bureaucratic and autocratic features of their political past.

As to the other aspect of the Soviet experiment, its dedication to the achievement of the final stage of communism, several things may be said. In the first place, it is a tribute to the high aspirations of the Marxian utopia that, after a century, it is still so attractive as to evoke such great and sustained effort. It is, of course, not original with Marx; it is a combination of humanitarian elements from Hebrew, Christian, and Enlightenment thought. Yet, distant as the goal may be, it remains credible and progress can be seen to be made toward it. Second, utopian experiments are usually much smaller-scale affairs. The large new efforts, such as those of the American and French revolutions, submerge their utopian elements in so many practical considerations that they are lost from sight. To find a similarly utopian, yet narrow, undertaking on a comparable scale it is necessary to go back to the pursuit of universal peace by Chingis Khan—which was one of the influences on the history of Russia and China but not on that of the West. Third, an accepted common goal gives a society cohesion, optimism, and a sense of purpose that is lacking where public policy is decided by compromise among conflicting private interests. There is much to be said in favor of a choice of goals, but also much to be attained by the cooperative, planned pursuit of an accepted goal. But, fourth, even a utopian goal may be distorted if there is no mechanism for the correction of autocratic interpretations and policy decisions made at the center. The career of Stalin demonstrated that. From it, perhaps, much has been learned. Also, with growing levels of education the system may attain a type of self-correcting feedback from public opinion. On the other hand, the approach of economic plenty, if it approaches, may operate like the bread and circuses of the Romans as a prelude to indifference and decadence.

The Soviet spokesmen themselves are very much aware that they are conducting a vast social experiment. It would be well if Western statesmen also were able to keep their eyes on both the current situation and the distant vision.

NOTES

BIBLIOGRAPHY

INDEX

Notes

NOTES are numbered consecutively by chapter. Translations made for this volume are indicated by translators' names following the place and date of publication; published translations, by names preceding the place and date. The abbreviation *PSRL* is used for Russia, Arkheograficheskaia Kommissia, *Polnoe sobranie russkikh letopisei* (Complete Collection of Russian Chronicles), published in St. Petersburg beginning in 1841.

PART ONE

Chapter I. The City-States: The Slavs

1. Procopius, *History of the Wars*, Bk. 7, Chap. 14, sec. 22, trans. H. B. Dewing ("Loeb Classical Library," IV [Cambridge, Mass., 1954], 269).

2. Quoted in George Vernadsky, *Ancient Russia* (New Haven, 1943), p. 159, from Mauricius, *Strategicon*, XI, 5.

3. Quoted in B. Grekov, *Kiev Rus*, trans. Y. Sdobnikov (Moscow, 1959), p. 414.

4. *The Russian Primary Chronicle*, ed. and trans. Samuel H. Cross and Olgerd P. Sherbowitz-Wetzor (Cambridge, Mass., [1953]), pp. 59–60.

5. *PSRL*, I (1846), 160.

6. *Medieval Russian Laws*, ed. and trans. George Vernadsky (New York, 1947), p. 81.

7. *PSRL*, III (1841), 21; trans. Deborah Hardy.

8. Cross and Sherbowitz-Wetzor, *Russian Primary Chronicle*, p. 199.

9. *The Chronicle of Novgorod, 1016–1471*, trans. Robert Michell and Nevill Forbes ("Camden Third Series," XXV [London, 1914]), 39. Spelling slightly adapted.

10. *Pamiatniki Russkogo Prava*, ed. S. V. Iushkov, II (Moscow, 1953), 139; trans. Norman Henley.

11. Quoted in George Vernadsky, *Kievan Russia* (New Haven, 1948), p. 211, from *PSRL*, II (1843), 23. Cf. Vasili N. Tatishchev, *Istoriia Rossiiskaia*, II (Moscow, 1773), 279–284.

Chapter II. Fraternity: *The Varangians*

1. *The Russian Primary Chronicle*, ed. and trans. Samuel H. Cross and Olgerd P. Sherbowitz-Wetzor (Cambridge, Mass., [1953]), p. 142.

2. *PSRL*, II (1843), 50.

3. Cross and Sherbowitz-Wetzor, *Russian Primary Chronicle*, p. 185.

4. *Ibid.*, p. 187.

5. *PSRL*, II (1843), 108.

6. *Ibid.*, VII (1856), 117.

7. *Ibid.*, II (1843), 97.

Chapter III. Symphonia: *The Byzantines*

1. John Chrysostom, *The Priesthood*, trans. W. A. Jurgens (New York, 1955), verses 165, 189.

2. C. A. Spulber, *L'Eclogue des Isauriens, Texte—traduction—histoire* (Cernautzi, Romania, 1929), pp. 3–4; trans. William T. Avery.

3. *The Civil Code*, trans. S. P. Scott, XVI (Cincinnati, 1932), 30.

4. *The Russian Primary Chronicle*, ed. and trans. Samuel H. Cross and Olgerd P. Sherbowitz-Wetzor (Cambridge, Mass., [1953]), p. 117.

5. *Pamiatniki Russkogo Prava*, ed. S. V. Iushkov, I (Moscow, 1952), 244–246; trans. John T. Dorosh, Norman Henley, and the author. This is the version known as the Synodal MS.

6. *Medieval Russian Laws*, ed. and trans. George Vernadsky (New York, 1947), p. 62.

7. For example, in *PSRL*, I (1846), 157, where it is erroneously attributed to John Chrysostom. Other instances are cited in Ihor Shevchenko, "A Neglected Byzantine Source of Muscovite Political Ideology," *Harvard Slavic Studies*, II (Cambridge, 1954), 141–179, where the derivation from Agapetus is established.

8. Quoted in William K. Medlin, *Moscow and East Rome* (Geneva, 1952), p. 51.

9. *PSRL*, IX (1862), 83; trans. Norman Henley.

10. *Ibid.*, II (1843), 30.

11. Sergei M. Solov'ev, *Istoriia Rossii s drevneishikh vremen*, I (St. Petersburg, 1896), 725, citing Tatishchev's chronicles.

12. Quoted in *ibid.*, p. 727. See *PSRL*, II (1843), 127.

13. *PSRL*, IX (1862), 225–228; trans. Norman Henley.

NOTES

PART TWO

Chapter IV. World Empire: The Mongols

1. *Die geheime Geschichte der Mongolen,* ed. and trans. Erich Haenisch (Leipzig, 1948), secs. 21, 80, 113, 121, 187.

2. Juvaini, *History of the World Conqueror,* trans. John A. Boyle, I (Cambridge, Mass., 1958), 105.

3. Eric Voegelin, "The Mongol Orders of Submission to European Powers, 1245–1255," *Byzantion,* XV (1941), 404.

4. Eric Voegelin, *The New Science of Politics* (Chicago, 1952), pp. 56–57, except the first paragraph, which was translated by the author from Paul Pelliot, "Les Mongols et la Papauté," *Revue de l'orient chrétien,* 3d series, III (1922–1923), 18–23. This English version is based on Pelliot's French, which is based on Latin and Persian texts prepared in the khan's court. The Mongol original has not been found.

5. Sections 1 and 7 from *The Chronography of Gregory Abu'l Faraj,* ed. and trans. E. A. W. Budge, I (London, 1932), 354–355; sec. 5 from George Vernadsky, "Juwaini's Version of Chingis Khan's Yasa," *Annales de l'Institut Kondakov,* XI (Belgrade, 1940), 42; sections 10–34 from V. A. Riasanovsky, *Fundamental Principles of Mongol Law* (Tientsin, 1937), pp. 83–86.

Chapter V. The Church: Autonomy

1. *Pamiatniki Russkogo Prava,* ed. L. V. Cherepnin, III (Moscow, 1955), 467–468; trans. John T. Dorosh, Norman Henley, and the author.

2. A. N. Murav'ev, *A History of the Church of Russia,* trans. R. W. Blackmore (Oxford, 1842), pp. 58–59.

3. Russia, Arkheograficheskaia Kommissiia, *Russkaia Istoricheskaia Biblioteka,* VI (St. Petersburg, 1880), 272–274 (Prilozhenie); trans. Norman Henley and the author.

Chapter VI. The Rise of Moscow

1. Sergei M. Solov'ev, *Istoriia Rossii s drevneishikh vremen,* I (St. Petersburg, 1896), 1118.

2. Quoted in V. O. Kliuchevski, *A History of Russia,* trans. C. J. Hogarth, I (London, 1911), 290.

3. *Pamiatniki Russkogo Prava*, ed. L. V. Cherepnin, III (Moscow, 1955), 294, 296; trans. Norman Henley.

4. *Dukhovnye i dogovornye gramoty velikikh i udel'nykh kniazei XIV–XVI vv.*, ed. S. V. Bakhrushin and L. V. Cherepnin (Moscow, 1950), p. 35.

5. *PSRL*, IV (1848), 271.

6. A. D. Gradovski, *Istoriia mestnago upravleniia v Rossii* (St. Petersburg, 1868), p. 38.

7. Bakhrushin and Cherepnin, *Dukhovnye i dogovornye gramoty*, p. 58.

8. Quoted in M. A. D'iakonov, *Ocherki obshchestvennago i gosudarstvennago stroia drevnei Rusi* (4th ed.; St. Petersburg, 1912), p. 395; cf. German trans. Eugen Goluboff (Breslau, 1931), p. 354.

9. Solov'ev, *Istoriia Rossii*, I, 1379 and 1648; *Ustiuzhskii letopisnyi svod*, ed. K. N. Serbina (Moscow, 1950), pp. 97–98; *PSRL*, IV (1848), 282–288.

PART THREE

Chapter VII. The Third Rome

1. Russia, Gosudarstvennaia kollegiia inostrannykh del, *Sobranie gosudarstvennykh gramot i dogovorov*, II (Moscow, 1819), 29.

2. *PSRL*, VI (1853), 228, quoted in Michael Cherniavsky, "*Khan* or *Basileus*: An Aspect of Russian Mediaeval Political Theory," *Journal of the History of Ideas*, XX (Oct.–Dec. 1959), 472. Cf. George Vernadsky, *Russia at the Dawn of the Modern Age* (New Haven, 1959), pp. 74–75.

3. "Poslanie startsa Pskovskago Eleazarova Monastyria Filotheia k Velikomu Kniaziu Vasiliiu Ivanovichu," *Pravoslavnyi sobesednik* (Kazan), March 1863, pp. 343–344, 347; trans. Norman Henley.

4. *A Treasury of Russian Spirituality*, ed. George P. Fedotov, trans. Helen Iswolsky (London, 1950), pp. 91–92; slightly emended.

5. Quoted in Vasili Zhmakin, *Mitropolit Daniil i ego sochineniia* (Moscow, 1881), pp. 93–94; trans. Norman Henley.

6. Joseph Volotski, *Prosvetitel'* (Kazan, 1896), pp. 488–489, translated in Marc Raeff, "An Early Theorist of Absolutism: Joseph of Volokolamsk," *American Slavic and East European Review*, VIII (April 1949), 82, 85.

7. Volotski, *Prosvetitel'*, pp. 286–288, in Raeff, "An Early Theorist," p. 86.

8. Maximus the Greek, *Sochineniia v russkom perevode*, III (Trinity Monastery, 1911), 101. The last clause is quoted from Hebrews 7:7.

9. Quoted in V. O. Kliuchevski, *A History of Russia*, trans. C. J. Hogarth, II (London, 1912), 64.

Chapter VIII. The Reign of Ivan IV

1. Quoted in V. O. Kliuchevski, *A History of Russia*, trans. C. J. Hogarth, II (London, 1912), 58.

2. V. I. Sergeevich, *Russkie iuridicheskie drevnosti*, II (St. Petersburg, 1908), 404.

3. M. A. D'iakonov, *Ocherki obshchestvennago i gosudarstennago stroia drevnei Rusi* (4th ed.; St. Petersburg, 1912), pp. 438–441; German trans. Eugen Glouboff (Breslau, 1931), pp. 392–395.

4. Quoted in Kliuchevski, *History of Russia*, II, 292. Cf. S. F. Platonov, *Stat'i po russkoi istorii* (2d ed.; St. Petersburg, 1912), pp. 201–205, 283–291.

5. Kliuchevski, *History of Russia*, II, 302.

6. Quoted in Hans von Eckardt, *Ivan the Terrible*, trans. Catherine A. Phillips (New York, 1949), p. 159.

7. *Zakonodatel'nye pamiatniki XVI i XVII stoletii*, ed. N. P. Khitrovo (Moscow, 1905), pp. 166–169; trans. Norman Henley.

8. *The Correspondence between Prince A. M. Kurbsky and Tsar Ivan IV of Russia, 1564–1579*, ed. and trans. J. L. I. Fennell (Cambridge, 1955), p. 229; emended.

9. Andrei Kurbski, *Skazaniia Kniazia Kurbskago*, I (St. Petersburg, 1833), 56; trans. Deborah Hardy.

10. Fennell, *Correspondence between Kurbsky and Ivan*, p. 47.

11. *Ibid.*, pp. 153–155.

12. *Ibid.*, p. 61.

13. *Ibid.*, p. 47.

14. *Ibid.*, p. 25; slightly emended.

15. Kurbski, *Skazaniia*, I, 53; trans. Deborah Hardy.

Chapter IX. From Riurikides to Romanovs

1. Giles Fletcher, *Of the Russe Common Wealth* (1591), in *Russia at the Close of the Sixteenth Century*, ed. Edward A. Bond (London, 1856), p. 26.

2. A. N. Murav'ev, *A History of the Church of Russia*, trans. R. W. Blackmore (Oxford, 1842), p. 305. Cf. Anton V. Kartashev, *Ocherki po istorii russkoi tserkvi*, II (Paris, 1959), 10–47.

3. *The Patriarch and the Tsar*, ed. and trans. William Palmer, I (London, 1871), 658.

4. Murav'ev, *History of the Church of Russia*, pp. 338–339.

5. Russia, Gosudarstvennaia kollegiia inostrannykh del, *Sobranie gosu-darstvennykh gramot i dogovorov*, II (Moscow, 1819), 299–300; trans. Norman Henley and the author.

6. *Ibid.*, II, 393–396; trans. Norman Henley.

7. V. O. Kliuchevski, *A History of Russia*, trans. C. J. Hogarth, II (London, 1912), 320.

8. Félix de Rocca, *Les assemblées politiques dans la Russie ancienne: Les Zemskié Sobors* (Paris, 1899), p. 182.

Chapter X. The Patriarch and the Tsar

1. Russia, Laws, Statutes, etc. *Ulozhenie* (St. Petersburg, 1796), Preamble; this and subsequent passages trans. Kiril Jaszenko.

2. Quoted in Pierre Pascal, *Avvakum et les débuts du Raskol* (Paris, 1938), p. 354.

3. "Pis'mo Patriarkha Nikona k Tsaregradskomu Patriarkhu Dionisiiu (1666 god)," in Russkoe arkheologicheskoe obshchestvo (Leningrad), Otdelenie russkoi i slavianskoi arkheologii, *Zapiskii*, II (1861), 512–513; trans. by the author. On Nikon see N. F. Kapterev, *Patriarkh Nikon i tsar Aleksei Mikhailovich* (Sergev Posad, 1909), and Anton V. Kartashev, *Ocherki po istorii russkoi tserkvi*, II (Paris, 1959), 119–230.

4. Paul Stroev, *Opisanie staropechatnykh knig slavianskikh* (Moscow, 1841), pp. 163–165.

5. "Pis'mo Patriarkha Nikona," p. 515.

6. *The Patriarch and the Tsar*, ed. and trans. William Palmer, I (London, 1871), 252.

7. "Mneniia Patr. Nikona ob ulozhenii i proch.," *in* Russkoe arkheologicheskoe obshchestvo (Leningrad), Otdelenie russkoi i slavianskoi arkheologii, *Zapiskii*, II (1861), 427.

8. Palmer, *Patriarch and the Tsar*, I, 189.

9. *Ibid.*, I, 189–190.

10. *Ibid.*, I, 234, 238.

11. *Ibid.*, I, 252.

12. *Patrologiae Graeca*, ed. J. P. Migne, Vol. CXI (Paris, 1863), no. 32, quoted in Louis Bréhier, *Les institutions de l'empire byzantine* (Paris, 1949), p. 65; trans. from the French by the author.

13. Palmer, *Patriarch and the Tsar*, III (London, 1873), 188.

14. *Ibid.*, III, 227–228; *The Civil Code*, trans. S. P. Scott, XVII (Cincinnati, 1932), 20.

15. Palmer, *Patriarch and the Tsar*, III, 227.

16. *Ibid.*, III, 234.

NOTES

PART FOUR

Chapter XI. Revolution from Above: Peter and Anna

1. Russia, Laws, Statutes, etc., *Polnoe sobranie zakonov*, 1st series, VI (St. Petersburg, 1830), 490 (item 3890); trans. Deborah Hardy.

2. Quoted in Iuri Samarin, *Stefan Iavorskii i Feofan Prokopovich*, in his *Sochineniia*, V (Moscow, 1880), 266–268; trans. Deborah Hardy.

3. Quoted in *The Patriarch and the Tsar*, ed. and trans. William Palmer, VI (London, 1876), 1592.

4. *The Present State and Regulations of the Church of Russia*, ed. and trans. Thomas Consett, I (London, 1729), 4, 10.

5. *Monuments historiques, relatifs aux règnes d'Alexis Michailovitch, Fédor III et Pierre le Grand, Czars de Russie*, ed. Augustin Theiner (Rome, 1859), p. 384.

6. Mikhail Shcherbatov, *Ueber die Sittenverderbnis in Russland*, trans. Ina Friedländer and Sergjej Jacobsohn (Königsberg, 1925), p. 36.

7. [Feofan Prokopovich,] "Pravda voli monarshei," in Russia, Laws, Statutes, etc., *Polnoe sobranie zakonov*, 1st series, VII (St. Petersburg, 1830), 624 (item 4870); trans. Deborah Hardy.

8. *Ibid.*, pp. 626, 619.

9. Sergei M. Solov'ev, *Istoriia Rossii s drevneishikh vremen*, IV (St. Petersburg, 1896), 1150; trans. Deborah Hardy.

10. See, e.g., Harald Hjärne, "Ryska konstitutionsprojekt år 1730 efter svenska förebilder," *Historisk tidskrift*, IV (1884), 189–272.

11. Quoted in Walther Recke, "Die Verfassungspläne der russischen Oligarchen im Jahre 1730 und die Thronbesteigung der Kaiserin Anna Ivanovna," *Zeitschrift für osteuropäische Geschichte*, II (1911–1912), 33.

12. V. N. Tatishchev, "Proizvol'noe i soglasnoe razsuzhdenie i mnenie sobravshagosia shliakhetstva russkago o pravlenii gosudarstvennom," *Utro* (Moscow, 1859), p. 370; trans. Deborah Hardy.

13. *Ibid.*, pp. 370–373.

14. *Ibid.*, pp. 375–377.

15. *Diario del viaje á Moscovia del duque de Liria y Xérica*, in the *Colección de documentos inéditos para la historia de Espana*, XCIII (Madrid, 1889), 313; trans. the author.

Chapter XII. The Enlightenment: Catherine and Her Critics

1. Catherine's note on Radishchev's *Journey*, in A. N. Radishchev, *A Journey from St. Petersburg to Moscow*, ed. Roderick P. Thaler (Cambridge, Mass., 1958), p. 241.

2. Catherine II, *The Instructions to the Commissioners for Composing a New Code of Laws* (1767), in *Documents of Catherine the Great,* ed. W. F. Reddaway (Cambridge, 1931), p. 292 (Art. 511).

3. *Ibid.,* p. 216 (Arts. 9–11).

4. *Ibid.,* p. 219 (Arts. 37, 38).

5. *Ibid.,* pp. 217, 256 (Arts. 19, 250).

6. Quoted in Maurice Tourneux, *Diderot et Catherine II* (Paris, 1899), p. 143.

7. *Ibid.,* pp. 519–520; trans. the author from Catherine's French.

8. Mikhail Shcherbatov, "Zamechaniia na bol'shoi nakaz Ekateriny," in his *Neizdannye sochineniia* (Moscow, 1935), p. 22; trans. Norman Henley.

9. Mikhail Shcherbatov, "Razmyshleniia o zakonodatel'stve voobshche," in his *Sochineniia,* I (St. Petersburg, 1898), 387; trans. Deborah Hardy.

10. *Ibid.,* pp. 388–389.

11. *Ibid.,* pp. 390–391.

12. Quoted in David M. Lang, "Radishchev and the Legislative Commission of Alexander I," *American Slavic and East European Review,* VI, nos. 18–19 (Dec. 1947), 20.

13. Alexander Radishchev, *Putechestvie iz Peterburga v Moskvu* (1790; Moscow and Leningrad, 1950), p. 127; trans. Deborah Hardy.

14. *Ibid.,* p. 166.

15. Quoted in the Introduction to Radishchev, *Journey,* p. 6, from a note in Radishchev's translation of G. B. de Mably, *Observations sur l'histoire de la Grèce* (Geneva, 1766), which he published in 1773; see his *Polnoe sobranie sochinenii,* II (Moscow, 1941), 282.

16. Quoted in Lang, "Radishchev and the Legislative Commission," p. 17, from the Preamble of Radishchev's "Project of a Civil Code."

17. *Ibid.,* p. 19.

Chapter XIII. Promise and Denouement: Alexander and His Aides

1. Nikolai K. Schilder, *Imperator Aleksandr I,* II (St. Petersburg, 1897), 339; trans. Doris Blaisdell.

2. *Ibid.,* II, 339.

3. V. P. Semennikov, *Radishchev* (Moscow, 1923), p. 181.

4. Nicholas Mikhailovich, grand duke, *Graf Pavel Aleksandrovich Stroganov,* II (St. Petersburg, 1903), 77; French ed., *Le Comte Paul Stroganov,* trans. F. Billecocq, II (Paris, 1905), 40.

5. Schilder, *Imperator Aleksandr I,* II, 347; trans. Doris Blaisdell.

6. Mikhail Speranski, *Plan gosudarstvennago preobrazovaniia* (Moscow, 1905), pp. 187–188; trans. Deborah Hardy.

7. *Ibid.,* pp. 189, 215–216.

8. Mikhail Speranski, "O zakonakh—besedy [to Crown Prince Alexander]," in Russkoe Istoricheskoe Obshchestvo, Leningrad, *Sbornik*, XXX (1881), 341; quoted in Marc Raeff, "The Political Philosophy of Speranski," *American Slavic and East European Review*, XII (Feb. 1953), 15.

9. Mikhail Speranski, "Proekt ulozheniia gosudarstvennykh zakonov," *Istoricheskoe obozrenie*, X (1898), 4–6; trans. Deborah Hardy.

10. *Ibid.*, pp. 18, 58, and *passim*.

11. Benjamin Constant, *Cours de politique constitutionnelle*, I (Paris, 1836), 2.

12. *La charte constitutionnelle de l'Empire de Russie*, ed. Theodor Schiemann (Berlin, 1903), pp. 14–15; trans. the author from Novosiltsev's French. Cf. English text in *The Portfolio* (London), V (Feb.–Mar., 1837), 513–522, 611–639, and VI (Apr. 1837), 73–86.

13. *Karamzin's Memoir on Ancient and Modern Russia*, ed. and trans. Richard Pipes (Cambridge, Mass., 1959), pp. 155, 192, 139.

14. *Ibid.*, p. 200; Nikolai Karamzin, *Istoriia gosudarstva rossiiskago*, VIII (St. Petersburg, 1817), 93 (French ed., *Histoire de l'empire de Russie*, trans. St.-Thomas and Jauffret, VIII [Paris, 1820], 67–68).

15. Pipes, *Karamzin's Memoir*, pp. 122, 135.

16. *Ibid.*, pp. 137, 46, quoted by Pipes from Karamzin's *Sochineniia*, ed. Aleksandra Smirdina, III (St. Petersburg, 1848), 585–586.

17. Pipes, *Karamzin's Memoir*, p. 135.

18. Speranski, "O zakonakh—besedy," pp. 359, 366, 437, 367, and *V Pamiat' Grafa Mikhaila Mikhailovicha Speranskago*, ed. A. T. Bychkov (St. Petersburg, 1872), p. 802.

Chapter XIV. Revolution from Below: The Decembrists

1. *Vosstanie Dekabristov: Materialy*, ed. M. N. Pokrovski, IV (Moscow, 1927), 90; trans. by the author.

2. *Ibid.*, V (Moscow, 1926), 31, quoted in Anatole G. Mazour, *The First Russian Revolution, 1825* (Berkeley, 1937), p. 151.

3. Pokrovski, *Vosstanie Dekabristov*, I (Moscow, 1925), 116; trans. Deborah Hardy.

4. *Ibid.*, I, 117.

5. *Dekabristy: otryvki iz istochnikov*, ed. Iuri G. Oksman (Moscow, 1926), p. 236; trans. Deborah Hardy.

6. Pokrovski, *Vosstanie Dekabristov*, IV, 91; trans. Deborah Hardy.

7. Paul Pestel, *Russkaia Pravda* (St. Petersburg, 1906), p. 9; trans. Deborah Hardy.

8. *Ibid.*

9. *Ibid.*, pp. 214, 66.

10. *Ibid.*, pp. 203–204.

11. *Ibid.*, pp. 204–205.

12. *Ibid.*, p. 205.

13. Paul Pestel, *Prakticheskie nachala politicheskoi ekonomii* (1819 or 1820), in *Krasnyi Arkhiv*, XIII (1925), 174–249, excerpted in translation by Leonid S. Rubinchek in *A Digest of the Krasnyi Arkhiv*, I (Cleveland, 1947), 122.

14. Pestel, *Russkaia Pravda*, pp. 71–72.

15. *Ibid.*, p. 89.

16. Paul Pestel, "Konstitutsiia gosudarstvennyi zavet," *Krasnyi Arkhiv*, XIII (1925), 280–284, quoted in Arthur E. Adams, "The Character of Pestel's Thought," *American Slavic and East European Review*, XII (April 1953), 158, in which parts are translated.

17. Pestel, *Russkaia Pravda*, pp. 237–238.

18. Quoted in Paul Miliukov, "La place du Décabrisme dans l'évolution de l'*intelligencija* russe," *Le monde slave*, N.S. II (Dec. 1925), 341.

19. Modest A. Korf, *The Accession of Nicholas I* (London, 1857), pp. 276–277 (an official translation of an official history).

PART FIVE

Chapter XV. The Official Ideology

1. Circular of March 21, 1833, in *Zhurnal ministerstva narodnogo prosveshcheniia*, I, no. 1 (1834), xlix.

2. Faddei Bulgarin, *Rossiia v istoricheskom, statisticheskom, geografiches-kom i literaturnom otnosheniiakh, Istorii*, IV (St. Petersburg, 1837) 291; and Stepan Shevyrev, letter of February 10, 1852, to K. S. Serbinovich, in *Russkaia starina*, XXXV (Feb. 1904), 427.

3. Sergei Uvarov, *Essay on the Eleusinian Mysteries*, trans. J. D. Price (London, 1817), p. 32; Nikolai Gogol, *Vybrannyia mesta iz perepiski s druz'iami*, in his *Sochineniia*, ed. V. Kallash, VIII (St. Petersburg, n.d.), 49, 45; Vasili Zhukovski, *Sochineniia V. A. Zhukovskago*, ed. P. V. Smirnovski (Moscow, 1915), p. 171 of the prose section; and Iakov Rostovtsev, "Nastavlenii dlia obrazovaniia vospitannikov voenno-uchebnykh zavedenii" (1848), quoted and paraphrased in Aleksandr Presniakov, *Apogei samoderzhaviia Nikolai I.* (Leningrad, 1925), p. 13.

4. Nicholas V. Riasanovsky, *Nicholas I and Official Nationality in Russia, 1825–1855* (Berkeley, 1959), p. 95.

5. Quoted in Alexandre Koyré, *La philosophie et le problème national en Russie au début du XIXᵉ siècle* (Paris, 1929), p. 198; trans. by the author.

6. Sergei Uvarov, Preface to *Zhurnal ministerstva narodnogo prosveshcheniia*, I (1834), iv; trans. by the author.

7. Quoted in Paul Miliukov, Ch. Seignobos, and L. Eisenmann, *Histoire de Russie*, II (Paris, 1932), 785.

8. Quoted in Alexander V. Nikitenko, *Zapiski i dnevnik*, I (2d ed.; St. Petersburg, 1893), 360, dated August 8, 1835.

9. Quoted in *Desiatiletie ministerstva narodnogo prosveshcheniia, 1833–1843* (St. Petersburg, 1864), p. 8.

10. Nikolai P. Barsukov, *Zhizn i trudy M. P. Pogodina*, IV (St. Petersburg, 1891), 98, and IX (St. Petersburg, 1895), 305–308.

11. Mikhail Pogodin, *Rechi, proiznesennie v torzhestvennykh i prochikh sobraniiakh, 1830–1872*, in his *Sochineniia*, III (Moscow, 1872), 90.

12. *Ibid.*, p. 388.

13. Mikhail Pogodin, *Ostzeiskii vopros* (Moscow, 1869), pp. 108, 111.

14. Barsukov, *Zhizn i trudy Pogodina* II (St. Petersburg, 1889), 17.

15. Reprinted in Ivan S. Aksakov, *Polnoe sobranie sochinenii*, V (Moscow, 1886), 26–35, from *Rus'*, I (March 28, 1881).

16. Konstantin Pobedonostsev, *L'Autocratie russe* (Paris, 1927), p. 56; trans. Doris Blaisdell.

17. Konstantin Pobedonostsev, *Reflections of a Russian Statesman*, trans. Robert Crozier Long (London, 1898), pp. 32, 47, 33, 36.

18. *Ibid.*, p. 1.

19. *Ibid.*, pp. 19, 23–24.

20. Sergei Witte, *Printsip zheleznodorozhnykh tarifov po perevozke gruzov* (1883), summarized in Theodore H. Von Laue, *Sergei Witte and the Industrialization of Russia* (New York, 1963), pp. 50–54.

21. Sergei Witte, "Manufakturnoe krepostnichestvo," *Rus'*, V (Jan. 19, 1885), 18–19.

22. Friedrich List, *The National System of Political Economy*, trans. G. A. Matile (Philadelphia, 1856), pp. 253, 74.

23. *Russkiia vedomosti* (Moscow), January 3, 1893, p. 5, col. 4.

Chapter XVI. The Westerners

1. Alexander Herzen, *Byloe i dumy*, II (Moscow, 1937), 383.

2. Peter Chaadaev, *Sochineniia i pisma*, I (Moscow, 1913), 80, 84; trans. Doris Blaisdell.

3. *Ibid.*, I, 230–231.

4. *Ibid.*, I, 231, 234.

5. Quoted in Herbert E. Bowman, *Vissarion Belinski, 1811–1848* (Cambridge, Mass., 1954), pp. 113–114.

6. Letter to V. P. Botkin, September 8, 1841, in V. G. Belinski, *Selected Philosophical Works* (Moscow, 1948), pp. 159, 166.

7. Alexander Herzen, *Pis'ma iz Frantsii i Italii, 1847–1852*, in his *Sobranie sochinenii*, V (Moscow, 1955), 182; trans. Deborah Hardy.

8. Alexander Herzen, "Russia and the Old World," *The English Republic*, III (1854), 52.

9. Herzen, *Pis'ma iz Frantsii i Italii*, p. 179.

10. Alexander Herzen, *My Past and Thoughts*, trans. Constance Garnett, VI (London, 1927), 65.

11. Alexander Herzen, *Du développement des idées révolutionnaires en Russie* (Paris, 1851), pp. 127, 132; trans. by the author.

12. Herzen, "Russia and the Old World," p. 100.

13. *Kolokol*, no. 110 (Nov. 1, 1861), p. 918, quoted in Alexander Kornilov, *Modern Russian History*, trans. Alexander S. Kaun, II (New York, 1948), 208.

14. Alexander Herzen, "K staromu tovarishchu [Bakunin]," in his *Izbrannye filosofskie proizvedeniia*, II (Moscow, 1946), 285–286; trans. Deborah Hardy. Cf. his *Selected Philosophical Works* (Moscow, 1956), pp. 577–579.

15. Herzen, *My Past and Thoughts*, II, 278.

16. Quoted in Franco Venturi, *Roots of Revolution*, trans. Francis Haskell (London, 1960), p. 152.

17. Nikolai Chernyshevski, *Osnovaniia politicheskoi ekonomii Dzhona Stiuarta Millia*, in his *Izbrannye ekonomicheskie proizvedeniia*, III (Moscow, 1948), 308; trans. Deborah Hardy.

18. Nikolai Chernyshevski, *A Vital Question; or, What Is to Be Done?*, trans. Nathan H. Dole and S. S. Skidelsky (New York, 1886), p. 316, end of part 3.

Chapter XVII. The Slavophils

1. Nil P. Koliupanov, *Biografiia Aleksandra Ivanovicha Kosheleva*, II (Moscow, 1892), 82.

2. Alexis S. Khomiakov, *Polnoe sobranie sochinenii*, VIII (Moscow, 1900), 178.

3. *Ibid.*, I (Moscow, 1900), 327; this and other quotations from Khomiakov are translated by the author.

4. *Ibid.*, I, 254–255.

5. Alexis Khomiakov, *Quelques mots par un chrétien orthodoxe sur les communions occidentales, à l'occasion d'un brochure de M. Laurentie* (Paris, 1853), in his *L'Eglise latine et le Protestantisme* (Lausanne, 1872), p. 38.

NOTES

6. Khomiakov, *Polnoe sobranie sochinenii*, I, 149–150.

7. *Ibid.*, I, 283.

8. *Ibid.*, I, 161.

9. *Ibid.*, III (Moscow, 1900), 462, 464–465.

10. *Ibid.*, VIII, 273–274.

11. Ivan Kireevski, "O neobkhodimosti i vozmozhnosti novykh nachal dlia filosofii," *Polnoe sobranie sochinenii*, ed. M. Gershenzon, I (Moscow, 1911), 240–241. This and other quotations from Kireevski are translated by Deborah Hardy.

12. *Ibid.*, I, 237–238.

13. *Ibid.*, I, 251; and his "O kharaktere prosveshcheniia Evropy i o ego otnoshenii k prosveshcheniiu Rossii," *ibid.*, I, 199, 201.

14. Kireevski, "O kharaktere prosveshcheniia Evropy," *ibid.*, I, 208–209.

15. Konstantin Aksakov, "O sovremennom literaturnom spore," *Rus'*, III (April 1, 1883), 21–22.

16. Konstantin Aksakov, "Po povodu VII toma istorii Rossii g. Solov'-eva," *Polnoe sobranie sochinenii*, I (Moscow, 1889), 241.

17. A. S. Nifontov, *Russland im Jahre 1848* (Berlin, 1954), p. 171; Aksakov, "Zapiska o vnutrennem sostoianii Rossii predstavlennaia Imperatoru Aleksandru II," *Polnoe sobranie sochinenii*, I, 602, 604.

18. Aksakov, "O sostoianii krest'ian v drevnei Rossii," *ibid.*, I, 396.

19. Aksakov, "Kratkii istoricheskii ocherk zemskikh soborov," *ibid.*, I, 280, 281; Konstantin Aksakov, *Zamechaniia na novoe administrativnoe ustroistvo krest'ian v Rossii* (Leipzig, 1861), pp. 53, 9, 13.

20. Thomas G. Masaryk, *The Spirit of Russia*, trans. Eden and Cedar Paul, I (London, 1955), 323.

21. Fedor Dostoevski, *The Diary of a Writer*, trans. Boris Brasol, II (New York, 1949), 780.

22. Fedor Dostoevski, *The Brothers Karamazov*, Bk. 5, Chap. 5; see Modern Library ed., p. 313.

Chapter XVIII. The Anarchists

1. Mikhail Bakunin, Address at the Congress of the League of Peace and Freedom at Berne in 1868, quoted in *Lettres à un Français sur la crise actuelle* [1870], in his *Oeuvres*, IV (Paris, 1910), 54–55.

2. Mikhail Bakunin, *God and the State* (New York, [1916?]), pp. 30, 33.

3. Bakunin, *Circulaire à mes amis d'Italie*, in *Oeuvres*, VI (Paris, 1913), 351.

4. Mikhail Bakunin, *Catéchisme révolutionnaire* (1866), quoted in Max Nettlau, *Michael Bakunin, eine Biographie*, I (London, 1896), 225–226.

5. Bakunin, *God and the State*, pp. 23–24, 27–28.

6. Mikhail Bakunin, *Estatismo y Anarquía*, in his *Obras completas*, V (Buenos Aires, 1929), 288–289, trans. in *The Political Philosophy of Bakunin: Scientific Anarchism*, ed. G. P. Maximoff (Glencoe, Ill., 1953), pp. 297–298.

7. Bakunin, Continuation of *L'Empire knouto-germanique et la révolution sociale*, in *Oeuvres*, IV, 413–414; cf. translation in his *Marxism, Freedom and the State*, ed. K. J. Kenafick (London, 1950), p. 47.

8. Mikhail Bakunin, Letter to Herzen and Ogarev, July 19, 1866, in *Correspondance de Michel Bakounine*, ed. Mikhail Dragomanov (Paris, 1896), pp. 223–224.

9. *The Private Diary of Leo Tolstóy, 1853–1857*, ed. Aylmer Maude (London, 1927), p. 114.

10. Leo Tolstoi, *The Slavery of Our Times*, trans. Aylmer Maude (New York, [1900?]), p. 124.

11. *Ibid.*, pp. 139–140.

12. *Ibid.*, pp. 171–172.

13. *Ibid.*, p. 148.

14. V. I. Lenin, "Tolstoy and the Proletarian Struggle," (1910), reprinted in his *Articles on Tolstoy* (Moscow, 1951), p. 33.

15. Peter Kropotkin, *Mutual Aid, a Factor of Evolution* (London, 1902), p. 58.

16. Peter Kropotkin, *The State: Its Historic Role* (1898; London, 1946), p. 44.

17. *Ibid.*, p. 41; Peter Kropotkin, *Revolutionary Government* (1880; London, 1945), p. 11.

18. Peter Kropotkin, *The Conquest of Bread* (1892; London, 1906), pp. 62, 31.

19. *Ibid.*, pp. 213, 15.

20. Peter Kropotkin, *Anarchist Morality* (1890; 9th ed., London, n.d.), p. 28.

Chapter XIX. The Narodniki

1. Nikolai V. Shelgunov, *Vospominaniia*, ed. A. S. Shilov (Moscow, 1923), Appendix I ("K molodomu pokoleniiu"), p. 293.

2. *Politicheskie protsessy 60-kh gg.*, ed. B. P. Koz'min, I (Moscow, 1923), 261, 264.

3. A. I. Herzen, "Zhurnalisty i terroristy," *Kolokol*, no. 141 (Aug. 15, 1862), 1166–1167, reprinted in his *Sobranie sochinenii*, XVI (Moscow, 1959), 222, 225.

4. P. L. Mirtov [Lavrov], *Istoricheskiia pis'ma* (1870), ed. M. P. Negreskul (St. Petersburg, 1906), p. 51.

5. *Ibid.*, pp. 319–320.

6. *Ibid.*, p. 233.

7. *Ibid.*, p. 237.

8. *Ibid.*, pp. 240–242.

9. *Ibid.*, pp. 305, 306.

10. Peter Tkachev, "Zadachi revoliutsionnoi propagandy v rossii," in his *Izbrannye sochineniia*, ed. B. P. Koz'min, III (Moscow, 1932), 64.

11. Tkachev, "Chto takoe partiia progressa," (on Lavrov's *Historical Letters*, 1870), in *ibid.*, II (Moscow, 1932), 206–207.

12. Tkachev, "Retsenziia na Sobranie sochinenii Gerberta Spensera," *ibid.*, V (Moscow, 1935), 302.

13. Tkachev, "Zadachi revoliutsionnoi propagandy v rossii," *ibid.*, III, 70.

14. Tkachev, *Offener Brief an Herrn Friedrich Engels* (Zurich, 1874), translated in *ibid.*, III, 89, 90.

15. Tkachev, "Razbitye illiuzii," *ibid.*, I (Moscow, 1932), 367–368.

16. Tkachev, *Offener Brief*, in *ibid.*, III, 91–92.

17. Lev Tikhomirov, *Andrei Ivanovich Zheliabov* (1882; Geneva, 1899), p. 36.

18. *Narodnaia volia*, no. 3 (Jan. 1, 1880), reprinted in *Literatura partii narodnoi voli*, ed. B. Bazilevski (Paris, 1905), p. 165; cf. translation in George Kennan, *Siberia and the Exile System*, II (New York, 1891), 498.

19. *Ibid.*, p. 162; cf. Kennan, *Siberia*, p. 495.

20. *Narodnaia volia*, no. 4 (Dec. 5, 1880), in *ibid.*, pp. 291–292.

21. *Ibid.*, p. 164; cf. Kennan, *Siberia* p. 497.

22. Nikolai K. Mikhailovski, *Sochineniia*, I (St. Petersburg, 1896), 703–704.

23. Victor Chernov, *Zapiski sotsialista-revoliutsionera* (Berlin, 1922), pp. 128–129; Nikolai K. Mikhailovski, "Literatura i zhizn'," *Russkoe bogatstvo*, XII, no. 10, (Oct. 1893), 108–139.

24. V. V. [Vasili Vorontsov], *Ocherki teoreticheskoi ekonomii* (St. Petersburg, 1895), p. 310.

25. *Ibid.*, p. 196.

26. Nikolai —on [Nikolai Danielson], *Ocherki nashego poreformennago khoziaistva* (St. Petersburg, 1893), p. 346.

27. Victor Chernov [?], "Klassovaia bor'ba v derevne" (editorial), *Revoliutsionnaia Rossiia*, no. 11 (Sept. 1902), p. 7.

28. *Protokoly pervago s"ezda Partii S-R* (n.p., 1906), p. 220.

29. Victor Chernov, *The Great Russian Revolution*, trans. and abridged by Philip E. Mosley (New Haven, 1936), p. 114.

30. *Ibid.*, pp. 112–115.

NOTES

Chapter XX. The Liberals

1. *Vestnik Evropy*, CLXXV (Oct. 1895), 788.

2. Boris Chicherin, *Vospominaniia Borisa Nikolaevicha Chicherina*, ed. V. I. Nevski, IV (Moscow, 1934), 173–174.

3. Dmitri Shipov, *Vospominaniia i dumy o perezhitom* (Moscow, 1918), p. 146.

4. Ivan Petrunkevich, "Blizhaishiia zdachi zemstva," in *Arkhiv russkoi revoliutsii*, XXI (Berlin, 1934), 455–456; full text of pamphlet in *Iubeleinyi zemskii sbornik*, ed. B. B. Vselovski and Z. G. Frenkel (St. Petersburg, 1914), pp. 429–436.

5. *The Times* (London), July 22, 1905, p. 5. Speech reported in third person.

6. Boris Chicherin, Note of March 6, 1881, quoted in Sergei Witte, *Samoderzhavie i zemstvo* (2d ed.; Stuttgart, 1903), p. 122.

7. Boris Chicherin, *Rossiia nakanune dvadtsatago stoletiia* (4th ed.; Berlin, 1901), pp. 146–147.

8. Mikhail Dragomanov [Drahomaniv], *Liberalizm i zemstvo v Rossii* (Geneva, 1889), pp. 41–42.

9. Full text in Peter Struve, "My Contacts with Rodichev," *Slavonic and East European Review*, XII (Jan. 1934), 350; cf. *The Times* (London), Jan. 30, 1895, p. 5.

10. Full text in George Fischer, *Russian Liberalism from Gentry to Intelligentsia* (Cambridge, Mass., 1958), p. 147, from *Listok Osvobozhdeniia*, no. 17 (Nov. 19, 1904), p. 2.

11. Reprinted in *Osvobozhdenie*, no. 57 (Oct. 15, 1904), p. 120.

12. *Loi fondamentale de l'empire Russe* (Paris, 1905), pp. 41, 61.

13. Full text in D. I. Shakhovskoi, "Soiuz osvobozhdeniia," *Zarnitsy*, no. 2, part 2 (St. Petersburg, 1909), p. 121.

14. *Chastnoe soveshchanie zemskikh deiatelei* (Moscow, 1905), pp. 56, 141–145; resolutions also in *Zemski s"ezd 6-go i sl. noiabria 1904 g., kratkii otchet* (Paris, 1905), p. 17.

15. Peter Struve, *Kriticheskiia zametki k voprosu ob ekonomicheskom razvitii Rossii* (St. Petersburg, 1894), p. 287.

16. Peter Struve, "Die Marxische Theorie der sozialen Entwicklung," *Archiv für soziale Gesetzgebung und Statistik*, XIV (1899), 664–688.

17. *Ibid.*, pp. 667–684.

18. Peter Struve, "K kritike nekotorykh osnovnykh problem i polozhenii politicheskoi ekonomii," *Zhizn'*, no. 3 (March 1900), pp. 361–392.

19. Struve, "Die Marxische Theorie," p. 698.

20. Peter Struve, "Manifest rossiiskoi sotsial-demokraticheskoi rabochei partii" (1898), *Vsesoiuznaia kommunisticheskaia partiia (b) v rezoliutsiiakh*

i resheniiakh s"ezdov, konferentsii i plenumov tsk (*1898–1935*), I (5th ed.; Moscow, 1936), 5.

21. Peter Struve, Introduction to Nikolai Berdiaev, *Sub"ektivizm i individualizm v obshchestvennoi filosofii* (St. Petersburg, 1901), p. lxiv.

22. Peter Struve, "Ot redaktora," *Osvobozhdenie*, no. 1 (June 18, 1902), p. 5.

23. Peter Struve, "Kak naiti sebia?," *Osvobozhdenie*, no. 71 (May 31, 1905), pp. 337–343.

24. Peter Struve, "Velikaia Rossiia: Iz razmyshlenii o probleme russkago mogushchestva," *Russkaia mysl'*, XXIX (Jan. 1908), 143–157.

25. Paul Miliukov, "Ot russkikh konstitutsionalistov," *Osvobozhdenie*, no. 1 (June 18, 1902), pp. 7–12.

26. Paul Miliukov, "K ocherednym voprosam," *Osvobozhdenie*, no. 17 (Feb. 16, 1903), pp. 289–292.

27. Paul Miliukov, "Voina i russkaia oppozitsiia," *Osvobozhdenie*, no. 43 (March 7, 1904), pp. 329–330, and no. 45 (April 2, 1904), pp. 377–379; and "Ocherednyia zadachi russkikh konstitutsionalistov," *Osvobozhdenie*, no. 52 (July 19, 1904), pp. 36–39.

28. Paul Miliukov, *Russia and Its Crisis* (Chicago, 1905), p. 518.

29. *Rech'* (St. Petersburg), no. 167 (June 21 [July 4], 1909), p. 3; cf. *Morning Post* (London), July 3, 1909, p. 7.

30. Paul Miliukov, *Russia Today and Tomorrow* (New York, 1922), p. 31.

Chapter XXI. The Marxists

1. Karl Marx and Friedrich Engels, *Selected Correspondence* (Moscow, n.d.), pp. 378, 412.

2. Marx and Engels, Preface to the Russian edition of *The Manifesto of the Communist Party* (1882), in their *Selected Works*, I (Moscow, 1951), 24.

3. Marx and Engels, *Selected Correspondence*, pp. 546–547.

4. *Ibid.*, p. 459.

5. George V. Plekhanov, *In Defense of Materialism: The Development of the Monist View of History* (1895), trans. Andrew Rothstein (London, 1947), pp. 244–245; also in his *Selected Philosophical Works*, I (Moscow, 1961), 741.

6. Plekhanov, *Our Differences* (1884), in *Selected Philosophical Works*, trans. R. Dixon, I, 379.

7. Plekhanov, "Programme of the Social-Democratic Emancipation of Labour Group" (1884), *ibid.*, p. 402.

8. Plekhanov, *Socialism and the Political Struggle* (1883), *ibid.*, p. 117.

9. Arkadie Kremer, *Ob Agitatsii* (Geneva, 1896), esp. pp. 20–24.

10. V. I. Lenin, *What Is To Be Done?* (1902), in his *Selected Works*, ed. J. Fineberg, II (London, 1936), 53, 62.

11. *Ibid.*, pp. 139, 140.

12. *Vtoroi ocherednoi s"ezd, RSDRP, polnyi tekst protokolov* (Geneva, 1903), pp. 239, 240.

13. V. I. Lenin, *One Step Forward, Two Steps Back* (London, 1941), pp. 218, 214.

14. Lenin, *What Is To Be Done?*, in *Selected Works*, II, 154, and *One Step Forward, Two Steps Back*, in *Selected Works*, II, p. 465.

15. Leon Trotsky, *Do deviatago Ianvaria* (Geneva, 1905), pp. xi–xii; cf. Isaac Deutscher, *The Prophet Armed* (London, 1954), pp. 112–113.

16. Lenin, "Social-Democracy and the Provisional Revolutionary Government," *Selected Works*, III (London, 1936), 35.

17. Leon Trotsky, *Results and Prospects* (1906), trans. Brian Pearce (London, 1962), p. 212 (bound with Trotsky's *Permanent Revolution*).

18. *Ibid.*, p. 208.

19. *Ibid.*, p. 247.

20. Lenin, "Social-Democracy and the Provisional Revolutionary Government," *Selected Works*, III, 31; *The Two Tactics of Social-Democracy in the Democratic Revolution*, in *ibid.*, pp. 99–100; "The Struggle of the Proletariat and the Servility of the Bourgeoisie," *ibid.*, p. 307; "The Attitude of Social-Democracy toward the Peasant Movement," *ibid.*, p. 145.

21. Leon Trotsky, *1905*, in his *Sochineniia*, II, part 2 (Moscow, 1925), 186.

22. Julius Martov (*pseud.* El'mar), *Narod i Gosudarstvennaia Duma* (St. Petersburg, 1906), p. 20.

23. *Piatyi s"ezd RSDRP, protokoly* (Moscow, 1935), p. 715.

24. V. I. Lenin, "The Tasks of Revolutionary Social-Democracy in the European War," *Collected Works*, XVIII (New York, 1930), 63–64, and "The War and Russian Social-Democracy," *ibid.*, p. 81.

25. Lenin, "The United States of Europe Slogan," *Selected Works*, V (London, 1936), 139–141.

PART SIX

Chapter XXII. The First Decade: Left, Then Right

1. V. I. Lenin, "April Theses" on "The Tasks of the Proletariat in the Present Revolution," *Selected Works*, ed. J. Fineberg, VI (London, 1936), 22–24.

2. Lenin, "A Dual Power," *ibid.*, p. 27, and "Letters on Tactics," *ibid.*, p. 34.

3. Lenin, *The State and Revolution*, in *ibid.*, VII (London, 1937), 21.

4. N. I. Bukharin, "Der imperialistische Raubstaat," *Jugend-Internationale*, no. 6 (Dec. 1, 1916), pp. 7–9.

5. Cf. Lenin, "The Youth International," *Selected Works*, V (London, 1936), 244.

6. Quoted in Robert V. Daniels, *The Conscience of the Revolution* (Cambridge, Mass., 1960), p. 78.

7. V. I. Lenin, "Draft Resolution on Measures to Overcome Economic Chaos," *Collected Works*, XX (New York, 1929), part 2, p. 136.

8. Lenin, *The State and Revolution*, in *Selected Works*, VII, 92, 93 (Chap. 5).

9. *Pervyi vserossiiskii s"ezd professional'nykh soiuzov, polnyi stenograficheski otchet* (Moscow, 1918), p. 80.

10. *Ibid.*, p. 364.

11. Lenin, "The Immediate Tasks of the Soviet Government," *Selected Works*, VII, 322, 342.

12. Bukharin, "Tezisy o tekushchem momente," *Kommunist* (Moscow), no. 1 (April 20, 1918), p. 8, quoted in Lenin, " 'Left-Wing' Childishness and Petty-Bourgeois Mentality," *Selected Works*, VII, 373.

13. V. V. [N.] Osinski, "O stroitel'stvo sotsializma," *Kommunist*, no. 2 (April 27, 1918), p. 5, quoted in Daniels, *Conscience of the Revolution*, p. 85.

14. Quoted in Lenin, " 'Left-Wing' Childishness," *Selected Works*, VII, 372, from *Vpered*, April 25, 1918.

15. *Program of the All-Russian Communist Party (Bolsheviks)* (1919), Art. 5 of the economic section; trans. the author.

16. Leon Trotsky, "The Fundamental Questions of the Food and Agrarian Policy" (1920), in his *The New Course*, trans. Max Shachtman (New York, 1943), p. 70.

17. Leon Trotsky, *Dictatorship vs. Democracy (Terrorism and Communism)* (1920; New York, 1922), pp. 135, 137.

18. *Ibid.*, p. 142.

19. *Deviatyi s"ezd RKP(B), protokoly* (Moscow, 1934), p. 101.

20. *Ibid.*, p. 564.

21. Eugene Preobrazhenski, "S"ezd neobkhodim," *Kommunist*, no. 4 (May, 1918), p. 13, quoted in Daniels, *Conscience of the Revolution*, p. 84.

22. *Deviatyi s"ezd RKP(B), protokoly*, pp. 534–537.

23. Lenin, "Report of the Central Committee" to the Ninth Party Congress, *Selected Works*, VIII (London, n.d. [1937]), 89.

24. *Deviatyi s"ezd RKP(B), protokoly*, pp. 538, 431–432.

25. Lenin, "Once Again on the Trade Unions, the Present Situation and the Mistakes of Comrades Trotsky and Bukharin," *Selected Works*, IX (London, 1937), 54.

26. *Desiatyi s"ezd RKP(B), protokoly* (Moscow, 1933), p. 802.

27. *Ibid.*, pp. 789–793.

28. Lenin, "The Trade Unions, the Present Situation and the Mistakes of Comrade Trotsky," *Selected Works*, IX, 4.

29. Alexandra Kollontai, *The Workers' Opposition In Russia* (Chicago, [1921?]), pp. 10–12, 19–20, 30–31, 36–40.

30. *Desiatyi s"ezd RKP(B), protokoly*, p. 301.

31. *Ibid.*, 353, quoted in Isaac Deutscher, *The Prophet Armed* (New York, 1954), pp. 508–509.

32. *Desiatyi s"ezd RKP(B), protokoly*, pp. 410, 415–416, translated as "The Tax in Kind" in Lenin, *Selected Works*, IX, 113, 119.

33. N. I. Bukharin, *Put' k sotsializmu i raboche-krest'ianskii soiuz* (Moscow, 1925), pp. 48–59, 65–66, 70–74.

34. N. I. Bukharin, "Observations of an Economist," *International Press Correspondence*, VIII (Oct. 26, 1928), 1377.

35. Eugene Preobrazhenski, "Osnovnye printsipy politiki RKP v sovremennoi derevne" (1922), in V. I. Lenin, *Sochineniia*, XXVII (3d ed.; Moscow, 1932), 446; and Eugene Preobrazhenski, *Novaia ekonomika* (2d ed.; Moscow, 1926), p. 99.

36. Trotsky, Letter of December 8, 1923 (*Pravda*, Dec. 11, 1923, p. 4), *The New Course*, p. 94.

37. A. G. Shliapnikov, "Nashi raznoglasiia," *Pravda*, Jan. 18, 1924, p. 5.

38. Lenin, "The Tax In Kind," *Selected Works*, IX, 108.

39. Leon Trotsky, *The Lessons of October*, trans. John G. Wright (New York, 1937), pp. 37, 63–75, 82.

40. Lenin, "The United States of Europe Slogan," *Selected Works*, V, 141.

41. Joseph Stalin, *The Foundations of Leninism* (1st ed., 1924), quoted in his *Works*, VIII (Moscow, 1954), 64–65. This passage was revised in subsequent editions.

42. Lenin, "On Co-operation," *Selected Works*, IX, 403.

43. Stalin, "The October Revolution and the Tactics of the Russian Communists," *Works*, VI (Moscow, 1953), 395, 391, 387.

44. Stalin, "Concerning Questions of Leninism," *Works*, VIII, 67–80.

45. Quoted in Daniels, *Conscience of the Revolution*, p. 284.

Chapter XXIII. The Autocrat and After

1. J. V. Stalin, "Grain Procurements and the Prospects for the Development of Agriculture," *Works*, XI (Moscow, 1954), 7.

2. Stalin, "The Work of the April Joint Plenum of the Central Committee and Central Control Commission," *ibid.*, p. 52.

3. *Ibid.*, pp. 44–45.

4. Stalin, "Report to the Seventeenth Party Congress on the Work of the Central Committee of the CPSU(B)," *ibid.*, XIII (Moscow, 1955), 374.

5. *Ibid.*, pp. 362–363.

6. Stalin, "The International Situation and the Defence of the USSR," *ibid.*, X (Moscow, 1954), 10–39, and "Political Report of the Central Committee," *ibid.*, pp. 291, 295, 296.

7. Stalin, "The Tasks of Business Executives," *ibid.*, XIII, 41.

8. Joseph Stalin, "On the Draft Constitution of the USSR," in his *Problems of Leninism* (Moscow, 1953), pp. 688, 690.

9. Stalin, "Report to the Eighteenth Congress of the CPSU(B) On the Work of the Central Committee," *ibid.*, pp. 790–797.

10. Stalin, "Dialectical and Historical Materialism," *ibid.*, pp. 725–727.

11. Joseph Stalin, *Marxism and Problems of Linguistics* (Moscow, 1954), p. 9.

12. *Ibid.*, pp. 38–39.

13. Joseph Stalin, *Economic Problems of Socialism in the USSR* (Moscow, 1953), pp. 6–8, 10–12.

14. *Ibid.*, pp. 103–105.

15. *Ibid.*, pp. 32–33, 75–77.

16. N. S. Khrushchev, *Report of the Central Committee of the CPSU to the 20th Party Congress* (Moscow, 1956), p. 119.

17. Nikita Khrushchev, *Speeches and Interviews on World Problems, 1957* (Moscow, 1958), pp. 16–17.

18. Quoted in Myron Rush, *The Rise of Khrushchev* (Washington, 1958), p. 29.

19. Nikita Khrushchev, "Accelerated Development of the Chemical Industry," *New Times* (Moscow), no. 19 (May 1958), supp., p. 7.

20. Khrushchev, *Report to the 20th Party Congress*, p. 40.

21. Nikita Khrushchev, *For Victory in Peaceful Competition with Capitalism* (New York, 1960), pp. 206–207.

22. Khrushchev, *Report to the 20th Party Congress*, p. 38; and *Report of the Central Committee of the CPSU to the 22nd Congress of the CPSU*, in *The Road to Communism, Documents of the 22nd Congress of the CPSU* (Moscow, [1962?]), p. 57.

23. Khrushchev, *Report to the 20th Party Congress*, p. 38.

24. *Programme of the CPSU*, in *The Road to Communism*, p. 588 (part 2, sec. 7); Khrushchev, Speech to World Youth Forum, *Current Digest of the Soviet Press*, XVI, no. 38 (Oct. 14, 1964), 9, from *Pravda*, Sept. 22, 1964, pp. 1–2.

25. Cf. V. I. Lenin, "A Caricature of Marxism and 'Imperialist Economism,'" *Collected Works*, XIX (New York, 1942), 256.

26. Khrushchev, *Report to the 20th Party Congress*, p. 44.

27. *Ibid.*, pp. 45–46.

28. Khrushchev, "On the Programme of the CPSU," in *The Road to Communism*, p. 274.

29. Nikita Khrushchev, *Forty Years of the Great October Socialist Revolution* (Moscow, 1957), pp. 57–58; *Control Figures for the Economic Development of the USSR for 1959–1965* (Moscow, 1959), pp. 133–134; and "On the Programme of the CPSU" and *Programme of the CPSU*, in *The Road to Communism*, pp. 270–271, 579.

30. Khrushchev, *Control Figures*, pp. 114–115, and "On the Programme of the CPSU," in *The Road to Communism*, p. 194.

31. *Programme of the CPSU*, in *The Road to Communism*, p. 589 (concluding sentence); Khrushchev, "On the Programme of the CPSU," in *ibid.*, pp. 194–196.

32. Khrushchev, "On the Programme of the CPSU," *ibid.*, pp. 250–251, 304.

33. *Ibid.*, pp. 249, 252.

34. "M.T.S. Reorganization: Khrushchev's Theses," *Current Digest of the Soviet Press*, X, no. 9 (April 9, 1958), 10, from *Pravda* and *Izvestia*, March 1, 1958.

35. Khrushchev, *Control Figures*, p. 124, and "On the Programme of the CPSU," *The Road to Communism*, p. 231.

36. Khrushchev, *Control Figures*, p. 123, and "On the Programme of the CPSU," *The Road to Communism*, p. 248.

37. Khrushchev, "On the Programme of the CPSU," *The Road to Communism*, pp. 261–266.

38. Khrushchev, *Control Figures*, pp. 123–124; *Programme of the CPSU*, in *The Road to Communism*, p. 514 (part 2, sec. 1).

39. T. A. Stepanian, "Oktiabr'skaia revoliutsiia i stanovlenie kommunisticheskoi formatsii," *Voprosy filosofii*, no. 10 (1958), p. 34.

40. Khrushchev, *Control Figures*, p. 135; *Programme of the CPSU*, in *The Road to Communism*, p. 581 (part 2, sec. 6).

41. *A Proposal Concerning the General Line of the International Communist Movement* (Peking, 1963), pp. 26–27, 21 (letter of June 14, 1963, from the Chinese Central Committee to the Central Committee of the CPSU).

42. Nikita Khrushchev, Address of January 16, 1963, to the Sixth Congress of the Socialist Unity Party of Germany, *Moscow News*, Jan. 17, 1963, pp. 10–11, 13.

43. Nine articles by the editorial departments of the Peking *People's Daily* and *Red Flag* (on the Open Letter of the Central Committee of the

CPSU of July 14, 1963) in *Peking Review*, September 13, 20, 27, Oct. 25, Nov. 22, and Dec. 20, 1963, and Feb. 7 and April 3, 1964.

44. Leonid Brezhnev, Speech at rally for cosmonauts, *Pravda*, Oct. 20, 1964, p. 1, in *Current Digest of the Soviet Press*, XVI, no. 41 (Nov. 4, 1964), 5.

45. G. Lisichkin, "Life Makes Corrections," *Current Digest of the Soviet Press*, XVIII, no. 9 (March 23, 1966), 4–5, from *Izvestia*, Feb. 27, 1966, p. 2.

46. *Ibid.*, p. 4.

47. *Pravda*, Jan. 14, 1966, p. 3, in *Current Digest of the Soviet Press*, XVIII, no. 2 (Feb. 2, 1966), 22.

48. Alexei Kosygin, "Report on the Directives for the Five-year Economic Development Plan of the USSR for 1966–1970," *23rd Congress of the Communist Party of the Soviet Union* (n.p., n.d. [Moscow, 1966]).

Bibliography

DESIGNED to facilitate further study by Western students, this bibliography largely excludes titles in Slavic languages. It should, however, be remembered that Russian titles, particularly in the eighteenth and early nineteenth centuries, frequently disguise contents written in French or German.

Some volumes, many of them extremely scarce, could not be obtained for use in this study, but they are included in the Bibliography for the reader's information. Such items are followed by an asterisk.

PART ONE

General Studies of the Kievan Period

Billington, James H. *The Icon and the Axe.* New York, 1966.

D'iakonov, Mikhail. *Skizzen zur Gesellschafts- und Staatsordnung des Alten Russlands.* Trans. Eugen Goluboff. Breslau, 1931.

Ewers, J. P. Gustav. *Das älteste Recht der Russen in seiner geschichtlichen Entwickelung dargestellt.* Dorpat, 1826.

Gitermann, Valentin. *Geschichte Russlands.* 3 vols. Zurich, 1944–1949. Vol. I. Also contains collection of primary materials.

Grekov, B. D. *The Culture of Kiev Rus.* Trans. Pauline Rose. Moscow, 1947.

——. *Der Kampf Russlands um seinen Staat.* Leipzig, 1948.

——. *Kiev Rus.* Trans. Y. Sdobnikov. Moscow, 1959.

Kliuchevski, V. O. *A History of Russia.* 5 vols. Trans. C. J. Hogarth. London, 1911–1931. Vol. I.

Krug, Johann Philipp. *Forschungen in der älteren Geschichte Russlands.* Part 2. St. Petersburg, 1848. Especially pp. 397–441: "Ideen über die älteste Verfassung und Verwaltung des Russischen Staats."

Vernadsky, George. *Kievan Russia.* New Haven, 1948.

Voronin, N. N., and M. K. Karger, eds. *Gesellschaftsordnung und geistige Kultur.* Berlin, 1962. This is Vol. II of B. D. Grekov and M. L. Artamonov, eds. *Geschichte der Kultur der alten Rus': Die vormongolische Periode.*

BIBLIOGRAPHY

Chapter I. The City-States: The Slavs

PRIMARY SOURCES

Chronicle of Novgorod, 1016–1471. Trans. Robert Michell and Nevill Forbes. ("Camden Third Series," Vol. XXV.) London, 1914. The first Novgorodian chronicle.

The Russian Primary Chronicle (Book of Annals). Trans. Samuel H. Cross and Olgerd P. Sherbowitz-Wetzor. Cambridge, 1953. Known as the chronicle of Nestor, coming to 1116. Also in French and German.

SECONDARY STUDIES

Anderssen, Walter. "Die Verfassungen vom Nowgorodtyp," *Zeitschrift für vergleichende Rechtswissenschaft,* XLVI (1931), 410–441.

Kadlec, Karel. *Introduction à l'étude comparative de l'histoire du droit public des peuples Slaves.* Paris, 1933.

Kovalevsky, Maxime. *Modern Customs and Ancient Laws of Russia.* London, 1891. Especially Chapters 3 and 4 on the village community and the *veche.*

Paszkiewicz, Henryk. *The Origin of Russia.* London, 1954.

———. *The Making of the Russian Nation.* Chicago, 1963.

Philipp, Werner. *Anzätze zum geschichtlichen und politischen Denken im Kiewer Russland.* Breslau, 1940.

Tikhomirov, M. *The Towns of Ancient Rus.* Trans. Y. Sdobnikov. Moscow, 1959.

Chapter II. Fraternity: The Varangians

PRIMARY SOURCES

Ewers, J. P. Gustav, and Moritz von Engelhardt, eds. *Beiträge zur Kenntnis Russlands und seiner Geschichte.* Vol. I, 1st half. Dorpat, 1816.*

Goetz, Leopold K. *Das russische Recht.* 4 vols. Stuttgart, 1910–1913. Reprinted from *Zeitschrift für vergleichende Rechtswissenschaft,* XXIV, XXVI, XXVIII, and XXXI (1910–1913). Iaroslav's code; texts and commentary.

———. *Deutsch-russische Handelsverträge des Mittelalters.* Hamburg, 1916.

Larson, Laurence M., ed. and trans. *The Earliest Norwegian Laws.* New York, 1935. Contains the Gulathing Law and the Frostathing Law.

Rafn, Carl C. *Antiquités russes d'après les monuments historiques des Islandais et des anciens Scandinaves.* 2 vols. Copenhagen, 1850–1852. In Islandic and Latin with French prefaces and notes.

Snorri Sturluson. *Heimskringla.* Trans. Erling Monsen and A. H. Smith. Cambridge, 1932. Norse sagas.

BIBLIOGRAPHY

Szeftel, Marc, ed. *Documents de droit public relatifs à la Russie médiévale.* Brussels, 1963. Contains Iaroslav's code, five church statutes, and other items.

Vernadsky, George, ed. and trans. *Medieval Russian Laws.* New York, 1947.

SECONDARY STUDIES

Gsovski, Vladimir. "Medieval Russian Laws," *American Slavic and East European Review*, VI, no. 18 (1947), 152–158. Review of Vernadsky, *Medieval Russian Laws.*

Ladreit de Lacharriere, G. *L'idée fédérale en Russie de Riourik à Staline.* Paris, 1945.

Maurer, Konrad. *Vorlesungen über altnordische Rechtsgeschichte.* 5 vols. Leipzig, 1907–1910. Especially Vol. I, *Altnorwegisches Staatsrecht.*

Ravndal, Gabriel B. *Stories of the East-Vikings.* Minneapolis, 1938.

Strinnholm, A. M. *Wikingszüge, Staatsverfassung und Sitten.* Trans. C. F. Frisch. 2 vols. Hamburg, 1839–1841.

Thomsen, Vilhelm L. P. *The Relations between Ancient Russia and Scandinavia and the Origin of the Russian State.* Oxford, 1877.

Chapter III. Symphonia: *The Byzantines*

PRIMARY SOURCES

Barker, Ernest, ed. and trans. *Social and Political Thought in Byzantium.* Oxford, 1957.

Freshfield, Edward H., ed. and trans. *A Manual of Eastern Roman Law.* Cambridge, 1928. The *Procheiros Nomos* or *Procheiron.*

——. *Roman Law in the Later Roman Empire.* Cambridge, 1932. The *Ecloga.*

Goetz, Leopold K. *Kirchenrechtliche und kulturgeschichtliche Denkmäler Altrusslands nebst Geschichte des russischen Kirchenrechts.* Stuttgart, 1905.

Rose, Karl, ed. *Grund und Quellort des russischen Geisteslebens.* Berlin, 1956.* Contains Hilarion's "Sermon on Law and Grace."

SECONDARY STUDIES

Anastos, M. "Political Theory in the Lives of the Slavic Saints Constantine and Methodius," *Harvard Slavic Studies*, II (1954), 11–38.

Bréhier, Louis. *Les institutions de l'Empire Byzantin.* Paris, 1949. Especially pp. 1–88, 430–446.

Bury, John B. *The Constitution of the Later Roman Empire.* Cambridge, 1910.

BIBLIOGRAPHY

Dvornik, Francis. "Byzantine Political Ideas in Kievan Russia," *Dumbarton Oaks Papers*, nos. 9 and 10 (1956), pp. 73–121.

Fabrège, Frédéric. "Saint Jean Chrysostome et les idées politiques des Pères de l'Église," *Revue générale*, N.S. II (Sept., Oct. 1868), 229–244, 356–370.

Gelzer, Heinrich K. G. "Das Verhältnis von Staat und Kirche in Byzanz," in his *Ausgewählte kleine Schriften* (Leipzig, 1907).

Goetz, Leopold K. *Staat und Kirche in Altrussland, Kiever Period 988–1240*. Berlin, 1908.

Mazon, André. "Byzance et la Russie," *Revue d'histoire de la philosophie et d'histoire générale de la civilisation*, N.S. V (July 1937), 261–277.

Medlin, William K. *Moscow and East Rome*. Geneva, 1952.

Mitrović, Chedomilj. *Nomokanon der slavischen morgenländischen Kirche oder die Kormtschaja Kniga*. Wien, 1898.

Obolensky, Dmitri. "Russia's Byzantine Heritage," *Oxford Slavonic Papers*, ed. S. Konovalov, I (1950), 37–63.

Runciman, Steven. "Byzantium, Russia and Caesaropapism," *Canadian Slavonic Papers*, II (1957), 1–10.

Seidler, Grzegorz L. *Soziale Ideen in Byzanz*. Berlin, 1960.

Shevčenko, Ihor. "A Neglected Byzantine Source of Muscovite Political Ideology," *Harvard Slavic Studies*, II (1954), 141–179.

Toynbee, Arnold J. "Russia's Byzantine Heritage," in his *Civilization on Trial* (London, 1948).

Treitinger, Otto. *Die oströmische Kaiser- und Reichsidee nach ihrer Gestaltung im höfischen Zeremoniell*. Jena, 1938.

———. "Vom oströmischen Staats- und Reichsgedanken," *Leipziger Vierteljahrschrift für Sudosteuropa*, IV (1940), 1–26.

Vernadsky, George. "Die kirchlich-politische Lehre der Epanagoge und ihr Einfluss auf das russische Leben im XVII Jahrhundert," *Byzantinisch-neugriechische Jahrbücher*, VI (1928), 119–142.

PART TWO

General Studies of the Mongolian Period

D'iakonov, Mikhail. *Skizzen zur Gesellschafts- und Staatsordnung des alten Russlands*. Trans. Eugen Goluboff. Breslau, 1931.

Eck, Alexandre. *Le moyen âge russe*. Paris, 1933. Also contains primary materials.

Gitermann, Valentin. *Geschichte Russlands*. 3 vols. Zurich, 1944–1949. Vol. I. Also contains primary materials.

Grekov, B. D., and A. Iakubovski. *La Horde d'Or*. Trans. François Thuret. Paris, 1939.

BIBLIOGRAPHY

Kliuchevski, V. O. *A History of Russia.* 5 vols. Trans. C. J. Hogarth. London, 1911–1931. Vols. I and II.

Vernadsky, George. *The Mongols and Russia.* New Haven, 1953.

Chapter IV. World Empire: The Mongols

PRIMARY SOURCES

Haenisch, Erich, ed. and trans. *Die geheime Geschichte der Mongolen.* 2d rev. ed. Leipzig, 1948.

Kei Kwei Sun, ed. and trans. *The Secret History of the Mongol Dynasty (Yuan-ch'ao pi-shi).* Aligarh, 1957.* Reprinted from *Medieval India Quarterly,* II (1957), 1–134.

Pelliot, Paul, ed. and trans. *Histoire secrète des Mongols.* Paris, 1949. Sections 1–185 only.

Riasanovsky, V. A. *Fundamental Principles of Mongol Law.* Tientsin, 1937. Contains fragments of the *Iasa* and the *Bilik,* or maxims of Chingis Khan.

Vernadsky, George. "Juwaini's Version of Chingis-Khan's Yasa," *Annales de l'Institut Kondakov,* XI (Belgrade, 1940), 33–45.

Voegelin, Eric. "The Mongol Orders of Submission to European Powers, 1245–1255," *Byzantion,* XV (1941), 378–413. Diplomatic letters.

Waley, Arthur. *The Secret History of the Mongols and Other Pieces.* New York, 1964.

SECONDARY STUDIES

Grousset, René. *L'empire Mongol (Ire phase).* Paris, 1941.

Hammer-Purgstall, Joseph. *Geschichte der goldenen Horde.* Pesth, 1840.

Kotwicz, Wladyslaw. "Les Mongols, promoteurs de l'idée de paix universelle au début du xiiie siècle," *La Pologne au VIIe Congrès International des Sciences Historiques,* I (1933), 199–204.

Krader, Lawrence. "Feudalism and the Tatar Polity of the Middle Ages," *Comparative Studies in Society and History,* I (Oct. 1958), 76–99.

Prawdin, Michael (Charol). *The Mongol Empire: Its Rise and Legacy.* London, 1952.

Seidler, Grzegorz L. *The Political Doctrine of the Mongols.* Lublin, 1960. Reprinted from *Annales Universitatis Mariae-Curie-Sklodowska,* VII (1959), 249–277.

Spuler, Bertold. *Die Goldene Horde, Die Mongolen in Russland, 1223–1502.* Leipzig, 1943.

Vernadsky, George. "The Scope and Contents of Chingis-Khan's Yasa," *Harvard Journal of Asiatic Studies,* III (1938), 337–360.

Vladimirtsov, B. *Le régime social des Mongols: Le féodalisme nomade.* Trans. Michel Carsow. Paris, 1948.

Chapter V. The Church: Autonomy

PRIMARY SOURCES

Hammer-Purgstall, Joseph. *Geschichte der goldenen Horde.* Pesth, 1840. Contains 36 iarlyks.

Pelliot, Paul. "Les Mongols et la papauté," *Revue de l'orient chrétien,* XXIII and XXIV (3d series, III and IV; 1922–1924).

Theiner, Augustin. *Vetera monumenta Poloniae et Lithuaniae.* 4 vols. Rome, 1860–1864.

Welykyj, Athanasius G. *Documenta pontificum romanorum historiam Ucrainae illustrantia.* Vol. I. Rome, 1953.

SECONDARY STUDIES

Ammann, Albert M. *Storia della Chiesa Russa e dei paesi limitrofi.* Turin, 1948. Also in German as *Abriss der ostslawischen Kirchengeschichte.* Vienna, 1950.

——. *Untersuchungen zur Geschichte der kirchlichen Kultur und des religiösen Lebens bei den Ostslawen.* Vol. I: *Die ostslawische Kirche im jurisdiktionellen Verband der byzantinischen Grosskirche, 988–1459.* Würzburg, 1955.

Fedotov, George P. *The Russian Religious Mind.* Vol. II. Cambridge, Mass., 1966.

Gorlin, Michel. "Le Dit de la ruine de la Terre Russe et de la mort du Grand-Prince Jaroslav," *Revue des études slaves,* XXIII (1947), 1–33.

——. "Sérapion de Vladimir, prédicateur de Kiev," *Revue des études slaves,* XXIV (1948), 21–28.

Murav'ev, A. N. *A History of the Church of Russia.* Trans. R. W. Blackmore. Oxford, 1842.

Soranzo, Giovanni. *Il Papato, l'Europa cristina e i Tartari.* Milan, 1930.

Winter, Eduard. *Russland und das Papsttum.* Berlin, 1960. Part 1.

Chapter VI. The Rise of Moscow

PRIMARY SOURCES

Eck, Alexandre. *Le moyen âge russe.* Paris, 1933. Contains documents and charters.

Ewers, J. P. Gustav, and Moritz von Engelhardt, eds. *Beiträge zur Kenntnis Russlands und seiner Geschichte.* Vol. I, 1st half. Dorpat, 1816.*

BIBLIOGRAPHY

Goetz, Leopold K. *Deutsch-russische Handelsverträge des Mittelalters.* Hamburg, 1916.

Tobien, Ewald S. *Sammlung kritisch bearbeiteter Quellen zur Geschichte des russischen Rechts.* Vol. I. Dorpat, 1845.*

Vernadsky, George, ed. and trans. *Medieval Russian Laws.* New York, 1947. Contains charters of Dvina Land, Novgorod, and Pskov.

SECONDARY STUDIES

Alef, Gustave. "Das Erlöschen des Abzugsrecht der moskauer Bojaren," *Forschungen zur osteuropäischen Geschichte*, X (1965), 7–74.

Bächtold, Rudolf. *Südwestrussland im Spätmittelalter.* Basel, 1951.

Eck, Alexandre. "La vassalité et les immunités dans la Russie du moyen âge," *Revue de l'Institut de Sociologie* (Brussels), XXII (année 16; 1936), 103–118.

Eckardt, Hans von. "Die Kontinuität der russischen Wirtschaftspolitik von Alt-Moskau bis zur Union der S.S.R.," *Archiv für Sozialwissenschaft und Sozialpolitik*, LV, no. 3 (June 1926), 754–768.

Korff, S. A. "Die Errichtung der Selbstherrschaft im moskauischen Staate," *Zeitschrift für osteuropäische Geschichte*, IV (1914), 319–337.

Stökl, Günther. "Die politische Religiosität des Mittelalters und die Entstehung des Moskauer Staates," *Saeculum*, II (1951), 393–415.

Ziegler, Adolf. *Die Union des Konzils von Florenz in der russischen Kirche.* Würzburg, 1938.

PART THREE

General Studies of the Muscovite Period

Alexejew, N. N. "Der Ursprung der politischen Ideale des russischen Volkes," *Osteuropa*, VI (March 1931), 313–328.

Backus, Oswald P. "Was Muscovite Russia Imperialistic?," *American Slavic and East European Review*, XIII (Dec. 1954), 522–534.

D'iakonov, Mikhail. *Skizzen zur Gesellschafts- und Staatsordnung des alten Russlands.* Trans. Eugen Goluboff. Breslau, 1931.

Gitermann, Valentin. *Geschichte Russlands.* 3 vols. Zurich, 1944–1949. Vol. I. Also contains collection of primary materials.

Kliuchevski, V. O. *A History of Russia.* Trans. C. J. Hogarth. 5 vols. London, 1911–1931. Vols. II and III.

Korff, S. A. "Die Errichtung der Selbstherrschaft im moskauischen Staate," *Zeitschrift für osteuropäische Geschichte*, IV (1914), 319–337.

Kovalevsky, Maxime. *Russian Political Institutions.* Chicago, 1902.

Lappo-Danilevski, A. S. "L'idée de l'état et son évolution en Russie depuis les Troubles du 17ᵉ siècle jusqu'aux Réformes du 18ᵉ," in *Essays in Legal History*, ed. Paul Vinogradoff (London, 1913), pp. 356–385.

Medlin, William K. *Moscow and East Rome.* Geneva, 1952.

Miller, Alexandre. *Essai sur l'histoire des institutions agraires de la Russie centrale du XVIe au XVIIIe siècles.* Paris, 1926.

Olšr, Joseph. "Gli ultimi Rurikide e le basi ideologiche della sovranità dello stato Russo," *Orientalia christiana periodica*, XII (1946), 322–373.

———. "La Chiesa e lo Stato nel cerimoniale d'incoronazione degli ultimi sovrani Rurikidi," *Orientalia christiana periodica*, XVI (1950), 267–302.

Raptschinsky, Boris. "Het Ontstaan van de Autocratie in Rusland," *Tijdschrift voor Geschiedenis*, L (1935), 113–133.

Chapter VII. The Third Rome

PRIMARY SOURCES

Dewey, Horace W. "The Sudebnik of 1497." Unpublished Ph.D. dissertation, University of Michigan, 1955. Pp. 303–326 contain an English translation of the Sudebnik or code of Ivan III.

Fedotov, George P., ed. *A Treasury of Russian Spirituality.* New York, 1948. Contains some short pieces by Nil Sorski.

Herberstein, Sigismund von. *Notes upon Russia* [Rerum Moscoviticarum Commentarii]. Trans. R. H. Major. 2 vols. London, 1851–1852.

Szeftel, Marc. "Le 'Justicier' (Sudebnik) du Tsar Ivan III (1497)," *Revue historique de droit français et étranger*, Série IV, XXIV (Oct.–Dec. 1956), 531–568. Translation and commentary.

SECONDARY STUDIES

Alef, Gustave. "Muscovy and the Council of Florence," *Slavic Review*, XX (Oct. 1961), 384–401.

Andreyev, N. "Filofey and his Epistle to Ivan Vasil'yevich," *Slavonic and East European Review*, XXXVIII (1959), 1–31.

Denissoff, Élie. *Maxime le Grec et l'Occident.* Louvain, 1943.

———. "On the Origins of the Autonomous Russian Church," *Review of Politics*, XII (April 1950), 225–246.

Dewey, Horace W. "The 1497 Sudebnik, Muscovite Russia's First National Law Code," *American Slavic and East European Review*, XV (Oct. 1956), 325–338.

Fennell, J. L. I. "The Attitude of the Josephians and the Trans-Volga Elders to the Heresy of the Judaisers," *Slavonic and East European Review*, XXIX (1951), 486–509.

———. *Ivan the Great of Moscow.* New York, 1961.

Léger, L. "Un théologien grec de la Renaissance en Moscovie," *Journal des savants*, XIV (Aug. 1916), 337–346. On Maxim the Greek.

Olšr, Joseph. "Mosca la terza Roma," *Humanitas,* IV (Jan. 1949), 2–18.

Raeff, Marc. "An Early Theorist of Absolutism: Joseph of Volokolamsk," *American Slavic and East European Review,* VIII (April 1949), 77–89.

Schaeder, Hildegard. *Moscow das dritte Rom.* Hamburg, 1929.

Smolitsch, Igor. *Leben und Lehre der Starzen.* Vienna, 1936.

Strémooukhoff, Dmitri. "Moscow the Third Rome: Sources of the Doctrine," *Speculum,* XXVIII (Jan. 1953), 84–101.

Stupperich, Robert. "Der Moskauer Staat und die Moskauer Kirche im Mittelalter," *Zeichen der Zeit* (Berlin), III (1949).*

Vernadsky, George. "The Heresy of the Judaizers and the Policies of Ivan III of Moscow," *Speculum,* VIII (Oct. 1933), 436–454.

Wolff, Robert L. "The Three Romes: The Migration of an Ideology and the Making of an Autocrat," *Daedalus,* LXXXVIII (Spring 1959), 291–311.

Zernov, Nicholas. *Moscow the Third Rome.* London, 1937.

Chapter VIII. The Reign of Ivan IV

PRIMARY SOURCES

The Correspondence between Prince A. M. Kurbsky and Tsar Ivan IV of Russia, 1564–1579. Ed. and trans. J. L. I. Fennell. Cambridge, 1955. Also in German.

Le Domostroi. Ed. and trans. E. Duchesne. Paris, 1910. In part also in *Revue de l'histoire des religions,* L (July–Aug. 1904), 13–38.

Ewers, J. P. Gustav, and Moritz von Engelhardt, eds. *Beiträge zur Kenntnis Russlands und seiner Geschichte.* Vol. I, 2d half. Dorpat, 1818. Contains the *Sudebnik* or code of 1550.*

Prince A. M. Kurbsky's History of Ivan IV. Ed. and trans. J. L. I. Fennell. Cambridge, 1965.

Staden, Heinrich von. *Aufzeichnungen über den moskauer Staat.* Ed. Fritz Epstein. Hamburg, 1930. Notes of an *oprichnik.*

Le Stoglav. Ed. and trans. E. Duchesne. Paris, 1920.

Tolstoi, George. *The First Forty Years of Intercourse between England and Russia.* St. Petersburg, 1875.

SECONDARY STUDIES

Dewey, Horace W. "The 1550 Sudebnik as an Instrument of Reform," *Jahrbücher für Geschichte Osteuropas,* N.S. X (July, 1962), 161–180.

Eckardt, Hans von. *Ivan the Terrible.* Trans. C. Phillips. New York, 1949.

Graham, Stephen. *Ivan the Terrible.* New Haven, 1933.

Karamzin, Nikolai M. *Histoire de l'empire de Russie.* Various translators. 11 vols. (through 1606). Paris, 1819–1826. Vols. VIII and IX.

Koslow, Jules. *Ivan the Terrible.* New York, 1961.

BIBLIOGRAPHY

Kostomarov, Nikolai I. *Russische Geschichte in Biographien*. Trans. W. Henckel. Leipzig, 1889. Chapters on Ivan and Sylvester and Adashev.

Lamb, Harold. *The March of Muscovy; Ivan the Terrible and the Growth of the Russian Empire, 1400–1648*. Garden City, N.Y., 1948.

Leontovitsch, Victor. *Die Rechtsumwälzung unter Iwan dem Schreckli- chen und die Ideologie der russischen Selbstherrschaft*. Stuttgart, 1947.

Philipp, Werner. *Ivan Peresvetov und seine Schriften zur Erneuerung des moskauer Reiches*. Königsberg and Berlin, 1935.

Stratonov, I. A. "Die Reform der Lokalverwaltung unter Ivan IV," *Zeitschrift für osteuropäische Geschichte*, VII (N.S. III; 1932), 1–20.

Strémooukhoff, Dmitri. "L'idée impériale à Moscou au XVI siècle," *Annales de la Faculté des Lettres d'Aix*, XXXII (1958), 165–184.

Chapter IX. From Riurikides to Romanovs

PRIMARY SOURCES

Fletcher, Giles. *Of the Russe Common Wealth* (1591), in Edward A. Bond, ed., *Russia at the Close of the Sixteenth Century* (London, 1856).

Howe, Sonia E., ed. *The False Dmitri*. New York, 1916. Many documents in contemporary English.

Olearius, Adam. *The Voyages and Travels of the Ambassadors sent by Frederick duke of Holstein, to the great Duke of Muscovy, and the King of Persia* (1639). Trans. John Davies. 2 vols. London, 1662.

SECONDARY STUDIES

Fleischhacker, Hedwig. *Russland zwischen zwei Dynastien (1598–1613)*. Badn bei Wien, 1933.

Keep, J. L. H. "The Decline of the Zemsky Sobor," *Slavonic and East European Review*, XXXVI (1957), 100–122.

———. "The Régime of Filaret (1619–1633)," *Slavonic and East European Review*, XXXVIII (1960), 334–360.

Kovalevski, Maksim M. *Modern Customs and Ancient Laws of Russia*. London, 1891. Especially Chap. 5 on the zemski sobor.

Mérimée, Prosper. *Demetrius the Impostor*. Trans. Andrew R. Scoble. London, 1853.

Olšr, Joseph. "La chiesa e lo stato nel cerimoniale d'incoronazione degli zar russi nel periodo dei torbidi (1598–1613)," *Orientalia christiana periodica*, XVII (1951), 395–434.

Rocca, Félix de. *Les assemblées politiques dans la Russie ancienne: Les Zemskié Sobors*. Paris, 1899.

Stralenberg [Strahlenberg], Philip J. T. von. *An historico-geographical description of the north and eastern parts of Europe and Asia.* [No trans. given.] London, 1738.

Waliszewski, Kazimierz. *Les origines de la Russie moderne: La crise révolutionnaire, 1584–1614.* Paris, 1906.

Chapter X. The Patriarch and the Tsar

PRIMARY SOURCES

Fedotov, George P., ed. *A Treasury of Russian Spirituality.* New York, 1948. Includes the autobiography of Avvakum.

Palmer, William, ed. and trans. *The Patriarch and the Tsar.* 6 vols. London, 1871–1876. Contains many contemporary documents on or by Nikon.

Pascal, Pierre, ed. and trans. *La Vie de l'Archiprêtre Avvakum.* Paris, 1938. Also in German trans. by Rudolf Jagoditsch (Königsberg and Berlin, 1930) and less scholarly English trans. by Jane Harrison and Hope Mirrlees (London, 1924).

Struve, Burkhard G., ed. and trans. *Allgemeines russisches Land-Recht.* Danzig, 1723. The *Ulozhenie* or code of 1649.

SECONDARY STUDIES

Brückner, Alexander G. *Beiträge zur Kulturgeschichte Russlands im XVII. Jahrhundert.* Leipzig, 1887. Especially Chap. 9 (pp. 279–354) on V. V. Golitsyn.

——. *Die Europäiserung Russlands, Land und Volk.* Gotha, 1888.

Field, Cecil. *The Great Cossack.* London, 1947. On Stenka Razin.

Melgunov, S. "Les mouvements religieux et sociaux en Russie aux XVIIᵉ–XVIIIᵉ siècles," *Le monde slave,* N.S. III, no. 12 (Dec. 1926), 381–410.

Olšr, Joseph. "La Chiesa e lo Stato nel cerimoniale d'incoronazione degli zar Romanov," *Orientalia christiana periodica,* XVIII (1952), 344–376.

Pascal, Pierre. *Avvakum et les débuts du Raskol.* Paris, 1938.

Spinka, Matthew. "Patriarch Nikon and the Subjugation of the Russian Church to the State," *Church History,* X (Dec. 1941), 347–366.

Vernadsky, George. "Die kirchlich-politische Lehre der Epanagoge und ihr Einfluss auf das russische Leben in XVII. Jahrhundert," *Byzantinisch-neugriechische Jahrbücher,* VI (1928), 119–142.

PART FOUR

General Studies of the Period 1689–1825

Bächtold, Rudolf. *Karamzins Weg zur Geschichte.* Basel, 1946.

Gitermann, Valentin. *Geschichte Russlands.* 3 vols. Zurich, 1944–1949. Vol. II. Contains primary materials.

Giusti, Wolfango. *Studi sul pensiero illuministico e liberale russo nei secoli XVIII–XIX.* Rome, 1938.

——. *Due secoli di pensiero politico russo: Le correnti progressiste.* Florence, 1943.

Honigsheim, P. "Russische Gesellschafts-, Staats-, und Wirtschaftsauffassungen," in the *Handwörterbuch der Sozialwissenschaften,* ed. E. v. Beckerath (2d ed.; Stuttgart, 1953).

Kovalevsky, Maxime. *Russian Political Institutions.* Chicago, 1902.

Masaryk, Thomas G. *The Spirit of Russia* (1913). 2 vols. London, 1955.

Miliukov, Paul. *Le mouvement intellectuel russe.* Paris, 1918.

Raeff, Marc. *Plans for Political Reform in Imperial Russia, 1730–1905.* Englewood Cliffs, N.J., 1966. Documents with commentary.

Stralenberg [Strahlenberg], Philip J. T. von. *An historico-geographical description of the north and eastern parts of Europe and Asia.* Trans. [no trans. given]. London, 1738.

Tompkins, Stuart R. *The Russian Mind from Peter the Great through the Enlightenment.* Norman, Okla., 1953.

Chapter XI. Revolution from Above: Peter and Anna

PRIMARY SOURCES

Consett, Thomas, ed. and trans. *The Present State and Regulations of the Church of Russia.* 2 vols. London, 1729. Peter's church statute and some short pieces by Prokopovich.

Ehrenberg, Hans, ed. *Östliches Christentum.* 2 vols. Munich, 1925. Vol. I, pp. 220–233, contains the sectarian attack on Peter, "Auszug aus der heiligen Schrift über den Antichrist."

Golitsyn, Augustin P. *La Russie au XVIIIᵉ siècle, mémoires inédits sur les règnes de Pierre le Grand, Catherine Iʳᵉ et Pierre IIᵉ.* Paris, 1863.

Liria y Xerica, James. *Diario del viaje á Moscovia,* in the *Collección de documentos ineditos para la historia de Espana,* XCIII (Madrid, 1889). Documents on Anna's accession, etc., not always accurate.

Prokopovich, Feofan. *Vorschläge wie ein Printz in der christlichen Religion soll unterrichtet werden.* N.p., n.d.*

——. *Das Recht der Monarchen, in willkühriger Bestellung der Reichs-Folge.* Berlin, 1724.

Schmidt-Phiseldek, Christoph. *Materielien zu der russischen Geschichte seit dem Tode Kaisers Peters des Grossen.* 3 vols. Riga, 1777 and 1784, and Frankfurt, 1788.*

Shmurlo, Evgeni F., ed. *Recueil de documents relatifs au règne de l'Empereur Pierre le Grand.* Dorpat, 1903. Relations with the Vatican, Venice, etc., mostly in Italian.

Tondini, C., ed. *Le Reglement Ecclésiastique de Pierre le Grand*. Paris, 1874.

SECONDARY STUDIES

Brückner, Alexander G. "Fürst W. W. Golizyn 1643–1714," *Russische Revue*, XIII (1878), 193–223.

——. *Iwan Possoschkow: Ideen und Zustände in Russland zur Zeit Peters des Grossen*. Leipzig, 1878.

——. "Die Thronbesteigung der Kaiserin Anna im Jahre 1730," *Russische Revue*, XX (1882), 1–42.

Danilov, N. N. "V. V. Golicyn bis zum Staatsstreich vom Mai 1682," *Jahrbücher für Geschichte Osteuropas*, I (1936), 1–33.

——. "Vasilij Vasil'evič Golicyn (1682–1714)," *Jahrbücher für Geschichte Osteuropas*, II (1937), 539–596.

Dorošenko, D. "Hetman Mazepa. Sein Leben und Wirken," *Zeitschrift für osteuropäische Geschichte*, VII (1933), 51–73.

Fleischhacker, Hedig. "1730, das Nachspiel der petrinischen Reform," *Jahrbücher für Geschichte Osteuropas*, VI (1941), 201–274.

Grau, Conrad. *Der Wirtschaftsorganisator, Staatsmann und Wissenschafter Vasilij N. Tatiščev (1686–1750)*. Berlin, 1963.

Hjärne, Harald. "Ryska konstitutionsprojekt år 1730 efter svenska förebilder," *Historisk Tidskrift*, IV (1884), 189–272.

Miliukov, Paul. "Pierre le Grand et sa réforme," *Le monde slave*, N.S. II (Feb. 1925), 157–185.

O'Brien, Carl B. *Russia Under Two Tsars, 1682–1689*. Berkeley, 1952.

Recke, Walther. "Die Verfassungspläne der russischen Oligarchen im Jahre 1730 und die Thronbesteigung der Kaiserin Anna Ivanovna," *Zeitschrift für osteuropäische Geschichte*, II (1911–1912), 11–64, 161–203.

Sherech, Jurij. "Stefan Iavorski and the Conflict of Ideologies in the Age of Peter the Great," *Slavonic and East European Review*, XXX (1951), 40–62.

Stupperich, Robert. "Feofan Prokopovič in Rom," *Zeitschrift für osteuropäische Geschichte*, V (1931), 327–339.

——. "Feofan Prokopovič und Johann Franz Buddeus," *Zeitschrift für osteuropäische Geschichte*, IX (1935), 341–362.

——. *Staatsgedanke und Religionspolitik Peters des Grossen*. Berlin, 1936.

——. "Feofan Prokopovič und seine akademische Wirksamkeit in Kiev," *Zeitschrift für Slavische Philologie*, XVII (1940), 70–102.

Venturi, Franco. "Feofan Prokopovič," *Annali delle facoltà di lettere filosofia e magistero dell'università di Cagliari*, XXI, part 1 (1953), 625–680.*

BIBLIOGRAPHY

Wittram, Reinhard. "Peters des Grossen Verhältnis zur Religion und den Kirchen," *Historische Zeitschrift*, CLXXIII (April 1952), 261–296.

——. *Peter der Erste*. Göttingen, 1964.

Chapter XII. *The Enlightenment: Catherine and Her Critics*

PRIMARY SOURCES

Catherine II. *The Memoirs of Catherine the Great*. Trans. Moura Budberg. New York, 1955. Includes only early years, to 1759.

——. *Instruction de Sa Majesté Imperiale Catherine II pour la Commission chargée de dresser le projet d'un nouveau code de loix*. St. Petersburg, 1769.* See Reddaway, below, for English.

——. *Verordnungen zur Verwaltung der Gouvernments des russischen Reiches*. St. Petersburg, 1776.* Also in French.*

Diderot, Denis. *Observations sur l'Instruction de Sa Majesté Impériale aux députés pour la confection des lois* (1774). Paris, 1921. Reprinted from *Revue d'histoire économique et sociale*, VIII (1920), 273–412. Also ed. in French, 2 vols. (New York, 1953).

Radishchev, Alexander N. *A Journey from St. Petersburg to Moscow.* Ed. Roderick P. Thaler. Trans. Leo Wiener. Cambridge, Mass., 1958. The London, 1858, and Paris, 1921, editions are in Russian. Also available in German.

Reddaway, W. F., ed. *Documents of Catherine the Great*. Cambridge, 1931. Contains *Instruction* and correspondence with Voltaire.

Shcherbatov, Mikhail. *Ueber die Sittenverderbnis in Russland*. Trans. Ina Friedländer. Berlin, 1925. The London, 1858, edition is in Russian.

Turgenev, Alexander I., ed. *La cour de Russie il y à cent ans, 1725–1783*. Berlin and Paris, 1858.

SECONDARY STUDIES

Backvis, Claude. "Nicolas Novikov et la Franc-maçonnerie russe au XVIII siècle," *Revue de l'Université de Bruxelles*, XLI (May–July 1936), 365–390.

Brückner, A. "Die Instruktion der Kaiserin Katharina II: 1767," *Russische Revue*, XVIII (1881), 385–438.

Clardy, Jesse V. *The Philosophical Ideas of Alexander Radishchev*. New York, 1964.

Cotta, Sergio. "L'illuminisme et la science politique: Montesquieu, Diderot et Catherine II," *Revue internationale d'histoire politique et constitutionnelle*, IV (N.S. no. 16; Oct.–Dec. 1954), 273–287.

Evgeniev, Boris. *Alexander Radishchev*. London, 1946.

Galitzyne, Nicolas. "La question de l'émancipation des serfs sous l'impératrice Catherine II," *Annales internationales d'histoire* (Congrès de Paris, 1900), sec. 2 (1902), pp. 83–102.

Lang, David M. "Radishchev and the Legislative Commission of Alexander I," *American Slavic and East European Review*, VI, nos. 18–19 (Dec. 1947), 11–24.

——. "Some Forerunners of the Decembrists," *Cambridge Journal*, I (1948), 623–634. Reprinted in *The Making of Modern Europe*, ed. Herman Ausubel, 2 vols. (New York, 1951), I.

——. "Some Western Sources of Radiščev's Political Thought," *Revue des études slaves*, XXV (1949), 73–86.

McConnell, Allen. *A Russian Philosophe, Alexander Radishchev, 1749–1802.* The Hague, 1964.

Pascal, Pierre. "De Pierre le Grand à Lénine," *Revue d'histoire de la philosophie et d'histoire générale de la civilisation*, V (July 1937), 294–308.

Raeff, Marc. "State and Nobility in the Ideology of M. M. Shcherbatov," *American Slavic and East European Review*, XIX (Oct., 1960), 363–379.

Sacke, Georg. "Zur Charakteristik der gesetzgebenden Kommission Katharinas II von Russland," *Archiv für Kulturgeschichte*, XXI (1931), 166–191.

——. *Graf A. Voroncov, A. N. Radiščev und der "Gnadenbrief für das russische Volk."* Emsdetten, n.d. [1938?].

——. "Fürst Michael Schčerbatov und seine Schriften," *Zeitschrift für slavische Philologie*, XVI (1939), 353–361.

——. *Die gesetzgebende Kommission Katharinas II: Ein Beitrag zur Geschichte des Absolutismus in Russland.* Breslau, 1940.

Singer, Eugenie. "Alexander Nikolaevič Radiščev," *Jahrbücher für Kultur und Geschichte der Slaven*, N.S. VII (Breslau, 1931), 113–162.

Thaler, Roderick P. "A. N. Radishchev's *A Journey from St. Petersburg to Moscow* (1790)." Unpublished Ph.D. dissertation, Harvard University, 1955.*

Venturi, Franco. "Beccaria in Russia," *El Ponte*, IX (Feb. 1953), 163–174. In Italian.

Chapter XIII. Promise and Denouement: Alexander and His Aides

PRIMARY SOURCES

"Constitutional Charter of the Russian Empire," *The Portfolio* (London), V (Feb.–March 1837), 513–522, 611–639, and VI (April 1837), 73–86. Also French edition, V (1837), 379–419. Novosiltsev's constitution of 1820.

Czartoryski, Adam. *Memoirs and Correspondence with Alexander I.* London, 1888.

Nikolai Mikhailovich, grand duke. *Le Comte Paul Stroganov.* Trans. F. Billecocq. 3 vols. Paris, 1905. Vols. II and III contain Stroganov's records of the unofficial committee and other materials. Also in French in the Russian edition.

Pipes, Richard, ed. and trans. *Karamzin's Memoir on Ancient and Modern Russia.* Cambridge, Mass., 1959.

Schiemann, Theodor, ed. *La charte constitutionelle de l'empire de Russie.* Berlin, 1903. Best edition of Novosiltsev's constitution of 1820.

Schilder, Nikolai K. *Imperator Aleksandr I.* 2 vols. St. Petersburg, 1897. Vol. II contains part of Stroganov's records in French.

Turgenev, Nikolai I. *La Russie et les Russes.* 3 vols. Paris, 1847. Vol. III, pp. 425–501, contain letters and projects of Speranski.

SECONDARY STUDIES

Budin, G. "Un réformateur Russe: Spéranski, ses projets de réforme; sa disgrâce," *Annales des sciences politiques*, XVIII (Sept. 15, 1903), 612–628.

Fateev, Arkadii N. "La constitution russe de 1809," *Bulletin de l'association russe pour les recherches scientifiques à Prague*, II, no. 7 (1935).

——. *La disgrâce d'un homme d'état* [Speranski]. Prague, 1940.

Koyré, Alexandre. "Un chapitre de l'histoire intellectuelle de la Russie: La persécution des philosophes sous Alexandre Iᵉʳ," *Le monde slave*, N.S. III, no. 10 (Oct. 1926), 90–117.

Leontovitsch, Victor. *Geschichte des Liberalismus in Russland.* Frankfort on Main, 1957.

McGrew, R. E. "Notes on the Princely Role in Karamzin's *Istorija gosudarstva rossijskago*," *American Slavic and East European Review*, XVIII (Feb. 1959), 12–24.

Mitter, Wolfgang. "Die Entwicklung der politischen Anschauungen Karamzins," *Forschungen zur osteuropaischen Geschichte*, II (1955), 165–285.

Nolde, Boris. "L'autocratie russe et la doctrine de la séparation des pouvoirs dans la première moitié du XIXᵉ siècle," *Revue du droit public*, XLI (Jan.–March 1924), 5–41.

Pipes, Richard. "Karamzin's Conception of the Monarchy," *Harvard Slavic Studies*, IV (The Hague, 1957), 35–58.

Raeff, Marc. "The Political Philosophy of Speranskii," *American Slavic and East European Review*, XII (Feb. 1953), 1–21.

——. *Michael Speransky.* The Hague, 1957.

Sacke, Georg. "M. M. Speranskij: politische Ideologie und reformatorische Tätigkeit," *Jahrbücher für Geschichte Osteuropas*, IV (1939), 331–350.

Svatikov, Sergius. *Die Entwürfe der Aenderung der russischen Staatsver-*

fassung: *Zur Entwicklung der konstitutionellen Ideen in Russland* (*1730–1819*). Heidelberg, 1904.

Taillandier, St.-René. "Le Comte Speranski," *Revue des deux mondes,* N.S. V (Oct. 15, 1856), 802–835. A biographical study.

Vernadsky, George. "Un projet de déclaration des droits de l'homme et du citoyen en Russie en 1801," *Revue historique de droit français et étranger,* 4th ser., IV (1925), 436–445.

——. *La charte constitutionnelle de l'empire russe de l'an 1820.* Paris, 1933.

——. "Reforms under Czar Alexander I," *Review of Politics,* IX (Jan. 1947), 47–64.

Chapter XIV. Revolution from Below: The Decembrists

PRIMARY SOURCES

Goldschmidt, Adda, ed. *Aus der Dekabristenzeit.* Hamburg, 1907. Memoirs of Iakushkin, Obolenski, and Volkonski.

Raeff, Marc, ed. *The Decembrist Movement.* Englewood Cliffs, 1966.

Russia. Sledstvennaia Kommissiia, 1825. *The Report of the Commission of Inquiry.* Trans. G. Elliott. St. Petersburg, 1826. Also in French.

Schiemann, Theodor. "Zur Geschichte des Dezemberaufstandes 1825," in his *Die Ermordung Pauls und die Thronbesteigung Nikolaus I* (Berlin, 1902), pp. 93–258. Contains documents, letters, etc.

Turgenev, Nikolai I. *La Russie et les Russes: Mémoires d'un proscrit.* 3 vols. Paris, 1847. His texts of documents are not always exact.

Wolkonskij, Michael. *Die Dekabristen.* Zürich, 1946. The most extensive collection of materials in a Western language.

SECONDARY STUDIES

Herzen, Alexander I. *La conspiration russe de 1825.* London, 1858. An answer to Korff.

Korff, Modest A. *The Accession of Nicholas I.* London, 1857. The official history.

Kulczycki, Ludwig. "Die sozialen und politischen Theorien der Dekabristen," in his *Geschichte der russischen Revolution,* 3 vols. (Gotha, 1910–1914), I, 132–170.

Lemberg, Hans. *Die nationale Gedankenwelt der Dekabristen.* Cologne, 1963.

Lubin, Israel M. *Zur Charakteristik und zur Quellenanalyse von Pestels 'Russkaja Pravda.'* Hamburg, 1930.

Mazour, Anatole G. *The First Russian Revolution, 1825.* Berkeley, 1937. The most complete historical study; some attention to theory.

Le monde slave, Dec. 1925. Entire issue devoted to Decembrists.

Salkind, Eugenie. "Die Dekabristen in ihrer Beziehung zu Westeuropa,"

BIBLIOGRAPHY

Jahrbücher für Kultur und Geschichte der Slaven, N.S. IV (1928), 380–410, 505–573.

Schwarz-Sochor, Jenny. "P. I. Pestel, the Beginnings of Jacobin Thought in Russia," *International Review of Social History*, III (1958), 71–96.

Wischnitzer, Markus. "Nikolaj Turgenews politische Ideale," in *Beiträge zur russischen Geschichte Theodor Schiemann*, ed. Otto Hötzsch (Berlin, 1907), pp. 215–240.

——. *Die Universität Göttingen und die Entwicklung der liberalen Ideen in Russland im ersten Viertel des 19. Jahrhunderts*. Berlin, 1907.

Zetlin, Mikhail O. *The Decembrists*. Trans. G. Panin. New York, 1958.

PART FIVE

General Studies of the Nineteenth Century

Berti, Giuseppe, and M. B. Gallinaro, eds. *Il pensiero democratico russo del XIX secolo*. Florence, 1950. Translations.

Cherniavsky, Michael. *Tsar and People*. New Haven, 1961.

Chyzhevsky, Dmytro I. "Hegel in Russland," in his *Hegel bei den Slaven* (Reichenberg, 1934), pp. 145–396.

Edie, James M., *et al.*, eds. *Russian Philosophy*. 3 vols. Chicago, 1965. Translations of Russian thinkers.

Friedmann, Georges. "La révolution de 1789 et quelques courants de la pensée sociale en Russie au XIXe siècle," *Revue philosophique*, CXXVIII, nos. 9–12 (Sept.–Dec. 1939), 172–192.

Giusti, Wolfango. *Studi sul pensiero illuministico e liberale russo nei secoli XVIII–XIX*. Rome, 1938. From Peter I to Nicholas II.

——. *Il pensiero politico russo dal Decabrismo alla Guerra Mondiale*. Milan, 1939. Selected readings.

Granjard, H. *Ivan Tourguénev et les courants politiques et sociaux de son temps*. Paris, 1954.

Hare, Richard. *Pioneers of Russian Social Thought*. London, 1951.

——. *Portraits of Russian Personalities Between Reform and Revolution*. New York, 1959.

Hecker, Julius F. *Russian Sociology*. Rev. ed. New York, 1934.

Iakovenko, Boris. *Filosofi russi: saggio di storia della filosofia russa*. Florence, 1927.

——. *Geschichte des Hegelianismus in Russland*. Prague, 1938.

Kohn, Hans, ed. *The Mind of Modern Russia*. New Brunswick, N.J., 1955. Selected readings.

Koyré, Alexandre. *La philosophie et le problèm national en Russie au début du XIXe siècle*. Paris, 1929.

Lourié, Ossip. *La philosophie russe contemporaine*. Paris, 1902.

McLean, Hugh, *et al.*, eds. *Russian Thought and Politics*. The Hague, 1957.

Masaryk, Thomas G. *The Spirit of Russia* (1913). 2 vols. London, 1955.

Philipp, Werner. "Historische Voraussetzungen des politischen Denkens in Russland," *Forschungen zur osteuropäischen Geschichte*, I (1954), 7–22.

Radlov, Ernest L. *Russische Philosophie.* Trans. M. Woltner. Breslau, 1925.

Raeff, Marc. *Plans for Political Reform in Imperial Russia, 1730–1905.* Englewood Cliffs, N.J., 1966. Documents and commentary.

Raeff, Marc, ed. *Russian Intellectual History.* New York, 1966.

Schelting, Alexander von. *Russland und Europa im Russischen Geschichtsdenken.* Bern, 1948.

Schultze, Bernhard. *Russische Denker, Ihre Stellung zu Christus, Kirche und Papsttum.* Vienna, 1950. Religious thought.

Simmons, Ernest J., ed. *Continuity and Change in Russian and Soviet Thought.* Cambridge, Mass., 1955.

Utechin, S. V. *Russian Political Thought.* New York, 1963.

Zenkovski, V. V. *A History of Russian Philosophy.* 2 vols. London, 1953.

Chapter XV. The Official Ideology

PRIMARY SOURCES

Grech, N. *Examen de l'ouvrage de M. le Marquis de Custine intitulé la Russie en 1839.* Paris, 1844.

Pobedonostsev, Konstantin P. *Reflections of a Russian Statesman.* Trans. Robert C. Long. London, 1898.

———. *L'autocratie russe, Mémoires politiques, correspondance et documents.* Paris, 1927. On the period 1880–1895.

Pogodin, Mikhail. *Historische Aphorismen.* Leipzig, 1836.

———. *Politische Briefe aus Russland.* Leipzig, 1860.

Steinmann, Friedrich, and Elias Hurwicz. *Konstantin Petrowitsch Pobjedonoszew.* Königsberg and Berlin, 1933. Contains a collection *Aus dem Archiv Pobjedonoszews.*

Uvarov, Sergei. *Esquisses politique et littéraires.* Paris, 1848.

———. *La certitude historique est-elle en progrès?* St. Petersburg, 1850.

Witte, Sergei. *The Memoirs of Count Witte.* Trans. and ed. Abraham Yarmolinsky. Garden City, N.Y., 1921.

———. *Vorlesungen über Volks- und Staatswirtschaft.* Trans. J. Melnik. 2 vols. Stuttgart, 1913.*

SECONDARY STUDIES

Byrnes, Robert F. "Pobedonostsev's Conception of the Good Society," *Review of Politics*, XIII (April 1951), 169–190.

Custine, Astolphe. *The Empire of the Czar*. London, 1843.

Görlitz, Walter. *Russische Gestalten*. Heidelberg, 1941. Pp. 183–211 are on Pobedonostsev.

Khomiakov, Dmitri A. "Orthodoxie, Autocratie, Nationalité," in Albert Gratieux, *Le mouvement slavophile à la veille de la révolution: Dmitri A. Khomiakov* (Paris, 1953), pp. 135–186.

Lanin, E. B. "Constantine Pobedonostseff," *Contemporary Review*, LXIII (April 1893), 584–608.

McGrew, Roderick E. "Nicholas I and the Genesis of Russian Officialism." Unpublished Ph.D. dissertation, University of Minnesota, 1955.

Petrovich, Michael B. *The Emergence of Russian Panslavism, 1856–1870*. New York, 1956.

Raeff, Marc. "The Russian Autocracy and its Officials," *Harvard Slavic Studies*, IV (The Hague, 1957), 77–91. Reprinted in *Readings in Russian History*, ed. Sidney Harcave (New York, 1962).

Rauch, Georg. "J. Ph. Fallmerayer und der russiche Reichsgedanke bei F. I. Tjutčev," *Jahrbücher für Geschichte Osteuropas*, N.S. I (1953), 54–96.

Riasanovsky, Nicholas V. *Nicholas I and Official Nationality in Russia, 1825–1855*. Berkeley, 1959.

Shoob, Leo. "Konstantin Petrovich Pobedonostsev: A Study in Reaction." Unpublished Ph.D. dissertation, University of California, 1947.

Strakhovsky, Leonid I. *L'Empereur Nicolas Ier et l'ésprit national russe*. Louvain, 1928.

——. "The Statesmanship of Peter Stolypin: A Reappraisal," *Slavonic and East European Review*, XXXVII (1959), 348–370.

Strémoukhov, D. *La poésie et l'idéologie de Tiouttchev*. Strasbourg, 1937.

Stupperich, Robert. *Die Anfänge der Bauernbefreiung in Russland*. Berlin, 1939. On Iuri Samarin.

Thaden, Edward C. *Conservative Nationalism in Nineteenth-Century Russia*. Seattle, 1964.

Von Laue, Theodore H. "Count Witte and the Russian Revolution of 1905," *American Slavic and East European Review*, XVII (Jan. 1958), 25–46.

——. *Sergei Witte and the Industrialization of Russia*. New York, 1963.

Chapter XVI. The Westerners

PRIMARY SOURCES

Belinski, Vissarion G. *Selected Philosophical Works*. Moscow, 1948.

Chaadaev, Peter I. "Lettres philosophiques" and "Apologie," ed. Raymond T. McNally, *Forschungen zur osteuropäischen Geschichte*, XI (1966), 24–129.* In French.

——. "Philosophical Letters," in James M. Edie *et al.*, eds., *Russian Philosophy*, I (Chicago, 1965), 106–154. The first letter and parts of others.

Chernyshevski, Nikolai G. *L'économie politique jugée par la science* (1860). Trans. A. Tveritinov and C. de Paepe. Brussels, 1874. A part of his translation and commentary on Mill's *Political Economy*.

——. *A Vital Question; or, What Is to Be Done?* Trans. Nathan H. Dole and S. S. Skidelsky. New York, 1886.

——. *La possession communale du sol.* Trans. E. Laran-Tamarkine. Paris, 1903.

——. *Selected Philosophical Essays.* Moscow, 1953.

Dobroliubov, N. A. *Selected Philosophical Essays.* Trans. J. Fineberg. Moscow, 1948.

Falk, H. *Das Weltbild Peter J. Tschaadajews nach seinen acht 'Philosophischen Briefen.'* Munich, 1954. Four additional letters.

Herzen, Alexander I. *Du développement des idées révolutionnaires en Russie.* Paris, 1851.

——. *From the Other Shore* (1847–1850). Trans. Moura Budberg. London, 1956.

——. *My Past and Thoughts.* Trans. Constance Garnett. 6 vols. London, 1924–1927.

——. *Selected Philosophical Works.* Trans. L. Navrozov. Moscow, 1956.

Pisarev, Dmitri. *Selected Philosophical, Social and Political Essays.* Moscow, 1958.

SECONDARY STUDIES

Barghoorn, Frederick C. "D. I. Pisarev: A Representative of Russian Nihilism," *Review of Politics*, X (April 1948), 190–212.

——. "Russian Radicals and the West European Revolutions of 1848," *Review of Politics*, XI (July 1949), 338–354.

Belchikov, Nikolai F. *Tschernyschewskij, eine kritisch-biographische Skizze.* Berlin, 1948. Soviet interpretation.

Bowman, Herbert E. *Vissarion Belinski, 1811–1848.* Cambridge, Mass., 1954.

Brown, Edward J. *Stankevich and His Moscow Circle, 1830–1840.* Stanford, 1966.

Coquart, Armand. *Dmitri Pisarev (1840–1868) et l'idéologie du nihilisme russe.* Paris, 1946.

Hurwicz, Elias. "Russische Geschichtsphilosophie," *Preussische Jahrbücher*, CLXXXI (July 1920), 185–202.

Jollos, Gregor. "Alexander Herzens socialpolitische Ideen," *Jahrbuch für Gesetzgebung*, XXII (Jan. 1898), 119–140.

Kobilinski-Ellis, L. "Sur P. Tchaadaïev," *Irénikon*, VI (Sept.–Oct. 1929), 527–543.

Kostka, Edmund. "At the Roots of Russian Westernism: N. V. Stankevich and His Circle," *Slavic and East European Studies,* VI (1961), 158–176.

Koyré, Alexandre. *Études sur l'histoire de la pensée philosophique en Russie.* Paris, 1950.

Labry, Raoul. *Alexandre Ivanovič Herzen, 1812–1870.* Paris, 1928.

Lampert, E. *Studies in Rebellion.* London, 1957.

McConnell, Allen. *Against All Idols—Alexander Herzen and the Revolutions of 1848.* Ann Arbor, University Microfilms, 1954.

Malia, Martin. *Alexander Herzen and the Birth of Russian Socialism.* Cambridge, Mass., 1961.

Mazour, Anatole G. "Petr Jakovlevič Čaadaev," *Le monde slave,* XIV (Nov. 1937), 243–266.

Plekhanov, George V. *N. G. Tschernischewsky.* Stuttgart, 1894.

Quenet, Charles. *Tchaadaev et les lettres philosophique.* Paris, 1931.

Rosen, Hans von. *Die socialpolitischen Ideen Alexander Herzens.* Halle, 1893.

Schultze, Bernhard. *Wissarion Grigorjewitsch Belinskij, Wegbereiter des revolutionären Atheismus in Russland.* Munich, 1958.

Silberstein, Leopold. "Belinskij und Černyševskij; Versuch einer geistesgeschichtlichen Orientierungsskizze," *Jahrbücher für Kultur und Geschichte der Slaven,* N.S. VII (1931), 163–189.

Sperber, Otto von. *Die socialpolitischen Ideen A. Herzens.* Leipzig, 1894. Chap. 3 appears in French as *Les vues théoriques de A. Herzen* (Brussels, 1894).

Steklow, Georg. "Alexander Herzen und Nikolai Tschernischewsky," *Archiv für die Geschichte der Sozialismus und der Arbeiterbewegung,* VIII (1918), 1–39.

Teriaev, G. V. *A. I. Herzen, Great Russian Thinker and Revolutionary Democrat.* Moscow, 1954. Soviet interpretation.

Valentinov, N. "Tchernychevski et Lénine," *Le contrat social,* I (May, June 1957), 101–110, 162–172.

Venturi, Franco. "Il populismo di Černyševskij," *Ricerche Slavistiche,* I (1952), 93–123.

Chapter XVII. The Slavophils

PRIMARY SOURCES

Birkbeck, William J., ed. *Russia and the English Church during the Last Fifty Years.* London, 1895. Correspondence of Khomiakov.

Bodenstedt, Friedrich, ed. *Russische Fragmente.* 2 vols. Leipzig, 1862. Essays by the Aksakovs, Khomiakov, Koshelev, and others.

Brianchaninov, Alexander N. *Ideological Foundations of Russian Slavonism.* Trans. Sophie de Bellegarde. London, 1916.

Danilevski, Nikolai I. *Russland und Europa.* Trans. Karl Nötzel. Stuttgart, 1920.

Dostoevski, Fedor. *Diary of a Writer* (1873–1877). Trans. Boris Brasol. New York, 1949.

——. "The Grand Inquisitor," in *The Brothers Karamazov* (1880). Several translations and separate editions.

Khomiakov, Alexis S. *L'Église latine et le Protestantisme.* Lausanne, 1872. A collection.

Kireevski, Ivan. *Drei Essays.* Trans. Harald von Hoerschelmann. Munich, 1921. Contains "The Nineteenth Century" (1832) (also in *Archives de philosophie*, XIX, no. 4 [1956], 34–54), "On the Character of European Enlightenment and its Relationship to Russian Enlightenment" (1852) (also in *Russlands Kritik an Europa*, trans. Nikolai Bubnoff [Stuttgart, 1923]), and "On the Need for and Possibility of New Foundations for Philosophy" (1856) (also in James M. Edie *et al.*, eds., *Russian Philosophy*, I [Chicago, 1965], 171–213).

Samarin, Iuri. *Préface aux oeuvres théologiques de A. S. Khomiakov.* Ed. and trans. A. Gratieux. Paris, 1939.

SECONDARY STUDIES

Astrow, Wladimir. "Kirejewski, der Slavophile," *Die weissen Blätter,* VI (Nov. 1919), 481–494.

Baron, Pierre. *Un théologien laïc orthodoxe au XIXᵉ siècle: Alexis Stépanovitch Khomiakov* (*1804–1860*). Rome, 1940.

Berdiaev, Nikolai. *Constantin Leontieff.* Trans. Hélène Iswolsky. Paris, n.d.

Bohatec, Josef. *Der Imperialismusgedanke und die Lebensphilosophie Dostojewskijs.* Graz and Cologne, 1951.

Chmielewski, Edward. *Tribune of the Slavophiles, Konstantin Aksakov.* Gainesville, Fla., 1961.

Christoff, Peter K. *An Introduction to Nineteenth-Century Russian Slavophilism.* Vol. I: *A. S. Xomjakov.* The Hague, 1961.

Galván, Enrique T. "Concepción del mundo e ideas políticas en la obra de Dostoyevsky," *Revista de estudios políticos,* XLVIII, no. 70 (July–Aug. 1953), 83–105.

Giusti, Wolf. *Dostoievskij e il mondo russo dell '800.* Naples, 1952.

Gratieux, A. *A. S. Khomiakov* (*1804–1860*). 2 vols. Paris, 1939.

——. *Le mouvement slavophile à le veille de la Révolution: Dmitri A. Khomiakov.* Paris, 1953.

Hacker, Andrew. "Dostoevsky's Disciples: Man and Sheep in Political Theory," *Journal of Politics*, XVII (Nov. 1955), 590–613.

Kohn, Hans. "Dostoyevski and Danilevsky: Nationalist Messianism," *Occidente* (Torino), X (July–Aug. 1954), 349–366.

Lanz, Henry. "The Philosophy of Ivan Kireyevsky," *The Slavonic Review*, IV (March 1926), 594–604.

Maceina, Antanas. *Der Grossinquisitor*. Heidelberg, 1952.

Masaryk, Thomas G. "Der erste Slavophile," *Die Zukunft*, LXXXIV (Sept. 20, 1913), 391–404. On Kireevski.

Pypin, A. "Die russischen Slawophilen im vierten bis zum achten Jahrzehnt dieses Jahrhunderts," *Russische Revue*, II (1873), 45–56, 160–175, 261–286.

Rahv, Philip. "The Legend of the Grand Inquisitor," *Partisan Review*, XXI (May–June 1954), 249–271.

Riasanovsky, Nicholas V. *Russia and the West in the Teaching of the Slavophiles*. Cambridge, Mass., 1952.

Smolitsch, Igor. *Ivan Vasil'evič Kireevskij, Leben und Weltanschauung*. Breslau, 1934. Reprinted from *Jahrbücher für Kultur und Geschichte der Slaven*, N.S. IX (1933), 390–427, 463–492.

Stojanović, J. D. "The First Slavophils: Homyakov and Kireyevsky," *Slavonic Review*, VI (March 1928), 561–578.

Wortman, Richard. "Koshelev, Samarin, and Cherkassky and the Fate of Liberal Slavophilism," *Slavic Review*, XXI (June 1962), 261–279.

Chapter XVIII. The Anarchists

PRIMARY SOURCES

Bakunin, Mikhail. *Fédéralisme, socialisme et antithéologisme* (1867). Paris, 1895.

——. *Dieu et l'état* (1871). Many editions and translations, including two into English.

——. *L'empire knoutogermanique et la révolution sociale* (1871). Geneva, 1871. Also known as *La révolution sociale ou la dictature militaire*.

——. *Estatismo y Anarquía* (1873). Trans. A. Chapiro and D. Abad de Santillán. Buenos Aires, 1929. Vol. V of the Spanish edition of his works.

——. *Oeuvres*. 6 vols. Paris, 1895–1913. These are also German, Italian, Russian and Spanish editions. All are incomplete.

——. *The Political Philosophy of Bakunin*. Ed. G. P. Maximoff. Glencoe, Ill., 1953. Writings rearranged by subjects.

Kropotkin, Peter. *Ethics: Origin and Development*. Trans. Louis S. Friedland and Joseph R. Piroshnikoff. New York, 1924.

——. *Fields, Factories and Workships*. London, 1898. Economics.

——. *Mutual Aid, A Factor of Evolution*. London, 1902.

BIBLIOGRAPHY

——. *The State: Its Historic Role.* London, 1903.

——. *Modern Science and Anarchism.* London, 1912.

Tolstoi, Leo. *Power and Liberty.* Trans. Huntington Smith. New York, 1888.

——. *Church and State and Other Essays.* Trans. Victor Yarros and George Schumm. Boston, 1891.

——. *Christianity and Patriotism* (1894). Trans. Constance Garnett. London, 1922.

——. *The Slavery of Our Times* (1899). Trans. Aylmer Maude. Maldon, Essex, 1900.

——. *On Socialism* (1910). Trans. Ludvig Perno. London, 1936.

SECONDARY STUDIES

Bernstein, Eduard. "Karl Marx und Michael Bakunin," *Archiv für Sozialwissenschaft und Sozialpolitik,* XXX (1910), 1–29.

Bourdeau, Jean. *Tolstoï, Lénine, et la révolution Russe.* Paris, 1921.

Friedmann, Aurel. *Das anarcho-kommunistische System des Fürsten Peter Kropotkin.* Cologne, 1931.

Jaffé-Gerschun, Nadeschda. *Bakunin und sein Einfluss auf die russische revolutionäre Bewegung.* Berlin, 1928.

Kvitko, David. *A Philosophic Study of Tolstoy.* New York, 1927.

Lampert, E. *Studies in Rebellion.* London, 1957. Chap. 3 on Bakunin.

Laurila, Kaarle S. "Leo Tolstois politische Ansichten," *Suomalaisen Tiedeakatemian Toimituksia* (Annales Academiae Scientiarum Fennicae), Ser. B, XVII (Helsinki, 1923), 1–158.

Markovitch, Milan I. *Tolstoï et Gandhi.* Paris, 1928.

Nettlau, Max. *Michael Bakunin, Eine Biographie.* 3 vols. London, 1896–1900. The most scholarly biography, but very scarce.

——. "Bakunin und die russische revolutionäre Bewegung in den Jahren 1868–1873," *Archiv für die Geschichte des Sozialismus und der Arbeiterbewegung,* V (1914), 357–422.

Plekhanov, George. *Anarchism and Socialism* (1894). Trans. E. M. Aveling. London, 1895.

Pyziur, Eugene. *The Doctrine of Anarchism of Michael A. Bakunin.* Milwaukee, 1955.

Rezneck, Samuel. "The Political and Social Theory of Michael Bakunin," *American Political Science Review,* XXI (May 1927), 270–296.

Rogers, James A. "Prince Peter Kropotkin, Scientist and Anarchist." Unpublished Ph.D. dissertation, Harvard University, 1957.*

Schuwal, Maxim. *Zur Theorie des Anarchismus.* Königsberg, 1927.

Stalin, Joseph. *Anarchism or Socialism?* (1906). Moscow, 1950.

Walter, Michael. *Tolstoi nach seinen sozialökonomischen, staatstheoretischen und politischen Anschauungen.* Zurich, 1906.

Woodcock, George, and Ivan Avakumovich. *The Anarchist Prince.* London, 1950.

Yaroslavsky, E. *History of Anarchism in Russia.* New York, 1937.

Chapter XIX. The Narodniki

PRIMARY SOURCES

Breshkovskaia, Ekaterina. *Hidden Springs of the Russian Revolution.* London, 1931.

Chernov, Victor. *Gregori Gershuni, sein Leben und Tätigkeit.* New York, 1934.*

——. *The Great Russian Revolution.* Trans. and abridged by Philip E. Mosely. New Haven, 1936.

Figner, Vera N. *Memoirs of a Revolutionist.* London, 1927.

Kravchinski, S. M. [Stepniak]. *Underground Russia, Revolutionary Profiles and Sketches from Life.* New York, 1883.

——. *The Career of a Nihilist.* New York, 1889. A novel by a revolutionary.

Lavrov, Peter. "Die sozialistische Bewegung in Russland," *Jahrbuch für Sozialwissenschaft und Sozialpolitik,* I (1879), 267–305.

——. *La propagande socialiste.* Paris, 1898.

——. *Lettres historiques.* Trans. Marie Goldsmith. Paris, 1903.

Mikhailovski, Nikolai K. *Qu'est ce que le progrès?* (1869). Trans. Paul Louis. Paris, 1897.

Tikhomirov, Lev. *Andrei Ivanovich Zheliabov* (1882). Geneva, 1899. In Russian.

——. *Russia, Political and Social.* Trans. Edward Aveling. London, 1888.

Tkachev, Peter. *Offener Brief an Herrn Friedrich Engels.* Zurich, 1874.*

SECONDARY STUDIES

Aleksinski, Grigori A. *La Russie révolutionnaire.* Paris, 1947.

Bienstock, J. W. *Histoire du mouvement révolutionnaire en Russie.* Paris, 1920.

Billington, James H. *Mikhailovsky and Russian Populism.* Oxford, 1958.

Branfoot, A. I. S. "A Critical Survey of the Narodnik Movement." Unpublished Ph.D. dissertation, London University, 1926.*

Cannac, R. *Aux sources de la révolution russe; Netchaiev du nihilisme au terrorisme.* Paris, 1961.

Duran, James A. *Lev Alexandrovich Tikhomirov and the End of the Age of Populism in Russia.* Ann Arbor: University Microfilms, 1957.

Footman, David. *Red Prelude, the Life of the Russian Terrorist Zhelyabov.* New Haven, 1945.

Hare, Richard. "A Repentant Social Revolutionary," *Slavonic and East European Review,* XXXVII (1958), 242–246. On Tikhomirov.

Kamkow, B. *Les Socialistes-révolutionnaires de gauche.* Geneva, 1918.

Karpovich, Michael. "A Forerunner of Lenin: P. N. Tkachev," *Review of Politics,* VI (July 1944), 336–350.

——. "P. L. Lavrov and Russian Socialism," *California Slavic Studies,* II (1963), 21–38.

Kulczycki, Ludwig. *Geschichte der russischen Revolution.* 3 vols. Gotha, 1910–1914.

Kupczanko, Gregor. *Der russische Nihilismus.* Leipzig, 1884.

Lampert, Eugene. *Sons against Fathers: Studies in Russian Radicalism and Revolution.* Oxford, 1965.

Lavigne, Ernest. *Introduction à l'histoire du nihilisme Russe.* Paris, 1880. Contains documents.

Mendel, Arthur P. *Dilemmas of Progress in Tsarist Russia: Legal Marxism and Legal Populism.* Cambridge, Mass., 1961.

Olgin, Moissaye J. *The Soul of the Russian Revolution.* New York, 1917.

Owen, Launcelot A. *The Russian Peasant Movement, 1906–1917.* London, 1937.

Pipes, Richard. "*Narodnichestvo:* A Semantic Inquiry," *Slavic Review,* XXIII (Sept. 1964), 440–458.

Prawdin, Michael (Charol). *The Unmentionable Nechaev, a Key to Bolshevism.* London, 1961.

Radkey, Oliver H. *The Agrarian Foes of Bolshevism.* New York, 1958. The SR's from February to October 1917.

——. *The Sickle Under the Hammer.* New York, 1963. The SR's in 1918.

Randall, Francis B. "The Major Prophets of Russian Peasant Socialism; A Study in the Social Thought of N. K. Mikhailovskii and V. M. Chernov." Unpublished Ph.D. dissertation, Columbia University, 1961.

Rappoport, Charles. *La philosophie sociale de Pierre Lavroff.* Paris, 1900.* Reprinted from *La revue socialiste,* XXXI (April–June 1900), 392–404, 528–557, 678–715, and XXXII (July 1900), 44–59.

Scheibert, P. *Von Bakunin zu Lenin. Geschichte der russischen revolutionären Ideologien 1840–1895.* Leiden, 1956.

Simkhovich, Vladimir G. "Die sozial-ökonomischen Lehren der russischen Narodniki," *Jahrbücher für Nationalökonomie und Statistik,* LXIX (3d series, XIV; Nov. 1897), 641–678.

Stepun, Fedor. "The Russian Intelligentsia and Bolshevism," *Russian Review,* XVII (Oct. 1958), 263–277.

Thun, Alphons. *Geschichte der revolutionären Bewegungen in Russland.* Leipzig, 1883.

Venturi, Franco. *Roots of Revolution.* Trans. Francis Haskell. London, 1960. Monumental study, ending about 1881.

Walker, F. A. "The Morality of Revolution in Pyotr Lavrovich Lavrov," *Slavonic and East European Review*, XLI (1962), 196–207.

Yaroslavsky, Emelian. *History of Anarchism in Russia.* New York, 1937.

Zaleski, Eugene. *Mouvements ouvriers et socialistes: La Russie.* Paris, 1956. A bibliography.

Chapter XX. The Liberals

PRIMARY SOURCES

Miliukov, Paul. *Russia and Its Crisis.* Chicago, 1905.

——. "The Representative System in Russia," in *Russian Realities and Problems,* ed. James Duff (Cambridge, 1917), pp. 25–46.

——. *Russia, To-day and To-morrow.* New York, 1922.

——. "The Influence of English Political Thought in Russia," *Slavonic Review,* V (Dec. 1926), 258–270.

Petrunkevich, Ivan. *Zur Agrarbewegung in Russland.* Leipzig, 1907.

Rodichev, Fedor. "The Liberal Movement in Russia," *The Slavonic Review,* II (June and Dec. 1923), 1–13, 249–262. From 1855 to 1905.

Struve, Peter B. "Die Marxische Theorie der sozialen Entwicklung," *Archiv für sozial Gesetzgebung und Statistik,* XIV (1899), 658–704.

——. "My Contacts with Rodichev," *Slavonic and East European Review,* XII (Jan. 1934), 347–367.

——. "My Contacts and Conflicts With Lenin," *Slavonic and East European Review,* XII (April 1934), 573–595, and XIII (July 1934), 66–84.

SECONDARY STUDIES

Fischer, George. *Russian Liberalism, From Gentry to Intelligentsia.* Cambridge, Mass., 1958.

Hammer, Darrell P. "Two Russian Liberals: The Political Thought of B. N. Chicherin and K. D. Kavelin." Unpublished Ph.D. dissertation, Columbia University, 1962.

Kantchalovski, Dmitri. "L'intelligentsia avant la révolution," *Revue des études slaves,* XXXVII (1960), 119–155.

Karpovich, Michael. "Two Types of Russian Liberalism: Maklakov and Miliukov," in *Continuity and Change in Russian and Soviet Thought,* ed. Ernest J. Simmons (Cambridge, Mass., 1955), pp. 129–143.

Leontowitsch, Victor. *Geschichte des Liberalismus in Russland.* Frankfurt, 1957.

Nahirny, Vladimir C. "The Russian Intelligentsia: From Men of Ideas to Men of Convictions," *Comparative Studies in Social History,* IV (July 1962), 403–435.

Pipes, Richard, ed. *The Russian Intelligentsia.* New York, 1961.

Raeff, Marc. "The Peasant Commune in the Political Thinking of Russian Publicists: Laissez-faire Liberalism in the Reign of Alexander II." Unpublished Ph.D. dissertation, Harvard University, 1950.

——. "A Reactionary Liberal: M. N. Katkov," *Russian Review,* XI (July 1952), 157–167.

——. "Some Reflections on Russian Liberalism," *Russian Review,* XVIII (July 1959), 218–230.

Rodichev, Fedor. "The Veteran of Russian Liberalism: Ivan Petrunkevich," *Slavonic and East European Review,* VII (Jan. 1929), 316–326.

Sachs, Hermine. *Peter von Struve, ein Beitrag zur russischen Nationalökonomie.* Breslau, 1904.

Smith, Nathan. "The Constitutional-Democratic Movement in Russia, 1902–1906." Unpublished Ph.D. dissertation, University of Illinois, 1958.

Treadgold, Donald W. "The Constitutional Democrats and the Russian Liberal Tradition," *American Slavic and East European Review,* X (April 1951), 85–94.

Weber, Max. "Zur Lage der bürgerlichen Demokratie in Russland," *Archiv für Sozialwissenschaft und Sozialpolitik,* XXII (1906), 234–353.

Zagorin, Bernard L. "The Political Thought of Peter B. Struve, 1870–1917." Unpublished Ph.D. dissertation, University of Illinois, 1957.

Chapter XXI. The Marxists

PRIMARY SOURCES

Axelrod (Akselrod), Paul. *Die Entwicklung der sozialrevolutionären Bewegung in Russland.* Zurich, 1881. Reprinted from *Jahrbuch für Sozialwissenschaft und Sozialpolitik,* II (1881), 261–306.

——. *Die russische Revolution und die sozialistische Internationale.* Ed. I. Tseretelli and W. Woytinsky. Jena, 1932.

Bukharin, Nikolai. *Imperialism and World Economy* (1915). New York, 1929.

——. "Der imperialistische Raubstaat," *Jugend-Internationale,* no. 6 (Dec. 1, 1916), 7–9. Trans. in part in *The Bolsheviks and the World War,* ed. Olga H. Gankin and Harold H. Fisher (London, 1940), pp. 236–239.

Lenin, Vladimir I. *Collected Works.* Moscow, 1960—. The Moscow and New York, 1927–1945, edition in seven scattered volumes was not completed.

——. *Selected Works.* Many editions; the Moscow, 1934–1938, edition in 12 volumes is best and identical in pagination with the London, 1936–1939, and New York undated editions.

BIBLIOGRAPHY

——. *What the "Friends of the People" Are and How They Fight the Social Democrats* (1894).

——. *What Is To Be Done?* (1902).

——. *One Step Forward, Two Steps Back* (1904).

——. *Two Tactics of Social Democracy in the Democratic Revolution* (1905).

——. *Imperialism, the Highest Stage of Capitalism* (1916).

Martov, Julius. *Geschichte der russischen Sozialdemokratie.* Trans. Alexander Stein. Berlin, 1926. Continued after 1908 by Fedor Dan.

——. "Die preussische Diskussion und die russische Erfahrung," *Die Neue Zeit*, XXVIII (Sept. 16, 1910), 907–919.

Plekhanov, George V. *Selected Philosophical Works.* Moscow and London, 1961—. To be issued in five volumes.

——. *Anarchism and Socialism* (1894). Trans. Eleanor Marx Aveling. London, 1895.

——. *Concerning the Evolution of the Monist View of History* (1895). Trans. Andrew Rothstein as *In Defence of Materialism* (London, 1947).

——. *Essays in Historical Materialism.* New York, 1940. Contains two essays, *The Materialist Conception of History* (1897) and *The Role of the Individual in History* (1898), also available separately.

——. *Fundamental Problems of Marxism* (1908). Trans. Eden and Cedar Paul. London, 1929.

Prokopovich, Sergei N. *Ueber die Bedingungen der industrieller Entwicklung Russlands.* Tübingen, 1913.

Stalin, Joseph. *Anarchism or Socialism?* (1906–1907). Moscow, 1950.

——. *Marxism and the National Question* (1913–1936). New York, 1942. A collection.

——. *The Foundations of Leninism.* (1924). Several editions.

Trotsky, Leon. *Our Revolution* (1906). Trans. Moissaye J. Olgin. New York, 1918.

——. *Results and Prospects* (1906), trans. Brian Pearce, in Trotsky's *The Permanent Revolution* (London, 1962). Also as *A Review and Some Perspectives*, trans. J. Fineberg (Moscow, 1921).

——. *Russland in der Revolution.* Dresden, [1910]. Also as *Die russische Revolution, 1905* (Berlin, 1923). In French as *1905* (Paris, 1923).

SECONDARY STUDIES

Abramovitch, Raphael. "Julius Martow und das russische Proletariat," *Der Kampf*, XVI (June, 1923), 180–188.

Abramovitch, Raphael, and others. *Julius Martow: Sein Werk und seine Bedeutung für den Sozialismus.* Berlin, 1924.*

Adler, Charles C. "The Politics of Socialism: The Thought of George V.

Plekhanov." Unpublished Ph.D. dissertation, Harvard University, 1958. 241 pp.*

Anderson, Robert V. "Nicholas Berdyaev's Critique of Marxism," *American Journal of Economics and Sociology*, XXI (July 1962), 271–284.

Baron, Samuel H. *Plekhanov: The Father of Russian Marxism*. Stanford, 1963.

Berdiaev, Nikolai. *The Origin of Russian Communism*. London, 1937.

Brennan, James F. "The Origins, Development and Failure of Russian Social-Democratic *Economism* 1886–1903." Unpublished Ph.D dissertation, University of California, 1963.

Bystrianski, V. A. [W. Bystranski]. *Die Menschewiki und die Sozial-Revolutionäre in der russischen Revolution*. Hamburg, 1922.

Dan, Fedor. "Aus dem Nachlass J. Martows," *Der Kampf*, XVIII (May 1925), 166–170.

Deutscher, Isaac. *The Prophet Armed, Trotsky: 1879–1921*. New York, 1954.

Fomina, V. A. *Die philosophischen Anschauungen G. W. Plechanows*. Trans. Nikolai Shcherbina. Berlin, 1957.

Freymond, Jacques. *Lénine et l'imperialisme*. Lausanne, 1951.

Getzler, I. "Julius Martov: His Role and Place in Russian Social Democracy." Unpublished Ph.D. dissertation, London University, 1965.*

Geyer, Dietrich. *Lenin in der russischen Sozialdemokratie*. Cologne, 1962.

Haimson, Leopold H. *The Russian Marxists and the Origins of Bolshevism*. Cambridge, Mass., 1955.

Hammond, Thomas T. *Lenin on Trade Unions and Revolution, 1893–1917*. New York, 1957.

Harper, J. *Lenin als Philosoph; Kritische Betrachtung der philosophischen Grundlagen des Leninismus*. Amsterdam, 1938.

Keep, J. L. H. *The Rise of Social Democracy in Russia 1898–1907*. Oxford, 1963.

Kindersley, R. H. *The First Russian Revisionists*. Oxford, 1962. On the legal Marxists.

Klein, Matthäus, and Alfred Kosing, eds. *Philosophie im Klassenkampf: fünfzig Jahre W. I. Lenin: Materialismus und Empiriokritizismus*. Berlin, 1959.

Kulczycki, Ludwig. *Geschichte der russischen Revolution*. 3 vols. Gotha, 1910–1914. Vol. III on early Marxists.

Leont'ev, Lev A. *Ueber das Werk W. I. Lenins 'Der Imperialismus als höchstes Stadium des Kapitalismus.'* Berlin, 1951.

Luppol, Ivan K. *Lenin und die Philosophie*. Vienna, 1929. A thorough Marxist study.

Mendel, Arthur P. *Dilemmas of Progress in Tsarist Russia: Legal Marxism and Legal Populism*. Cambridge, Mass., 1961.

Page, Stanley W. "The Russian Proletariat and World Revolution: Lenin's Views to 1914," *American Slavic and East European Review*, X (Feb. 1951), 1–13.

Pannekoek, Anton. *Lenin as Philosopher* (1938). New York, 1948.

Pipes, Richard. "Russian Marxism and its Populist Background: The Late Nineteenth Century," *Russian Review*, XIX (Oct. 1960), 316–337.

——. *Social Democracy and the St. Petersburg Labor Movement, 1885–1897.* Cambridge, Mass., 1963.

Schapiro, Leonard. "Plechanov als Politiker," *Forschungen zur osteuropäischen Geschichte*, VIII (1962), 282–298.

Scharlau, Winfried B. "Parvus und Trockij: 1904–1914: Ein Beitrag zur Theorie der permanenten Revolution," *Jahrbücher für Geschichte Osteuropas*, X (1962), 349–380.

Schwarz, Solomon M. *The Russian Revolution of 1905: The Workers' Movement and the Formation of Bolshevism and Menshevism.* Trans. Gertrude Vakar. Chicago, 1967.* Volume I of the "History of Menshevism" series.

Smith, David C. "Lenin's 'Imperialism': A Study in the Unity of Theory and Practice," *Journal of Politics*, XVII (Nov. 1955), 546–569.

Treadgold, Donald W. *Lenin and His Rivals.* London, 1955.

Vardin [Wardin], I. V. *Die Partei der Menschewiki in der russischen Revolution.* Hamburg, 1922.

PART SIX

General Studies of Russian Marxism

Anderson, Thornton. *Masters of Russian Marxism.* New York, 1963.

Bochenski, I. M. *Soviet Dialectical Materialism.* Trans. N. Sollohub. Dordrecht, 1963. Also in German and Italian.

Carr, Edward H. *A History of Soviet Russia.* Multivolume. London, 1950—.

Kuusinen, O., ed. *Fundamentals of Marxism-Leninism.* Moscow, 1960. The official textbook.

McNeal, Robert H. *The Bolshevik Tradition: Lenin, Stalin, Khrushchev.* Englewood Cliffs, 1963.

Plamenatz, John. *German Marxism and Russian Communism.* London, 1954.

Russell, Bertrand. *The Practice and Theory of Bolshevism* (1920). New York, 1964.

Seton-Watson, Hugh. *From Lenin to Khrushchev: The History of World Communism.* New York, 1960.

Somerville, John. *Soviet Philosophy: A Study of Theory and Practice.* New York, 1946.

——. "Some Perspectives on Russia and the West," *Philosophy and Phenomenological Research*, XIII (March 1953), 324–336.

Ulam, Adam. *The Unfinished Revolution*. New York, 1960.

——. *The Bolsheviks: The Intellectual and Political History of the Triumph of Communism in Russia*. New York, 1965.

Von Laue, Theodore H. *Why Lenin? Why Stalin?: A Reappraisal of the Russian Revolution, 1900–1930*. Philadelphia, 1964.

Vostokov, P. "La philosophie russe durant la période post-révolutionnaire," *Le monde slave*, N.S. IX, no. 4 (Nov.–Dec. 1932), 286–305 (on Marxists) and 432–457 (on émigrés).

Wetter, Gustav A. *Dialectical Materialism, a Historical and Systematic Survey of Philosophy in the Soviet Union*. Trans. Peter Heath. London, 1958.

Wolfe, Bertram D. *Three Who Made a Revolution* (1948). Boston, 1955. On Lenin, Trotsky, and Stalin.

Chapter XXII. The First Decade: Left, Then Right

PRIMARY SOURCES

Bukharin, Nikolai. *Die Oekonomik der Transformationsperiode* (1920). Hamburg, 1922.

——. "The New Economic Policy of Soviet Russia," in V. I. Lenin *et al.*, *The New Policies of Soviet Russia* (Chicago, 1921).

——. *Le chemin du socialisme et le bloc ouvrièr-paysan*. Paris, 1925. Also in German.

——. *Capitalist Stabilisation and Proletarian Revolution*. Moscow, 1926.

——. *Der Imperialismus und die Akkumulation des Kapitals*. Berlin, 1927. Reprinted from *Unter dem Banner des Marxismus*, I (March and July 1925), 21–63, 231–290.

Kollontai, Alexandra. *La femme nouvelle et la classe ouvrière* (1918). Trans. Marie Bor. Paris, 1932. Also in German as *Die neue Moral und die Arbeiterklasse* (Berlin, 1920).

——. *The Workers' Opposition in Russia*. Chicago, [1921?].

Lenin, V. I. *The State and Revolution* (1917).

——. *The Tasks of the Proletariat in Our Revolution* (1917).

——. *The Proletarian Revolution and the Renegade Kautsky* (1918).

——. "The Trade Unions, the Present Situation and the Mistakes of Comrade Trotsky" (Dec. 1920), *Selected Works*, IX (New York, 1943), 3–27.

——. "Once Again on the Trade Unions, the Present Situation and the Mistakes of Comrades Trotsky and Bukharin," (Jan. 1921), *Selected Works*, IX (New York, 1943), 40–80.

——. *The Tax In Kind* (1921).

Martov, Julius. *Das Problem der Internationale und die russische Revolution.* Trans. A. Stein. Magdeburg, 1920.

——. "Das Problem der Internationale," *Der Kampf,* XVI (Jan. 1923), 1–9.

——. *Le bolchevisme mondial* (1919–1921). Trans. V. Mayer. Paris, 1934.

——. *The State and the Socialist Revolution.* Trans. Integer. New York, 1938. Chapters from *Le bolchevisme mondial.*

Preobrazhenski, E. A. *Moral und die Klassennormen.* Hamburg, 1923.

——. *The New Economics* (1926). Trans. Brian Pearce. Oxford, 1965.

Spulber, Nicolas, ed. *Foundations of Soviet Strategy for Economic Growth: Selected Soviet Essays, 1924–1930.* Bloomington, Ind., 1964.

Stalin, J. V. *Works.* 13 vols. Moscow, 1952–1955. Contains works written through January 1934.

——. *Problems of Leninism.* Moscow, 1953. Works from 1924 to 1939.

——. *The October Revolution and the Tactics of the Russian Communists* (1924).

——. *On the Problems of Leninism* (1926).

Trotsky, Leon. *From October to Brest-Litovsk* (1918). New York, 1919. Also known as *The October Revolution.*

——. *The First Five Years of the Communist International* (1919–1924). Trans. John G. Wright. Vol. I, New York, 1945; Vol. II, London, 1953.

——. *Terrorism and Communism, A Reply to Karl Kautsky* (1920). Ann Arbor, 1961. Also as *Dictatorship vs. Democracy* (New York, 1922) and as *The Defence of Terrorism* (London, 1921).

——. *The New Course* (1923). Trans. Max Shachtman. New York, 1943.

——. *Communism and Syndicalism* (1923–1931). Trans. Max Shachtman. New York, 1931.

——. *The Lessons of October, 1917* (1924). Trans. Susan Lawrence and I. Olshan. London, 1925. Also trans. John G. Wright (New York, 1937).

——. *The Permanent Revolution* (1928–1930). Trans. Max Shachtman. New York, 1931.

Zinov'ev, Gregory. *War and the Crisis of Socialism.* Petrograd, 1920.

SECONDARY STUDIES

Bell, Daniel. "One Road from Marx: On the Vision of Socialism, and the Fate of Workers' Control, in Socialist Thought," *World Politics,* XI (1959), 491–512.

Carr, Edward H. "Lenin's Theory of the State," in his *The Bolshevik Revolution,* I (London, 1950), 233–249.

Daniels, Robert V. "The State and Revolution: A Case Study in the Genesis and Transformation of Communist Ideology," *American Slavic and East European Review,* XII (Feb. 1953), 22–43.

Deutscher, Isaac. *The Prophet Unarmed, Trotsky: 1921–1929.* New York, 1959.

Dimitriev, Grigori, ed. *Die Tragödie Trotzki.* Berlin, 1925. Essays by leading Marxists.

Giusti, Wolfango. *Il pensiero di Trotzky.* Florence, 1949.

Heitman, Sidney. "Nikolai Burkarin's Theory of Revolution." Unpublished Ph.D. dissertation, Columbia University, 1963.

Johnson, J. R. "Trotsky's Place in History," *New International,* VI (Sept. 1940), 151–167.

Kautsky, Karl. *The Dictatorship of the Proletariat* (1918). London, 1919.

———. *Terrorism and Communism* (1919). London, 1920.

———. *Von der Demokratie zur Staats-Sklaverei.* Berlin, 1921.

Kelsen, Hans. *The Political Theory of Bolshevism, A Critical Analysis.* Berkeley, 1949.

Korey, William. "Zinoviev's Critique of Stalin's Theory of Socialism in One Country, December, 1925—December, 1926," *American Slavic and East European Review,* IX (Dec. 1950), 255–267.

Limon, Didier L. "Lénine et le contrôle ouvrier," *Revue internationale,* I (April, May 1946), 366–379, 455–470.

Luxemburg, Rosa. *Leninism or Marxism.* Glasgow, 1935.

———. *The Russian Revolution.* Trans. Bertram D. Wolfe. New York, 1940.

Meyer, Alfred G. *Leninism.* Cambridge, Mass., 1957.

Mignot, John. *Le Léninisme.* Louvain and Paris, 1933.

Murphy, John T., ed. *The Errors of Trotskyism.* London, 1925. Includes five items from *Um den Oktober.*

Sarel, Benno. "Lénine, Trotski, Staline et le problème du parti révolutionnaire," *Temps modernes,* VII (Nov. 1951), 848–879.

Schapiro, Leonard. *The Origin of the Communist Autocracy, Political Opposition in the Soviet State—First Phase, 1917–1922.* London, 1955.

Schlesinger, Rudolf. *The Spirit of Post-War Russia: Soviet Ideology, 1917–1946.* London, 1947.

Shachtman, Max. *The Struggle for the New Course.* New York, 1943. Bound with Trotsky's *The New Course.*

Trotsky, Leon, *et al. Um den Oktober.* Hamburg, 1925. Trotsky's *Die Lehren des Oktober* and critiques by six leading Bolsheviks.

Valentinov, N. "Boukharine, sa doctrine, son 'école,'" *Le contrat social,* VI (Nov.–Dec. 1962), 331–339.

———. "De Boukharine au Stalinisme," *Le contrat social,* VII (March–April 1963), 69–78.

Zinov'ev, Gregory E., *et al. Leninism or Trotskyism.* Chicago, 1925. Contains three items from *Um den Oktober.*

BIBLIOGRAPHY

Chapter XXIII. The Autocrat and After

PRIMARY SOURCES

Bukharin, Nikolai. "Notes of an Economist" (1928), in Bertram D. Wolfe, *Khrushchev and Stalin's Ghost* (New York, 1957), pp. 295–315.

Khrushchev, Nikita. *Report of the Central Committee of the CPSU to the 20th Party Congress.* Moscow, 1956.

——. *On Peaceful Co-existence: A Collection.* Moscow, 1961. Speeches, articles, and interviews, 1956–1960.

——. *For Victory in Peaceful Competition with Capitalism.* New York, 1960. Speeches and interviews in 1958.

——. *Control Figures for the Economic Development of the USSR for 1959–1965.* Moscow, 1959. His report to the Twenty-first Party Congress.

——. *Disarmament and Colonial Freedom; Speeches and Interviews at the United Nations General Assembly, September–October, 1960.* London, 1961.

The Road to Communism. Moscow, 1962. Khrushchev's reports to the Twenty-second Party Congress and the Party Program.

Spulber, Nicolas, ed. *Foundations of Soviet Strategy for Economic Growth: Selected Soviet Essays, 1924–1930.* Bloomington, Ind., 1964.

Stalin, Joseph. *The Right Deviation in the CPSU(B)* (1929). Several eds.

——. *Dialectical and Historical Materialism* (1938). Several eds.

——. *Marxism and Problems of Linguistics* (1950). Moscow, 1954.

——. *Economic Problems of Socialism in the USSR.* Moscow, 1952.

Trotsky, Leon. *The Third International After Lenin* (1928). Trans. John G. Wright. New York, 1936.

——. *Écrits 1928–1940.* 3 vols. Paris, 1955–1959.

——. *In Defense of Marxism* (1939–1940). New York, 1942.

SECONDARY STUDIES

Achiminow, Herman. "Khrushchev's 'Creative Development' of Marxism-Leninism," *Studies on the Soviet Union,* N.S. II, no. 3 (1962), 3–17.

Bataille, Georges. "Le Communisme et le Stalinisme," *Critique,* IX (May, June 1953), 415–428, 514–535.

Beyer, Wilhelm R. "Stalins sprachwissenschaftliche Arbeit," *Archiv für Rechts- und Sozialphilosophie,* XL (1952), 436–447.

Brinkley, George A. "The 'Withering' of the State Under Khrushchev," *Review of Politics,* XXIII (Jan. 1961), 37–51.

Brodersen, Arvid. "New Trends in Soviet Social Theory," *American Slavic and East European Review,* XVII (Oct. 1958), 282–292.

Denno, Theodore. *The Communist Millennium: The Soviet View.* The Hague, 1964.

Deutscher, Isaac. *Stalin.* London, 1949.

——. "Dogma and Reality in Stalin's 'Economic Problems,' " *Soviet Studies,* IV (April 1953), 349–363.

——. *The Prophet Outcast, Trotsky: 1929–1940.* New York, 1963.

Erlich, Alexander. "Preobrazhenski and the Economics of Soviet Industrialization," *Quarterly Journal of Economics,* LXIV (Feb. 1950), 57–88.

——. *The Soviet Industrialization Debate, 1924–1928.* Cambridge, Mass., 1960.

Fainsod, Merle. "The 22nd Party Congress," *Problems of Communism,* X (Nov.–Dec. 1961), special supp.

Griffith, William E. *The Sino-Soviet Rift.* Cambridge, Mass., 1964.

Historicus (*pseud.*). "Stalin on Revolution," *Foreign Affairs,* XXVII (Jan. 1949), 175–214.

Karol, K. S. *Khrouchtchev et l'occident.* Paris, 1960.

Knirsch, Peter. *Die ökonomischen Anschauungen Nikolaj I. Bucharins.* Berlin, 1959.

Kux, E. "Von Stalin zu Chruschtschew," *Politische Studien* (Munich), IX (Jan.–June 1958), 13–19, 88–89, 161–167, 312–317, 398–402.

Labedz, Leopold, ed. *Revisionism: Essays on the History of Marxist Ideas.* New York, 1962.

Lange, Max G. *Marxismus, Leninismus, Stalinismus; zur Kritik des dialektischen Materialismus.* Stuttgart, 1955.

Lapenna, Ivo. *State and Law: Soviet and Yugoslav Theory.* New Haven, 1964.

Laqueur, Walter, and Leopold Labedz, eds. *The Future of Communist Society.* New York, 1962. Reprint of *Survey* for October 1961.

Linden, Carl A. *Khrushchev and the Soviet Leadership: 1957–1964.* Baltimore, 1966.

Marcuse, Herbert. *Soviet Marxism, a Critical Analysis.* New York, 1958.

Meissner, Boris. *Russland unter Chruschtschow.* Munich, 1960.

——. "Die Sowjetunion vor dem XXII. Parteikongress der KPdSU," *Osteuropa,* XI (Feb., Sept., and Oct. 1961), 81–97, 601–619, 685–712.

——. "Die Ergebnisse des 22. Parteikongresses der KPdSU," *Europa Archiv,* XVII (Feb. 10, 1962), 73–92.

Riasanovsky, Alexander V., and Alvin Z. Rubinstein. "Russian Utopia and Soviet Communism," *Social Science,* XXXVIII (June 1963), 151–167.

Sager, Peter. *Die theoretischen Grundlagen des Stalinismus und ihre Auswirkungen auf die Wirtschaftspolitik der Sowjetunion.* Bern, 1953.*

Santiago de Pablo, Luis. "El tránsito del socialismo al comunismo en la ideología soviética actual," *Revista de estudios políticos,* no. 121 (Jan.–Feb. 1962), 23–81.

Seydewitz, Max. *Stalin oder Trotzki, die UdSSR und der Trotzkismus.* London, 1938.

Souvarine, Boris. *Staline: Aperçu historique du bolchévisme.* Paris, 1940. Also in English without the bibliography.

Stern, Victor. *Stalin als Philosoph.* Berlin, 1949.

Trotsky, Leon. *Stalin: An Appraisal of the Man and His Influence.* London, 1947.

Tucker, Robert C. *The Soviet Political Mind.* New York, 1963.

——. "Stalin, Bukharin, and History As Conspiracy," *Dissent,* XII (Spring, 1965), 253–287. Also as an Introduction in his *The Great Purge Trial* (New York, 1965).

Wetter, Gustav A. *Dialectical Materialism: A Historical and Systematic Survey of Philosophy in the Soviet Union.* Trans. Peter Heath. London, 1958.

Wolfe, Bertram D. *Khrushchev and Stalin's Ghost.* New York, 1956. Contains text of Khrushchev's address, "The Crimes of Stalin."

Index

INDEX

INDEX

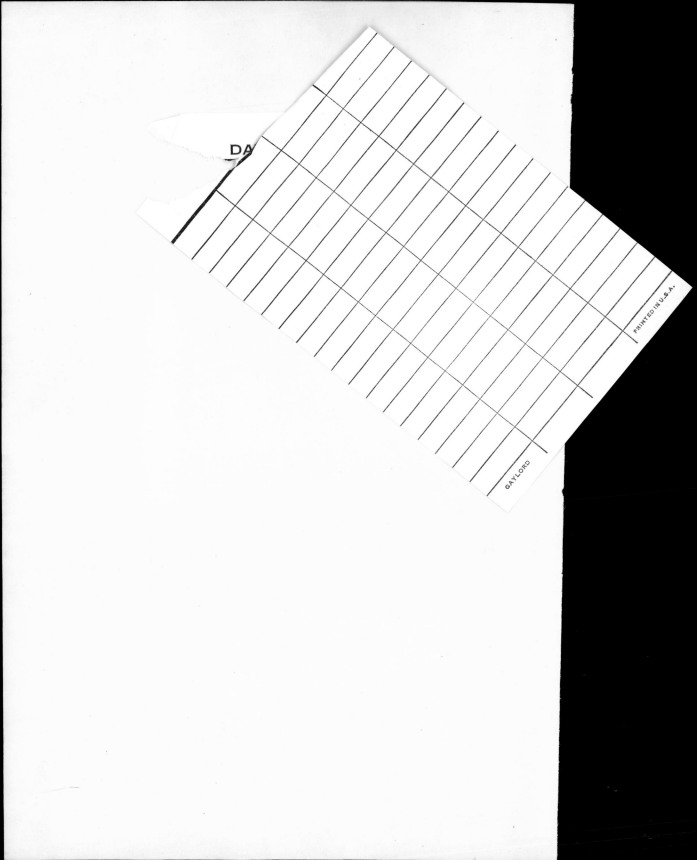

DA

GAYLORD

PRINTED IN U.S.A.